THE SOCIOLOGY OF VIRTUE

THE SOCIOLOGY OF VIRTUE

THE POLITICAL & SOCIAL THEORIES OF GEORGE SOREL

JOHN STANLEY

UNIVERSITY OF CALIFORNIA PRESS
BERKELEY, LOS ANGELES, LONDON

UNIVERSITY OF CALIFORNIA PRESS
BERKELEY AND LOS ANGELES, CALIFORNIA

UNIVERSITY OF CALIFORNIA PRESS, LTD
LONDON, ENGLAND

LIBRARY OF CONGRESS CATALOG CARD NUMBER 81-40318

ISBN: 9780520303874

FOR MY MOTHER AND FATHER
JOHN AND MARION STANLEY

CONTENTS

ACKNOWLEDGMENTS

Among the many individuals who helped me in writing this volume, I am especially grateful to Irving Louis Horowitz, whose own work on Sorel helped to inspire this one. I am also grateful for the advice of Robert A. Nisbet, Mario Einaudi, Mulford Q. Sibley, Thomas P. Jenkin, Neal Wood, Richard Vernon, Brian Davies, Selwyn Ryan, and John Schaar. A grant from the National Endowment for the Humanities made early stages of this research possible, and several intramural grants from the University of California, Riverside, supported both further research and clerical assistance. I am grateful to the editors of the University of California Press for permission to quote from the *Illusions of Progress.* Portions of the introduction and many quotations throughout this work are from *From Georges Sorel: Essays in Socialism and Philosophy*, edited, with an introduction, by John L. Stanley, copyright 1976 by Oxford University Press, Inc., and reprinted here with their kind permission. Finally, without the conscientious and cheerful help of my wife Charlotte in typing, editing, and translating, and, above all, without her constant encouragement, this book would not have been possible.

J.L.S.
Riverside, California

INTRODUCTION

In a letter to his friend Benedetto Croce, Georges Sorel succinctly defined the fundamental purpose of his work: "If I were to sum up the great concern of my entire life, it would be to investigate the historical genesis of morals."[1] When the famous twistings and turnings of Sorel's political allegiances are seen in this light, many of the apparent contradictions of his thought give way to a quite coherent sociology of morals. From his first writings through the last, it is possible to view Sorel's thought as what he at least once referred to as "my system."

For this reason, I have paid particular attention to those writings of Sorel which have been relatively ignored in previous accounts. Traditionally, Sorel's early works on Socrates and on the Bible have been placed in the background, while Sorel's syndicalist views and his myth of the general strike have been spotlighted. The immense academic preoccupation with the history of socialism and Sorel's own rather severe self-criticism of his early works make this emphasis, however unfortunate, at least understandable.

One of these early works, *Le Procès de Socrate*, is an extremely detailed attempt to reconcile the historical relativity of thought with a system of ethics—an attempt which is replicated, with increasing refinement, in virtually every one of his later principal works, including *La Ruine du monde antique*, *The Illusions of Progress*, and the *Reflections on Violence*.

In treating these early books in such a detailed way there is, of course, a risk of imitating those trendy interpretations of Marx that see a complete world-view contained in jottings found in an attic. The present work does assume that changes in Sorel's thought occurred in his thirty-year writing career, but it also makes the assumption that his thinking had a solid base which, despite many changes in expression and detail, stood firm throughout his career. Changes in Sorel's thought were usually reactions to the series of historical and intellectual crises that occurred in his lifetime. From the débâcle of the Franco-Prussian war—which provoked a demand for a new spirit and a new vigor in French morals and culture to combat the national malaise, a malaise which persisted in the vulgarity and materialism of *la belle époque*—through the period of national dread—touched off by the Dreyfus Affair—and concluding with the First World War, the events of the time inspired a spirit of pessimism and the conviction that great effort and struggle would be needed to effect a cultural *ricorsi.*

The major intellectual crisis concerned Marxism. Early in his career, Sorel decided that the traditional social-democratic interpretation of events, the materialist conception of history, was inadequate for interpreting and, more importantly, for resolving cultural and social problems. They were, rather, problems of social *morale.* To Sorel *la morale* was not only etymologically but psychologically related to *moeurs,* that is, to manners, mores, and morals. Sorel soon came to say that Marxism was either devoid of moral concerns—dismissing them as ideology—or lacked the coherent set of transformative principles necessary for a revolutionary theory.

Ironically, although Sorel criticized the inadequacy of the Marxian theory of social action, of the class struggle, of the union of theory and practice, he was more of an ivory-tower theorist and metaphysician than Marx was. Even when Sorel discussed history and politics, he was usually looking at the world through theoretical lenses. Far more than Marx, Sorel was a solitary thinker, gathering a small group of devoted followers who discussed the trends of the day in Charles Péguy's cramped Paris bookshop. He founded no worldwide ideological movement, but contented himself with trying to influence other major intellectuals of his day.

It is proper, therefore, to treat Sorel as a theorist rather than an actor in the historical drama. The present work does not attempt to be a sociology of knowledge (Irving Louis Horowitz has already performed that task brilliantly); its aim is the exposition of the unfolding of Sorel's thought. It is not a history of ideas, but an intellectual cinematograph.

By living for so many years wrapped up in the thoughts of one man, the researcher almost invariably risks either excessive sympathy (masquerading as understanding) with the subject, or an antagonism caused by ideological debunking. Really to know Sorel is to admire him, if not to love him; he was a man of immense personal charm (if contemporary accounts are to be believed), as well as of astonishing and largely self-taught erudition. The careful student is almost invariably overwhelmed by the power of such a figure. I have avoided attacking Sorel as the bad boy of early fascism and have at times editorialized on the desirability of caution in labeling men as fascistic when they are merely, like most people, anti-democratic. This does not mean that I have denied or disguised Sorel's ethical warts. As the reader will discover shortly, before World War I he wrote incoherent anti-Semitic nonsense that was completely at odds with what he had written prior to that period. He was, for a short time, a credulous fan of Lenin, calling him the greatest Russian statesman since Peter the Great and a harbinger of a new era of workers' soviets—this at a time when the "Soviet" part of the Soviet Union was for export only. Part of Sorel's credulity was the result of misinformation—very scanty intelligence emerged from Russia at the time; part of it was simply inconsistency, which should not be ignored. On the other hand, it is a grave mistake to demand necessary causal relationships between a man's theoretical system and his practical politics: they are all too often at odds with each other even in the most brilliant men. My argument here is that Sorel's theoretical system is valuable for the social scientist, especially the Marxian social scientist as self-critic, whether or not that system was abused or misused by Sorel himself or by his erstwhile totalitarian admirers.

Georges Sorel was born in Cherbourg on 2 November 1847, to a traditionally pious mother, the daughter of the mayor of Barfleur, and a businessman father of unknown ancestry. Sorel's biographer and friend, Pierre Andreu, speculates that his father's bankruptcy might have disposed Sorel to accept socialist ideas because it "separated him from the life of his class," but there is very little to sustain that conclusion.[2] Sorel's youth was the epitome of bourgeois placidity. During summer vacations he, his brother, and his cousin Albert Sorel (later to become a great French historian and president of the French Senate) visited his grandmother at the seashore. Educated at the Collège de Cherbourg, he was graduated with distinction in 1864. He then enrolled in the Parisian Ecole Polytechnique, the summit of French technical and scientific achievement, from which he was graduated tenth in a class of 133. In 1867 he joined the Bureau of Bridges and Highways as an engineer and loyal servant of the Empire and, subsequently, of the Third Republic. Indeed, at this time Sorel was politically conservative. According to Andreu, he was an ardent royalist in his youth, a partisan of the Comte de Chambord against the Duc d'Orléans; he urged that the pretender invade Paris at the head of an army of volunteers and it was reported that the phrase *Vive Henri V* appeared at the head of his notebooks.[3]

In 1870 he was graduated eighteenth in his class from the school of the department of highways. After two brief missions as a student engineer in the Loire and in Finistère, he took up a full-time appointment in Corsica, a few days after the outbreak of the Franco-Prussian war. There he remained until July 1871, when he moved to Albi. After the Commune period, he was transferred to Draguignan, to Gap, and then to Mostaganem. In 1876 he went to Algeria and in 1879 to Perpignan in the Eastern Pyrénées, where he worked until his retirement in 1892.[4]

Nothing in this conventional career suggests the making of a revolutionary theorist. Sorel apparently performed his engineering tasks with efficiency and diligence. Upon his retirement he received a letter of commendation from the Perpignan Municipal Council,[5] and was made a Chevalier of the Legion of Honor.

What makes a man think as he does? Sorel was a conventional conservative who had worn the military uniform of the Ecole Polytechnique and worked and lived among soldiers for three years in Algeria. Did this background lead to his hostility toward intellectualism, his respect for experienced workmen and technocrats over liberal-arts graduates, and his view that technical and "heroic" qualities can be combined on the workshop floor? But in his retirement Sorel was content to live the life of the independent intellectual, to roam the fields of thought as the "Socrates of the Latin Quarter," living quietly just outside Paris, at Boulogne-sur-Seine. He is interesting as an original figure, not as a member of a social group. The broadest and most deterministic theory of the sociology of knowledge does not tell us why Georges Sorel chose to concentrate on certain events and ignore others. It tells us little, in fact, about the positive and more subtle aspects of his thought—beyond the obvious: that it was a mixture of unknown proportions of personal background, history, literary tradition, upbringing, and perhaps a thousand other factors.

What, for example, led Sorel to his unique "socialism" and thence to the idea of the myth of the general strike? And why did he encase this theory in a severely Puritanical moralism, when some men in similar circumstances justified in their writings their own highly sybaritic lives? Andreu speculates that it may have been the influence of his life's companion, Marie-Euphrasie David.[6] Practically illiterate and two years his senior, she may have inspired his work by her devotion to the poor, her personal fidelity, her compassion and religious severity. Certainly she was close to that model of virtue against which Sorel measured so many of the events and personages of his time. His *Reflections on Violence* is dedicated to her memory as "entirely inspired by her spirit," and Sorel implies in a concluding note to the fourth edition of that work that it was she who revealed his genius to him.

Was Sorel's reaction to society's forcing him to live with Marie-Euphrasie in a common-law relationship an even more important factor in his condemnation of the hypocrisy of bourgeois society? Marie's lowly birth and the objections of Sorel's parents may have prevented formal marriage between her and the rather dashing graduate of the Ecole Polytechnique. Yet Sorel respected the sanctity of marriage, along with many of the characteristics of traditional society expressed in "tribal" conventions. His earlier writings are certainly devoid of socialist concepts as such, and a rebellion against bourgeois society does not explain why he selected certain aspects of socialism and rejected others. In Andreu's list of the books Sorel borrowed from the library at Perpignan, the works of Marx are not included.[7] It is evident that he read Proudhon—*Le Procès de Socrate* is infused with Proudhonian references rather than specifically Marxist or socialist ones—but this only indicates that intellectual history and the ideas of Proudhon provided Sorel with the basis of his social thought. It is Proudhon who is cited in his early writings: Marie-Euphrasie is never mentioned in his short autobiography.[8] His autobiography does so little, in fact, to explain Sorel's gravitation toward particular viewpoints that even Andreu finally throws up his hands. We will never know, he says, why Sorel adopted certain views.[9]

The thread connecting the various phases of Sorel's thought is provided by those writers who influenced him most deeply early in his career. These figures, in the tradition of the French moralists, wrote of political and religious matters with an eye to the decadence of existing society. Care must be taken not to include all moralists in this stable of Sorelian influences. Only the most severe of them seemed to appeal to Sorel—which makes it dangerous to draw close parallels between Rousseau and Sorel. To be sure, both Rousseau and Sorel saw the importance of a simple society of limited size and rigid and severe morals; both were anti-intellectual and opposed to the idea of progress; both saw virtue resting in a regime of warrior-producers; and, in a way, for both "the heart has its reasons." But Sorel's debt to Rousseau had to be filtered through pessimism and an abhorrence of abstractions: for Sorel, Rousseau's concept of the general will embodies all the worst features of the chicanery and double-talk of philosophic politicians.[10] Sorel noted that Rousseau would have been horrified at the use to which the Jacobins put this idea, but that its very vagueness encouraged this misuse. For these reasons, Sorel approved of Joseph de Maistre's condemnation of Rousseau's abstract man.[11] It might be objected that both Sorel and de Maistre were closer to Rousseau than either was willing to admit; as anti-rationalists both could find comparisons in the ideas of the "father of romanticism." But Sorel rejected the notion of "natural sympathy" or of sentimentalizing about the downtrodden, in order to stress his conviction that only effort and sacrifice can bring about social improvement.

Sorel also expressed a preference for classicism over romanticism in literature. He lauded Corneille's subordination of passion to duty.[12] He wrote sympathetically of Boileau's satires against the fashionable partisans of literary "progress" in the seventeenth century, even though the Romantics attempted to rehabilitate some of the victims of the satires.[13] But Rousseau, too, had scoffed at the notion of progress in any field; it may well be that the two were, indeed, closer than Sorel realized.

In any event, while Sorel obviously shared some of Rousseau's concerns, the latter's positive view of human nature stands in marked contrast to the Augustinian morality that Sorel lauded in the works of Pascal, of whom he wrote with great sympathy. Like Sorel, Pascal had a pessimistic view of man, and he too was a man of science who believed strongly in the limits of rationality. "It is likely," Sorel wrote, "that Pascal wrote his *Pensées* against the Cartesians," who gave the impression of being able to explain everything in order to please the "aristocratic modes of thought."[14] Pascal attacked not reason but a rationalism that used pseudo-mathematical reasoning for answering moral questions. In fact, mathematical reasoning, to Pascal, constituted a very limited area in the field of knowledge. In the face of scientistic *hubris*, Pascal and Sorel were strongly attracted by the miracle. Although Sorel was not a believer like Pascal, he recognized the importance that mystery plays in human affairs: there are some things that cannot be answered by science properly understood.

Sorel's acceptance of the non-scientific dimension of thought was not a late development. His early appreciation of the importance of at least the moral function of religion led him (probably in the early 1880's) to the works of the religious historian Ernest Renan (1823-1892). The author of *La Réforme intellectuelle et morale*, *The Life of Jesus*, and *The History of Christianity*, Renan held the Chair of Hebrew at the Sorbonne. He astounded his contemporaries by placing Christianity in an historical sweep of grandeur and comprehensiveness unknown to the rationalist works of the eighteenth century. Writing under the shadow of the disasters of 1870, Renan felt that since the 1851 coup of Napoleon III, France had been immersed .n an era of the most debased plutocracy:

> Every rebel is, with us, more or less a soldier who has missed his vocation, a being made for the heroic life. . . . The European race is a race of masters and soldiers. If you reduce this noble race to work in a slaves' prison like Negroes or Chinamen, it will rebel.[15]

> Moral values decline; sacrifice has almost disappeared; one sees the day coming when everything will be syndicalized, when organized egoism will replace love and devotion. There will be strange upheavals. . . . The two things which until now have alone resisted the decline of respect, the army and the church, will soon be swept away by the general torrent.[16]

Sorel was impressed by Renan's "remarkable insight"; at a time when men were optimistic about progressive elements in the church, Renan had been struck by the decay of religious ideas: "An immense moral and *perhaps intellectual* decline," Renan had said, "will follow the disappearance of religion from the world. We, at the present time, can dispense with religion, because others have it for us . . . but on the day when the majority loses this sentiment, the men of spirit themselves will go feebly on the attack."[17]

It was, according to Sorel, the absence of the spirit of sublimity that Renan dreaded: "Man is of value in proportion to the religious sentiment that he brings from his early education and that affects his whole life."[18] But the source of the sublime had dried up. Jesuitical Catholicism was in danger of becoming the accomplice of a servile humanitarian socialism. A general renewal was needed, a new religion: "Tremble! At this moment perhaps the religion of the future is being made . . . without us." Sorel insisted that his concept of the class war was compatible with Renan's: regeneration in society is brought about, in Renan's words, by "the source of life forces always returning to the surface," that is, by a class that worked subterraneously and was in the process of separating itself from the modern world as Judaism had from the ancient world.[19]

Sorel's criticism was that Renan played the role of the apostle of heroism and Protestant preacher, but that this was only one of the many roles he performed throughout his career. In Renan's *Souvenirs*, he virtually confesses his role-playing and his avoidance of all action:

> Teachers have inculcated in me the idea that the man who does not have a noble mission is the blackguard of creation. I have always been instinctively very unjust toward the bourgeoisie. On the other hand, I have a vivid liking for the people, for the poor. . . . [My dream is to be] lodged, nourished, clothed, and warmed, without having to think about it, by someone who will take the enterprise from me and allow me all my freedom. . . . I will leave life without having possessed anything other than what I consume by use, according to the Franciscan rule.[20]

Even here, according to Sorel, Renan has concealed his real reason for proclaiming the ascetic concept that "values give income without giving anyone any cares." Unlike the man in charge of an enterprise, the ascetic intellectual can enjoy benefits without accepting any responsibility. Although he preached heroism, Renan's rebellion against the civilization of Chinese coolies was predicated entirely on an almost Platonic distaste for the material civilization of capitalism.

Sorel sympathized with Renan's antagonism to bourgeois materialism, but the latter''s solution was the opposite of that which Sorel desired. Sorel sought a world of *homo faber*, while Renan wanted a world free from the cares of labor. But, according to Sorel, the thinker who starts out by condemning the world of coolies must eventually help to create it: a world that rejects all material value and speaks only of the "ethereal and the lofty" ideal subjects the world of labor to vassalage and produces an intellectual feudalism. Bearing this out, in *Les Apôtres* Renan proclaims that the materialists will be hunted down and whipped, and the scholars will live in the manner of medieval Franciscan monks. The great souls will form an "alliance against vulgarity. . . . One will assume that possessing things represents inferiority."[21]

Except for Renan's early writings in *La Réforme*, which he found to be deeply moving, Sorel judged Renan as fundamentally a liberal and a positivist-rationalist who attempted to "please a frivolous public" by explaining Christianity to them. By giving quasi-scientific "explanations" for religious phenomena, Renan ended by partly debunking Christianity. In fact, Sorel felt, Renan profoundly misunderstood Christianity. Sorel insisted that to probe religious phenomena one must take them on their own terms and look at their results rather than their causes. This approach demands non-scientific methods of speculation; Renan failed to comprehend adequately the radical difference in method of understanding between science and religion. Like Pascal, Sorel called for a truce between the two, a recognition of their equal validity.

Sorel's highest tribute was reserved not for a religious but a political writer, Pierre-Joseph Proudhon (1809-1865). Variously labeled an *anarchist* (he is said to have coined the term) and a *mutualist*, Proudhon is no easier to categorize than Sorel. Sorel and Proudhon share Rousseau's love for classical culture, his egalitarianism, his bias in favor of rural life, his contempt for social decadence, and his contradictions. The outlines of Sorelian thought begin to be visible in Proudhon's contradictions: this often confused and complex writer, the author of the phrase "Property is theft," was himself a great defender of property, a defender of war and enemy of militarism, an anarchist who upheld the old traditions, a proponent of progress who was, toward the end of his life, plunged into despair.

Proudhon's reputation, like Sorel's, is just now emerging from the overshadowing of his ideas by Marxism and social democracy. His recent obscurity is ironic, for it was Proudhon, not Marx, who dominated the French working-class movement during the early years of its development—the workers of the Paris Commune, for example, were led by men who called themselves mutualists and followers of Proudhon. However, the complexity of his thought at least partially explains the neglect from which it has suffered. Although Proudhon's thought, like Sorel's, was dominated by a few basic concepts—justice, liberty, love, virtue—its expression, also like Sorel's, was complicated by disorder of presentation and by fluidity.

Proudhon, like Hobbes, viewed man as seeking the greatest possible good for himself, and, he argued, those who seek to restructure society can ill afford to ignore this trait:

> It is ridiculous to want to submit the human masses, in the name of their own sovereignty, to laws against which their instincts rebel; on the contrary, it is a sane policy, and it is just and truly revolutionary, to prepare to give them what their egoism seeks and what they want to demand enthusiastically. The egoism of the people in political matters is the first law.[22]

Sorel shared this view and argued that this egoism is overcome only in periods of great effort and struggle. Proudhon balances this view with the seemingly contradictory notion that man is inherently just. Proudhon's "idea of justice," which is bound up with a sense of balance, is central to his philosophy—to understand Sorel it is necessary to understand the ramifications of this concept in Proudhon's thought as well as Sorel's modifications of it. Justice is not a mere harmony of selfish interests; rather, selfish interests are balanced by an individual's recognition of the dignity of his fellow creatures. This is the basis of the equality necessary to justice.

This idea is apparent in Proudhon's view of property: opponents of *laissez-faire* are for the most part wrong, because their solutions call for a tyrannical kind of state communism. Liberty is as essential to justice as equality is, and when tempered by rules it becomes a "collective sovereign force" which thrives only with voluntary social institutions and associations. Thus civil liberty means liberty of property as well. Yet Proudhon is aware that the distribution of property tends to be unequal and that this imbalance is reflected in the public force: "Government must be property's creature."[23] Men of property tend to dominate governments and, thus, other men. Consequently, Proudhon tends, as does Sorel, to be hostile to government as such, opposing its attempts to dominate everything it touches. Yet Proudhon, in contrast to Rousseau, insists that property is the preserver of liberty and a balance against state power. It is not the creation of law but its counterweight, produced spontaneously by society and insuring the limitation of law.

Proudhon asserts that a kind of balance should exist not only between altruism and egoism, property and the state, but in other areas as well: among economic forces, among countries, and among groups. It is the totality of the balance of forces in society that Proudhon calls justice. In the political and economic realm he calls this justice "mutualism," a system based on balance and reciprocity. In the realm of punishment it means "an eye for an eye"; in society it means voluntary associations, cooperatives and mutual-aid societies rather than the state; it is essentially a form of federalist anarchism.

According to Proudhon, men come together in mutual societies only insofar as this is required by the demands of production. The mechanism that he sees as preserving economic justice is competition, but here Proudhon gives his thought a twist which places him at odds with the *laissez-faire* theorists. The natural desire for more goods is the motive of social progress. Luxury is synonymous with progress; it is, at each moment of social life, the expression of maximum well-being realized by labor, and "it is the right, as it is the destiny, of everyone to attain it." It is the desire for luxury that in our times, lacking religious principles, maintains the social movement and "reveals to the inferior classes their dignity."[24] But this is balanced by the existence of poverty. The poverty arising from increasing population requires men to work harder and to create new productive forces. Unlike Malthus, Proudhon sees poverty as a beneficial social force: "It is celebrated by antiquity and by Christianity. The hero is poor, temperate, and surrounded by a large family: the ideal of those revealers of beauty [the poets]. . . . [Poverty] is not an object of fear for men imbued with the idea of justice."[25]

Proudhon's "idea of justice" is not contingent upon social circumstances, nor does it arise like some mechanism from the social order—it is not an "ideology" in the Marxist sense. The idea of justice is as much a part of ourselves and our nature as the emotion of love. In fact, Proudhon sees love as a major force for justice and a strong family life with conjugal fidelity as its institutional basis:

> For myself, the more I think of it, the less I am able to imagine woman outside the family and marriage. I see nothing between the state of courtesan and that of homemaker (I say homemaker, not servant). . . . Mankind is created male and female: from this results the necessity of the ménage and of property. The two sexes are united: at once from this mystical union, the most astonishing of all human institutions is created, by an irreconcilable marvel—property, the division of the common patrimony into individual sovereignties.[26]

If marriage based on love is institutionally at the basis of justice, the same "balance" prevailing in the just society must prevail within the household. The physical distinction between the sexes is transformed into a balance between the force and productivity of men and the grace and ideals of women. If woman does not personify her qualities by accepting the feminine role, ideal values will be degraded and the union between idealism and productivity, between justice and economics, will be shattered. It is when the male represents the warrior, the embodiment of productivity and force, organizer of the city and leader of social movement, and the female is mother, educator of children and mistress of the household, that the union of the ideal and the real is found in marriage.[27]

An economic realm is needed to unite the household with production. Agriculture best performs this function. No enemy of the "idiocy of rural life" as Marx is, Proudhon proclaims that "when I turn the tracks made by my plow, I am king."[28] The regime of farming allows woman to remain in the home, uncorrupted by the life of the factory. Only when agrarian virtue is brought into the new industrial society will justice and honor prevail; only then will the sense of possession and pride that has characterized the peasant be found in the industrial worker. Again justice is a balance, this time between the peasant and the industrial worker. Marx believed that agrarian life was destined to disappear; Proudhon believed that the peasant provides the model of the best human being, and that rural life should therefore be preserved.

The love and harmony which pervade the household reinforce the self-sustaining nature of the ménage. Each household is an independent unit, a kind of Roman *dominium*, and (as in the *dominium*) the *pater familias* must be able to defend it. Therefore, Proudhon believed, to maintain justice a certain militancy is necessary. Like patriotism, justice must be armed, for it is not only the enemy within that must be vanquished but also the one from outside:

> War is linked at a very deep level, and in a way we are just beginning to perceive, with man's sense of religion, justice, beauty, and morality. War is the basis of our history, our life, and our whole being. . . . People . . . do not see that if man takes away war . . . nothing in his past remains, and not an atom is left on which to build the future. I would ask these inept peacemakers, as I myself was once asked in connection with property, "What sort of society do you envisage once you have abolished war? . . . What will become of mankind in this state of permanent *siesta*?"[29]

Proudhon's solution, as always, was on an institutional basis. Since mutualism calls for a justice based on reciprocity—an eye for an eye—and since the ineptitude of the legislator is universal and he deals with only the least dangerous part of wrongdoing, voluntary groups known as *justiciers* (lovers of justice) are necessary to balance state-administered justice. These vigilantes he defined as "juries of honor with the right of pursuit, judgment, and execution." The Roman *pater familias* of Proudhon's vision can, like Cincinnatus, leave his home to defend it; he creates an equivalent of the upright Roman soldier-laborer.

These views horrify us today: they lend credence to the view that the tradition of Proudhon (and Sorel) is closer to that of the Ku Klux Klan than it is to an enlightened path of social understanding. But we should not condemn Proudhon quite so precipitously. He was well aware that modern warfare leads to appalling butchery, and that the Bonapartist regime under which he lived used militaristic and chauvinistic slogans to sustain its power. Louis Napoleon's empire was a hierarchy upheld by despots and demagogues that bore no similarity to the amateur soldier fighting to preserve freedom in the ancient world. In the modern world, Proudhon saw a balance of power between one country and another as the salvation from militarism. Sovereignty in the modern sense represents not justice but only one force or territory opposed to another; justice is found in the balance between and among those sovereignties.[30]

More importantly, Proudhon's *justiciers* anticipate Sorel's thought in another way: Proudhon says that even if the two sides are equal in strength and justice, there is justification for battle—or at least for preparation for battle:

> Man first dreamed of glory and immortality as he stood over the body of an enemy he had slain. Our philanthropic souls are horrified by blood that is spilled so freely and by fratricidal carnage. I am afraid this squeamishness may indicate that our virtue is failing in strength. What is so terrible in supporting a great cause in heroic combat, at the risk of killing or being killed, if both sides are equally honorable and their claims equally just? . . . Death is the crown of life. How could man, who is a thinking, moral, free being, have a more noble end?[31]

Proudhon feels that the just and good society is possible only through action, obtained when men are stimulated to fight an enemy: "Action is the principal condition of life, health, and strength in an organized being. . . . For there to be action . . . there must be some ground that exists in relation to the acting subject . . . and that resists and opposes the acting self. Action, therefore, is a struggle. To act is to fight."[32] Proudhon was not the first theorist (nor, as we see from Sorel, the last) to assert that a society in torpor abdicates its self-rule to the parasitic few.

But a serious problem in Proudhon's thought emerged from this, in Sorel's view. If competing sovereignties are, as such, only balanced competing forces, can dispassionate judgment, rather than mere force, result from Proudhonian *justiciers*? What is to prevent those excesses of vigilantism that are now the common experience of humanity? Proudhon seemed well aware of this problem when he made it clear that this "supplemental justice" is to be directed against immoral and ignominious acts rather than strictly criminal ones. This means, however, that vigilantism, which is a very logical anarchist replacement for officers of police, presumes a counterbalancing force—an "official," or state, mechanism to cope with the most disruptive acts. Still, after Proudhon has dispensed with the state as an objective, dispassionate, and interest-free institution, the problem of the dispassionate judge remains. If justice is balance, rather than objectivity and detachment, if the "umpire" of the liberal state is a myth, as Proudhon implied that it is, then where do we find detached *judgment*? One response is that it is only the balance itself, irrespective of what is being balanced, that Proudhon regarded as justice, and that the innate justice in men corresponds to that balance.

From this generalization, Proudhon argued that only balance will provide the creative tension necessary for human progress. In this respect Proudhon's idealization of war could easily be conflated into a respect for other kinds of struggle and tension, and it was now possible for Proudhon to condemn war as dishonorable in practice, however noble it may be in theory. Most wars do not embody the principles of justice; they are struggles between two unequal forces driven by greed, poverty, and unequal wealth. War must be transformed back into justice by changing the arena in which struggle takes place. Proudhon argued that if justice is practically impossible in the *droit de force*, it is still possible in the *droit économique*, in the very realm which undermines the balance of the political-military world. Politics is no longer the arena in which justice is to be found—the law of force has been replaced by the law of labor: the worker replaces the soldier, and his battle is against poverty and nature rather than his fellow man. Had Proudhon, in the manner of certain liberal economists, merely replaced the idealization of war with an equally misplaced idealization of the economic world?

It is at this point that Sorel found Proudhon's thought problematic. Despite Proudhon's linking of the idea of justice to specific social and economic institutions and his attempt to balance those institutions, Sorel shared Marx's opinion that Proudhon remained a prisoner of subjective and abstract ideals. In some writings Proudhon admitted this himself; for example, in his assertion that justice is not merely the attribute of some authority: "Justice is the attribute of man that no *raison d'état* ought to despoil." But since Proudhon made justice as much an attribute of human nature as of the balance of forces in society, Sorel (still echoing Marx's criticism) wondered if Proudhon was "the victim of a strange illusion when he assumed that our nature leads us toward justice. On the contrary, it would seem that law was imposed on man by historical accidents."[33] Sorel finally perceived a utopian element in Proudhonian concepts. If justice is not a power play and the truly "candid judge" must be above all interest, Sorel said that justice then becomes absolute: "It is an idea that can comprehend relations among men only in the mythical city conceived by reason."[34]

For Sorel the great challenge was to disentangle and discard the idealistic and metaphysical remnants in Proudhon's writing. Proudhon was well aware that justice, as such, is subject to that grave dilemma which Sorel spelled out in some detail. Sorel intended to replace the theory of natural right, however conceived, by a theory of historical justice with its focus on the productive warrior. What this means in a practical sense is that the problem of distributive justice, either as regards rotation of offices or distribution of wealth, was made by Sorel into a secondary question; the primary problem involved the idea of virtue in the producers. We can gain some insight into this from the *Reflections on Violence*:

> The Napoleonic soldier's sacrifice of his life in return for the honor of working in an "eternal" epoch and of living in the glory of France, all the while saying that "he would always be a poor man"; the extraordinary virtues shown by the Romans who resigned themselves to a frightful inequality and who endured such sacrifices to conquer the world; "the faith in glory of unequaled value" created by the Greeks and thanks to which "a selection was made from the teeming throng of humanity, all showed that life had a purpose, that there was reward here for those who pursued the good and beautiful."[35]

Men should not work without recompense, but their reward should be epochal and not financial or political. It is not economic inequality nor even human suffering which, for Sorel, constituted the prime injustice, but the sapping of the incentive for glory and thus victimization by the "pride of a few," by "historical superiorities"—that is, by repressive force.[36]

Sorel was indebted to Proudhon for the idea of a strong family structure based on the productive household, for the warrior ethic, and for his distrust of state power and its corollary that it is among voluntary associations based on production that one finds the freest institutions.

It was primarily the two early influences, Renan and Proudhon, who bequeathed to Sorel the basis of his thought. Rejecting the theory of abstract natural right and replacing it with a vague formula of "the protest against historical superiorities," Sorel set himself a double task: he had to elaborate his attack on the theory of natural right; and he had to replace this notion with a theory of morality better adapted to the Proudhonian institutions, that is, based on productive life itself. Seen in this light, Sorel's many variations on this theme can be viewed as experimental attempts, testing these Proudhonian hypotheses on various subjects. Sorel's thought, like any experiment, can be seen as being in a continuous state of evolution, of Bergsonian flux; it is, therefore, best explicated chronologically, starting with his first "experimenting" on the historical situation of Socrates and ending with modern European ideologies.

This seemingly complicated task of chronological exposition has been made somewhat easier by Sorel's tendency to concentrate on certain themes during the various stages or "experiments" of his intellectual development: for example, the period from 1897 to about 1902 was focused primarily on theoretical discussions of Marxism, while the stages preceding and following World War I dealt primarily with contemporary European politics. Sorel certainly discussed other matters—sometimes at length—during these periods, and, conversely, dealt with the main subject matter of each period at other times, but the "center of gravity," so to speak, of each of these periods is weighty enough to give an evolutionary coherence to Sorel's writings. Furthermore, it allows the commentator in good conscience (provided that proper scholarly precautions are taken) to cite writings from outside the period in order to bring greater clarity and crispness to the analyses.

Six stages—five main movements and a coda—may be perceived in the course of the development of Sorel's thought. The first stage extends from his first writings in 1886 until 1892; here Sorel laid the groundwork for his sociology of morals. This stage includes three principal works, *La Contribution à l'étude profane de la Bible* and *Le Procès de Socrate* (both published in 1889), and an essay on Proudhon (published three years later). During this time he was working in Perpignan; little that is specifically socialist can be found in the writings of this period. They are moral portraits with a deeply conservative bent and obviously reflect his early intellectual interests. The first work, that on the Bible, reflects and echoes many of Renan's concerns: the origins of the Christian faith, the interpretation of biblical books such as the Song of Songs, and, most importantly, the social relevance of the Bible as a vehicle for the restoration of a civilization reduced to despair by defeat in the Franco-Prussian war. In the introduction to the *Contribution*, Sorel asserted that the Bible is an heroic work, a modern *Iliad* teaching civic virtues.[37] In *Le Procès de Socrate* he reflected on many of the theories discussed in the Proudhon essay and elaborated on the relationship of heroism to the productive life. Sorel remained with many of these themes after accepting the revolutionary idea, that is, after his 1892 switch to Marxism. In 1894 in *La Ruine du monde antique*,[38] he attempted to put these problems in a Marxist framework within the context of the history of early Christianity. Here we find a sociology of morals remarkably similar to that in the "conservative" work on Socrates (cf. Chapter 1, below).

The second, or methodological, stage of Sorel's thought extends from 1893 until 1897 (see Chapters 2 and 3). In 1894 he acted as editor of a short-lived journal, *Ere Nouvelle*, and in the following year he edited a somewhat longer-lived periodical, *Le Devenir Social*, whose purpose, according to Sorel, was to "probe Marxism in depth."[39] Yet Sorel's chief concern at this time was not the content of Marx's writings but the scientific assumptions behind them, that is, the problem of sorting out the various elements of Marx's social theory from other theories. Sorel's more important writings for both *Ere Nouvelle* and *Devenir Social* are concerned with the philosophical and metaphysical presuppositions underlying the methods of scientific investigation and the limits of applying those scientific methods to social phenomena. Here Sorel adopted the late-nineteenth-century philosophy of science, noting that the investigation of phenomena in the laboratory (and, still more, in society) cannot result in that totality and completeness of understanding which men of the previous age had expected from it. Sorel understood science to be a fragmentary method of investigating particular phenomena whose relationship to other areas of investigation was often tenuous. Sorel's highly skeptical view of social science as it was practiced implied a criticism, not yet made explicit, of Marx's own scientific assumptions, a balancing of Marxism with positivism and psychologism.

It was not until 1897 or 1898 that Sorel began to discuss extensively the Marxian texts themselves (see Chapter 4). He resigned from *Devenir Social* in 1897, disappointed with the journal's rather stale orthodoxy and with the low level of its contributions. At that time the official German social democracy as personified by its leader, Karl Kautsky, had influenced the entire European socialist movement. Academic, scientific, and deterministic, its spokesmen appeared to abandon all moral aspirations and to pursue either narrow economic ends or political domination for its own sake. At this time, Sorel sided with Eduard Bernstein's attacks on official Marxism, insisting that it was not Marx's "predictions" that were important but his ambition to better, in every sense of the word, the life of the working class. In Sorel's view, Bernstein was attempting to restore moral integrity to Marxism and—because he was closer to understanding reality than Kautsky was—to science as well. Thus, for a time Sorel did see some hope in a kind of parliamentary revisionism. "I thought then," he recalled later, "that a temporary coalition established with a quite determined goal and alien to economic considerations between men of groups regarded as fatal enemies by Marxist theorists would not necessarily hurt the autonomy of socialist thought."[40]

In this period Sorel was constantly wrangling with the distinctions among state socialism, economic socialism, and the working-class movement itself; it was the last that Sorel came to recognize as the "true" socialism, considering the others faulty impersonations of Marx's true intentions. The movement was of prime concern for Sorel, and he had to distinguish this movement from mere state distribution of wealth. For Marx this was an unnecessary distinction;

parliamentary democratic parties in his day did not speak for the working class, nor did they claim to do so. With the development of what was called social democracy and the active participation of socialist parties in politics, it was increasingly difficult to proclaim democracy a "bourgeois mask." By the early 1890s, socialism, progress, reason, democracy, and the strengthening of the state all seemed to blur into a dry academicism which obscured the exclusively working-class nature of genuine socialism.

By 1902 Sorel departed from revisionism and precipitated a breach with political socialism (see Chapter 8). In his introduction to Fernand Pelloutier's *L'Histoire des bourses du travail* Sorel for the first time—by his own later admission—came to grips with the true differences between what he called "proletarian socialism" and "political socialism."[41] From 1902 until 1908 was what Sorel called his period of "socialist autonomy," wherein he brought his distrust of politics to its logical conclusion. The historical event that precipitated this period was the Dreyfus Affair, the facts of which are well known: Alfred Dreyfus, an army captain, was convicted of espionage; because new evidence was uncovered implicating a Major Esterhazy as the real culprit, the original conviction was placed under a cloud of suspicion. The army failed to exonerate Dreyfus, and Esterhazy was acquitted. By 1898 practically the whole of French society had become polarized on the question—the left staunchly supporting Dreyfus and demanding a reopening of the case, the right defending the increasingly beleaguered army. The rightists acted in such a way as to make it appear that they were attacking the republic itself rather than the Dreyfusards, or so the partisans of Dreyfus claimed. The latter saw in the case an ideal opportunity to gain power by "defending the republic." The many leftist radicals coalesced around the Dreyfus cause in order to excoriate the army with the demagogic shrillness earlier French republican governments had used in attacks on the church, and they assumed power by the same method—or so Sorel thought.

At first Sorel was sympathetic to the Dreyfus cause and its socialist allies. But in June 1899, Millerand, who orchestrated the coalition of Dreyfus factions, was invited into the new government by Premier Waldeck-Rousseau; the furthest left government since that of the Commune of 1870, Sorel dubbed it "the Dreyfus revolution."[42] When the government, in July 1901, passed a law limiting the autonomy of the religious orders, Sorel saw a similarity between the government of his time and the repressive Jacobinism of earlier times: the "autonomy" of socialism was being swallowed by the office-seeking and corruption of what Sorel called the "democratic ocean."[43] He believed that Jean Jaurès was leading socialism to a kind of Jacobinism and statist dictatorship and was substituting economic redistribution and confiscation for the demands of the Third Estate in the earlier Revolution.

Only by thoroughly freeing itself from statism could socialism effect moral reform. According to Sorel, the institutions best able to carry out this reform in France were the *syndicats* (unions) and their corollary organizations, the *bourses du travail* (labor exchanges). The *bourses du travail* were, roughly speaking, employment agencies run by the *syndicats* independently of parallel state organizations. Together with the unions, the *bourses* established themselves as virtual states within states. In this period Sorel focused on theories of history, on early Christianity, on the myths surrounding the working-class movement, and on psychological questions relating to them. This was Sorel's most productive period: his studies on Bergson, Renan, the *Illusions of Progress*, and the myth of the general strike were written during these years; five of his thirteen full-length books and numerous studies for *Mouvement Socialiste* were published. Many of these writings revolve around one great question: what is the psychology of a revolutionary class? In the *Illusions of Progress* Sorel attacks rationalism, supplanting it with his theory of myths, inspired by his critique of Renan's views on Christianity as well as by Bergson's *Elan vital.*

In 1909 began the fifth and perhaps most paradoxical stage of Sorel's thought (see Chapters 9 and 10). Syndicalism, "working-class autonomy," had not lived up to Sorel''s expectations. Strikes had become bitter and hate-filled, betraying Sorel's hopes for an ethical limitation to brutality. The unions themselves had inclined toward reformism, that is, toward accommodation with the existing order. In 1909, also, Sorel abandoned the *Mouvement Socialiste* and in 1910 wrote to Missiroli that "the proletariat is still too divided as regards the ordering of the wonderful democracy. . . . Syndicalism has slid down the same incline that socialism has already traveled—toward a pure outbidding of demagogues." Bergson had "exhausted everything he has to say," Sorel later asserted, while Croce would be considered a great thinker in years to come. To Croce he had written of his intention never to work on syndicalism again.[44]

From the theory of syndicalism and ideological studies Sorel turned to pragmatism and to studies of contemporary non-socialist politics. These new themes mark a sudden departure from his earlier undertakings. Sorel's writings on contemporary politics before 1909 number only about a dozen articles. After 1909 his work mainly concerns the development of French and European politics after

1870. In 1909 he wrote a pamphlet on the Dreyfus revolution, and, after an abortive attempt to start the journal *La Cité Française*, Jean Variot established the journal *L'Indépendance* especially for Sorel.

Sorel's turn to pragmatism was just as abrupt. As late as May 1908 he had written to Croce that "there is something frightening in making success the proof of the legitimacy of an idea," and noted that it had led to the decline of Greek civilization.[45] Indeed, Sorel had attacked the cult of success in his early work on Socrates.[46] By November of 1909 he was applauding James's pluralism and his insights into evil; in the following year he wrote an extensive article on the philosophical ramifications of pragmatism. Sudden as this reversal was, it was consistent with many of the statements he made about the myth of the general strike, for this myth was a deeply pragmatic one.

In this period of pragmatism an apparently quixotic series of changes took place in Sorel's political allegiances. Shortly after having despaired of the future of syndicalism, he wrote a flattering letter to Maurras extolling the idea of traditional monarchy;[47] at the same time, he was bemoaning the weakening of the old republican ruling class in France. It is apparent that Sorel adopted these various stances for many of the same reasons that he adopted the idea of the myth of the general strike: they were pragmatic attempts to inculcate heroic virtues. The only difference between the syndicalist myth and those of his later allegiances was that Sorel, after 1910, was a conscious pragmatist, but underlying this pragmatism was the same set of moral principles he had possessed before.

With the coming of the First World War, Sorel saw the impossibility of success for any of the groups to whom he had previously given allegiance. The Third Republic had, in his eyes, sunk to an even lower level of demagogy than it had reached in peacetime. This was the period of Sorel's deepest disillusionment and despair. The only bright spot Sorel found in it was the coming of the Russian Revolution; 1917 might be identified as the beginning of a sixth and last stage of thought (see Chapter 11). It was for him a revival of syndicalist hopes. He was under the quite illusory impression that Lenin had strengthened the autonomy of the workers through the Soviets. Here at last, it seemed, a vehicle for the restoration of the great virtues had been discovered. From 1918 until his death in 1922, Sorel was sympathetic to the communist cause, his final articles appearing in communist journals. "Cursed be the plutocratic democracies which starve Russia!" he wrote. "I am only an old man whose life is at the mercy of slight accidents, but may I, before descending into the tomb, see humiliated the arrogant bourgeois democracies, today cynically triumphant."[48] In his final days, he saw still another apparent repository of virtue wrecked at the hands of political ambition. Alone and impoverished in a small Paris apartment, Sorel died in October 1922, at the age of seventy-four.

His biography is interesting not, as we have said, because of the uneventful course of Sorel's engineering career but because of the intellectual migration that took place after his retirement. It is the variety of the "stages," or tendencies, in Sorel's thought that makes succinct interpretation of it so difficult and challenging. What sense can we make of a man who speaks of social revolution one year and of monarchy in the following year; of independence from the state in one breath and of tradition and community in the next? Writers looking for contradictions in Sorelian thought will meet with no resistance from their author, who not only confessed to such changes but flaunted them. In *Matériaux d'une théorie du prolétariat* he said, "I have never hidden variations in my thought, and one can do nothing but admit that I have always conducted my research in complete good faith."[49]

Furthermore, Sorel's writing style would not earn him any awards. In the *Reflections* he maintained that the "incorrigible vice" of his prose was due to his continual effort "to escape the constraints of what had previously been constructed for everyone in order to find what is personal in it. To me, it seems interesting to put in my notebooks only what I have not encountered elsewhere. I willingly avoid the transitions because they are always found among commonplaces."[50] Sorel thought it was better to appeal to a few readers to stimulate personal inquiry:

> I do not think that I praise myself needlessly in saying that I have sometimes succeeded in stimulating the spirit of invention in my readers; and it is the spirit of invention which it is above all necessary to provoke in the world. It is better to have obtained this result than to have gained the banal approbation of people who repeat formulas and enslave their thought in scholastic disputes.[51]

The question of Sorel's originality is perplexing partly because of his style and partly because so much of his writing consists in criticism of others, but the careful student will find something fascinating in this writer. Inventiveness is indeed there, and it is this very creativity that makes categorizing Sorel such a challenging undertaking.

There remains the question of why this book was written. The final chapter attempts to show Sorel's importance for understanding the writers he influenced and his relevance to contemporary civil and political issues. Sorel is an important figure in intellectual history, as well as a formidable social-science theorist. One can recite the list of theoreticians of French syndicalism whom he influenced—Berth, Lagardelle, Platon—but these men were of small consequence in the decades after the Second World War. More important, I think, is his influence on Camus, whose *L'Homme révolté* incorporates many of the internal restraints on violence to be found in the *Reflections* and whose distinction between rebellion and revolution was inspired by Sorel's distinction between violence and force.[52] Furthermore, Sorel's critique of Marxism—in his theory of the plural and limited nature of the sciences and in his view of progress—is found in the works of Camus and other existential critics of Marxism.

More important in a general sense is Sorel's overall critique of social-science assumptions. In his early writings Sorel criticizes the natural-law assumptions of the old political theory as well as the organic theories of Durkheim, but in doing so refuses to replace them with the "empirical" theories which assume that some sort of order in history allows the movement of peoples to be considered natural and predictable. For Sorel, beyond certain general tendencies, no predictability in human affairs is possible. He thus places himself on the side of modernity, of the essential historicity of human affairs, without espousing the Marxian elevation of history itself to a position as the new criterion of legitimacy.

What is most interesting about Sorel is that he did not fall into vulgar positivism or cultural relativism. For Sorel, the challenge for the new social science was to find some criterion of moral order, some standard by which man could still judge good and evil. Nietzsche in his generation and Péguy in his tried in their different ways to deal with the same problems. But to my knowledge few have attempted to do so with the specificity and exactitude of Sorel. Only Sorel faced squarely the problems of socialism and the textual exegesis of Marxism. Only Sorel had enough sophistication in the sciences, in scientific theory as well as engineering practice, to be able to talk authoritatively on the limited role of science within the context of specific social-science theories. That is why reading Sorel has become mandatory for modern scholars who wish an understanding of the theory of social science.

Notes

1. Letter to Croce, 6 May 1907. This series of letters appeared in *Critica* 25-28 (1927-1930). See 26, no. 2 (20 March 1928): 100.

2. Pierre Andreu, *Notre maître Georges Sorel* (Paris: Grasset, 1953), p. 26.

3. Ibid., p. 32. Andreu's source for this was Gilbert Maire, a fellow student of Sorel's.

4. Ibid., pp. 31-35.

5. See ibid., p. 319, where the commendation is reprinted.

6. Ibid., pp. 41-42.

7. Ibid., pp. 320-23.

8. Published as "Mes raisons du syndicalisme" in *Matériaux d'une théorie du prolétariat* (Paris: Rivière, 1919).

9. Andreu, *Notre maître*, p. 43.

10. Sorel, *Les Illusions du progrès* (5th ed., Paris: Rivière, 1947), p. 95.

11. Ibid., p. 9; American edition, *The Illusions of Progress*, translated by John and Charlotte Stanley (Berkeley and Los Angeles: University of California, 1969), p. xlv.

12. Sorel, *Le Procès de Socrate* (Paris: Alcan, 1889), pp. 47-48.

13. Sorel, *Illusions du progrès*, pp. 22-25 (American edition, pp. 5-7).

14. Ibid., pp. 38-42.

15. Ernest Renan, *La Réforme intellectuelle et morale* (14th ed., Paris: Calmann-Lévy, n.d.), p. 94.

16. Renan, *Feuilles détachées* (Paris: Calmann-Lévy, 1892), p. *xiv.*

17. Ibid., pp. *xvii-xviii.*

18. Ibid.

19. Renan, *Histoire du peuple d'Israël* (Paris: Calmann-Lévy, 1887-1893), vol. 5, p. 420; *Feuilles détachées*, p. 14. Cited in Sorel's *Réflexions sur la violence* (6th ed. revised, Paris: Rivière, 1925), p. 348; translated by T. E. Hulme and J. Roth, *Reflections on Violence*, (New York and London: Macmillan, 1950), pp. 225-26. (Hereafter referred to as: *Réflexions* and *Reflections*, respectively).

20. Renan, *Souvenirs d'enfance et de jeunesse* (Paris: Calmann-Lévy, n.d.), pp. 348-49.

21. Sorel, *Système historique de Renan* (Paris: Jacques, 1905), p. 65, citing Renan's *Les Apôtres.*

22. Pierre-Joseph Proudhon, *L'Idée générale de la révolution au XIXe siècle* (Paris: Lacroix, 1867), p. 225. See also Edouard Berth, *Du "Capital" aux "Réflexions sur la violence"* (Paris: Rivière, 1932), p. 120. The body of literature in English on Proudhon is growing. For a competent biography, see George Woodcock, *Pierre-Joseph Proudhon* (London: Routledge and Kegan Paul, 1956); for a study of his philosophy, see Alan Ritter, *The Political Thought of Pierre-Joseph Proudhon* (Princeton: Princeton University Press, 1969). A brief anthology of this prolific writer's works can be found in a collection of excerpted segments in English translation, *Selected Writings of Pierre-Joseph Proudhon*, edited by Stewart Edwards and translated by Elizabeth Fraser (New York: Doubleday, 1969). A recent essay is William H. Harbold: "Justice in the Thought of Pierre-Joseph Proudhon," *Western Political Quarterly* 22, no. 4 (Dec. 1969): 723. For a comment on Proudhon by Sorel's chief disciple, see the first chapter of Berth, *Du "Capital" aux "Réflexions sur la violence."*

23. Proudhon, *Théorie de la propriété* (2nd ed., Paris: Lacroix, 1866), p. 131; *Selected Writings*, p. 133.

24. Proudhon, *Philosophie de la misère* (Paris: Lacroix, 1875), vol. 1, p. 285.

25. Sorel, "Essai sur la philosophie de Proudhon," *Revue Philosophique* 33-34 (1892): 633.

26. Proudhon, *Système des contradictions économiques* (3rd ed., Paris: Lacroix, 1867), ch. 11, sec. 2. Cf. *La Pornocratie ou les femmes dans les temps modernes* (Paris: Lacroix, 1875), p. 5.

27. Proudhon, *De la justice dans la révolution et dans l'église* (Paris: Lacroix, 1868-1870), vol. 4, pp. 276-79. See also Proudhon's *Selected Writings*, pp. 254-56, and Berth, *Du "Capital" aux "Réflexions sur la Violence,"* p. 162.

28. Berth, *Du "Capital" aux "Réflexions sur la violence,"* p. 130, citing Proudhon, *De la justice dans la révolution et dans l'église.*

29. Proudhon, *La Guerre et la paix* (Paris: Lacroix, 1869), pp. 71-72; translated in *Selected Writings*, p. 207.

30. For a discussion of the role that *balance* plays in Proudhon's notion of justice, see *De la justice*, pp. 60-61, and *De la capacité politique des classes ouvrières* (Paris: Lacroix, 1873), pp. 124-26; Sorel, "Essai sur Proudhon," p. 42.

31. Proudhon, *La Guerre et la paix*, p. 31 (cited in *Selected Writings*, p. 203).

32. Ibid., p. 54 (cited in *Selected Writings*, p. 204).

33. Sorel, *Illusions du Progrès*, p. 307 (American edition, p. 170).

34. Sorel, "Essai sur Proudhon," p. 47.

35. Sorel, *Réflexions*, pp. 35-36, citing Renan, *Histoire du peuple d'Israël.*

36. Ibid., p. 36; Sorel, "The Ethics of Socialism," *From Georges Sorel*, ed. John Stanley (New York: Oxford University Press, 1976), p. 103 (hereafter referred to as *FGS*). For the distinction between force (state repression) and violence (rebellion against the state), see *Réflexions*, pp. 256-57.

37. Sorel, *Contribution à l'étude profane de la Bible* (Paris: Ghio, 1889), esp. p. vii.

38. First published in *Ere Nouvelle* in 1894; reprinted with three editions as a book (Paris: Rivière, 1st ed., 1901, 2nd ed., 1925, 3rd ed., 1933).

39. Sorel, *Matériaux*, p. 250.

40. Ibid., p. 263.

41. *L'Histoire* was published in Paris by Schleicher in 1902 (reprinted Paris and London: Gordon and Breach, 1971, in their Publications Gramma series). His admission came in *Matériaux*, p. 268.

42. See Sorel's *La Révolution Dreyfusienne* (Paris: Rivière, 1909).

43. Sorel, *Matériaux*, p. 263.

44. Letter to Mario Missiroli, 13 August 1910, in Georges Sorel, *'Da Proudhon a Lenin' e 'L'Europa sotto la tormenta,'* ed. Gabriele de Rosa (Rome: Edizioni di Storia e Letteratura, 1974), p. 449; letter to Missiroli, 17 June 1915, in ibid., p. 537; letter to Croce, 19 February 1911, *Critica* 26, no. 5 (20 Sept. 1928): 347.

45. Letter to Croce, 27 May 1908, *Critica* 26, no. 2 (20 March 1928): 106.

46. *FGS*, pp. 64, 68-69.

47. Dated 6 July 1909: reproduced in Andreu, *Notre maître*, pp. 325-26.

48. Sorel, *Réflexions*, p. 454.

49. Sorel, *Matériaux*, p. 3.

50. Sorel, *Réflexions*, p. 9.

51. Ibid., p. 12.

52. See, for example, Albert Camus, *The Rebel,* trans. Arthur Bower (New York: Vintage, 1968), esp. p. 194.

I

THE TRIAL AND DEATH OF SOCRATES

"Young man, France is dying; do not be disturbed by her agony." Renan's apparently sanguine words to Déroulède in 1882 were reflected in the political thought of the next decade as well as in parliamentary *immobilisme.* The inertia of liberal institutions following the establishment of the Third Republic had provoked a challenge from the right in which Royalists and Bonapartists formed a coalition to support Minister of War Boulanger in his demand for a reformed constitution and a more spirited foreign policy. The political malaise that had plagued France since her defeat by Germany in the Franco-Prussian war had taken its toll. Defeat had not unified the country; it had merely opened the sores of conflict between the forces of radicalism and conservatism, clericalism and anti-clericalism, socialism and liberalism.

By 1879 the principal area of conflict between radical and conservative forces was that of education. Renan, a moderate liberal and a positivist as well as one of the most popular authors of his day, echoed the common opinion that the Prussian victory was

> the victory of discipline over indiscipline; of men who were respectful, careful, attentive, and methodical over those who were not. While it was the victory of science and reason, it was at the same time the victory of the old regime, of the principle that denies the sovereignty of the people and the right of the people to determine their destiny, for these democratic ideas, far from strengthening a race, disarm them and render them incapable of any military action.[1]

Most liberal critics complained that the example of the *ancien régime* did not provide the answer to the problem of education. Renan condemned the education of "the Jesuits of the seventeenth and eighteenth centuries in which the child, separated from his family, sequestered from the world and from the company of the opposite sex, could acquire neither distinction nor delicacy."[2] He predicted that the state "would end up by running gigantic boarding schools, the unfortunate heritage of the Jesuits."[3] State education would produce only uniformity and an "official spirit" which would be the intellectual death of the nation.[4] To Renan, the proposals to make education a state monopoly reflected the agony in the moderate liberal forces; on the other hand, he recalled the Greek *polis* as an ideal in which education, like religion, was entirely a creature of the state: "The slightest details of education were regulated; everyone devoted himself to the same physical exercises, all learned the same songs, participated in the same religious ceremonies, and went through the same rites of initiation."[5] On the other hand, to Renan "a society is all the more perfect insofar as the state is concerned with fewer things."[6] The *polis* was really a family. "The struggles among us which divide the family, the church, the state did not exist then; our ideas on the separation of church and state or on private versus public schools had no meaning. The city was the family, the church, and the state at the same time."[7] Such an organization was impossible in a modern society, and Renan hesitated even over the question of whether the state should provide a certain minimum education.[8] Only the profoundly serious and moral influence of the family—especially the mother—"can cure the wounds of our times, reform the education of men, and revive the taste for the good and the beautiful."[9]

Into this climate of opinion stepped Jules Ferry, the Minister of Education, who attempted to remove from the schools the clerical influence that had frustrated educational reform throughout the 1870s. In 1879, Ferry expelled the bishops from the Conseil Supérieur de l'Instruction Publique and gave state institutions a monopoly in the awarding of degrees. Most controversial of all was his prohibition of religious education in state schools and his exclusion of teachers who were members of any religious order unrecognized by the state. As a result of the conflicts which developed from this decree, some 300 unauthorized religious houses were dissolved.[10]

Sorel granted that this move toward secularization had some positive results, but at least before the turn of the century he saw it primarily as a return to the tyrannical excesses of Jacobinism. On the one hand, he opposed complete secularization, and on the other, he thought that the secularized state schools, as Renan had predicted, had become, ironically, very much like the mediocre Jesuit schools of the past.

In 1889 Sorel's first two books were published—both on the subject of education. Since he was at that time working as an engineer in Perpignan, he was forced to rely on the limited resources of the Perpignan library. For that reason, Sorel's first book, *Contribution à l'étude profane de la Bible*, was a somewhat fragmentary attempt to demonstrate the heroic teachings of the Bible.[11] As he later said, the Bible embodied new morals while "the error of most philosophers . . . is that they take as their starting point . . . books written for declining societies; when Aristotle wrote the *Nichomachean Ethics*, Greece had already lost her own reasons for morality."[12] Secularization would only accelerate the decline of the heroic virtues necessary for the recomposition of the French national spirit. Like Renan, Sorel saw no solution in a return to the Jesuitical practices which he felt produced mediocrity in both students and curriculum.[13] Unlike Renan, however, Sorel upheld the Athenian *polis* as a valid model for the modern state, at least as a model from whose fate at the hands of the Sophists and Socrates several important lessons could be learned. Like the Jacobins and their Jesuitical predecessors, the philosophers of the classical Athenian *polis* had desired, according to Sorel, to upset the old teaching methods and to substitute a hierarchy based on examinations.

Sorel's opposition to what he regarded as the subversive tendencies of these philosophers was codified in a second and far more coherent book, published the same year as his work on the Bible. *Le Procès de Socrate* contains Sorel's fundamental ideas on the function of education in society. Indeed, this work goes far beyond an exposition of an educational theory: it is, rather, the first systematic exposition of Sorel's historical theory of morals. It is hard to agree with James Meisel's judgment that the book on Socrates did not establish "the seminal unity of Sorel's thought at the very beginning of his writing career." Meisel argues that Sorel does not yet appreciate the central force of the social myth. "The author is, to the exclusion of everything else, concerned with the negative task of belaboring the 'logical faith' of the Jacobin *émeute*, the faith in reason which produces utopias and their sequence."[14] Besides overemphasizing the importance of the role of myth, Meisel ignores Sorel's fundamental purpose: the exposition of a genealogy of morals based partly on the superiority of poetry over philosophy. Chapter 1 is an attempt to outline the Proudhonian moral system of Sorel as reflected in his indictment of Socrates' teaching. The argument is not that Sorel failed to change any of his subsequent views, only that the basic framework of his moral system, of whose existence Meisel is so skeptical, is to be found in this important, if flawed, book.

One does not have to probe very deeply to discover that Sorel (like Proudhon) deeply admired the ancient *polis*—especially the *polis* of early Greece before the Peloponnesian War:

> [The culture], so simple in appearance and so unified, nonetheless involved the whole person, all the more profoundly and energetically as these young minds, not being distracted by multiple tasks, could more freely profit from what was offered to them as spiritual nourishment . . . the Homeric epic, with its magnificent portrayal of the world, which inspires heroic feelings and the passion for lofty deeds; liturgical hymns, with their rich treasure of sacred legends originating in the temples . . . finally, the elegy in its infinite diversity . . . which expressed with striking clarity everything that a brave citizen of Athens should know and attempt! . . . As the young man had happily grown up assimilating the best of the intellectual richness of the people, participation in public life became for him a superior school in which he perfected himself and demonstrated his ability. Each new progress in poetry was at the same time an extension of popular education.[15]

Sorel's *Le Procès de Socrate* (1889), published in the same year as the *Contribution à l'étude profane de la Bible*, contains one of the most complete outlines of the social basis of a moral society to be found anywhere in his works. In it Sorel attempts to sketch the political and ideological movements that sabotaged the poetic spirit, the product of the Homeric education that had played such an important educational role in early Athens. Sorel maintains that through an examination of certain philosophical and dramatic texts we can discover that philosophers in general and Socrates in particular were the chief culprits in the movement toward moral decay which took place in Athens' transition from a rural to an urban society during the time of Pericles.

The moral ideas on which this old system relied for its ethical code rested, according to Sorel, on three principles. These principles were substantially the same ones as those Sorel inherited from Proudhon; moreover, they are substantially the same as those which stand at the heart of Sorel's criticism of the European bourgeoisie. They are: (1) there must be a strong family structure based on the productive household, and this ménage is cemented by both sentimental and erotic love between husband and wife; (2) legal and political institutions cannot be strong when they are separated from military life; and (3) estrangement of military and family life comes about when an ethic of productivity is replaced by a society based on consumption and leisure, for this consumers' society replaces a democratic and egalitarian division of labor with a hierarchical and meritocratic one.

Sorel's case against Socrates is faulty—in particular, it either misinterprets Xenophon or confuses his ideas with those of Socrates—but his failures themselves foreshadow Sorel's later efforts to combine traditional virtues with modern productivity.

I

Sorel saw Socrates as one of the chief agents in the ideological subversion of the ancient Athenian ethical system. This was brought about primarily through Socrates' cult of political expertise, through the proposition that the best government is the rule of knowledgeable men who have a special mission in life. To Sorel this was Socrates' basic agreement with the Sophists; together they provided justification for the new oligarchy of politicians who engineered the destruction of the old moral code.

Sorel represents philosophic teaching—both Socratic and Sophistic—as "elitist," opposed to the teaching of ancient Athens, which was not complex and was consequently available to all citizens. In "old" Athens, poetry—first in the form of the epic, then in the form of Aeschylean or "heroic" tragedy—reduced the distance between the aristocratic families and the citizens, for poetry was the fundamental civic teaching for everyone. Thus, what Sorel calls "the alliance between poets and the great sacerdotal families"[16] really meant an alliance between classes, a true democracy, and a union of politics and poetry, thought and action.

According to Sorel, "the development of the Sophist schools completely changed this situation. . . . The Sophists sought to determine on what basis democratic equality could be founded, and it was soon concluded to be absurd in both fact and law."[17] The old alliance between poetry and politics was challenged by another alliance between Sophist philosophers and a newer breed of politicians who had learned the arts of rhetoric from their Sophist masters. The young generation was imbued with the new philosophy, and, imitating Euripides' subtle and amiable citizen against the Aeschylean hero, scorned the old faith.[18] Thus was constituted a new oligarchy of intelligence and oratory, a union of philosophy and politics that opposed the old *polis* of simple rural citizens and teachers of the poetic heritage.

While Sorel admits that Socrates was not instrumental in forging this new oligarchy (that had already been done by the Sophists), he maintains that Socrates helped Sophist efforts to break the old poetic civility by his attacks on poetry: "Socrates says that tragedy is a form of popular rhetoric intended to flatter without edifying . . . that the supposed practical lessons drawn from Homer and so praised by the ancients really do not amount to much."[19]

Socrates' attack on both rhetoric and poetry was adopted by Plato, who saw the trial of Socrates as a revenge of poets and orators against philosophy. In Plato's eyes philosophy had exposed the falsehood of both politics and poetry. But, in Sorel's view, to accept this Platonic account is to accept both the purity of philosophy and the corruptibility of poetry. Poetry, not philosophy, thus was put on the defensive in Plato's account.

According to Sorel, the antagonism between philosophy and power was not as clear-cut as Plato had supposedly made it: in Plato, philosophy was represented by professional philosophers who dearly wanted to take power.[20] Sorel admits that a critical tension often prevails between philosophy and politics, and that the alliance between orators and philosophers was an unstable one. He notes that Anytus wished to attack all philosophy when he attacked Socrates.[21] While sharing Plato's antagonism toward the political world, Sorel labels such hostility as characteristic of one who is jealous of the power of others. Sorel takes care to make it appear that Anytus was not a good orator and therefore relied on Meletus to undertake the active work of the prosecution.[22] Sorel asserts, with little justification, that the Meletus depicted in Aristophanes' *Frogs* as attacking the old poets is the same Meletus as he who prosecuted Socrates. Sorel interprets Meletus's appeals to the jury as being utterly cynical, and asserts (in the face of overwhelming contrary evidence showing that Meletus was indeed a religious fanatic as well as a poet) that "Meletus never passed for a great poet" and that "the alliance between poetry and the great sacerdotal families was broken." Neither Meletus nor Lycon could pose as a champion of great literature.[23]

The real reason that Sorel attempted to show the division between poets and politicians was the obvious fact that the trial itself was unjust. Meletus' accusations had to be simple to appeal to the jury of old soldiers and, as such, were distorted and oversimplified. Meletus was "careful to place his accusation in vague terms suitable for motivating declamations against the oligarchs. This method is always held in strong repute by philistines."[24] At a political trial oversimplifications are inevitable, and that is Sorel's explanation for the apparent severing of philosophy and politics during the trial—a separation that Plato took to be characteristic of philosophy and politics in general. Sorel admits that Socrates was attacked for personal and political reasons, and that political trials are intrinsically unjust; truly great political trials—as Sorel would later remind us during the Dreyfus Affair—are vicious by their very nature: the more important the judgment, the more elevated the situation of the accused, the less equity there will be in the proceedings and the more likely it is that the jurors will, for political reasons, struggle against their consciences.[25]

It was therefore imperative for Sorel to make it appear that the poets are dissociated from an unjust procedure. He wanted to transform Plato's depiction of the prosecution as a cabal of poets and orators into an account which condemns both orators and philosophers while sparing the poets. Plato's scholarship stands condemned: the *Apology* "developed several accessory aspects in an exaggerated way and has not approached the question rigorously." Furthermore, Sorel argues *ad hominem*, Plato "belonged by birth and ideas to the oligarchic party."[26]

But is Sorel himself attacking Plato for political reasons and injuring his own case? Not only does he misrepresent the ideas of Meletus, but he brings no strong counter-evidence to bear against Plato's *Apology*. The latter represents the trial as an alliance between poets and orators, and Xenophon's account, on which Sorel relies, distinguishes only between those jurors who are jealous of Socrates and those who simply disbelieve him.[27] Since Plato's account is generally held to be superior to Xenophon's, if only because of Plato's proximity to the event, Sorel can be suspected of basing his case on an inferior source to suit his own polemical purposes.

Sorel found Xenophon to be a far more suitable witness against Socrates than Aristophanes' comic exaggeration, for poetry cannot be a judge in its own case any more than philosophy can. Xenophon was not a poet but an historian, and he had the incomparable advantage of being a student of Socrates without being a philosopher himself.[28] It is true that we should not trust a defender of Socrates any more than his poetic opponents, but Sorel suggests that Xenophon is a strong witness against Socrates precisely because he defended him: Xenophon unwittingly convicts Socrates while attempting to place the master in the best light. Since Xenophon is really a traditionalist, an "old Athenian," not a Socratic, in reporting the words of the master Xenophon naturally attempted to make Socrates' ideas as close as possible to his own. Any misreporting would err in the direction of conventionality rather than subversion. If Xenophon's testimony can be used against Socrates, the conviction is all the more secure. Sorel not only reports the sayings of Socrates found in Xenophon's writings but establishes Xenophon's own credentials as a traditionalist. Sorel does not have to proceed in this way, of course; indeed, he exposes himself to the risk of unwittingly "proving" Socrates' conservatism. As we shall see, this course proved fatal to Sorel's case.

II

Sorel claims that Xenophon's traditional ethics were established in the *Oeconomicus*, a treatise on household management unique among Xenophon's Socratic writings. The *Apology*, the *Memorabilia*, and the *Symposium* are true Socratic dialogues that do not reflect Xenophon's own ideas; the *Oeconomicus* is not genuinely Socratic but "completely honors Xenophon's mind, which is so just and so Greek." Sorel adds that Xenophon was never really Socratic at all, for "he did not derive from the master anything but grace of exposition and the finesse of dialectical distinctions."[29]

The basic problem with Sorel's proof of the extraordinary character of the *Oeconomicus* rests with the question of what role Socrates really plays in the work. At one point Sorel argues that "Socrates figures the same way in the dialogue as he does in the Platonic dialogues. . . . In the name of Socrates, it is really Xenophon who is speaking."[30] Sorel argues that the "Socratic speeches" in the *Oeconomicus* praising Cyrus could not have been spoken by Socrates; they could only have been the opinion of Xenophon, the old campaigner who had served Cyrus.[31] But in fact it is not clear in this comparison whether Socrates really is the vehicle for Xenophon. Sorel notes quite correctly that Socrates is confessedly ignorant of the agricultural subjects in the dialogue and seems to be content to recount the conversations he held with Ischomachus, a man whose strong resemblance to Xenophon Sorel admits (in agreement with most scholars). It is from Ischomachus, not "Socrates," that we hear a considerable portion of the technical knowledge.[32]

To identify Xenophon's real ideas we must determine whether it is Socrates or Ischomachus through whom Xenophon is speaking, or whether he is using both as his spokesmen. This is important, as we shall see, because Socrates only appears to play a passive role in the discourse. In any event, after reading Sorel's interpretation of the *Oeconomicus* one remains unsure as to whether Xenophon is an earnest country bumpkin, speaking through the rustic and unphilosophic character of Ischomachus without understanding the implications of Socrates' character, or whether he is a philosopher in his own right speaking through Socrates. Sorel rejects, as he must, the possibility that Xenophon had sufficient "dialectical finesse" to be able to reconcile the *Oeconomicus* with the other Socratic works. Not to do so would open the possibility of a more complete reconciliation of Socrates and Xenophon, and would constitute an affirmation of either the Xenophontic Socrates' traditionalism—which would invalidate Sorel's thesis—or of the "Socratism" of Xenophon's ethics—which would weaken Sorel's case by drastically undermining the credibility of the chief witness.[33]

The principles enunciated in the *Oeconomicus* as interpreted by Sorel reflect the principles of rustic Attic society. Sorel may indeed be right in attributing to that dialogue a highly Xenophontic (as opposed to Socratic) character. Sorel's exposition of the *Oeconomicus* leaves no doubt that the dialogue is entirely at one with Sorel's own principles of morality. It combines the three Proudhonian principles of domesticity, struggle, and productivity in the art of household management.

The *Oeconomicus* begins with Socrates discussing the art of household management with Critobulous. Socrates professes no great knowledge of the art but establishes that wealth is not really one's own unless it has been mastered: for example, we cannot count a horse among our wealth unless we can ride it.[34] If a household is to be counted among our goods, it should be well-ordered, in accordance with the science of household management. The benefits of this "science of husbandry" are threefold: (1) it provides for the necessities of life efficiently; (2) it makes its practitioners strong and bold for the defense of their city; and (3) it is beautiful. Thus, Xenophon links the efficient and productive practice of household management to the virtues of the soldier.[35]

As Sorel notes, Xenophon asserts that men and women are joined for their mutual advantage—the man to gather substance from abroad, and the woman to manage and improve the home. The partners being similarly endowed with memory and diligence, marriage of man and woman is a partnership between equals united divinely and by law in a sort of domestic division of labor—a duality of functions—ordained by the gods for the purpose of procreation and by law for the preservation of the household. Only when the proper division of labor is maintained is the household well-ordered.[36] There is nothing "which is more commendable or profitable than to preserve good order in everything." This division of labor in the household is necessary to the production of goods, and both the division of labor and the resulting well-ordered household are necessary to a good army and a strong state. Sorel interprets Xenophon's essay, then, as viewing the Greek citizen less as *homo politicus*, the man who spends his time in the city, than as an economic and military being. He is *animal laborans*, whose fulfillment is found in the world of agricultural production, and he is military man, whose civic being is defined by his role as defender of the city.

If a strong family structure is needed to produce warriors, war and its epics are the schoolrooms in which that virtue is given its civic qualities. Sorel insists that it is impossible to understand antique constitutions without understanding their relationship to military institutions. War was the basis of citizenship. The aristocratic period of Greek history—the period in which the few (wealthy) ruled—was associated with the expensive ownership of cavalry horses and equipment; the increased use of infantry and of oarsmen for naval triremes brought about the expansion of citizenship.[37] Sorel depicts both the aristocratic and democratic warrior as appreciating the practical and warlike basis of the state itself: the ancient *polis* gave power to the warrior because he was the only man who could keep it free.[38] In the activity of defense "man discovers his own best qualities: courage, patience, disregard of death, devotion to glory, and the good of his fellows: in one word, his virtue."[39]

Sorel interprets Xenophon as saying that parallels can be drawn among war and citizenship and home economics. In all three, tradition dominates instruction, and one learns by rote. Sorel insists that in the traditional society anyone could learn the simple military tactics and that "obedience was the school of command."[40] Xenophon explicitly said that the ordering of any ship or the supplying of cavalry is exactly analogous to housekeeping,[41] and Aristotle noted that excellence in military matters is the kind of excellence that can show itself in a crowd.[42] Xenophon maintains that the same is true of household management: anyone can master it, all men can be excellent if they only apply themselves, and this excellence can be combined with routine performance of tasks.[43]

It is in the writings on classical military virtues that Sorel reveals his solution to the problem of the "iron law of oligarchy." As long as obedience is the school of command, no meritocracy or science of military tactics really exists, and the distance between commander and private is not great; in the Xenophontic household, according to Sorel, wifely obedience is certainly the school of command, but a rough equality prevails between husband and wife. Sorel despairs of elevating the moral stature of modern military organization, because it is organized on opposite principles: being based on expertise, it resembles a post office more than an arena fit for heroes.[44]

III

In the main argument of *Le Procès de Socrate*, Sorel attempts to demonstrate how Socrates' teaching as reflected in Xenophon's "Socratic" dialogues undermined the principles discussed above.

Sorel accuses Socrates of subverting the moral basis of the family. Xenophon's *Oeconomicus* gives prime importance to domestic institutions, and, in Sorel's view, "the constitution of the family (influenced by political life) is the principal source of our moral ideas."[45] Sorel argues that "the world will become more just in proportion as it becomes more chaste."[46] For him, the integrity of the family is essential for the moral improvement of society. Sorel's "psycho-erotic law," that sexual usages are perhaps the most important element in the constitution of society, helps us to understand his condemnation of Socrates. In accusing Socrates of replacing the social family with the moral one, Sorel really means that an abstract family has replaced the flesh-and-blood family of the old system. The poets praise *eros*: according to Sorel, Socrates suppressed *eros*. It is on this basis that he cites Xenophon as sustaining Aristophanes' accusations against Socrates.

In "putting the body out to pasture," in his contempt for the physical, Socrates argues for a strong spiritual connection between men as an alternative to pederasty. To Sorel, this teaching had the effect of a "true crime" in which Socrates, in reality, gives a perfect theory of homosexual love. Sorel believes that this abstract male love is all too easily corrupted, and the apparent contempt for conjugal love which Socrates evinces by his conception of an abstract family really destroys *eros* completely; Socratic heterosexual love seems to be aimed solely at procreation. The moral force of woman's erotic and moral love is replaced by a mere social contract.[47]

According to Sorel, the final shock to the ordered family life was Socrates' undermining of Greek religion. Sorel notes that Socrates was innocent in a formal way of the charges leveled against him. He was not impious any more than he was a pederast; he was perfectly correct in the homage that he paid to the gods.[48] In fact, Sorel believes that Socrates was not even hypocritical in this regard: it was the nature of his sincerity which had such disastrous consequences for Hellas.

Sorel describes Socrates as a "cultist and a hierophant." The communication between Socrates and the gods was established with the help of extraordinary mental states in which Socrates' mind felt itself dominated completely by superior forces. The ecstatic condition was inadvertently admired by Xenophon, who said that divinity gave Socrates signs and that these all-powerful daemonic councils were infallible. By establishing a permanent link with the gods, Socrates transformed the oracular nature of Greek religion, rooted in institutions—especially the family—into something personal, spontaneous—in a word, mystical.[49]

But if the character of the Socratic religion was, in Sorel's eyes, misguided, its social consequences were similar to those produced by the Stoic. Sorel notes that in Xenophon's account, Socrates accused of folly those who acted against the advice of the gods on the grounds that they were anxious to avoid the poor opinion of other men. By combining divination with prophecy such religious teaching, in Sorel's view, "transforms the infant into a novitiate against his family. His masters must shape his mind in such a way that he will never forget his lessons." The result tended toward theocracy and resulted in a confusion of legal, religious, and political laws.[50] "It appears that Socrates related divination to Providence, without caring to examine too closely how compatible this thesis was with the existence of a well-ordered world. The philosopher was not far from that Stoic conception which likens the world to an organized being continuously directed by a great soul."[51]

To Sorel, Socrates as depicted by Xenophon became the purveyor of the great and all-encompassing idea of unity in the political world, and, in a sense, foreshadowed the Saint-Simonian and Comptean utopias. Here freedom vanishes, and the ties which held the citizen to military discipline were broken, to be replaced by the discipline of theocracy. Sorel sees Socrates' corrupting influence extending into the classical military virtues precisely because his conception of military expertise undermined the traditional egalitarian basis of Athenian military organization. This organization led to political equality, but Socrates' ideas on military expertise were of a far different nature from those found in Xenophon's *Oeconomicus*: there, a certain expertise flourishes, but it is of a kind universally attainable. In the "genuinely" Socratic works of Xenophon, Socrates insists that only the few can become adept at military science. In the *Memorabilia*, Socrates proves to Nichomachides that to command an army one must have more than the experience of routine in the inferior ranks, and that the Athenians would do well to modify their armaments.[52] By introducing the role of "science" into military affairs, Socrates "proved" that the old ways were insufficient for military excellence. The old basis of Athenian democratic virtue in which mass action could be combined with excellence and in which heroism could emerge from anywhere in the ranks is now called into question.

The Socratic tradition is guilty of destroying the democratic qualities which came out of the military tradition. The old notion in civic affairs was to ostracize any citizen of such marked superiority that his excellence would be compromised by obedience to the laws; anyone, in short, who would demean both himself and the laws if he were to remain a part of the city. According to Aristotle, however, who represents for Sorel the later stages of the Socratic tradition, the truly superior citizen should not be ostracized: absolute genius is above the law. "There can be no law contrary to men who are utterly superior to others." According to Sorel, once this doctrine is admitted, "the principle of Oligarchy is posed."[53] Ostracism, which was a form of democratic compromise between absolute excellence and mediocrity, gave way to the principle of absolute privilege—a privilege that, though it is reserved to genius, can be reserved to all talented men. Superior beings are, in the Socratic tradition, "those who know," who have participated in divine grace. To Sorel, this Socratic doctrine helped to separate the old-fashioned doctrines of excellence—of performing well—on the one hand and democratic equality on the other; the traditional household/military virtues reconciled these two principles, whereas to Socrates the removing of all privileges and the return to traditional practices in which all citizen-soldier-farmers are equal is considered a crime against divinity. The philosophers, with Socrates at their head, maintained that the legitimate government belonged to the *savants.* As Sorel exclaims sarcastically, "How nice it would be if the assembly had dialecticians instead of old sailors! Then natural laws could really be discovered and infallible decisions taken."[54] Is not the right to rule of "those who know" a natural right, superior to a purely formal legality? To Sorel, in late Athens the old uniformity of culture on which tradition always rests had broken down, partly out of economic reasons such as increasing international commerce. As a consequence, there appeared a new urban class—an oligarchy of artisans and "*boutiquiers*"—far different from the farmers who had been the backbone of the old democracy.[55]

Xenophon and Aristophanes shared the opinion that the farming class was essential to democracy. In Xenophon's words, "those who had been used to the labor of the field would rather go out to fight and deliver their country, and the artificers would choose rather to sit still in the way they had been brought up."[56] These new sedentary urban men were an ideal constituency for the Sophists; they could afford "lessons" in rhetoric which the old farmers could not. This produced, in effect, a class division between the new urban "*boutiquiers*" and the old warrior-farmers. The economic basis of the former consisted in consumption and leisure, while the old class was concerned with production and action. The urban class, needing leisure for political activity, increased the demand for slaves. This leisure class, despising labor and relying on slavery, became the great moving agent of corruption. To Sorel, one of the primary laws of nature is that demoralization sets in when one gives up labor to devote one's life to living for power.[57]

The great question that Sorel attempts to answer is: to what degree does Socrates share with the Sophists the responsibility of changing the moral climate of the *polis* to such an extent that it undermined the classic virtues and the legitimacy of the old democracy? Sorel maintains that there were great differences between the Sophists and Socrates: Socrates was a philosopher, searching for an absolute basis for the state, who ignored the importance of historical law, while the Sophists were neither absolutist nor naturalistic in their perspective. "From a political point of view, Socrates was almost as bad as the Sophists."[58] In effect, Sorel's charge against Socrates was that he was guilty of corrupting the old institutions primarily because of the *strength* of his differences from the Sophists. Socrates' philosophical power made him as liable for the moral responsibility of Athenian decline as the Sophists. The latter were not as great a threat, according to Sorel, because they rarely acted at all and they never acted on principle. Sorel insists that Socrates' refusal of payment and his rejection of Sophistic demagogy added to his effectiveness. Like the Sophists, Socrates pretended to a science; there was a ready-made constituency eager and able to absorb Socratic teaching solely for their own political purposes. Socrates wished to wean the Sophistic customers away from their masters; but his philosophical success meant that he, not the Sophists, was used by the new urbanites to help formulate the ideology of the new urban oligarchy.[59] For Sorel, Socrates' excellence as a dialectician gave these men abilities they would not have possessed had they been content to study rhetoric with unprincipled Sophists.

Sorel admits that these new followers of Socrates perverted Socratic teaching; Socrates' failure was one not of commission but of omission. Far from questioning the sincerity of Socrates' intentions, Sorel says that the philosopher's failure was his inability to perceive that his teaching, though strong enough to give the *coup de grâce* to the old alliance of poets and orators, was not sufficient to sustain a lasting alliance between philosophy and politics. Strong as his teaching may have been, Socrates' failure lay in his inability to perceive the arrogance of his followers, to realize that his students would not remain chaste. Regarding themselves as possessing a "special science" of political things, they anticipated the worst form of government: the union of philosophy and politics in which the wealthy (who can afford expertise) and the able share power.[60]

Socratic morality brought forward the question of theory and practice that was to mark Sorel's study of Marx in future years. While the Platonic Socrates disdains politics, Sorel's Xenophontic Socrates insisted that the *savants* perform the mission of action—that they cannot merely cross their arms and laugh at the stupidities of fools.[61] But Socratic morals, as expounded by Xenophon the non-philosopher, can in Sorel's view succeed only if either power or philosophy itself is sacrificed. The unity of theory and practice brings two different moral qualities into play: prudence, the virtue connected with activity, and knowledge or science, the virtue connected with thought. Socratic political thought distinguishes between prudence and science; Sorel points to the familiar examples of Critias and Alcibiades to demonstrate the incompatibility of these two virtues. These two students of Socrates remained at the feet of the master only long enough to absorb lessons from him, and they remained perfectly virtuous as long as they stayed near him,[62] but upon entering the political world they were corrupted. Philosophy had imposed temperance on them, but this quality is not a science in the ordinary sense of the word.[63] It is a kind of virtue which requires propaganda by continuous teaching, as the Franciscan monks understand.[64] Socratic temperance consists in detaching oneself from the world; this is reflected in Socrates' asceticism. In attempting to "put the body out to pasture," only the intellect can be relied upon to be temperate—the body must be supervised continuously. But unlike the Franciscans, who must voluntarily take an oath of separation from the world, Alcibiades left his exemplar and went into the world of politics, leaving morals behind. Self-denial concerning secular goods "in the world" is more difficult. Part of the problem, as Sorel sees it, is basic to the character of all intellectuals: "Men of science do not interfere in active politics. It is remarkable enough that they are all the more timid as they are all the more firm and radical in their doctrines. In general, men who resort to violence are the most theoretically weak. Our revolutionary assemblies are the best proof of this."[65]

In addition to the farmer-soldiers, we now have professional politicians and professional intellectuals. The politicians use the philosophers as their ideologues, while he are incapable of practical action. In Sorel's view, this leads to the corruption of both. The professional politicians become more arbitrary, while the philosophers, having no practical ties, become more and more utopian and less and less tolerant of opposing opinions. By reducing all political problems to formulas, the philosophers tend to place everything in rigid molds; the result is the loss not only of the old virtues but of freedom itself.[66] Sorel's Socrates has placed the intellectual in a double bind. The constant supervision of a philosopher's pupils makes attention to politics impossible, and attention to philosophy must result eventually in the separation of philosophy from politics. The unity of theory and practice is ironically presented in such a way as to conform to the lesson of Plato's cave: the rule of philosophers negates itself. Since practical politicians can only use philosophy in an improper way and the intellectuals can do nothing to stop them, men of intellect become divorced from men of politics, and the old farmer-soldier class which had united the two with poetic myths is shunted aside. Without access to the "science" of the men of intellect, the old Athenian warriors found themselves shut off from power. For these old soldiers, good citizenship meant a virile education based on mythology. In Sorel's eyes, when Socrates replaced this with study he replaced the souls of free men with the minds of *savants.*[67] Thought became abstracted from reality and politics lost its moral roots. As a consequence of the inevitable separation of philosophy from action, Socrates' attempt at moral reconstruction of the city only sped his own death; the advance of philosophy continued.

Much of Sorel's effort is spent in arguing against the Socratic natural-law theory itself. To Xenophon's Socrates (though not to Plato's) the just man is he who obeys the laws of his country, and there is no clear distinction in Xenophon between the just and the legal. Socrates, wishing to prove to his son that he ought to honor his mother, establishes a theory of the family based on civil law, noting that the state punishes men who are uncivil to their parents. Hence the rules become juridical: they do not carry certitude in themselves, but are demonstrated by the consequences of transgression, by the existence of sanctions revealed by observation.[68] In another instance, Xenophon's Socrates gives as his argument against physical pederasty the opprobrium attached to it.

Sorel takes care to dissociate Socrates from utilitarianism, however. Utilitarianism sees the motive of a thing determined in the agent, while Socrates, speaking from a juridical standpoint, asserts that the "science of the law" has as its object to recognize what is best ordered and consequently what is most useful for men.[69] How does Sorel distinguish Socrates' equation of law and morals from Xenophon's traditionalism which, like any traditionalism, does the same thing? A traditional orientation tends to equate the just with the legal. Sorel attempts to get out of this by saying that if the just man obeys the laws of his country, the search for justice must focus on the search for a just law, an absolute law of nature: the political decision of an assembly is just only if it conforms to that natural law. But why does Sorel insist that this *begins* with a unity between law and morality? How can Sorel say that Socrates is subversive in starting his logic from the most conventional and traditional observations and then accuse him of subverting these traditions?[70] Could he have taken any other tack?

The Sophists, Sorel is the first to admit, had disturbed tradition through philosophy by demonstrating the break between nature and convention. Socrates could only restore traditional virtues on the Sophists' own philosophical grounds rather than by appeal to tradition. Sorel takes a different view, criticizing the Socratic theory of knowledge: on the one hand, Socrates pretends to legislate scientifically for pure essences which do not exist in nature, and on the other hand, he is obliged to have recourse to observation and phenomenology in order to posit his juridical rules. The dialectical method, according to Sorel, is a very embarrassing one for Socrates. During the Socratic dialogue, commonsense observation is used in order to posit unwritten laws and to discover among these unwritten laws some which have codified equivalents and penal sanctions. Thus morality becomes juridical and law becomes the expression of truth; but Sorel asks, "Who will say this truth?" No one really knows, and we arrive at the absence of certitude in morals; since we lose certitude, "the principle of legitimacy disappears from the law itself."[71]

There is another difficulty with natural law, according to Sorel. If morality is equated with law, if the search for justice focuses on a search for absolute reason and natural law is thought to be discovered, force and repression may be used to enforce it. This use of force, in Sorel's view, leads to the complete disappearance of both tradition and freedom except for the freedom of the philosopher to discover the good. What repressive regime, asks Sorel in a later work, has not justified itself on the basis that it was the possessor of truth? "The philosophy of natural justice is in perfect agreement with that of force." Sorel cites Pascal: "Justice is subject to dispute; might is easily recognized and not disputed. Thus it is not possible to attribute might to justice, because might has often contradicted justice and said that it itself was just. And thus not being able to make what was just strong, what was strong has been made just."[72] Moreover, mere observation showed Pascal the absurdity of the theory of natural right; if this theory was correct, we ought to find laws which are universally admitted; but actions which we regard as criminal have at other times been regarded as virtuous: "Three degrees of latitude nearer the pole reverse all jurisprudence, a meridian decides what is truth. . . . Truth on one side of the Pyrenees becomes error on the other. . . . We must, it is said, go back to the natural and fundamental laws of the state, which an unjust custom has abolished. This is a game certain to result in the loss of all; nothing will be just on the balance."[73]

Sorel asserts that Pascal's criticism of natural right has not the perfect clearness that we could give it at the present day, because we now know that economics has a type of force that has attained absolutely uncontrolled development and thus can be identified naturally with right. This is precisely Sorel's focus in his attack on Socrates. It is in economics that the original soldier-farmers of Sorel's primitive Greek society had their roots. Virtue for him is found in a system run by the producers themselves. Only those who themselves produce can act to run the society in which that production takes place, and it is in this combination of productive activity and the action necessary to preserve it that man discovers his virtue. It is therefore interesting that Sorel's assertion that natural law with its corollary theory of justice should lead to repression is combined with an affirmation of the concept of virtue. Sorel ends by driving a wedge between justice and virtue. "Natural justice" is not really natural at all; it is an abstract intellectual construction—something Sorel rejects—while real virtue is integral to the productive life. In noting that the life of production is the most fruitful for moral science and that only in the historical course of economic activity can one truly understand and discover the underlying forces of moral advancement, Sorel was led to Marxism. But in recognizing that custom was part of that historical development, that Marxism itself was intellectualistic, i.e., that Marxism preferred abstract justice to virtue, he was led away from it again.

IV

It remains for us to evaluate the overall validity of Sorel's indictment, not, we hasten to add, because Socrates is in any great need of rescue; it is not the purpose of this volume to preserve the philosopher's reputation against Sorel's assaults, any more than it is to fend off those of Nietzsche or Hegel, which Sorel's resembles in several points.[74] It is important for our understanding of Sorel, however, to understand the attack, for it reflects Sorel's own moral system. We inquired above whether Sorel's invocation of and representation of Xenophon were accurate. If Xenophon's "pseudo-Socratic"

Oeconomicus is in fact similar to his "Socratic" discourses, it would either make Sorel's Xenophon into a Socratic or the Xenophontic Socrates into something that was closer to Xenophon himself. The first transformation would force Sorel to disconnect himself from Xenophon; the second would ruin Sorel's case against Socrates. In any case, a closer reading of Xenophon reveals that the *Oeconomicus* is in some respects far more similar to the other dialogues than Sorel claims they are.

The *Oeconomicus* seems to uphold many of those "corrupt" characteristics with regard to the arrangement of the household and the morals that hold it together which Sorel denies in that dialogue but which he claims permeate the so-called "genuinely" Socratic works. In the *Oeconomicus*, Ischomachus, the expert in economics and the virtual personification of Xenophon, argues that marriage is primarily for the purpose of procreation and for security. Nothing is said about love, which Sorel calls the basis of social sentiments. On the contrary, Xenophon's Ischomachus goes so far as to argue that he did not choose his wife "for want of someone to sleep with—this is obvious, I know, to you too. . . . I considered . . . whom I might take as the best partner for the household."[75] Conversely, Socrates—in, of all places, the *Memorabilia*—praises *eros* as a gift from the gods who "limited the season of the year in which they gave other animals the pleasures of sexual intercourse, but to us they granted these continuously until old age."[76] It appears that if Xenophon and Socrates are indeed different, it is Xenophon who comes closer to reducing marriage to a legal contract while Socrates preserves *eros*[77] —the reverse of Sorel's interpretation. This is not to say that the *Oeconomicus* is in fact very different from the other dialogues; merely, on the contrary, that Sorel does not make a very strong case for that proposition.

There is a far more serious problem concerning the economic aspects of household management. In the *Memorabilia* Socrates discusses household management in a manner which is quite similar to the intent of the *Oeconomicus*: Aristarchus is advised by Socrates to give his relatives work in order to make them productive; by "productive" is meant useful and beneficial for both worker and master.[78] If the two dialogues indeed contain the same teaching on this question, then either the *Oeconomicus* is Socratic or the *Memorabilia* is not (at least in respect to the question of household management).

This leads in turn to a still more important difficulty in Sorel's interpretation. It is not at all clear that the *Oeconomicus* is much more egalitarian than the so-called "genuine" Socratic dialogues of

Xenophon. Indeed, one can see considerable similarities of sentiment and outlook among all of them. In the first place, surely Xenophon did not really mean a general equality between husband and wife in household duties. It might be said that Xenophon, in endowing woman with memory and diligence equal to that of the male, is somewhat more liberal than Aristotle, but household organization is still, as in Aristotle, a four-level hierarchy of husband, wife, supervisors, and slaves.[79] The difference between men and women is not a simple horizontal division of labor between indoor and outdoor work but a vertical or hierarchical one as well: Xenophon makes it clear that women's work is inferior, for it is due to the sedentary nature of indoor work that Xenophon condemns the new urban artisans as inferior to farmer-gentlemen.[80]

Perhaps more than any other ancient writer, Xenophon emphasized the importance of hierarchy and expertise in military affairs as well as the household. It is significant that Xenophon's *Education of Cyrus*, in which Socrates does not appear, has as its main theme the replacement of the amateur and generalist in military affairs and the establishment of a hierarchy of carefully trained specialists and experts. This is, of course, hardly surprising, in light of the fact that Xenophon was one of the great military innovators of history. It was he who was responsible for transforming the inflexible Greek phalanx into a highly adaptable military instrument, employing such novelties as reserve forces, light infantry tactics suitable for mountain warfare, and the like.[81]

This hierarchic characteristic is not at all absent from the *Oeconomicus*, in which Xenophon repeats his admiration for King Cyrus's great Oriental empire. In the conclusion of the work, Xenophon compares estate managers to generals and both generals and household management to rulers. Ischomachus states that "as to that which is common to all pursuits, agricultural, political, domestic, or military, namely, that he who would excel in them must be capable of directing others, I entirely agree with you, Socrates, that some persons greatly excel others in judgment." Xenophon also makes it clear that excellence in all these areas is manifested by ability in "the art of ruling over willing subjects" and, as such, this excellence has "something of a kingly character."[82] Xenophon compares the housewife to a queen bee, while the relationship between master and field hands is a tyrannical one "suitable only for brutes."[83] The role of the expert seems not only as important for Xenophon as it does for Plato, but seems directed toward "having more obedient human beings for my use,"[84] and this in turn is directed toward the end of order and efficiency.

Perhaps the supreme shortcoming of *Le Procès de Socrate* is that the man whom Sorel regards as the embodiment of the old virtues is in fact the supreme technocrat and bureaucrat—the closest thing in Hellenic antiquity to an advocate of a highly centralized, meritocratic, and technocratic society.[85] This confusion on Sorel's part stems in part from his attempt to distill the pure Socratic teaching from that of Xenophon. Sorel is aware of the difficulties of this undertaking, noting that "if the *Education of Cyrus* is replete with the Socratic spirit, it also contains many parts in which Xenophon has expressed his own ideas."[86] But this is certainly as true for the other dialogues. It is easy for Sorel to transpose the Xenophontic characteristics and the Socratic ones, but it is hardly consistent for him to admit the partly Socratic nature of the Xenophontic Cyrus and then extol the *Oeconomicus* for its egalitarianism, when both praise Cyrus's monarchy.[87]

The retroflection of Socrates and Xenophon becomes even more complicated when we try to distinguish Ischomachus' teaching from that of Socrates in the *Oeconomicus.* It certainly appears that Socrates is the student in this dialogue, learning from Ischomachus about things of which he (Socrates) is confessedly ignorant. But Ischomachus, who appears to personify Xenophon, notes the money-making potential of home economics. "Know well," says Ischomachus, that "we have made many parcels of land worth many times their old value." To which Socrates replies that by nature Ischomachus and his family are "really no less lovers of farming than the merchants are lovers of grain,"[88] in which profit rather than use becomes the standard of value. Ischomachus thinks Socrates is joking[89] but apparently (along with Sorel) misses the point: that he may not be a farmer in the traditional understanding of the word but a businessman, a practitioner of that part of the art of acquisition (*chrematistic*) which includes usury or retail trade for profit. Aristotle distinguishes this commercial side of *chrematistic* from that side which is devoted to home economics or natural acquisition for use; it appears that Ischomachus is unaware of this distinction.[90] Is there not a touch of Socratic irony in a dialogue which commences by praising home economics and concludes by appearing to extol the urban arts of profit-making? Either Xenophon is aware of Socrates' meaning and hence, through Ischomachus, is gently mocking himself, or he is making Socrates legitimate his own ideas—ideas which seem to want to import urban ideas into traditional areas.[91]

There is considerable similarity between this admiration for profit in the *Oeconomicus* and Socrates' defense in the *Memorabilia* of businessmen as generals, against Nichomachides' claim to a generalship based on experience.[92] Here again obedience as the school of command is challenged by urban expertise. Since Sorel's thesis requires that the Xenophontic be distinguished from the purely Socratic elements in these writings, it would seem that Sorel's case against Socrates has been weakened. There is less difference among Xenophon's dialogues than Sorel would have us believe.

Finally, there appear to be no great differences between the rural and anti-urban sentiments of Xenophon and those of Plato's *Laws* and Aristotle's *Politics.* All three writers seem concerned with placing citizenship on a modest middle class of gentlemen who rely in part on the labor of others and who seem a bit more socially elevated than Sorel's peasant ideal. Indeed, Xenophon's admiration for profits places him at a somewhat greater distance from the traditional practices extolled by Plato and Aristotle.[93]

Sixteen years after he wrote his work on Socrates, Sorel persisted in referring to Xenophon as an "old Athenian" and condemned Marx for saying that the profit-oriented author of the *Oeconomicus* had a bourgeois instinct.[94] Sorel did change his mind in regard to the *Memorabilia*, however, saying that that work reflects Xenophon himself rather than Socrates.[95] Thus Sorel is consistent in maintaining that Xenophon was old-fashioned, but in so doing he must now admit that the *Memorabilia* is old-fashioned. In Sorel's eyes, Xenophon's integrity remains intact; it is his own indictment of Socrates which must fall. Xenophon's "dialectical finesse" has won out over his unwitting conviction. Sorel later confessed to Croce that *Le Procès du Socrate* "was composed in the provinces, without much knowledge and with vagueness on many points," and discouraged its re-publication.[96]

But the very fact that Sorel upheld the rusticity of Xenophon and the moral values contained in the *Oeconomicus* led him to retain the moral basis on which Socrates was indicted in his early work. In the final chapter of what Sorel calls his "standard work," the *Reflections on Violence*, we see a substantially similar praise of work, family, and the warrior and a condemnation of intellectuals.[97] Even the laudatory treatment of Xenophon remains.

The transposition of Socrates and Xenophon in *Le Procès du Socrate* later takes the form of a blend of bourgeois and traditional characteristics coloring Sorel's vision of industrial life. In his later works on socialism and Marxism, Sorel seems to take as ambiguous a view of the division of labor as he did of Xenophon's attempts to introduce order and rationality into traditional affairs. Sorel's entire syndicalist outlook is affected by an attempt to restore traditional virtues while offsetting these virtues by a respect for constant improvement and innovation in industry, improvement that is usually subversive of those traditional values. The ease with which different and varied tasks are mastered is counterbalanced in Sorel's writings with an agonal portrait of the modern industrial worker, straining to overcome the Sisyphusian resistance that nature exerts on all of man's efforts. We can say that Xenophon's mixture of new and old ideas was reflected in Sorel's failure to disentangle the Socratic from the Xenophontic elements in the dialogues. Sorel attempted in his own way to graft traditional values onto modern industrial practice without ever quite embracing the cult of expertise that developed out of the relentless division of labor characterizing modern production. Sorel, in contrast to Xenophon, assumed that those traditional productive virtues would lessen the need for experts. For Sorel, the modern industrial laborer would be the equivalent of the old soldier, and the myth of the general strike would be the new Homeric social poetry. That Xenophon had little use for the old soldiers (or, it would seem, the poetic teaching that inspired them) is obscured by Sorel's simplified understanding of Xenophon as a representative of traditional values.

Notes

1. Renan, *La Réforme intellectuelle et morale*, p. 55.
2. Ibid., p. 327.
3. Ibid.
4. Ibid., p. 325.
5. Ibid., p. 315.
6. Ibid., p. 314.
7. Ibid., p. 316.
8. Ibid., p. 325.
9. Ibid., p. 329.
10. For Sorel's general reaction to this development see Chapter 6.
11. Sorel, *Contribution à l'étude profane de la Bible*, p. vii.
12. Sorel, review of Fouillée, *Eléments sociologiques de la morale*, in *Revue générale de bibliographie* (Dec. 1905): 489.
13. Sorel, *Illusions* (American ed.), pp. 25-26.
14. James H. Meisel, *The Genesis of Georges Sorel* (Ann Arbor: George Wahr, 1951), p. 60.
15. Sorel, *Le Procès de Socrate*, pp. 172-73. The quotation is actually taken by Sorel from Ernst Curtius, *Histoire grecque* (Paris: Leroux, 1883-1884), translated from the German by A. Bouche-Leclercq, vol. 2, p. 460 (*FGS*, p. 63).
16. Sorel, *Le Procès de Socrate*, p. 222.
17. Ibid., p. 176 (*FGS*, p. 64).
18. Ibid., p. 213 (*FGS*, p. 69).
19. Ibid., pp. 213-15, citing Plato's *Gorgias* LXVII and Xenophon's *Symposium* IV.6 (*FGS*, pp. 69-70).

20. Ibid., p. 8.
21. Ibid., p. 13.
22. Ibid., p. 222.
23. Ibid., p. 223.
24. Ibid., p. 245.
25. Ibid., p. 242. Sorel says practically the same thing in *La Révolution Dreyfusienne* with respect to the Dreyfus Affair, attacking the Dreyfusards for undermining traditional virtues while conceding that the trial of Dreyfus may have been unfairly conducted.
26. Sorel, *Le Procès de Socrate*, p. 34.
27. Plato's *Apology* also distinguishes between the "old accusers" and the "present" (or "later") accusers of Socrates. The old accusers were the traditionalists and poets, including Aristophanes, who "got hold of most of you when you were children," Socrates said, "and I fear them more than I fear Anytus." Rooted in sincere conviction, their opinions are "hardest to cope with." The very strength of their traditional beliefs make their accusations "much more compelling" and, since they are based on a mass belief, they cannot be cross-examined: Plato *Apology* 18, trans. by F. J. Church (Indianapolis: Bobbs-Merrill, 1956). Anytus and Meletus, both associated with the "later accusers," are guilty of insincerity, "of playing a solemn joke by casually bringing men to trial." These new accusers are cross-examined (Apology 24). Compare Xenophon's *Apology* at 14.
28. Sorel seems to anticipate the confessedly eccentric notion put forth in our day by Leo Strauss, who maintains that "Xenophon is the only one who, while knowing Socrates himself, showed by deed that he was willing to be a historian. Hence it would appear that the primary source for our knowledge of Socrates should be the Socratic writings of Xenophon." Against the common judgment of Xenophon as simple-minded and philistine, Strauss maintains that our age "is surely blind to the greatness of Xenophon," and upholds Winckelmann's comparisons of Xenophon to Raphael with Thucydides to Michelangelo: Leo Strauss, *Xenophon's Socratic Discourse: An Interpretation of the 'Oeconomicus'* (Ithaca: Cornell University Press, 1970), pp. 83-84, citing J. J. Winckelmann, *Ausgewahlte Schriften und Briefe*, ed. Walter Rehm (Wiesbaden: Dietrich, 1948), pp. 22, 37, 46, 119. Against this view, Neal Wood maintains that "primarily because of the meticulous researching of German scholarship, Xenophon is no longer generally considered a creditable source for the character of the intellect of Socrates. Upon careful scrutiny the *Hellenica* has failed to pass muster as either good history or chronology": "Xenophon's Theory of Leadership," *Classica et Mediaevalia* 25, no. 1 (1964): 33-66. Anton-Herman Chroust notes that although Xenophon records a total of forty-nine Socratic conversations, he himself participates in only one of them. "The Xenophontean *Socratica* are not so much historico-biographical reporting fact, but rather autobiographical . . . and, therefore, primarily the product of creative writing and unfettered imagination . . . and as such of extremely limited historical source value": *Socrates, Man and Myth: The Two Socratic Dialogues of Xenophon* (London: Routledge and Kegan Paul, 1957), pp. 9 and 15. Cf. Theodor Gomperz, *Greek Thinkers*, vol. 2, trans. by G. G. Berry (London: John Murray, 1949). Gomperz argues that, compared to Plato, Xenophon reveals "much less artistic freedom, and yet not much more historical fidelity" (p. 61). A somewhat more balanced view of Xenophon comes from J. K. Anderson, who says that "Xenophon seems to have found the 'Socratic

dialogue' a convenient medium for expressing his own opinions, but we may suppose that, if he is not always remembering what Socrates actually said on a particular topic, he is still asking himself 'What would Socrates have said?'": *Xenophon* (New York: Scribners, 1974), p. 20. But Anderson elsewhere distinguishes the historical from the Socratic works of Xenophon, saying that as an historian Xenophon is "far inferior" to his predecessor Thucydides "in almost all respects": *Military Theory and Practice in the Age of Xenophon* (Berkeley, Los Angeles, and London: University of California Press, 1970), p. 9. Eduard Delebecque has a similar conviction that Socrates' teaching permeates Xenophon's works, even the non-Socratic ones. "One must keep from citing the Socratic words of Xenophon as Gospel but we should not go so far as to deny all historical value to them. . . . If Xenophon is our best source of the knowledge of Socrates because he often relates words that were really said or exposes a thought which was his own, we must recognize nonetheless that this source is not always accurate, for it often concentrates on what Socrates said on a particular day." Furthermore, Xenophon is more of a bibliophile than Plato and certainly Socrates, who, in the *Phaedrus*, scorns books: Eduard Delebecque, *Essai sur la vie de Xénophon* (Paris: Klincksieck, 1957), pp. 239-41, citing Plato *Phaedrus* 275-76.

29. Sorel, *Le Procès de Socrate*, pp. 375-89.

30. Ibid., pp. 375-76.

31. Ibid., p. 376. Sorel underscores this point by noting that there is an almost identical passage praising Cyrus in Xenophon's non-Socratic dialogue, the *Cyropaedia* (*Oeconomicus* IV. 7; *Cyropaedia* VIII. vi. 11). On the other hand, Leo Strauss maintains that Xenophon divides activity into the categories of speech, action, and thought, which would appear "to underlie the distinction among his three Socratic writings other than the *Memorabilia*. . . . This would mean that the *Oeconomicus* is devoted to Socrates speaking or conversing, the *Symposium* to Socrates' deeds, and the *Apology of Socrates* to Socrates deliberating (on a certain subject). Accordingly, the *Oeconomicus* would be Xenophon's Socratic *logos* or discourse par excellence" (*Xenophon's Socratic Discourse*, p. 86). But why assign the *Oeconomicus* to speech rather than action, and why assign the *Apology* to thought rather than speech? Though Strauss's views again seem extreme, W. K. C. Guthrie partially agrees with them when he says that Xenophon's purpose in the *Oeconomicus* is to illustrate the dialectical method, that is, "to illustrate a pedagogic principle that he had learned from Socrates": *Socrates* (Cambridge: Cambridge University Press, 1971), p. 17. Delebecque, on the other hand, is "struck by the strange analogy between the first chapters of the *Oeconomicus* and the first two books of the *Memorabilia*" (*Essai sur la vie de Xénophon*, p. 235). Chroust admits that the *Oeconomicus* is a vehicle for Xenophon's own ideas, but that this characteristic is "no less apparent in the remaining *Socratica* of Xenophon" (*Socrates, Man and Myth*, p. 11).

32. J. K. Davis has found an historical Ischomachus who appears to resemble Xenophon's tight-fisted and wealthy landowner and who might have been an acquaintance of Socrates: *Athenian Propertied Families* (Oxford: Oxford University Press, 1971), p. 267. Sorel and Plato are certainly in agreement on Socrates' own urban preferences, "never leaving town to cross the frontier nor even . . . so much as setting foot outside the walls." Socrates says, "I'm a lover of learning, and trees and open country won't teach me anything, whereas men in town do": Plato *Phaedrus* 230d, the R.

Hackforth translation (Indianapolis: Bobbs-Merrill, 1952), p. 25.

33. Despite the possibility that Xenophon might indeed have possessed some "dialectical finesse," Sorel admits that "the theses of Socrates are not formulated by Xenophon with the scientific rigor and precision which characterized the Peripatetic school" (*Le Procès de Socrate*, pp. 2-3).

34. Xenophon *Oeconomicus* I. 10. Contrast this with *Cyropaedia* I. iii. 17, in which a teacher of justice flogs young Cyrus for deciding in favor of allowing a large boy to exchange his small tunic for a larger tunic owned by a smaller boy on the grounds that the legal is right and the unlawful is wrong, that the boys were entitled to possess only that to which they were legally entitled. If the concept of *fitness* has any relation to the concept of *well-ordered*, then either Xenophon is not being consistent or he is not identifying his own views either with those of Cyrus's teacher or with those of Socrates.

35. Sorel, *Le Procès de Socrate*, pp. 376-80, citing *Oeconomicus* IV. 2-4. For an exposition of the Xenophontic view of war, see Neal Wood, "Xenophon's Theory of Leadership." For a general discussion of the relation between Xenophon and Sorel, see Neal Wood, "Some Reflections on Sorel and Machiavelli," *Political Science Quarterly* 83 (March 1968): 76-91.

36. Sorel, *Le Procès de Socrate*, p. 382, citing *Oeconomicus* VII. 18, 22, and 28.

37. Sorel, *Le Procès de Socrate*, p. 168.

38. Ibid., p. 175 (*FGS*, p. 63).

39. Sorel, "Essai sur la philosophie de Proudhon," p. 44, citing Proudhon's *La Guerre et la paix*.

40. Sorel, *Le Procès de Socrate*, p. 165. Here Sorel invokes Aristotle's *Politics* 1279b. Neal Wood maintains that "Plato and Aristotle see no similarity between the art of war on the one hand, and politics and economics on the other. . . . The crucial managerial function of the general is completely neglected" in Plato and Aristotle ("Xenophon's Theory of Leadership," p. 46).

41. Xenophon *Oeconomicus* VIII.8-10.

42. Aristotle *Politics* 1279b.

43. Xenophon *Oeconomicus* XX.1-5, XV.10.

44. Cf. W. Kendrick Pritchett, *The Greek State at War*, vol. 1 (Berkeley, Los Angeles, London: University of California Press, 1974): "There is no evidence that [Greek] military discipline was regularized and codified to the degree of the Roman. . . . From Xenophon we get the impression that discipline was lax." Popular odium prevented unmanly conduct; discipline was different from that in modern, expert mercenary armies "in which the slightest loosening of discipline results in barbarization" (pp. 244-45). W. W. Tarn says that "fighting was amateur fighting: men left their occupations to fight in the summer and there was little temptation to study the art of war": *Hellenistic Military and Naval Developments* (Cambridge: Cambridge University Press, 1930), p. 33. J. K. Anderson notes "how very far the officers were from forming a separate class, as in a modern European Army" (*Military Theory and Practice in the Age of Xenophon*, p. 99, citing *Cyropaidea* II.2.6-9).

45. Sorel, "Etude sur Vico," *Devenir Social* (November 1896): 925.

46. Sorel, *Matériaux*, p. 199.

47. Sorel, *Le Procès de Socrate*, pp. 87-101, citing Xenophon *Symposium* VIII. See the *Réflexions*, in which Sorel maintains that "love, by the

enthusiasm which it engenders, can produce the sublime without which there would be absolutely no effective morality" (American edition, p. 235; *FGS*, p. 216).

48. Sorel, *Le Procès de Socrate*, p. 106.

49. Ibid., pp. 126-32, 135, citing Xenophon *Memorabilia* I.i.4, iii. 4.

50. Sorel, *Le Procès de Socrate*, pp. 7-8.

51. Ibid., p. 132.

52. Ibid., p. 169n, citing Xenophon *Memorabilia* III. i, iv, v.

53. Sorel, *Le Procès de Socrate*, p. 198 (*FGS*, pp. 64-65).

54. Ibid., pp. 239, 239n (cf. *Memorabilia* III.ix.10-11).

55. Ibid., p. 179 (*FGS*, p. 65).

56. See Xenophon *Oeconomicus* IV.2, 3, and Sorel, *Le Procès de Socrate*, pp. 375-76.

57. Sorel, *Le Procès de Socrate*, p. 85.

58. Ibid., p. 203.

59. Ibid., p. 236: "We have seen that the secret societies had produced the greatest harm in Athens during the Peloponnesian War; we have noted with Curtius the destruction of family ties by the activity of these associations which were both political and religious at the same time. . . . Undoubtedly, Socrates was not connected with the formation of these lodges, but he was the most brilliant and forceful theoretician of the new organization based on the fictional family."

60. Ibid., p. 210 (*FGS*, p. 68).

61. Ibid., p. 199 (*FGS*, p. 65), citing Xenophon *Memorabilia* III. vii. Cf. Plato *Apology* 31 and *Republic* 592a-b.

62. Sorel, *Le Procès de Socrate*, pp. 286-87, citing Xenophon *Memorabilia* I.i.

63. Sorel, *Le Procès de Socrate*, p. 287.

64. Ibid., p. 294.

65. Ibid., p. 204 (*FGS*, p. 66).

66. Ibid., p. 205 (*FGS*, p. 67). Cf. p. 7, in which Sorel maintains that the only freedom left in Socrates' ideal world is the freedom of the philosopher to search for the good.

67. Ibid., p. 212 (*FGS*, p. 69): "Study could make a scholar out of a freed slave, but it could not give him the soul of a free man."

68. Ibid., pp. 301-2. Plato's Socrates presents a more complex relationship between law and morals. See *Apology* 29-30 and cf. *Crito* 51.

69. Sorel, *Le Procès de Socrate*, p. 303n.

70. Sorel himself refers to that speech of Socrates on obedience to the law in which he gets Hippias to admit that "the gods are therefore satisfied that the just and the lawful are the same thing," an assertion which is in close agreement with *Cyropaedia* I.iii.17 (see footnote 34, above). See *Memorabilia* IV.iv.24-25.

Leo Strauss notes that "Socrates has not proved that the legal and the just are the same. This explains why he abruptly turns to the unwritten laws . . . because its transgressors cannot possibly escape punishment. . . . In the case of incest between parents and children, however, the automatic punishment consists in the defective character of the offspring. . . . In other words, that divine punishment (and reward) is the same as the natural consequence of human action": Leo Strauss, *Xenophon's Socrates* (Ithaca: Cornell University Press, 1972), pp. 111-13.

71. Sorel, *Le Procès de Socrate*, p. 303.

72. Sorel, *Réflexions*, pp. 24, 26-27, citing Pascal, *Pensées*, frags. 297, 302, 303, 306, 307, 311 of the Brunschwig ed. (*FGS*, pp. 197-98; American edition, pp. 37-38).

73. Sorel, *Réflexions*, p. 26, citing Pascal, *Pensées*, frag. 294 (*FGS*, p. 198).

74. Hegel argues that "Socrates established in the place of the Delphic Oracle the principle that man must look within himself to know what is truth. . . . This inward certainty . . . is undoubtedly another new god, and not the god of the Athenians existing hitherto, and thus the accusation of Socrates was quite just": *The History of Philosophy*, trans. E. S. Haldane (New York: Humanities Press, 1955), vol. I, p. 435. He adds, however, that the Athenians "had come into a period of culture in which this individual consciousness made itself independent of the universal spirit and became itself. . . . The principle of Socrates is hence not a transgression of one individual, for all were implicated; the crime was one that the spirit of the people committed against itself" (ibid., p. 447). Sorel lauds Socrates for founding philosophy and, like Hegel, admits that no formal crime was committed. But whereas Hegel calls Socrates' death a tragedy, Sorel argues that it was, to use Hegelian terminology, "a rational misfortune" in which the course of events is "brought about by the will of the subject" (ibid., p. 446). This seems to be only a terminological difference. Hegel insists that Socrates brought on his fate by refusing to propose an alternative punishment, while Sorel says that Socrates planned a hero's death (ibid., p. 442; Sorel, *Le Procès de Socrate*, p. 261). It is interesting to note that Hegel's discussion of the trial of Socrates refers to Xenophon's account twelve times and to Plato's only four (Hegel, *The History of Philosophy*, pp. 425-48). There is no evidence that Sorel was influenced by a reading of Hegel's *History of Philosophy* any more than he had been by Nietzsche's *Birth of Tragedy*, which was not translated into French until 1901, twelve years after the publication of *Le Procès de Socrate*. It is doubtful that Sorel would have read it in German. Moreover, as Geneviève Bianquis says, "It is hardly possible to speak of [Nietzsche's] influence at this time (1893)." This is still four years after the publication in 1889 of *Le Procès de Socrate*, and the first articles on Nietzsche appeared in French journals in 1891 and 1892 (*Nietzsche en France* [Paris: Alcan, 1929], p. 10). In any case, the two figures look at art in somewhat different lights. Both side with Aeschyulus against Euripides, but Sorel does not distinguish between the epic and tragedy, as Nietzsche does. For Nietzsche, the death of Socrates restores a new poetry and a new art, whereas for Sorel (as for Hegel) the triumph of philosophy over poetry is complete.

Most authorities are in agreement that Nietzsche's influence on Sorel is minimal overall and non-existent in the early writings. Thus Fernand Rossignol says: "Nothing authorizes us, it would seem, to speak of a true influence of Nietzsche upon Sorel. The heroic theme exists in Sorel's writings, and he had often played on it before revealing the slightest trace of a reading of Nietzsche's works. And Georges Sorel did not have the habit of ignoring what he had read!": *Pour connaître la pensée de Georges Sorel* (Paris: Bordas, 1948), p. 52. Georges Goriely says that both writers were inspired by the prospect of social disintegration, of decadence and prevailing mediocrity, and concludes that we "ought to attribute to Nietzsche only a very occasional influence on Sorel's thought": *Le Pluralisme dramatique de Georges Sorel* (Paris: Rivière, 1962), pp. 54-55. It is true that at a later date,

Sorel consorted with Daniel Halévy and other Nietzsche pioneers; but even Geneviève Bianquis, who mistakenly attributes a "Nietzschean imperialism" to Sorel, notes that Barrès, Péguy, and others did not take their nationalism from Nietzsche and that the pragmatic philosophy of Bergson "owes nothing to Nietzsche": *Nietzsche en France*, pp. 7, 79, 81 (see Chapter 8). I can find only four discussions of Nietzsche in Sorel's work in the *Reflections* (*FGS*, pp. 212-15); in Sorel's Preface to Serverio Merlino's *Formes et essence du socialisme* (Paris: Giard et Brière, 1898); and in two reviews of Pacheu's *Du Positivisme au mysticisme* in *Revue Générale de Bibliographie* (Feb. 1906): 30 and of Valois' *L'Homme qui vient* in ibid, (Dec. 1906): 453.

75. Xenophon *Oeconomicus* VII.11.

76. Xenophon *Memorabilia* I.iv.12.

77. Cf. Delebecque, *Essai sur la vie de Xénophon*, p. 225: "This utilitarian idea of marriage is closer to that of the author of the *Oeconomicus* than to that of Socrates."

78. Xenophon *Memorabilia* II.vii.10 (see footnote 95, below).

79. Later Sorel argues that such a hierarchy is a return to older customs, citing the *Memorabilia* II.vii to support this viewpoint: see *FGS*, p. 336n14.

80. Xenophon *Oeconomicus* VI.5, VII.3. Compare Aristotle *Politics*, which also implies a relative equality between men and women in its comparison of the head of the household to a statesman and the wife to a non-governing citizen rather than as king and subject (1259b). Aristotle undoes this equality immediately, however, by stating that "a modest silence is a woman's crown" (1260a). Since speech is essential to citizenship, to encourage silence is to reject claims to equal status.

81. See Wood, "Xenophon's Theory of Leadership," p. 36. J. K. Anderson says: "Modern scholars have sometimes held that the hoplite [phalanx] was obsolete in the fourth century, and blamed Xenophon and his Spartan contemporaries for not recognizing the fact. But although Xenophon may have underestimated the power of the new professional light armed infantry, it does not follow that the Greeks would have done well to rely on that power alone": *Military Theory and Practice in the Age of Xenophon*, pp. 111-12. Elsewhere, Anderson says that Xenophon admitted his errors and corrected them: "Xenophon also gives examples of his skill and imagination in adapting technical formations to the ground and to the enemies' position—a branch of generalship in which . . . he judged the professional drillmasters to be deficient": *Xenophon,* (New York: Scribners, 1974), p. 130, citing Xenophon *Anabasis* III.iii.1ff., and *Memorabilia* III.i.2.

82. Xenophon *Oeconomicus* XXI.10.

83. Ibid., VII.31-34, XIII.9.

84. Ibid., XIII.10.

85. In his work "On the Revenue of Athens," Xenophon advocates extensive nationalization projects.

86. Sorel, *Le Procès de Socrate*, p. 334.

87. Xenophon *Oeconomicus* IV.7; *Cyropaedia* VIII.vi.11.

88. Xenophon *Oeconomicus* XX.24, 27.

89. Ibid., XX.29.

90. Aristotle *Politics* 1256b-1258a. Aristotle distinguishes two types of *chremetistic* (the art of gain): one serves *oeconomicus* or household management; the other serves usury or retail trade for profit. The former is the only one Aristotle considers natural and acceptable. Although it is apparent

that "nature" cannot be Sorel's criterion of judgment, he accepts the view that *oeconomicus* produces robust and moral men, whereas the life based on trade does not. Sorel carries this antagonism toward trade into his analysis of capitalism, primarily condemning exchange rather than manufacturing capital.

91. This use of Socrates in the dialogue further complicates the role he plays in Xenophon's work. Most scholarship agrees with Eduard Delebecque that Ischomachus is the "image of Xenophon" (*Essai sur la vie de Xénophon*, p. 367) and that Socrates serves merely to legitimize his teaching. On the other hand, there is an implication here that Socrates has led Ischomachus down the garden path through his usual appearance of innocence. Guthrie states: "Xenophon is not usually credited with an appreciation of Socratic irony, the affectation that everyone else is wiser than he, but surely it is present here in double measure." Guthrie instances the "delighted surprise with which . . . he hails his discovery of what Ischomachus had been after with his questions" (*Socrates*, p. 17). Gomperz, on the other hand, sees the dialectical method, of which irony is a crucial support, fade into the background in favor of long-winded and dogmatic speechifying (*Greek Thinkers*, vol. 2, p. 137).

92. Xenophon *Memorabilia* III.iv.1-3.

93. Plato would have made alienation of landed property a crime (*Laws* 740).

94. Sorel, *Reflections*, p. 236n (*FGS*, p. 336n14).

95. Ibid., citing Xenophon *Memorabilia* II.vii, in which industry is extolled. Sorel regards this industriousness as a "return to ancient customs" rather than as bourgeoisification.

96. Letter to Croce 14 March 1915, in *Critica* 27 (1929): 119.

97. Sorel, *Reflections* (American ed.), pp. 229-37 (*FGS*, pp. 212-17).

II

THE PHILOSOPHY OF SCIENCE, 1887–1896

Edward Shils has speculated that Sorel's training at the Ecole Polytechnique alienated him from the professional intellectuals of the Sorbonne and the Ecole Normale.[1] As we shall see, Sorel praised the foundation of the Ecole Polytechnique as a step forward in science, but was sharply critical of the intellectual tradition that had come to dominate this *grande école* since its founding. Rebellion against the Polytechnique constitutes at least a part of Sorel's scientific views.

The Ecole Polytechnique was founded during the Revolution and completed by Napoleon as part of the great reform undertaken in public and military administration. Historically, Sorel could look upon it as being a part of the technical and administrative hierarchy of the modern state, an institution of Jacobin domination. Terry Clark has noted that, in Sorel's time, among the great "cultural configurations" in French society the most prominent was Cartesianism, which became identified with reason, order, and authority and was based in the administrative institutions.[2]

The most important intellectual center of Cartesianism in the first part of the nineteenth century was the Ecole Polytechnique. This great engineering school was, in fact, an heir to Jacobinism. It was here that young men, steeped in the Cartesian tradition of viewing the world in terms of mathematical laws, attempted to adapt these laws to society. The Ecole propagated the ideas of Saint-Simon and his disciple Comte, proposing an elaborate techno-scientific hierarchy inspired by Cartesian ideas. This "positive philosophy"—to use Comte's term—looked upon mathematics "not so much as a constituent part of natural philosophy, properly so-called, but as having been since Descartes and Newton the true fundamental basis of the whole of that philosophy."[3] The Saint-Simonians and Comteans took it upon themselves to "complete the vast intellectual operation commenced by Bacon, Descartes, and Galileo, by furnishing the positive philosophy with the system of general ideas that is destined to prevail henceforth, and for an indefinite future, among the human race."[4]

This positive philosophy was inspired by Saint-Simon's early attempt at unification of all knowledge, on the basis of Newton's law of gravity. A new synopticon would replace the *summa theologica* as the ideological guide for the new order; the new temporal power would be placed in the hands of the property-holders, and this power would be buttressed by a new religion of science with scholars as its priests. The Saint-Simonians "ventured to create a religion as one learns at the Ecole to build a bridge or a road."[5] The whole of society was looked upon as a single vast scientific enterprise whose completion awaited only the perfection of the social sciences to equal that of the sciences of nature. Comte, himself a graduate of the Ecole Polytechnique, undertook the completion of this task in his *Cours de philosophie positive.* Now that the human mind had founded celestial, mechanical, and organic physics, "it only remain[ed] to complete the system of observational sciences by the foundation of social physics . . . the greatest and most pressing of our cognitive needs."[6]

In *Le Procès de Socrate*, Sorel explicitly likens Socratic teaching to the Comtean tendencies of modern socialist schools, whose aim was to give everyone an understanding of the principles of all branches of knowledge. Like Socrates, the positivist school "proposes organizing society by science. But could there be a more atrocious government than that of academicians?" The "social physics" sought by the Comteans would, in Sorel's view, lead to mandarinism, a system which "rejects all talents which have not been classified at a given time," and which produces stultifying routinization.[7] Indeed, it is startling to note that the positivists represented in Sorel's eyes a retrogression from Socratic philosophy. By refusing to answer cosmological questions that had no practical value, Socrates at least had ignored questions involving cause and purpose in which he saw little usefulness.[8] This practicality brought Socrates slightly closer to the modern scientific viewpoint than the Comteans who, inspired by the awesome predictability of the Laplacean solar system, wanted to merge all branches of knowledge in an integrated system.

Sorel's opposition to the positivistic world-view entailed emphasizing the practicality of each science and the necessity of divorcing the scientific enterprise from the holistic Cartesian viewpoint. Science could no longer remain abstract; it had to be brought down from the heavens, as philosophy had been under Socrates. Henceforth, science should be viewed only as the theoretical product of men interacting with nature.

Sorel's criticism of positivism is somewhat analogous to the criticism Marx made of Feuerbach: in both cases, there is an attempt to override an ahistorical view of nature which regards phenomena as an integrated whole. To Marx (and to Sorel) this Feuerbachian view legitimizes exploitation and justifies every occurrence as the natural order of things. At a later stage, Sorel would accuse Marxism of retaining too much of the old Feuerbachian viewpoint: by shattering the unity of the sciences more than Marx did, Sorel moved closer to *modern* positivism than Marx, who unified the sciences on another plane. But in the early 1890s Sorel, like Marx before him, stressed the importance of the productive process in understanding the processes of nature.

Sorel adopted the idea, following Vico and Marx, that man's knowledge is acquired through his own mind and labor; it is the mediating function of the productive process which Sorel finds important. How, he asks, can production tell us anything about the world that cannot be learned in other ways? To answer this question, Sorel asks what the relationship is between the construction, say, of a cotton-spinning mill and our general understanding of nature or of the scientific properties of machinery. Having outlined certain ideas on this relationship, Sorel then proceeds to inquire into the connections between our understanding of the physical world and our understanding of the social world.

I

Shortly after *Le Procès de Socrate* was published, Sorel wrote for *La Revue Scientifique* a series of short scientific articles on technical subjects. These articles culminated in a long piece published in his new journal *Ere Nouvelle* in 1894. The article, entitled "L'Ancienne et la nouvelle métaphysique," had as its purpose to demonstrate that science was a collective rather than an individual undertaking. As such, scientific development was partly historical, and therefore its methods were not absolute and all-pervasive through every field of knowledge. This, as we shall see in later chapters, makes the distinction between science and social science all the more difficult and challenging, since scientific development takes on a social character. In order to continue to distinguish between science and social science, it was necessary for Sorel to follow the reconstruction of scientific philosophy which had been undertaken in his lifetime.

It is fair to say that prior to the late nineteenth century—that is to say, until Sorel's time—the practitioners of the scientific enterprise had a far more elevated view of their calling than they do today. Well into the last century, according to Sorel, physics and most scientific theory were based on an assumption of a general unity in nature, a unity usually associated with the universality of cause and of discoverable laws. In the nineteenth century the emerging field of the philosophy of science helped to undermine this assumption of unity. Sorel, up-to-date on some of the latest developments in scientific philosophy, participated in this enterprise of debunking the assumption of unity and to a certain extent helped create awareness of the plural nature of experimentation, of the futility of viewing natural-science methods as a path to total knowledge based on universal laws, and of the limits of the scientific undertaking.

At the beginning of the modern era, according to Sorel, the concept of knowledge of any kind was founded on the Cartesian process, starting from the individual and projecting outward. It was Sorel's view that Descartes's maxim "I think, therefore I am" was introduced primarily for moral and political reasons.[9] By placing man at the center of the moral universe, the individualist principle was introduced. Indeed, "at a time when the entire world was strongly preoccupied with consciousness, it was impossible for each man not to place himself at the center of the world as being the true center and the true creator."[10] Moreover, Descartes's corollary idea of universal doubt, of viewing man as a doubting animal, meant that the doubting person is also a thinking one. This doubting individual's connection to the outside world is through the science which relies solely on thought—in short, through mathematics.

Mathematics leads to explanations in which all phenomena are reducible to general, universal laws. To Sorel, Descartes's reputation as the first modern master obscures his rather antiquated attitudes toward physics. With much more knowledge than Aristotle, Descartes fashioned, like Aristotle, "cosmic hypotheses that our science today regards as useless."[11] Even in such practical questions as the calculation of artillery projectiles, mathematical formulas were constructed in such a way as to give these projectiles the same qualities as those possessed by the planets and stars, "that is, they were regarded as eternal and they conserved their movement indefinitely; *matter was thus made divine* and thanks to this divinization, it became capable of providing a complete explanation of the world."[12] Cartesianism is a dogma which embraces the entirety of human knowledge, a dogma organized by its founder to become the basis of a kind of teaching and which, consequently, "claims to play a role analogous to that played by scholasticism."[13] Under the common heading of thought, Descartes places all the various phenomena of consciousness without making any differentiation among them; from this generality, the Cartesian axiom becomes so universal that it can really be applied to anything. Descartes starts with subjective consciousness as the only real knowledge, but ends by projecting this knowledge externally. Subjectivity ends in competing doctrines of universal order—a kind of epistemological anarchy, according to Sorel.[14] Thus, Sorel says later that the creator of a Cartesian system "operates like an artist who interprets everything around him with extreme freedom."[15]

The superficiality of Cartesian ideas, according to Sorel, made them "infinitely better suited to conversation than to scientific study."[16] Men of society, having received a good education, could converse with professionals and "a good intellect familiar with Cartesian reasoning could find an answer to anything."[17] This philosophy was perfectly suited to the habitués of the salons, an "example of the adoption of an ideology by a class that has found in it certain formulas to express its class propensities."[18]

Sorel notes that both Pascal and Newton protested against "the fantastic and often fraudulent" procedures Cartesians used to give the impression of explaining the whole world. The trouble, according to these critics, is that the Cartesians' attempt to explain the essential nature of all phenomena led them, by virtue of their dependence on the concept of cause, to primitive scientific theories which attributed a "soul" to matter. To Sorel, such a notion of cause, unless proved by strict scientific methods, is either anthropomorphic—returning to the idea of a world soul—or it is inspired by the idea of movements transmitted between bodies touching one another—returning to the theory of the aether. In any case, "scientists" seek cause-and-effect relations in everything, and are tempted to reduce all relations to forces that are as simple and as general as possible.[19] The idea of cause thus grows out of primitive magic. Sorel notes that Newton, following Galileo, dealt with celestial gravitation through mathematical procedures without providing any Cartesian explanatory mechanism. Couched in terms of mathematical laws, Newton's celestial mechanics rendered Descartes useless by avoiding any explanations of the essence of matter or of the mechanisms which produce movement. Henceforth, science would be based on observation; philosophic explanations were superfluous.

For Sorel, the problem of holism remained. Newton's system embraced all questions of a natural order. From this science, the synthetic principles of pure understanding were drawn up by Kant, in whose hands "the axioms of intuition and the anticipations of perception reduce all phenomena to mathematical control because one finds in them either extension or degrees of intensity."[20] Kant founded his theory of knowledge on the hypothesis of an absolute harmony between the universal exigencies of reason and the methods of Newtonian physics.[21] Thus, according to Sorel, science in the eighteenth century had, because of this "universalism," such immense prestige "that people did not think of regarding it, as they do today, as a product of intelligence, capable of only limited application."[22]

For Sorel, a good example of this "scientistic *hubris*" is found in Laplace, who, inspired by the idea of absolute harmony in science, asserted that everything is produced in a way analogous to that found in the solar system. The world was looked upon through the same deterministic lenses as those which were used to predict the movement of the planets in their orbits. Thus Laplace predicted the development of

> an intelligence which, in a given instant, will know all the forces by which nature is animated as well as the respective situations of the beings which compose it; if, moreover, it is extensive enough to submit these givens to an analysis, it will include, in the same formula, the movements of the greatest body of the universe as well as of the slightest atom: nothing will be uncertain for it. . . . The human mind offers a weak sketch of this intelligence in the perfection that it has given to astronomy.[23]

Up to the middle of the nineteenth century the idea of certainty and universality still played a central role in the development of scientific thought. The French physician Claude Bernard (1813-1878) maintained that a given set of conditions will inevitably end in the same result and that failure to predict a result is due to ignorance of the underlying law. Bernard came close to asserting the ultimate unity of all natural phenomena in claiming that there was little difference between the scientific method used to study biological beings and that used to examine the laws governing inert matter; in other words, the study of medicine should be as precise as the study of physics.

But by Bernard's time philosophers were beginning to have doubts about the limitless possibilities of science through the reduction of all human activity to certain formulas. There arose a kind of radical empiricism that restricted theoretical concepts or hypotheses to observable phenomena and that viewed the laws of nature as (in Mach's words) "the mental reproduction of facts in thought."[24]

In France the empirical tradition did not go that far. Instead, there existed a kind of middling position: theories and hypotheses were convenient devices on which to build knowledge, but their inherent truth was dubious. Cournot (1801-1877) argued that order in a group of phenomena must not be taken to imply cause. Cournot replaced the idea of universal laws governing all phenomena with the idea that many things can be considered only from the point of view of mathematical probability. Furthermore, chance occurrences unattributable to any hidden law are as much a part of reality as are the more ordered aspects of nature. Cournot thus introduces a plural dimension to science—indeed, to all knowledge. Some occurrences are governed by strict laws, some by probability, others by chance. The area of activity (or the phenomenon) with which we are concerned is sometimes governed by a determinism that may be absent from other areas.

Jules Henri Poincaré (1854-1912), a contemporary of Sorel's, was probably, after Cournot, the greatest influence on Sorel's scientific thought. Poincaré regarded scientific theories as linguistic conventions; his method, called *conventionalism*, stipulated that geometry is a method of representing spatial facts rather than a set of facts themselves, and it is not necessarily possessed with intrinsic truth. Scientific theories are useful concepts, to be continuously validated through empirical research, and it is only through such testing that concepts are viewed as superior or as valid. It has been pointed out that such a view leads to a kind of pragmatism, as it certainly did in Sorel's later thought.

This conventionalism is found in the earlier scientific procedures of the Scottish physicist James Maxwell (1831-1879), who, adopting an agnostic attitude toward many phenomena, advocated the construction of physical models to supplement mathematical theories so that one can show partial similarities between one science and another (by allowing one to illustrate another). These models did not represent absolute truth; they were attempts to show a "temporary theory." Sorel says of models what Maxwell said of the "temporary theories": their chief merit was that they should guide experimentation without producing falsehood, that is, without preventing a true theory from appearing. Models can help construct temporary theories about electricity in spite of our ignorance of the "essence" of electricity.

Maxwell was not embarrassed by the limited application of scientific model-building, for its purpose was to deal with a specific problem: the very limitation of these applications strengthened the Maxwellian model (other things being equal). The problem with the very different "model" of the Laplacean solar system (along with many other universalistic theories of science), according to Sorel, is that expressing laws in such a general way—reducing all phenomena to actions approximating "planetary" behavior, in Laplace's case—risks distorting the truth through false analogies or inappropriate applications. Sorel feels that it is a mistake to assume that the most general is the most true, and he further notes that "such generalities do not have a very great influence on modern science and technology."[25]

II

Sorel commences his discussion of modern science by attacking models which are inappropriate according to the canons of Maxwell's own method. Sorel says that general weaknesses in scientific undertaking can be traced to the inadequacies of what he calls "expressive supports"—hypothetical models (or conventions, in Poincaré's sense of the term), which are used as explanations. "Expressive support" is a general concept, which can include not only Maxwellian models but also the Laplacean system. To Sorel these theoretical reference points are often used for purposes other than those for which they were originally intended; they are incomplete; they are transformed from mere theoretical analogies through reification into objective reality.[26] These supports can be valuable, but we must always keep in mind that they are intended only to clarify or to illustrate hypotheses and that ultimately they must always be subordinated to reality. The necessity of such subordination is "the first principle of science."

Unfortunately, in Sorel's eyes, these expressive supports have been so badly misused that we are driven toward a metaphysical science. This science, applying logical deduction to such problems as the substance of things and the first causes of changes, steers us either toward the assumptions of ancient science or toward pantheism. Sorel cites the example of eighteenth- and nineteenth-century physicists who used to invoke "life" in order to explain such physico-chemical phenomena as the doubling factor of the leavening of beer. "There is here a vitalist explanation which explains nothing"; using "life" as a concept is no more advantageous in advancing the science of brewing than knowledge of the essence of matter would be in the construction of a house.[27] Sorel is enlarging on Maxwell's comment that our knowledge, or lack of it, of the "properties" of electricity has little bearing on successful construction of electronic equipment.

Despite its subsequent Saint-Simonism, the establishment of the Ecole Polytechnique had rejuvenated science because it replaced the stale recitation of formulas until then regarded as invariable and immutable (a recitation, moreover, which had as its object the preparation of philosophical research into causes and essences) with a practical preparation in the problems of industrial mechanics. For the military engineers who founded the school, "the entire question was of discovering rules which are practical and sufficiently exact to enable us to resolve day-to-day problems."[28] Science does not have as its object the determination of essences, of natures, but the determination of relations.[29] If the function of science is to solve such everyday problems, it is absurd to try to reduce all science to a single mathematical system.

Sorel regards modern science as a social undertaking, not a development from the thinking individual of Descartes. Today "the isolation of the innovative scholar is more apparent than real; he does not rely on a separation between himself and contemporary thought, but, rather, on the difficulty of introducing into usage certain new formulas, which at first seem quite obscure, but which appear subsequently to be very simple, once the habit of using them has taken hold."[30]

Modern science is the activity of a community—a *Cité savante*, as Sorel would later call it—with its own values, customs, and traditions. Perfect objectivity is "an old Platonic concept." Consequently, science has a history which could have been constructed in another way. On the other hand, science is linked to society and community, but is not mere ideology.[31] The development of modern science does not come simply from the judgment of scientists and from the process of its explication to students. If this were the case, there would be no certainty: science "would be subject to all the caprices which depend on our own emotions and interests."[32]

How can Sorel say that science is social and yet above our emotions and interests? Society too has interests, and an entire scientific community can be in error. If we cannot be sure of our own mind, how can we be sure of others'? Sorel's rebellion against a purely intellectual or mathematical science enters in here. Our knowledge always comes from the relations in the environment, either among men or between man and matter. In Vico's terms, men are cognizant of phenomena, including mathematics, because they are products of their own invention. From this simple precept, Sorel was led to Marx's adaptation of the Vicoian notion that it is not passive, intellectual man who is the true scientist, but active man who is constantly intervening in the processes of nature. "I think, therefore I am" has been replaced by the precept "I make, therefore I know." Sorel and Marx depend for this idea on the concept of *homo faber*, man the toolmaker and constructor of devices. Science is social, not individual, because the machine is "more social than language itself."[33] Since the machine mediates the relations among men and between men and nature, this mediation provides us with control over procedures which would otherwise be subjective and uncertain. Machines receive and utilize natural forces: "they are devices placing nature under an experiment, only they are no longer concerned with a temporary and individual experiment, but with a permanent and social one."[34]

Thus Sorel's earliest scientific viewpoint is based on a parallel between the scientific laboratory and the industrial workshop: he equates the industrial world with "an immense physics laboratory in which one acts on industrial energies."[35] Thus, all modes of reason "should be examined from the perspective of the real industrial combinations to which they correspond."[36] As the workshop becomes a laboratory, the milieu of the scientist is increasingly proximate to that of the workshop. Isolated facts are reunited materially by the mechanical apparatus which engenders them. The gap between the two realms, experimentation and productivity, is bridged by the power of invention—in most cases, the invention of either machines or of mechanical models which preserve the unity of the abstractions of science with the industrial world which was science's original inspiration. Thus "mechanical invention differs from science (as we would normally understand that term) only by the mode of exposition."[37] The laboratory is "a small workshop where instruments are used that are more precise than those in manufacturing, but there is no essential difference between the two types of establishment."[38]

These models, the new expressive supports, should be judged solely according to their potential utility in understanding certain phenomena. The construction of these models performs approximately the same task in the area of physical science as that which laboring activity plays in activity in general, according to Marxian theory: that is, a parallel still exists between social science and natural science. In both fields, laboring is an active task that mediates the gulf between the knower and the thing known. Nevertheless, just as Sorel had seen the gap between subject and object bridged in good scientific fashion (a way which would be superficially appealing to Marx himself), he embarked on an elaboration of the themes he had commenced by separating the world of man-made science—the science of the physics laboratory—from the scientific study of natural phenomena that are not fashioned by machines, by models, or by artificial devices. This separation had ramifications that went far beyond an affirmation of Marxism; it ended, in fact, by helping to undermine Marxism.

III

After the 1894 publication of "L'Ancienne et la nouvelle métaphysique," in which Sorel developed his early ideas on natural science, he soon realized that he had relied in his analysis too much on the manufacturing process as the great explanatory device in modern science. In the following year, *Ere Nouvelle* failed and Sorel helped found *Le Devenir Social.* It was in its pages that an article was published in 1896 entitled "La Science dans l'éducation."[39] In this work and in the later "The Metaphysical Foundations of Modern Physics" (1901)[40] Sorel developed the implications of the modern view of science.

In "L'Ancienne et la nouvelle métaphysique," Sorel had maintained that machines serve as geometric verifications of change wrought on matter. Their construction and successful operation constituted a sort of proof of scientific processes and resulted in the analogy between laboratory and workshop that led this industrialized science to assume that the scientific world could be transformed into an immense factory. But what if, as Bergson believed, the scope of scientific activity itself is limited? As early as 1894, Sorel had begun to study some of Bergson's writings. Bergson distinguished between intellectual and intuitive thought (cf. Chapter 5). For Bergson, intellectual thought had as its object the geometrical and the scientific, while intuition did not. Its object was the vital, the fluid. While, as we shall see, Sorel did not follow Bergson very far before deviating from his ideas, Bergson had succeeded in making Sorel aware that nature, the object of science, had many aspects that were not geometric at all and hence were outside the highly specialized area of the laboratory. Only after the publication of his early scientific writings were the full consequences of this view revealed to him. Sorel later wrote that in 1894 "my theses were vitiated by a fundamental error: I thought that science is applied perfectly to nature" and that a harmony exists between natural processes and the scientist who manipulates them.[41]

By 1896, however, Sorel began to draw the pluralistic philosophy of science to its logical conclusion: some scientific activities lay outside the world of manipulable nature. If this were not the case, Sorel would merely have succeeded in replacing the all-encompassing

Laplacean world of mathematics with an all-encompassing laboratory. Sorel came to believe that since not all of our scientific activity could be reproduced in mechanical models, other scientific methods were necessary; science varied greatly in precision and predictability from one field to another.

This problem led Sorel to a critique of the French physician Claude Bernard, who asserted that no question was fully answered unless it could meet the standards of the most precise sciences. Bernard's faith in the scientific method was boundless; experimentation was a means of producing the same level of precision, the same absolute determinism, in all natural as well as physical sciences. Since there should be no essential difference in level of precision among the various natural sciences, Bernard insisted that the more we depart from mathematics and the closer we get to the complex problems of individual living beings, "the more minutely we ought to submit our particular conclusions to experimental verification in order to be sure that we have not forgotten any cause."[42]

Bernard thought our theories or laboratory mechanisms or procedures are at fault if no causal relations between phenomena are discovered; Sorel argues that experimental methods applicable in mechanics may be inappropriate when applied to other subject matter, especially matter which is not as subject to reversability and manipulation as that studied in physics. For Sorel, if an experimental method has failed to reveal results in a science like biology, the method itself has, through a kind of falsification process, revealed qualitative differences among fields of study. Sorel concludes that if science can no longer rely on universal mathematical laws, there is no reason to believe in an experimental methodology common to all branches of science. If, as Sorel says, "only the vulgar believe that the most general is the most true," then it is almost as vulgar to subject all phenomena to the same kind of scientific procedures as those found in physics:

> When we make an experiment, we do not imitate nature: we employ combinations, devices, which are very much our own; we try to produce movements which are never realized in the cosmic milieu. Experimentation is thus a creation; it belongs entirely to the artificial world: it is fact and truth at the same time. Experimentation differs from mathematical exposition through the difference which exists between (to use Vico's expression) the unspoken language and the spoken or written language.[43]

The difference between a science like biology and a laboratory science like physics leads Sorel not only to fragment science and its methods but also to bifurcate the "nature" it investigates. Sorel argues that the experimental method, when subject to the controlling influence of Maxwellian models, places limits on itself by virtue of the transformation that the active experimenter fashions in nature itself. Just as the toolmaker must change nature through active intervention in natural processes, a laboratory science such as physics is more closely connected to what it creates in the world by its control mechanisms than it is to those aspects of nature it has not altered, that is, to the given world. The physicist gets answers to the problems he poses by effecting changes in nature and by cutting himself off from that part of nature which remains "untouched." Sorel calls this process of transforming nature through intervening in it "artificial nature," as differentiated from "natural nature"—for example, meteorological phenomena, in which man does not intervene directly and which he therefore cannot alter. In Sorel's view, biological phenomena, which Bernard was so anxious to understand in the precise way of artificial nature, can never be subject to the kind of laws known in laboratory physics because the subject matter of biology is closer to "natural nature" than it is to "artificial nature." No one, Sorel maintains, "would ever dream of assuming that an animal can be looked at as equivalent to a combination of geometric figures."[44]

One of the principal methods of distinguishing between the two aspects of nature, according to Sorel, is by their determinism (predictability). "Natural nature," in many of its phenomena, is far less determined, and occurrences are produced by chance more than in the "artificial nature" of the workshop or laboratory. Indeed, "there are an infinite number of forms of indetermination."[45] On the other hand, according to Sorel, when we are "masters" of phenomena, then "we can say that scientific facts are those which are produced by mechanisms having a movement and forms that are determined (by the experimenter) in an absolute way."[46] Thus, for example, the geometrically designed machines of a laboratory are much more "determined" than outside phenomena such as the natural lifespan of an animal, because "absolute qualitative laws" can be discovered in laboratories and the results of their operations are predictable.

This implies neither the inferiority of "natural" sciences (for in Sorel's view such comparison is devoid of meaning) nor that "natural" sciences are necessarily given over to arbitrariness; they are merely less determined. Chance occurrences do not, in Sorel's view, always imply arbitrary happenings. Following Cournot, Sorel sees order in the statistical clustering of, for example, longevity in the actuarial tables of life-insurance companies, even though individual longevity is impossible to predict.[47] "Similar groupings are found in the existence of periods of heat and cold, of agricultural abundance and sterility, of economic prosperity and depression."[48] Random phenomena can therefore be shown to have a superior degree of order "when they are concentrated around a median position in a compact way, so that the numerical value of this position can be used to characterize a whole."[49] This "characterization" is often little more than descriptive. Sorel does not maintain, however, that limiting certain investigations to statistical indexes in some fields is slovenly or incorrect on the simplified ground that no cause, determinism, or law can be imputed to them. Statistics do not always lead to a natural law: "There are an infinite number of cases in which observation can permit only statements of past fact and can lead to nothing more than approximated tables or to empirical formulas."[50] Sorel maintains that only dreamers still try "to imitate natural processes, and, by disproportionate sacrifices of time and money, arrive at the conclusion that the rigorous study of nature ought to have the discovery of laws as its sole purpose."[51]

IV

Because of the disparate nature of the kinds of discoveries that are made among the various sciences, the discoveries in one science cannot necessarily inform us about phenomena in general or about another science. This holds true generally of the relationship between natural nature and artificial nature. Sorel subscribes to an "uncertainty principle": "natural nature" cannot be transformed by *homo faber* through laboratory procedures without changing the quality of the subject matter and the laws which govern them. Furthermore, the more technology advances, that is, the more "artificial" the phenomena of the laboratory become, the more disparate the two "natures" become. "Natural nature," which surrounds us in everyday life, according to Sorel, "is separated from the entirely geometrical 'artificial nature' by a zone that does not fit into mathematical law. . . . The two systems do not belong to the same type as had been true of the universe of the ancients."[52]

The increasing divergence between the two natures is furthered, in Sorel's view, by the theory of entropy derived from the second law of thermodynamics. This law, whereby energy is transformed into heat, thus resulting in a general degradation of energy, was "the germ of a far-reaching revolution in thought whose significance we cannot yet surmise."[53] Sorel notes that until the nineteenth century nature was believed to be an inexhaustible source of energy. Huge amounts of labor power, for example, were available for the construction of pyramids, and water power seemed an infinite source of energy. The industrial revolution changed this viewpoint. When it occurred, "one saw the necessity of better recognizing the malfeasant causes that entered into a struggle against the spirit of men during the functioning of machines."[54] For example, the introduction of steam in the great textile mills forced theorists to examine closely the cost of daily motor power: "It was recognized that it is advantageous to speed up some machines in order to conserve heat."[55] Furthermore, heat loss is not always predictable. The friction which develops in running machines constitutes an agglomeration of unpredictable accidents involving energy loss and machine malfunction. With research into thermodynamics, the loss of energy seemed to conform to the less determined area of "natural nature." Sorel found it likely that the phenomena of friction should be akin to meteorology rather than to the phenomena of strictly controlled physical laws. Paradoxically, the more precise research into heat became, the more precise the scientific methods employed, "the more the hypothesis of the indeterminism of friction is affirmed."[56]

The implications of this for Sorel's original viewpoint were far-ranging. Not only was the world no longer merely a huge laboratory, not only were natural and artificial nature separated, but the realm of artificial nature itself risked incursion and constant violations from the realm that at least resembled "natural nature." In reading Sorel's mature philosophy of science, one receives the impression that natural and artificial nature are locked in a kind of permanent guerrilla war of attrition that requires constant patching and filling on the part of the practitioner of artificial nature. The more practical or industrial a scientific device becomes, the more the two realms escalate the conflict. What started in Sorel's early writings as a close parallel between the practitioner of the laboratory and the industrial practitioner now ends in a divergence in methods: the industrialist must put up with the more unpredictable aspects of friction; the laboratory theorist must possess "a liberty of judgment which brings [science] close to art."[57] The industrialist or industrial inventor is like a soldier who must constantly revise his projections as the battle against degraded energy continues. The physicist, on the other hand, resembles the general drawing up battle plans. It is not surprising that in the *Reflections on Violence* Sorel would not include the scientist in his drawing of parallels—among the soldier, the industrial worker, the inventor, and the artist.

The doctrine of entropy affected Sorel's views, and he realized the effect that the transformations it wrought on the philosophy of science would have for social philosophy or what is called "social science."

V

The concept of universal physical laws had consequences that went far beyond laboratory practice. In the optimistic period of the eighteenth century, the idea of universal laws often meant exactly what the term implies. If laws could be applied to all physical nature, could not "natural philosophy" (the old term for physics) be applied to man as well? If men and society are natural phenomena, it appeared to the men of the Enlightenment that laws of society, a kind of "social astronomy," could be formulated to propound a "science of society" as precise and as predictive as that dealing with the course of phenomena observed in laboratory experiments.

We have noted that Laplace was inspired by the idea of an absolute harmony in nature: Laplacean science was based on the "expressive support" of an all-encompassing solar system in which phenomena are predicted in a manner similar to prediction of the location of the planets. In Laplace's view, this predictability is extensible to all "animate nature," and he envisioned a perfect social (as well as natural) science.

Sorel's chief criticism of Laplace's science is easily comprehended: its difficulty is its source in an "expressive support" which is terribly misleading. Laplace's principal model is the solar system. "Natural nature" is generally less predictable than artificial nature, but the one great exception to this rule, according to Sorel, is astronomy, in which the positions of phenomena are as predictable as they are in most areas of "artificial nature." In using the solar system as its expressive support, Laplacean science, in Sorel's view, prevented many scholars from distinguishing between artificial and natural nature. The result of this unfortunate mistake in natural science was the perpetuation of the idea of unified science, an error which created a series of false assumptions about the nature of social science. By ignoring what would later become Sorel's distinction between natural and artificial nature, by failing to distinguish between areas of science in which men actively intervene and those in which they do not, Laplace invited a host of future utopians to develop sciences of society that "are constructed in the same way as philosophical explanations of matter."[58] In using his planetary model, Laplace "reconstructs the world and makes a utopia having no other reason than its own logic."[59] In short, like the philosophers of matter, the utopians confuse the expressive support with reality.

Sorel found an example of such utopian thinking in the liberal theories of the social contract, originally hypothesized as an expressive support or model for a view or views of human nature, but taking on in later theories, a dimension of reality.

To Sorel, utopias, like Laplacean science, consist of an ensemble "of quite clear and distinct propositions, very well connected by logic, capable of being applied with fairly high accuracy."[60] Like Laplace, the utopian attempts to eliminate chance from the realm of human affairs. That is why eighteenth-century utopians so admired Chinese despotism:

> Everything was reduced to prefigured formulas; it was decided that knowledge of the world could not surpass a certain moment of perfectly determined thought. . . . All attempts at emancipation were stifled in the name of given principles; idealism was adapted in an absolute way to a routine, and has given to it the aspect of a philosophy which has attained perfect maturity."[61]

Sorel implies that the perfectly ordered, old-fashioned science of Laplace's time is almost analagous to an independently ordered mental picture. Despite the strictures of the Newtonian tradition against Descartes, there is for Sorel an almost Cartesian tendency in early-nineteenth-century science to project one's own mentality onto the physical world; only in our mind, in the realm of abstractions, are we "used never to pose questions about the real world, but about the world that is truly subjective, more perfect and truer (because it conforms more to the laws of the mind). This world—which is sometimes called metaphysics—is the only one which lends itself to the movements of the intelligence. Here, all is logical."[62]

The new philosophy of science, of which Sorel was an advocate, came as a great shock to old-fashioned scientists and theorists, and even more so to nineteenth-century "advanced" liberals. As Sorel phrased it, the old science relied on the metaphysical notion that "the immobile is worth more than the mobile, equality more than inequality, unity more than diversity."[63] The essential balance and harmony of nature embodied in the old formulas were replaced in the new vision by mobility, disequilibrium, and fragmentation. In moving from science (so-called) to social science, the immense energy and prestige which had gone into adapting natural and physical science to society, the "scientific" bolstering of democracy, harmony, and unity amid a welter of utopian visions, had to be replaced, according to Sorel, by more realistic ideas. The utopian vision of mankind was severely undermined from a genuinely scientific point of view. Immense logico-utopian systems—constructed by such theorists as Saint-Simon and Fourier—should give way to Marxism and to conservative thought. Ideal solutions must yield to historical ones.

Finally, the doctrine of entropy or energy loss also had an adverse effect on social optimism because, in Sorel's words, it "made men feel vividly the evil-mindedness of a nature which leads the world to its own ruination."[64] What would happen to social science in a scientific world which was faced with the annihilation of utopian hopes of historical progress to match the advances in science. Was this world one which could ultimately be understood and hence mastered in accordance with a coordinated social plan? In Sorel's view, social science, or what was left of it, had to be rebuilt; it was necessary for the would-be architect of that effort first to undertake a critique of social science.

Notes

1. Edward A. Shils, Introduction to *Reflections on Violence*, (American ed.), p. 19n.
2. Terry Clark, ed., *Gabriel Tarde: On Communication and Social Influence* (Chicago: University of Chicago Press, 1969), p. 8.
3. Auguste Comte, *Introduction to the Positive Philosophy*, ed. and trans. by Frederick Ferré (Indianapolis: Bobbs-Merrill, 1970), pp. 65-66.
4. Ibid., p. 30.
5. Edward von Hayak, *The Counter-Revolution in Science* (New York: Free Press, 1969), p. 113, citing Gouhier, *La Jeunesse d'Auguste Comte*, vol. 1, p. 146.
6. Comte, *Introduction*, p. 13.
7. Sorel, *Le Procès de Socrate*, pp. 182-83.
8. Ibid., p. 313, citing Xenophon *Memorabilia* IV.vii.5.
9. Sorel, "L'Ancienne et la nouvelle métaphysique," *Ere Nouvelle* (1894), republished under the title *D'Aristote à Marx*, ed. by Eduard Berth (Paris: Rivière, 1935), p. 190. All references will be to the later edition.
10. Sorel, *D'Aristote*, p. 191.
11. Sorel, "Vues sur les problèmes de la philosophie," *Revue de Métaphysique et de Morale* 18 (Dec. 1910): 584.
12. Ibid., p. 589. Italics are Sorel's. Cf. *De l'utilité du pragmatisme* (2nd ed., Paris: Rivière, 1928), p. 333.
13. Sorel, "Vues," p. 602.
14. Ibid., p. 605.
15. Sorel, *Illusions*, p. 37 (American edition, p. 14).
16. Ibid. (American edition), p. 18.
17. Ibid., p. 19.
18. Ibid., p. 14.
19. Sorel, "De la cause en physique," *Revue Philosophique* 26 (1888): 465-66.
20. Sorel, "Vues," p. 606.
21. Ibid., p. 609.
22. Sorel, *Illusions* (American edition), p. 89.
23. Sorel, "La Science dans l'éducation," *Devenir Social*, vol. 1, no. 12

(1896): 217-18.

24. See Peter Alexander's article on Ernst Mach in *The Encyclopedia of Philosophy* (New York: Collier-Macmillan, 1967), vol. 5, p. 118.

25. Sorel, *D'Aristote*, p. 131; "La Science dans l'éducation," *Devenir Social* 2, no. 1 (April 1896): 354.

26. Sorel, *D'Aristote*, p. 131.

27. Ibid., p. 136.

28. Sorel, "La Science dans l'éducation," *Devenir Social* 1, no. 11 (Feb. 1896): 133.

29. Sorel, *D'Aristote*, p. 140.

30. Sorel, *D'Aristote*, p. 197.

31. Sorel, *Insegnamenti sociale della economia contemporanea* (Palermo: Sandron, 1906), pp. 62-3 (Hereafter *Insegnamenti*).

32. Sorel, *D'Aristote*, p. 199.

33. Ibid., p. 201.

34. Ibid., p. 203.

35. Ibid., p. 205.

36. Ibid., p. 227.

37. Ibid., p. 208.

38. Sorel, *Insegnamenti*, p. 64.

39. *Devenir Social* (Feb.-May 1896).

40. *Cahiers de la Quinzaine* (16th Cahier of the 8th series, 1901), and largely incorporated into chapter 4 of *De l'utilité du pragmatisme* under the title "L'Expérience dans la physique moderne."

41. Sorel, "Critique de 'L'Evolution créatrice,'" *Mouvement Socialiste* (Oct., Nov., Dec. 1907): 482.

42. Sorel, *De l'utilité du pragmatisme*, p. 292, paraphrasing Claude Bernard, *Introduction à l'étude de la médecine expérimentale.*

43. Sorel, "Etude sur Vico," *Devenir Social* (Oct. 1896): 817.

44. Sorel, *De l'utilité du pragmatisme*, p. 352.

45. Ibid., p. 346.

46. "La Science dans l'éducation," p. 348.

47. Sorel, *D'Aristote*, p. 121. Cf. "Les Préoccupations métaphysiques des physiciens modernes," preface by Julien Benda; he says, paraphrasing this point: If the relations between, say, a^5 and b^5 extend to a^6 and b^6 and to a thousand other pairs through experimental verification, "then it will be declared that it also exists for still others according to the same formula. We see that the consistency of a relation is something that is declared . . . an act of faith . . . a belief." The correlations existing in the world are not necessarily logical or explainable; they are only observable.

48. Sorel, *De l'utilité du pragmatisme*, p. 344.

49. Ibid., pp. 344-45; Sorel, *D'Aristote*, pp. 121-22.

50. Sorel, "Idées socialistes et faits économiques au XIXe siècle," *Revue Socialiste* (1902): 406.

51. Sorel, *De l'utilité du pragmatisme*, pp. 340-41, citing Franz Reuleaux, *Cinématique* (Paris: Savy, 1877), p. 554.

52. Sorel, *De l'utilité du pragmatisme*, p. 343.

53. Ibid., p. 322.

54. Ibid., p. 312.

55. Ibid., p. 314.

56. Ibid., p. 319.

57. Ibid., pp. 320-21.

58. Sorel, *D'Aristote*, p. 149.
59. Ibid., p. 151.
60. Sorel, "La Science dans l'éducation," *Devenir Social* 1, no. 12 (1896): p. 216.
61. Ibid., p. 340.
62. Ibid., pp. 216-17.
63. Sorel, *De l'utilité du pragmatisme*, pp. 327-28.
64. Ibid., p. 325.

III

PSYCHOLOGISM, POSITIVISM, AND MARXISM, 1893–1897

It is fair to say that Sorel's early thought was pulled in three separate (though not always distinct) directions—toward positivism, toward Marxism, and, to a lesser extent, toward the school of psychological spontaneity. Sorel's writings before 1895 embody all three of these tendencies; from 1895 to 1897 his efforts were directed toward analyzing and clarifying the three vectors in his earlier thought. This undertaking showed no great results until his critique of Marxism in 1898-1900, his critique of Renan's positivism in 1904, and his critique of Bergsonian "spontaneity" in 1907. The writings of the 1895-1897 period are useful for their illumination of the background and inspiration of these later critiques, for it was in 1896 that Sorel developed his conception of the laboring process as performing the function of integrating, while upholding separate methods for evaluating, science and morals.

When Sorel assumed the editorship of *Ere Nouvelle*, he published "L'Ancienne et la nouvelle métaphysique," an apology for the social nature of natural science, and "La Fin du paganisme," which contained a plea for the social nature of political and societal investigations.[1] In the latter work, Sorel strove to apply the genealogy of morals presented in *Le Procès de Socrate* to the decline of Rome, using historical materialism as the method of analysis. This work embodied many of the problems faced by his pre-1896 view of physical science.

Sorel's analysis is characterized by an ambiguous positivism: he attempts to meet the requirements of scientific detachment while accepting the Marxian idea of inevitable social bias. Thus, he insists that historians cannot view their own work objectively. The historian's failure to examine his own values and biases means that "science cannot hope to concern itself with the merits and demerits of the actors of the historical drama; it cannot claim to penetrate into the consciousness of men; all that it can do is to classify verifiable phenomena."[2] On the surface, this appears to be an absurd statement for the author of *Le Procès de Socrate* to make, and, indeed, Sorel admitted in a later edition that ambiguous positivism, a viewpoint that claimed both value-free and biased standpoints, had infected the mainstream of Marxist criticism; additionally, Marxism had not successfully distinguished itself from positivism, especially in Germany. "The desire to lead everything back to a scientific perspective almost necessarily leads to utopianism or state socialism." It is far removed from the "true spirit" of historical materialism.[3]

The discovery of Comtean positivist tendencies in Marxism later caused Sorel virtually to abandon Marxism; yet, Sorel's early scientism paved the way for his later thought. The manner in which he opposed positivism reflected the positivist dilemma: in increasingly denying the positivist unity of the sciences, he was led to exclude human values from scientific study. In detaching himself from positivism, Sorel became interested in the idea of a separate, nonscientific, "spontaneous" approach to an increasingly wide range of human activities, which ended in his proclaiming the general strike to be secure from refutation yet subject to scientific study.

After about 1895, Sorel's ambiguous positivism was superseded by his version of Marxism, made equally ambiguous by his depiction of a continuous Bergsonian struggle between geometric and spontaneous thought or, in Sorel's terms, a struggle between scientific and poetic content. Indeed, the conflict between science on the one hand and spontaneity on the other was a far more important struggle in the schools of sociological thought in France in the *fin de siècle* period than any would-be struggle between Marxism and positivism.

The evolution of Sorel's thought in the years before and after his participation in *Devenir Social* may be made clearer if we understand the struggle between the Durkheimian positivists and the so-called "Tardians." Emile Durkheim had inherited the mantle of dean of French scientific sociology from Comte, Renan, and Taine. He had succeeded in placing his protégés in influential positions in the French university system. Durkheim's teaching, which derived fundamentally from Comte, spread from the Ecole Polytechnique to the Ecole Normale and thence to the Sorbonne. It became apparent to Sorel after 1895 that Durkheim was playing an ideological role in his support of the Third Republic.[4] In Sorel's view, in attempting to build a secular morality to replace Catholic dogma Durkheim offered a systematic justification for the subjugation of corporate groups to "the existing order of the state" and provided a rationale for state supervision of religious orders and trade unions.[5]

Opposition to the Durkheimians came from the school of "spontaneity," a mélange of aesthetic romanticism and subjectivism led by Gabriel Tarde of the Collège de France. Tarde centered his analysis on the individual, asserting that Durkheim's view of crime as a normal phenomenon was morally irresponsible. Responsibility must remain with the individual. Terry Clark asserts that Tarde's school of spontaneity was a "continuous source of inspiration" to Sorel.[6] Henri Bergson, Tarde's successor at the Collège de France, provided the same kind of inspiration, but not without considerable modification and criticism from Sorel (as we shall see in Chapter 5).

Because of Sorel's own early positivism, it is an oversimplification to argue that he immediately threw in his lot with the anti-Durkheimians and rejected them out of hand. Sorel was less critical of Durkheim before 1895, and his admiration for Renan made his opposition to the positivist tradition more qualified than it would be in later years. In 1894, Sorel criticized Tarde's reliance on the spontaneity of the individual as implying that man can live independent of the industrial milieu in which he finds himself. Tarde's spontaneous individualism, Sorel complained, placed him in the old liberal tradition of eighteenth-century Whiggery and was no more revolutionary than positivism.[7] Sorel even criticized Tarde for his attacks on the nineteenth-century positivist Cesare Lombroso. Critical as he was of Lombroso's extreme biological determinism,[8] Sorel argued (against Tarde) that it was perfectly correct for Lombroso and Durkheim to employ statistics as measures of certain social trends.[9]

The real question, which was only gradually made clear to Sorel, is whether these statistics should have the same function as those employed in natural science. To what extent are analogies and parallels between the natural sciences and the social sciences at all justified? Concerned as he was with the physical law of entropy, Sorel wondered if this law could be applied to society as well. If the law of thermodynamics could be used as an "expressive support" for historical development, then how can Sorel justify using such a model without being subject to the same criticism that he was leveling against Laplacean social science? Was Sorel attempting to produce his own, less optimistic "social physics" simply by substituting the second law of thermodynamics for the Laplacean solar system? Sorel's criticism of Lombroso is conditioned by his sympathy for an analogy which he nonetheless knew was at bottom inadequate; this reasoning lay behind his criticism in the years following the failure of *Ere Nouvelle* (at the end of 1894) of so much of what was to pass as social science.

The inadequacy of physico-social analogies was one reason why Sorel moved toward the concept of psychological spontaneity. Not only did he reject Lombroso's socio-physical parallelism, he also rebelled against Lombroso's linkage of physiology and psychology. Sorel knew that for Lombroso "Misoneism is not a simple nominal concept but a reality fundamental to our individual constitution," and he summarizes Lombroso accordingly:

> The principle of inertia which engenders social misoneism depends, in a more or less direct way, on a physiological cause: that is why one sees it appear in all epochs, in all civilizations and social classes. One finds *roots* to this law of inertia in the study of animals, infants, savages—that is, in all creatures most subject to the laws of the sentient life. Furthermore, it is to this rudimentary psychology that we should always refer in order to find out if a principle is really structural.[10]

Superficially, Sorel's exposition of Lombroso seems approving: it greatly resembles what Sorel was later to say about the tendency of civilizations to return to barbarism. Furthermore, Lombroso's theory gives the lie to the facile optimism of Tarde. Yet, even in 1893 Sorel was critical of Lombroso's atavism, first as "too vague," as presuming the "unity of the human species" and ignoring the fact that "certain characteristics can become rare and even unique among civilized people."[11] Second, Sorel complains that Lombroso explained atavistic tendencies in physiological terms, and he wonders whether social science should be reduced to what he terms "a fragment of physiological psychology." Sorel sides with Wilhelm Wundt and Ribot in denouncing the "purely metaphysical" assumption that psychological facts ought always to be derived from physiological causes.[12] It is better to argue that there are physical processes parallel to psychic ones: "physiological idealism" is in the same situation as historical idealism. Rather like the biologist who attempts to ape the physicist, the physiological idealist permits theoretical constructions to intervene in the course of experimentation, and this in turn allows us to coordinate phenomena (in a most unsatisfactory manner) that we view as connected deterministically but whose real laws we cannot succeed in knowing.

Sorel's assertion that psychological phenomena are easier to study than those of a physiological nature[13] highlights the principal difficulties in Sorel's attempt to resolve the general Marxist-positivist dilemma. How does this assertion square with his notion, projected at about the same time, that science cannot probe human consciousness? Furthermore, Sorel had maintained that "it is quite difficult to account for the influence that economics exercises on human thought in a general way."[14] Yet there is no doubt in Sorel's mind that some such relationship between the economy and thought exists, for in the same work Sorel says that "economic conditions provide men with a framework from which it is very difficult to free oneself. Isolated thinkers can think in an independent way, but this is not possible for numerous groups; a collectivity is riveted to economic categories just as the individual is fastened to his nervous system."[15] Finally, this scientific—physiological—comparison again highlighted the problem of how social phenomena can be at all related to natural scientific phenomena.

I

The complex relationship among social, physical, and psychological phenomena was the subject of much of Sorel's writings in *Devenir Social* after 1895, when he attempted to sort out many of the positivist, Marxist, and Tardian psychological elements in his thought.

Sorel's first publication in *Devenir Social* was an attempt to disentangle the positivistic from the metaphysical elements in Durkheim's thought: attempting to distinguish the social from the psychological view. When Durkheim said that "the manner in which a phenomenon develops expresses its nature,"[16] this implied for Sorel a not-so-hidden Aristotelian doctrine of essences: a universal quality is revealed in the pattern shown by a phenomenon in the process of its unfolding—the essence of manhood, for example, is revealed in "boyhood," the condition of the unfolding of a fully developed man.

For Sorel, this idea may be unexceptional from a biological point of view, but it becomes dubious when one tries to determine "the nature" of what Durkheim calls a "social fact." To Durkheim, a social fact is a phenomenon that is general throughout society and which, though it can assume different forms in different cases, can still conserve its "essential" characteristics. But Sorel claims that as soon as one speaks of "essential characteristics" one becomes extremely susceptible to the idealism of the unitarist doctrines of the old Laplacean science, or to the metaphysical concept of the thing-in-itself. Sorel views Durkheim as a prime example of one who succumbed to these tendencies.[17] He displaces Durkheim's unitarist view with the contention that because the natural and physical sciences have, since Newton, largely dispensed with the determination of essences, social science should not attempt to discover the essence of a social fact. "Only the determination of relations" should be the goal of social science, as it is for natural science.[18]

Sorel claims that Durkheim's doctrine is inherited from an ancient metaphysical notion (also seen in Aristotle), wherein "all science ought to be constituted by analogy with the natural history of the habits of animals."[19] The misuse of organic analogies (or what might be called biological expressive supports) leads Durkheim, in Sorel's view, to look at society from the perspective of its pathology. As Durkheim himself expresses it, the role of the sociologist "is that of a physician; he prevents the eruption of maladies through good hygiene and when they are established he tries to cure them."[20] But applied to society, the activity of the physician finds analogy only in the activity of the statesman in his role as lawgiver, prescribing medicine for the ills of society. lawgiver. Sorel sees the sociologist as being led to some of the assumptions that a physician finds useful, but they are assumptions that prevent us from discovering accurate truths about society. The foremost of these assumptions is the concept of normality. Durkheim determines normality through clustering phenomena around an average pattern, but whereas such a clustering represents a statistical technique for Sorel, for Durkheim it is morally normative, i.e., the norms or averages which are discovered are by definition good. Furthermore, they are good because they are "useful," while the abnormal is bad because disadvantageous. Sorel sees this doctrine as a kind of covert Darwinism in which the fittest of social orders "survives" the diseases of the social order; in which the human will is excluded in the shaping of social institutions. The standard of utility is applied only to the victory itself, but, in Sorel's eyes, "it is puerile to say that those who adapt best are those who succeed, since the measure of the best adaptation is this very success."[21]

Durkheim, with most sociologists, goes beyond mere empiricism and assumes social laws that are both physical and normative. The idea that long-lasting institutions have some "natural" superiority is based on what is essentially a functional or closed system in which cause and effect have a reciprocal character: the effect cannot exist without its cause, and vice versa. According to Sorel, in this theory, which we would call functionalism, there is an affirmation of a very important ethical thesis, which Durkheim does not make obvious. When his system is applied to legal or political institutions, it becomes an utterly deterministic chain, an "empirical system of repression." Durkheim's system, according to Sorel, can thus be used as an ideology of the rule of the stronger.

In depicting his closed system, Durkheim has not only employed a law of cause-and-effect but has made the law so iron-clad that it has gone beyond biology to find analogies in physics and astronomy.[22]

Again Sorel quotes Durkheim: "Since the law of causality has been verified in the other provinces of nature, and since it has progressively extended its empire from the physico-chemical to the biological world and from the biological world to that of the psychological, we have the right to maintain that it is equally true in the social world."[23]

Sorel claims that this argument is so weak that Durkheim backtracks on the same page, in two important assertions: "The question of knowing whether the nature of the causal connection excludes all contingency is not decided for all this," and "Sociology affirms liberty no more than it affirms determinism."[24] For Sorel, these two phrases demonstrate quite clearly that in sociology the word *cause* has a very different meaning from that of its use in the physical sciences: "Physics and chemistry do not contain any relaxation of deterministic relations. . . . But how can one speak of causes analogous to those of physics in sociology, when things that are placed in relation to one another are fictions devoid of individual reality?"[25] To say that sociological laws are merely approximations or hypotheses of unknown relationships only serves to underscore the point that we cannot attribute causal relationships to entities whose very existence has yet to be conclusively established.

For Sorel, legitimate science starts from concrete realities and hypotheses based on those realities. Durkheim's method works in the opposite way. Such things as "social facts," "social body," and "normality" cannot be established as either cause or effect until their existence and properties have been irrefutably determined by scientific method. For Sorel, a "scientific system is not assumed; it proves itself by the regularity of its constitution and by its application."[26] In physics, the region of experimentation is rigorously limited. Here "we are obliged to experience the boredom and ignorance and, grumblingly, the failure to arrive at a total explanation," but the question cannot be posed in the same way for social phenomena: "We no longer feel as strongly the resistance of the exterior world and we can eliminate this disturbing area, which, in physics, corresponds to the unknown region."[27] The art of any scientific enterprise is in setting the proper boundaries in studying a phenomenon. Social science, more than any other, is susceptible to the double hazard of either ignoring factors which must be considered or, conversely, of taking all factors into consideration and thus of aiming at a holistic (i.e., utopian and fallacious) system.

Durkheim's tendency is to distinguish, in a rather artificial way, social from psychological phenomena. On the one hand, Durkheim maintains that "all economic life . . . is definitely dependent on a purely individual factor, the desire for wealth." On the other hand, he says that in social phenomena a change occurs: "Sociology is not a corollary of individual psychology. . . . We must, then, seek the explanation of social life in the nature of society itself."[28] For Durkheim, the whole is not identical to the sum of its parts. Social phenomena possess a different nature from our individual natures: "If the authority before which the individual bows when he acts, feels, or thinks socially governs him to this extent, it does so because it is a product of social forces which transcend him and for which he, consequently, cannot account. The external impulse to which he submits cannot come from him, nor can it be explained by whatever happens within him."[29] But, then, asks Sorel, why make sociology analogous to other sciences?

In his attempt to formalize sociology and to make it into a distinct discipline, Durkheim, in Sorel's view, has attributed a unique and mysterious quality to social phenomena which is entirely distinct from psychological phenomena. Sociology defends its autonomy, in Durkheim's words, "by refusing to explain the most complex by way of the most simple," the collective by way of the individual; "the association, by some mysterious alchemy, adds something (to individual psychology) and it is through this increment that the sociological phenomenon appears in reality."[30]

Yet Sorel was almost equally dubious about current attempts to unify psychological and social phenomena in the French schools of sociology. To his criticism of Tarde Sorel was to add a criticism of social psychology which he would not modify until much later.

II

Sorel's distrust of the Durkheimian idea of a "social alchemy" extended to his opinions concerning the school of "social suggestion" which Gustave Le Bon inherited from Théodule Ribot and Nordeau. Ribot (for whose journal Sorel had written several early articles) speaks of social facts in almost Rousseauian terms. The common life "demanded certain ways of acting and habits based on sympathy with the concerted end which everyone follows."[31] Others, like Nordeau in his *Sociological Paradoxes*, deal with the theory of social suggestion, of thoughts originating in the minds of great geniuses who inspire their followers to imitate them as if by hypnotism. Nordeau argues that all education is suggestion, and it is through suggestion that the actions of morality and corruption operate.[32] To Sorel, Ribot's "sympathy" and Nordeau's "suggestion" merely replace Durkheim's social facts with equally metaphysical social-psychological facts. The dimension of the "social" had transmuted psychology from subjective mental constructions into unique social phenomena whose content was exceedingly difficult to explain.

The most extensive attempt to trace the development of social psychology was perhaps that of Gustave Le Bon, for whom Sorel had considerable respect. To the studies of Nordeau and Ribot, Le Bon added theories inspired in part by the studies in hypnotic suggestion done by A. A. Liebeault. In *La Psychologie des foules*, Le Bon portrays mass belief as a state, bordering on hypnosis, which he later called "collective logic." This state was the result of a kind of osmotic pressure exerted on the subject by the sheer mass of public opinion. For Le Bon the self-generating effect of such opinions shows no respect for class or race. Crowd psychology is found equally in legislatures, juries, and mobs—even among otherwise isolated individuals sharing the same opinion sources. By ascribing collective logic to a natural tendency toward imitation, Le Bon verges on describing the trends of public opinion in terms of fads. From Le Bon's depiction of the adolescent character of crowds, as well as from the omnipresence of collective logic in any gathering, it would appear that no reasonable democratic politics, no collective intelligence, no rational decision-making by groups is possible. Indeed, nothing would appear to be further from Marxist socialism than Le Bon's utter anti-intellectualism, to which he added an equally strong commitment to Darwinian competition.[33]

As he does with much of social science, Sorel takes what he wants from Le Bon and discards the rest. He accepts the idea that there is a heterogeneity between knowledge and belief, and he approves Le Bon's skeptical view of democracy based on popular wisdom, but even in his later writings, Sorel cannot help thinking that "perhaps in some way we can submerge these baleful tendencies by harnessing the whole consciousness for the support of constructions that are satisfying to the mind and that also have strong roots in the heart" and without a further development of rationalism.[34] Sorel criticizes Le Bon's tendency to treat all manifestations of public opinion in the same way. In such a procedure, Sorel writes, all branches of knowledge are united and "very dissimilar things are designated by the same term." Le Bon erroneously reduces the history of ideas to a reproduction of gestures, to mimicry, contagion, and race. These categories Sorel regards as pseudo-explanations analogous to Durkheim's social facts, which really "explain nothing at all."[35]

Yet, Sorel agrees with Le Bon that group activities ought to be described in psychological terms, for it is our own psychology that we truly know. On the other hand, Durkheim's analysis, taken to its logical conclusion, shows the impossibility of treating sociological problems psychologically. Sorel wants the vagaries of Durkheim's social facts and Le Bon's mass society replaced by concrete social institutions: "Thanks to the theory of classes, the socialists do not relate their ends to imaginary entities, to the needs of the collective soul and to other sociological simplicities, but to real men gathered in groups that are active in social life. This opens up a new way of looking at psychological phenomena and allows it to play an important role in sociological investigations."[36] We can thus recognize "what is truly human in sociology"; that is, we can define these active groups correctly and observe the economic conditions in which they develop:

> Their movements ought to be described by psychological characteristics; all analogy drawn from physics can only induce error. We will observe to what degree *individuals* possess consciousness of the movements in which they participate; we shall seek the origins of sentimental illusions which most often hide from the classes, under ideological appearances, the true character of class struggles; and we will note carefully the variations in the sentiments of solidarity, etc.[37]

But Sorel is still highly reductionist. Psychology "provides sociology with explanatory elements [almost] as chemistry provides them for the natural sciences."[38] Sorel's inconsistent use of analogies drawn from natural science is illustrated in his parallel between psychology and a science based on the components of atoms, on the one hand, and the condemnation of "all analogy drawn from physics," on the other.

The Durkheim essay Sorel wrote in the winter and spring of 1896 was an attempt at self-clarification. His next such efforts were the articles on Vico and on science in education (mentioned in Chapter 2). The positivistic refusal in these articles to study morals scientifically did not lead to a rejection of moral studies altogether. On the contrary, Sorel was to call for a plurality of methods to study society. These methods were not clarified until his later critique of Bergson. In 1896, however, Sorel had already gone a considerable distance toward his mature view that "social poetry," as well as objective data, must be evaluated. To suppress all ideals in the practice of social science is to suppress all knowledge: "If there exist only facts capable of empirical knowledge, one can ask what intellectual interest these mountains of 'historical atoms' possess."[39]

The immense contradiction that dominated some of Durkheim's cruder positivistic forebears was to affirm the unity of all phenomena—including social phenomena—while arguing that values were immune from the scientific method. But, as Sorel said, "Moral evaluation plays a capital role both in the struggles of the old orders and in modern class struggles. It is because these evaluations are not scientific and demonstrable that they play this role: no one would ever struggle over a mechanical theory. Viewed in a certain way, moral judgments are the basis of all historical movement."[40] By emphasizing the primacy of the scientific method, positivists miss the essential ingredient of social order. Rather than exclude morals from study, Sorel is anticipating a call for new ways of understanding non-scientific phenomena. But Sorel had earlier stated that social science was the study of relations. How, then, is he to meet the challenge of connecting social, economic, psychological, and moral phenomena without himself engaging in metaphysical speculation on the one hand and reverting to scientifico-social parallelism on the other? How can he accept the heterogeneity of phenomena while at the same time seeing the connections between them?

Sorel's viewpoint, which he inherits from Vico and Marx, is that the categories of social classification are produced in our minds by our psychology. Sorel claims—true to the Vicoian spirit—that although it is necessary to combine events, one must do so under standards that are "concrete and living, by what is human, i.e., by the laws of psychology."[41] But if such psychological laws exist, then Sorel must admit the possibility (which he doubted in 1894) of penetrating into men's consciousness. To continue his old skepticism would make it absurd to speak of psychological laws.

III

In his "Etude sur Vico" Sorel for the first time spells out the relationship between the act of making and the act of thinking. "The social world is certainly the work of men," he quotes Vico as saying, "which results in the fact that man should find in it the principle of the changes in human intelligence."[42] Sorel cites a passage from *Capital* in which Marx acknowledges his debt to the great Neapolitan thinker: "As Vico says, human history differs from natural history in that we have made the former but not the latter. . . . Technology discloses man's mode of dealing with nature, the process of production by which he sustains his life, and thereby lays bare the mode of formation of his social relations and of the mental conceptions which flow from them."[43] From this statement Sorel derives the notion that implicit in the Vicoian notion that "man knows what he makes" is the distinction between artificial and natural nature: the social world belongs to artificial nature that man can know because it is his work.[44] This is a crucial interpretation for Sorel. Instead of emphasizing the aspects of Marx in which all sciences are unified in the Comtean way, he views Marx as an apostle of the two natures and infers from this that Marx advocated partial studies in which the "social question" in its broader aspects would play second fiddle to the accomplishment of immediate tasks. In this respect, Marxian social science simultaneously imitates science and affirms separation from it. Furthermore, by this very separation social science can reincorporate moral phenomena into studies through psychological investigations.

It is at this point that the Maxwellian industrial-factory model that so informed Sorel's view of science becomes applicable to his view of social science. Sorel rejects ideal systematizing in science as a means of satisfying idle curiosity; the discovery of the "true machine" has been replaced by solving limited problems suited to specific needs, "to discover some types which manifest lesser defects than in the existing mechanism, or to improve a particular device with a view to some particular application."[45]

Just as physical and natural sciences in modernity almost always propose problems of a practical nature, the implications of practicality extend beyond those fields. To confine science to a practical realm, Sorel implies, is to be concerned with the problems which are directly confronting us, those problems that are close to being solved. Sorel notes in a much later essay that Marx, in his preface to the *Critique of Political Economy*, laid down rules for the limits of social science in regard to socialism: productive forces create the material conditions for a solution of antagonism within the social processes of production; thus, no solution to the antagonisms of productive systems under capitalism is possible until capitalism matures, since capitalism is the only system with resources adequate to quell such antagonism. The solutions to the problems of capitalism, in short, are found within the capitalist system itself—in productive resources and in the proletarian class created by capitalist production. Therefore, according to Marx, new social relations do not replace the old ones until their material conditions have ripened in the womb of the old society. Mankind thus inevitably sets itself only those tasks whose material solutions already exist.[46] Both science and sociology are motivated by the impulse of urgent needs and are content with empirical procedures; both act on the present.

If, Sorel asks, science is not universal, if science deals with phenomena which are of immediate practical importance, "why proceed otherwise in social science?" Until now, social science has failed us because it pretends to do what even the more precise sciences cannot do: it claims to proceed toward a totality. Why object, for example, to the failure of the cooperative movement to resolve what is called "the social question? . . . They are criticized for not striking capitalism at its heart, for adapting to the present economic structure, for rendering service to only a fraction of the working class." But Sorel warns us not to reach "beyond the potentiality of human action under the present social conditions."[47]

It is Sorel's contention that the broader the scope of the scientific or social theory, the more it risks becoming utopian or ideological. Once a theory or hypothesis in physical science has been tested, the narrower it becomes, simply by virtue of the tightly knit organization of the experiment. The natural and physical sciences "control" for ideological distortion by, among other things, limiting the scope of their investigations. That is why artificial nature is more precise, more determined and more predictable in proportion to its insulation from spurious outside forces. Despite the vast gulf separating the two realms of physical and social theory, Sorel maintains that the latter should attempt to imitate the physical sciences by limiting its investigation to taking particular views on certain aspects of phenomena. To Sorel "the sole truth" of this self-limitation arises because the human mind itself is "divided into distinct ideologies whose provinces are increasingly separated as we embrace a more extensive range of knowledge. . . . This *philosophy of diremption* ought to replace that of unification."[48] At a later date, Sorel was to define the concept of "diremption" more precisely as the examination of certain parts of phenomena "without taking into account all their connections with the whole; determining in some way the nature of their activity by isolating them. When it has attained the most perfect knowledge in this way, social philosophy can no longer reconstruct the broken unity."[49] Even in 1897, he insists that social philosophy is as powerless to reconstruct the old unity as it is to reassemble the separated parts of physical nature. With a fragmented view of social theory, "we should no longer recognize in the social world a system analogous to that of astronomy. We are asked only to recognize that the intermingling of causes produces sufficiently regular and characteristic periods to allow them to become objects for an intelligent understanding of facts."[50]

It is now easier to see why Sorel seems to be extremely empiricist in his criticism of Durkheim. Sorel does not deny the validity of generalizing about social things; he merely places severe strictures on doing this, and consequently establishes a rough parallel between certain aspects of social science and natural science by making what he would later call *diremptions* into a rough social-science equivalent of the expressive supports of artificial nature—Sorel's ideal types.

The equation, for certain purposes, of science with industry helps to elucidate the differences and similarities among psychological, social, and physical phenomena. Comparison can be made with regard to the future of the three fields. In one sense, science and social science must avoid historical prediction. Although certain physical sciences (unlike social science) can predict the outcome of certain experiments under laboratory conditions (artificial nature), the course experimentation itself will take in the future cannot be predicted. Furthermore, the course of a productive process in a certain industry during a certain workday may be predictable, but it is impossible to predict the development of the steam engine (to use Sorel's example) over the course of the next hundred years.[51] Although physics is a separate discipline, the history of physics is part of intellectual history. Science, in Vico's words, "proceeds by a secure analysis of thinking which relates to the necessities and utilities of social life. . . . Viewed in this way, science becomes the history of human ideas."[52] Social research should, like science, cut itself off from most, if not all, extrapolation of present trends into future events; limited to proximate and practical needs, it is precluded from theorizing about the world of the future. For Marxists, this means that "research applies no longer to what society should be, but to what the proletariat can accomplish in the present class struggle."[53]

The difference between natural and social science lies in the fact that natural science can replicate events in controlled circumstances. Whereas in this respect natural science is "closed," the closed aspect of social science or history applies only to those occurrences which are *faits accomplis*. The open aspects of social phenomena, those which are oriented toward the future, are non-scientific and psychological. This futuristic knowledge Sorel calls "a personal poetic knowledge developed with a view to free action" which must never be compared to science and which is entirely separate from it.[54] This separation corresponds to the Kantian dualism between the mechanistic and analytical world of *phenomena* in which the whole is equal to the sum of its parts, and the *noumenal* world of our creative conscience, in which only the whole matters. Are we then to relegate Sorel's viewpoint to either a Kantian or a positivist duality?

Sorel realizes that to rest on this duality is to invite stagnation in science as well as in society. To exclude the poetic spirit altogether from scientific undertakings would be to lapse into the passive region of natural nature. Scientific knowledge is, as he later put it, "purely intellectual; it presents itself to us as something alien to our person."

Such entities are determined and operate in a realm of un-freedom. Insofar as we accept scientific laws without acting on them, "we attribute to them a determinant force on our will and we submit meekly to their tyranny."[55]

This circle of determinism can only be broken through innovation in devices or in the development of new laws which require the invention of new apparatuses. Sorel then argues that the development of devices precedes the development of scientific theory. Future creations of science are the purview of practical men—such as inventors—who see in theories only instruments destined to establish certain qualitative determinations that have already been constructed through empirical investigations. Such men never reason by applying scientific theories: "The architect combines all his pieces before *verifying* their stability; this verification is very useful; but it comes at the end as a contributory means of science."[56] That is why Sorel later pays great attention to the distinction between scientists and inventors. It is the creative man, the architect or inventor, who exhausts himself in the accomplishment of tasks which the existing scientific estate regards as ludicrous.

At this point Sorel's respect for the school of psychological spontaneity comes into play. In order for the practical man to act, he must break the chain of determinism by an act of will. This will is motivated by a "real spontaneity" rather than by determined science: Poetic fictions are stronger than scientific ones. We have in them "the ability to substitute an imaginary world for scientific truths which we populate with plastic creations and that we perceive with much greater clarity than the material world. It is these idols which penetrate our will and are the sisters of our soul."[57] To build a house is not a predetermined action but an action of the will and, hence, motivated by our poetic side. So too the development of new techniques: "Determinism reveals itself to be an adversary of science; for it always ends in affirming the powerlessness of our creative forces; we then *have science only to the extent that we have the force to govern the world*."[58] The more we advance in the study of nature, which is to say the more we understand our own methods of production, the more we see the "absolute incompatibility between natural processes and those of our technique."[59]

Social science, which deals with the human will, is linked to artificial nature by severing itself from natural nature in much the same way that experimental invention does. Since science and morals are connected to each other through an act of will driven by the poetic imagination, they rise and fall together. The same poetic imagination that inspires the inventor produces in him the moral certitude of the rightness of his task: "If man loses something of his confidence in scientific certitude, he loses much of his moral certitude at the same time."[60]

The poetic spirit can be shared by practitioners of both natural and social sciences. Indeed, refined into the myth of the general strike, the idea of a "social poetry" was to become Sorel's best-known contribution to sociology. A decade before he wrote *Reflections on Violence* we find him saying that knowledge of the future, a knowledge which is solely poetic, is accepted by Marx in the *Eighteenth Brumaire of Louis Bonaparte*:

> The social revolution of the nineteenth century cannot draw its poetry from the past, but only from the future. It cannot begin its own task until it has been rid of all superstition about the past. The revolutions of previous times had need of historical reminiscences in order to dazzle themselves with their own importance. . . . The proletarian revolutions recoil in fright before the indeterminate enormity of their own goals until the time when the situation becomes such that any return is impossible.[61]

Sorel remarks that in this statement Marx posed with great clarity the future of idealism as opposed to science. "Until now, revolutionaries have almost always been led to impose upon themselves an illusory theory patterned after legends of the past: they advanced with the complete certitude that they were repeating an experiment belonging to science; these historical reminiscences prevented seeing and discussing the facts which unfolded in reality."[62] What Marx argues is that such an approach to revolutions is only pseudo-scientific.

For Sorel, Marx is a true scientist because he employs anterior facts to create hypotheses that can and should be tested with an eye open only up to the present. These hypotheses are limited, as they are in physical science; they should never be used to predict future experiences, for reliance on models of past experience transforms social science into utopianism. The open-ended character of human behavior is constricted in formulas based on outmoded conditions:

> But the great *total revolution* can never be made in this way. In order to effect it, we must be certain that it will not be produced on any anterior model . . . and that *the future cannot be determined*. What we should ask of social science is to inform us of revolutionary forces; but while, in the past, people embraced the future in an hypothesis which was received with the deference that one accorded to a scientific theory, we can have only

> *indeterminate* views on the future, expressed solely in the language of the artistic imagination.[63]

This means that history cannot be conceived as a set of laws; it is at this point that social science becomes radically different from natural science. Historical laws do not, in Sorel's view, determine the effect from the cause; rather, they represent an infinite complexity of causes under an artificially unitary appearance: "What these hypotheses describe can never be produced and is never produced, because in order to find the reproduction of so many combinations whose coincidence is so accidental, we must construct an hypothesis having no probability whatsoever."[64]

Sorel's use of Marx in his exposition of the right principles of social science is novel—at least for Sorel's time. In place of the traditional holistic understanding of Marx, Sorel presents him as a pluralist who recognizes the multiple bases of hypotheses used in the various kinds of sciences. Furthermore, "Marx would show that all political, philosophical, and religious systems could not be considered complete systems, having their own fundamental roots."[65] Sorel sees in Marx the view that the struggle of interests and of economic competition demonstrates the absence of a coordinated social system. While, until now, "everything appeared to be subordinated to a certain (more or less ideal) unity in the state, the new philosophy perceived the fundamental (class) division which the old theories had viewed as accidental."[66]

By relegating the future to poetic imagination and placing it outside the purview of social science, Sorel—perhaps inadvertently—shatters the overall unity of Marxist thought. Indeed, Sorel admits that if someone adopts Marx's principles, "he can say that there is no longer any social question. He can even say that socialism (in the ordinary and historical sense of the word) is outgrown."[67] If the social revolution is total, it cannot be a subject of a piecemeal social science. If social science concerns itself with partial solutions, its way of understanding things must also be partial; and if a strictly controlled laboratory science renders, by its method, only a partial solution to a problem of limited scope, how much more pretentious it is of social science, whose only "laboratory" is the factory-workshop, to do otherwise. It is easy to see how, in *Reflections on Violence*, Sorel would transform the total revolution into myth. But the theory of diremption, which was certainly coming close to being spelled out by 1896, served only to sap the internal unity of Marxism as a system. In making Marxism "scientifically relevant," Sorel had to change Marx's and Engels's understanding of science and, in doing so, he "decomposed" it.[68]

IV

In order to make this clearer, let us depart from Sorel briefly and discuss Marx's and Engels's view of the scientific enterprise. There is a problem in interpretation here: although Engels did most of the writing on natural science, he has been accused of becoming more deterministic and holistic in his writings than Marx.[69] One can, of course, impute a certain pluralism to Engels's own views on science. In *Anti-Dühring*, Engels distinguishes between physical sciences, in which permanent truths operate, and the "historical sciences," which are relative beyond trivialities. "Anyone therefore who here sets out to hunt down final and ultimate truths, genuine, absolutely immutable truths, will bring home but little."[70]

However, Marx's and Engels's dedication to this pluralistic viewpoint was anything but clear-cut. Theirs was a nineteenth-century optimistic and progressive view of the world, inclined toward a universalistic understanding of science. Engels professed extensive research into mathematics and the natural sciences "in order to convince myself of what in general I was not in doubt—that in nature, amid the welter of innumerable changes, the same dialectical laws of motion force their way through as those which in history govern the apparent fortuitousness of events; the same laws as those which similarly form the thread running through the history of the development of human thought and gradually rise to consciousness in the mind of man."[71] Laws of external nature and laws which govern man's bodily and mental existence can be distinguished "only in thought, not in reality."[72]

There is some controversy as to whether Marx intended a unified view of science. Jurgen Habermas notes that in order to prove the scientific character of his analysis, Marx made repeated use of its analogy to the natural sciences. Thus, Marx says that "natural science will eventually subsume the science of man, just as the science of man will subsume natural science: there will be a *single* science."[73] Marx's science of society is looked upon as the "natural history of labor," in which social theory remains epistemologically unjustified because it is assumed to be ultimately identical to the natural sciences. These sciences in turn do not examine their own basis of understanding.

Marx's failure to develop a more detailed and systematic philosophy of science and of knowledge did not prevent him from anticipating a world in which the productive processes were fostering an increasingly unified social consciousness, allowing the worker a progressively more thorough knowledge of the process of "natural exchange" between man and nature. As Engels expressed it: "Freedom does not consist in emancipation from natural laws but in the knowledge of those laws, and in the possibility of making them work toward definite ends. . . . Therefore, the freedom of the will means nothing but the capacity to make decisions with knowledge of the subject. . . . The freer a man's judgment . . . the greater is the necessity with which the content of this judgment will be determined."[74] For Marx, capitalist society prevents this full-scale realization. The oppressive conditions of capitalism do not allow the worker to realize himself in this free state, and it is as a member of an oppressed class that he rebels; only after the social revolution, when men will fully appropriate the means of production and operate them in accordance with the needs of all humanity, will men be able to realize themselves as individual, creative, inventive beings. Only then will the science of man be applied consciously and rationally to the entire laboring and productive process. According to both Marx and Engels, in order for this new society to come into being, the division of labor which prevailed under capitalism must disappear:

> Its place must be taken by an organization of production in which, on the one hand, no individual can throw on the shoulders of others his share of productive labor, the natural condition of human existence; and in which, on the other hand, productive labor, instead of being a means of subjugating men, will become a means of their emancipation, by offering each individual the opportunity to develop all his faculties.[75]

If the division of labor under capitalism lies at the heart of man's alienation, then the abolition of this division is imperative. A solution to the problem is found in the development of technology and of large-scale production. "Since the notion of the whole system does not proceed from the workman, but from the machinery, a change of persons can take place at any time without an interruption,"[76] allowing us to do away with the outmoded specialization that occurs under capitalism and to become masters of production in accordance with a social plan. In the total revolution, man apprehends as well as controls, in cooperation with others, the totality of productive forces.

Habermas's claim that Marx's natural-social science is epistemologically unjustified is disputed by Paul Thomas, who quotes Marx as saying that nature as it unfolds in human society "is man's real nature; hence nature, as it develops through industry, albeit in alienated form, is truly anthropological nature."[77] This viewpoint, Thomas continues, is the reverse of Engels's attempted synthesis of Comte and Hegel, his attempt to deduce historical laws from those of nature (conceived as an independent reality external to man).

Engels and others derived their science *a priori* instead of through critical knowledge of what men actually do in society. As a methodological consequence of this view,

> work for Marx is not, for all its centrality, a metabolic process involving man, nature, and society, if this means that it involves a metaphysical conception of *praxis* which may be invoked as an absolute point of departure or as a pre-categorical postulate. The world is not a scientific laboratory writ large. Marx's emphasis on constitutive labor, indeed, depends upon his belief that there are no extrinsic principles, preceding empirical enquiry, that can be "applied" to the facts.[78]

There is strong support for this viewpoint in Marxian texts, and Sorel's own view of Marx approximates it. He condemned the "adaptation" of Engels's philosophy to Marxism, and insisted that *Anti-Dühring* was "written without the scientific spirit."[79] However, the reasons for Sorel's, and Thomas's, criticism of Engels are not the usual modern objections; Sorel's viewpoint is at odds with both the modern viewpoint, on the question of alienation, and that of old-fashioned Marxists, in regard to scientific analogies.

Let us note briefly the paradox produced by the Marxian solution to the problem of alienation: the unity of theory and practice includes a unity of natural science and social activity precisely because science is inextricably linked to social purposes. This implies that if Marx does not turn the world into a laboratory, he certainly anticipates a society self-constituted as a huge building-project engineered (and exquisitely designed) according to principles that do not contradict those of natural science. To deny this would be to assert that the utopian activities of "hunter, fisherman, shepherd, and critic" depicted in *The German Ideology*[80] would be divorced from scientific undertakings; hence, would be perpetuating the division of labor within knowledge (i.e., alienated thought). For Marx, then, science would indeed be "humanized," but if "there is to be only one science," humanistic endeavors must likewise be made scientific. On the other hand, if we are to affirm such a unity, then Marx's differences from Engels are hardly worth mentioning: the ethico-scientific presupposition that men should direct themselves toward a unified science appears as much a pre-categorical postulate and is just as doctrinaire and prescriptive as one that argues for the positivistic belief that all knowledge derives from the empirical analytical method. The only difference here between Marx and Comte is that Marx's view of science is more consistently unified than Comte's; Marx anticipates a more thorough merging of science and human values.

We must remember that Sorel's access to the works of Marx and Engels' was limited. Available translations were few in number and of mediocre quality. No Paris manuscripts had been discovered, no elaborate theory of alienated labor had been developed. Nevertheless, Sorel's reading of Marxist writings in the 1895-1897 period constitutes a fascinating hidden critique of both traditional and modern Marxian theory: What happens if Sorel's non-unitary interpretation of Marx replaces the conventional one? In other words, what are the consequences of Marx's and Engels's vision of a unified natural history of labor being replaced by a theory of science which insists on the plurality of means and ends? What, furthermore, emerges from Sorel's contention that in the realm of artificial nature all procedures should be regarded as provisional? In Sorel's understanding, the unity of science is a chimera; for Marx it was not.

V

Superficially, Sorel seems to have agreed with Marx: routine and alienation must be overcome through varying the tasks associated with work. But unlike Marx—or at least unlike many of his modern interpreters—Sorel believed that the nature of science and of modern machinery makes any full-scale attempt to overcome either the division of labor or the onerous burdens of labor a utopian scheme. This is so despite superficial appearances to the contrary. Sorel only *seems* to agree with Marx on the division of labor. He cites Ure: when the modern worker transfers his attention from one machine to another, "he varies his tasks and develops his ideas by reflecting on general combinations which result from his own works and those of his companions."[81] Furthermore, Sorel notes that Marx's *Capital* proclaims it necessary to replace "the fragmented individual, bearer of a detailed social function, by the totally developed individual, for whom different social functions are modes of activity."[82] Indeed, Sorel harks back to his own *Procès de Socrate*, in which the division of labor "existed only in a rudimentary state" and in which hierarchy and command were functions of seniority and experience.[83]

However, as we noted at the end of our discussion of Socrates, Sorel was later to modify his viewpoint on the division of labor, as consistent adherence to the Xenophontic morality required. By 1897, Sorel calls it an exaggeration to speak of the abolition of the division of labor in modern production. For him such an abolition signifies a naive "mixture of functions and passage of everyone to diverse positions in the workshop."[84]

For Sorel, the fragmentation that occurs in both science and industry means that the scope of our understanding must be specialized accordingly. If man becomes scientifically sophisticated through the use of materials which, by their very finitude, limit the scope of the laborer, how then can the integral realization of human nature be prepared for by philosophers to whom it appears that the division of labor "advances to an ever greater reduction of the value of the individual"?[85] The number of components of the manufacturing process with which the worker can familiarize himself is limited. The aim of education is, therefore, to "familiarize the student with the handling of a restricted number of combinations and to inculcate in him in a systematic way the *intellectual routine* needed to resolve problems."[86]

Sorel does not see the industrial revolution, with its attendant mechanization of industry, as containing the potential for total emancipation. Instead, there appears to be a certain balance between the harmony of the traditional community and the emancipation obtained from the mobility of modern society:

> The old occlusion of the individual in a strictly determined environment constituted a professional and local synthesis: man went through all the phases of production or of transformation, thus referring to a great number of techniques. Today this integration no longer exists; there is a rupture of the ensemble and a splitting of the various techniques. But the techniques themselves are no longer particular modes of making but reasoned branches of knowledge extending over a wide range of professions and of local methods. Thus, in this case, a synthesis based on common scientific reasoning is produced.[87]

Although one synthesis is exchanged for another, the new synthesis is no more total or comprehensive than the old one. On the contrary, since the regime of modern industry cannot be fixed at any one stage of development, and since, as we have seen, its future is unpredictable, Sorel later argues that it is all we can do to keep up with our own area of specialization. "Heads of factories, engineers, and workers are condemned to remain apprentices all their lives, even though men subjected to such a condition bitterly complain of the difficulty of their fate."[88] These complaints are for the future, for "the more scientific production becomes, the better we understand that our destiny is to struggle without a truce and thus to annihilate the dreams of paradisiacal happiness which the old socialists had taken for legitimate anticipation."[89]

This apprenticeship, under which man is irrevocably placed by the operation of modern industry, requires men to struggle against two forces that subjugate the worker: the resistance of the external nature of the objects of our labor; and the natural nature of our personality—that is, the inclination to relaxation, to sloth. These two forces, more than the capitalist organization of production, Sorel sees as the major obstacles that must be overcome. With regard to the nature of the materials worked on, Sorel argues:

> Nature does not let itself be reduced to the role of servant of humanity without protesting. Passive resistance warns us that we will never be able completely to subject phenomena to mathematical laws, that is to say, to our intelligence. We must destroy the enormous mass of accumulated forces in order to arrive at creating the new forces organized for our benefit. Nature never ceases working, with crafty slowness, for the ruination of all our works. . . . Matter imposes its own laws when the mind withdraws.[90]

Alienation, for Sorel, is never completely transcended, because man overcomes this entropy in natural nature only through continued struggle.

But this laboring process is all the more difficult because *our own* nature resists it. Loath as he is to characterize humanity as possessing any kind of "nature," Sorel says:

> The tendency to routine is the great danger that menaces the workshops which are not subject to the constraints of capitalism; the latter has appeared to triumph over the normal forces of our deepest psychology, always desirous of mediocrity, but our nature hastens to recapture its rights from the moment that it is free to do so. . . . It is not easy to realize the psychology which is contrary to the mediocrity that is defined above.[91]

It is, nevertheless, the obligation of socialism to assist in the self-overcoming process, to pit our wills against our inclinations and our creative activity against our day-to-day routine.

In saying that man's nature generally inclines us toward automatism rather than away from it, Sorel's view of man—insofar as he has one—is almost the opposite of Marx's (assuming that Marx too can be said to possess a view of human nature). In place of Marx's *animal laborens*, whose spirit is fragmented by the manufacturing process in capitalism, Sorel hints that the competitive nature of the capitalist economy prevents us from being enslaved by our own inertia and the forces of natural nature. Man can overcome this pull toward decline and decadence only *through* "incessant labor," rather than by emancipation from it, as Marx sometimes suggests.[92]

As we have said, at this stage in his writing career Sorel was not entirely conscious of his differences from Marx; but at this point Sorel seems to be replacing Marx's attempt to transcend alienation with an organization of production which is still partly alienated and partly routinized. Marx appears to envision a total victory over nature; Sorel regards it as a triumph if the struggle between man and nature is kept in some sort of balance. A *sturm und drang* view of labor replaces the Marxist one: man, for Sorel, if not for Marx, remains an alienated animal.

We have seen that Sorel is more sensitive to the need for a division of labor in the productive process than he appeared to be in *Le Procès de Socrate*. On the other hand, we can argue that more than a little of his view that obedience should be the school of command remains, and in this respect Sorel owes a debt to Marx. Although Sorel sees an inevitable limit placed on the division of labor *among* workers (and, by inference, between workers and inventor-engineers) he would abolish (along with Marx) the hierarchy in the management of production that set the *patron* or capitalist above the men who are actively engaged in the productive process. Thus, while rejecting the abolition, on a *horizontal* level, of the division of labor (among workers), Sorel sees the need for the abolition, on a *vertical* plane, of bossism. Capitalists "will be the masters [only] as long as they justify their *ability* in their capacity as producers."[93] However, according to Sorel, capitalists tend increasingly to justify their superiority on the grounds of a liberal-arts university education that is utterly separate from the world of production. The capitalists, once so able and so daring in the direction of production, have now become intellectuals—the modern equivalent of the Sophists or the Socratics—basing their superiority on the grounds of knowledge.

Citing Marx's *Capital*, Sorel notes that "the distinction between skilled and unskilled labor is often based on pure illusion," and that "at the present time a change is taking place which tends to spoil the prestige of the intellectuals."[94] The syndicalists, Sorel predicts, will triumph when they reveal the superiority of their own ability, when they demonstrate that it is they rather than the capitalists who are most adept in organizing production. "As the character and intelligence of the workers improve, the majority of the overseers can be eliminated."[95]

Ultimately, the problems of industrial society must be dealt with by the workers themselves, not the intellectuals who pretend to speak for them. The ultimate purpose behind Sorel's writings on social science is to point out that neither social science nor the socialist movement possesses answers to what is called the social question; the socialist movement and social scientists must beware of becoming a class of intellectuals who, separated from the life of work, impose upon society abstractions of justice for the ultimate purpose of gaining party advantage.

It was, of course, the galvanizing concept of the social myth that would later, for Sorel, make possible the emergence of the workman from his traditional somnolence. At this stage, Sorel relies on the unification of education with industrial practice to circumvent "the already excessively numerous class of demo-savants in an industry." By condemning man to perpetual apprenticeship, Sorel shifts the problem of education into the workplace; it is only there that the gap between intellectuals and workers can be overcome. Sorel notes that Marx's emphasis on industrial education will unite, for all children above a certain age, education and productive labor with gymnastic instruction "not only as a method of increasing social wealth but as *the sole and unique method of producing complete men.*"[96]

Sorel's heavy reliance on Marx to support his own views on factory life obviously meant that Sorel was not, in 1897, aware of how later scholars would characterize Marx's understanding of the overcoming of the problem of division of labor. It was apparent shortly after 1897 that Sorel was increasingly aware of the breach in ideas between himself and those who called themselves Marxists. At this time Sorel was to undertake a major revision of Marxian theory by attempting, in a manner far more explicit than the one he had used in *Le Devenir Social*, to remove once and for all both the positivistic and the metaphysical elements from Marxism. This was the first of his great revisions: later would come his revisions of positivism itself, and of the content of Bergson's theory of psychological spontaneity.

Notes

1. Sorel, "La Fin du paganisme," *Ere Nouvelle* (Aug.-Oct. 1894); reissued with corrections as *La Ruine du monde antique* (Paris: Rivière, 1901), and with further corrections in 1925 and 1933.

2. Ibid. (1925 edition), p. 198.

3. Ibid., p. xix.

4. See also Terry Clark, ed., *Gabriel Tarde*, p. 10.

5. Emile Durkheim, *Le Suicide* (Paris: F. Alcan, 1897), p. 439 (cited in *FGS*, p. 74).

6. Terry Clark, *Gabriel Tarde*, p. 11.

7. Sorel, "Les Théories pénales de MM. Durkheim et Tarde," *Archivio di Psichiatria e Scienze Penali* 16 (1895): 222, 221.

8. Sorel, "La Femme criminelle d'après M. Lombroso," *Revue Scientifique* 52 (1893): 467.

9. Sorel, "La Position du problème de M. Lombroso," *Revue Scientifique* 51 (1893): 207f.

10. Sorel, "Le Crime politique d'après M. Lombroso," *Revue Scientifique* 51 (1893): 561.

11. Sorel, "La Position du problème," p. 208.

12. Sorel, "La Femme criminelle," pp. 463-64; cf. Sorel, "La Science et la morale," in *Questions de morale* (Paris: Alcan, 1900), p. 18.

13. Ibid., p. 464.

14. Sorel, *La ruine*, p. 197.

15. Ibid., p. 168.

16. Sorel, "Les Théories de M. Durkheim," *Devenir Social* 1, nos. 1-2 (Apr.-May 1895): 13, citing Durkheim, *Les Règles de la méthode sociologique* (Paris: Alcan, 1895). See the English translation, *The Rules of the Sociological Method*, translated by Sarah A. Solovay and John H. Mueller (New York: Free Press, 1966), p. 131. All future references will be to this translation, hereafter cited as *Rules*.

17. Sorel, "Les Théories," pp. 3, 17. See Durkheim's *Rules*, p. 54, wherein Durkheim criticizes "premature attempts to grasp the essence of phenomena." Durkheim is rather abstract in his explanation of development, and he gives few examples. The example of boyhood is that of the present writer.

18. Sorel, "Les Théories," p. 3. Cf. Sorel, *D'Aristote*, p. 197.

19. Sorel, "Les Théories," p. 14.

20. Ibid., p. 4, citing Durkheim's *Rules*, p. 75.

21. Sorel, "Les Théories," p. 175. Sorel criticized Le Bon's theory that competition results in the triumph of the most competent: *Revue Internationale de Sociologie* (Feb. 1899): 152.

22. Sorel, "Les Théories," p. 11. Sorel notes here that in astronomy, the positions of the heavenly bodies form the material cause of changes and determine the forces, and, reciprocally, given the forces, the positions can be determined: "If we consider a rectangle ABCD we can construct the following schema:

A. Positions at a given instant.
B. Forces at the given instant.
C. Forces at that determined time.
D. Positions at that determined time.

The chain is absolutely closed. Durkheim gives as an example of social reciprocity a chain that is quite analogous. 'The social reaction that we call *punishment* is due to the intensity of the collective sentiments which the crime offends; but, from another angle, it has the useful function of maintaining these sentiments at the same degree of intensity, for they would soon diminish if offenses against them were not punished' [*Rules*, p. 96]. This doctrine can be translated into a four-element chain like that above:

A. The penal system in general.
B. The current system of ideas about justice.
C. Public opinion about a given crime.
D. Punishment decided for the crime.

As we see, there is nothing mysterious in this so-called reciprocity, but there is an affirmation of a very important ethical thesis that Durkheim's exposition does not make obvious: the system of legal ideas on the right of punishment derives from abstract philosophical principles based on the empirical system of repression. We start from the real considered in general for the determination of principles, then return to the particular reality."

23. Sorel, "Les Théories," p. 7, citing Durkheim's *Rules*, p. 141.

24. Ibid.

25. Ibid.

26. Sorel, "Les Théories," p. 8.

27. Sorel, "La Science dans l'éducation," *Devenir Social* 1, no. 12 (March 1896): 218-19.

28. Durkheim, *Rules*, pp. 101-2.

29. Ibid.

30. Sorel, "Les Théories," p. 19, citing Durkheim's *Rules*, p. xxxix.

31. Théodule Ribot, *La Psychologie des sentiments* (13th ed.,Paris: Alcan, 1930), p. 294; cf. Sorel's review of this work in "Les Sentiments sociaux," *Devenir Social* 2, nos. 5-6 (Aug.-Sept. 1896): 674ff. (signed "x").

32. See Sorel, "Sociologie de la suggestion," *Devenir Social* 3, nos. 5-6 (Aug.-Sept. 1897): 677 (signed "x").

33. See Le Bon's *La Psychologie des foules* (Paris: Alcan, 1895), translated as *The Crowd* (New York: Viking, 1960), pp. 155-59, and *The Psychology of Socialism* (New Brunswick, N.J.: Transaction Books, 1981), pp. 298, 321. For a comparison of Le Bon and Sorel, see Robert A. Nye, *The Origins of Crowd Psychology: Gustave Le Bon and the Crisis of Mass Democracy in the Third Republic* (London: Sage, 1975), chap. 5.

34. Sorel, "Sur la magie moderne," *Indépendance* (Sept. 1911): 4.

35. Review of *La Psychologie des foules* in *Devenir Social* 1, no. 8 (Nov. 1895): 767.

36. Sorel, "Les Théories," p. 24.

37. Ibid., p. 169.

38. Ibid., p. 24.

39. Sorel, "Etude sur Vico," *Devenir Social* 2, no. 7 (Oct. 1896): 797n.

40. Ibid.

41. Ibid., p. 912.

42. Ibid., pp. 809-10.

43. Ibid., p. 810, citing Marx's *Capital* (French edition, Paris: M. Lachatre, 1872-75), trans. J. Roy, p. 162. See the Modern Library edition (New York: Random House, n.d.), p. 406n2.

44. Sorel, "Etude sur Vico," p. 810.

45. Sorel, *Saggi di critica del marxismo* (Palermo: Sandron, 1902), p. 172.

46. Sorel, Preface to E. R. A. Seligman's *L'Interprétation économique de l'histoire* (Paris: Rivière, 1911), pp. xv-xvi. This book was originally published in English, under the title *The Economic Interpretation of History*. Sorel's introduction appears only in the French translation.

47. Sorel, *Saggi di critica del marxismo*, p. 172.

48. Sorel, "Léon XIII," *Etudes Socialistes* 1 (1903): 265-66 (italics are Sorel's).

49. Sorel, *Réflexions*, p. 407 (American ed., p. 259; cf. *FGS*, p. 228).

50. See Sorel's preface to the French translation of Antonio Labriola's *Essais sur la conception matérialiste de l'histoire* (Paris: Giard et Brière, 1897). A partial translation of this preface can be found in the English translation of a series of Labriola articles criticizing Sorel: *Socialism and Philosophy* (Chicago: Kerr, 1911), p. 186.

51. Sorel, "Economie et agriculture," *Revue Socialiste* (March 1901): 297. Cf. Sorel, *D'Aristote*, p. 115.

52. Sorel, "Etude sur Vico," p. 814, citing Vico, *La Science nouvelle*, French trans. Jules Michelet, 1894 ed.

53. Preface to Labriola, *Socialism and Philosophy*, p. 184. See also Preface to Serverio Merlino, *Formes et essence du socialisme*, p. *xxiv*.

54. Sorel, "L'Evolution créatrice," *Mouvement Socialiste* (Feb. 1908):

286, 289. Cf. *FGS*, p. 106, where Sorel distinguishes between the "exterior" and "interior" points of view; between defining society by its "correlations with institutions" and attempting "to treat it as the *behavior of free men* and to seek to understand the psychological state corresponding to a *just decision*. . . . This interior aspect, this collection of feelings . . . should be examined by the philosopher at the same time as the exterior; the two points of view can never be separated."

55. Sorel, "La Science et la morale," in *Questions de morale*, p. 7.

56. Ibid., p. 4 (italics are Sorel's).

57. Ibid., p. 7.

58. Ibid., p. 15 (italics are Sorel's).

59. Ibid., pp. 14-15.

60. Ibid., p. 2.

61. Sorel, "Les Théories," p. 163, citing Marx's *Eighteenth Brumaire of Louis Bonaparte*, French translation.

62. Ibid., p. 163.

63. Ibid., (Sorel's italics).

64. Sorel, "Etude sur Vico," p. 913.

65. Sorel, "Les Théories," p. 153.

66. Ibid., p. 153.

67. Sorel, Preface to Labriola, *Socialism and Philosophy*, p. 184.

68. Hence the title of Sorel's later work, *La Décomposition du Marxisme* (Paris: Rivière, 1908).

69. See, for example, George Lichtheim, *Marxism: An Historical and Critical Study* (New York: Praeger, 1962), pp. 236ff.

70. Friedrich Engels, *Anti-Dühring* (English ed., Moscow: Foreign Languages Publishing House, 1959), pp. 124-25.

71. Ibid., p. 17.

72. Ibid., p. 125.

73. Jurgen Habermas, *Knowledge and Human Interests*, trans. by J. J. Shapiro (Boston: Beacon, 1971), p. 46, citing the "Economic and Philosophical Manuscripts" (Marx's italics). See Karl Marx, *Early Writings*, ed. by T. B. Bottomore (New York: McGraw-Hill, 1964), p. 164.

74. Engels, *Anti-Dühring*, p. 157.

75. Ibid., p. 406, citing Marx's *Capital*.

76. Marx, *Capital* (Moscow: Foreign Languages Publishing House, 1958), vol. 1, p. 421.

77. Paul Thomas, "Marx and Science," *Political Studies* 24, no. 1 (1976): 16, citing Marx's *Early Writings*.

78. Thomas, "Marx and Science," p. 19.

79. Sorel, *Saggi di critica del marxismo*, p. 177.

80. Marx and Engels, *The German Ideology*, trans. by R. Pascal (New York: International Publishers, 1947), p. 22.

81. Sorel, "La Science dans l'éducation," *Devenir Social* 2 (May 1896): 446, citing Andrew Ure, *Philosophy of Manufactures* (French translation, Paris: L. Mathias, 1836). Sorel criticizes Ure for exaggeration but agrees with his views on the division of technique.

82. Sorel, "La Science dans l'éducation," pp. 435-36, citing Marx, *Capital* (French edition), p. 211, col. 1. Sorel notes that the French text speaks of the need to replace "l'individu morcelé porte douleur d'une fonction productrice de détail, par l'individu *intégral* qui ne donne, dans les fonctions alternées, qu'un libre essor à la diversité de ses *capacités* naturelles ou

acquises." Sorel argues that the first part of this sentence should read "l'individu totalement *developpé*, pour lequel des fonctions sociales différentes sont des modes d'activité." The Modern Library edition reads: "Modern Industry, indeed, compels society, under penalty of death, to replace the detail-worker of to-day, crippled by life-long repetition of one and the same trivial operation, and thus reduced to the mere fragment of a man, by the fully developed individual, fit for a variety of labors, ready to face any change of production, and to whom the different social functions he performs, are but so many modes of giving free scope to his own natural or acquired powers" (p. 534). The Stuttgart edition (J. W. N. Dietz Nachfolger, 1914) reads: "Das Teilindividuum, den blossen Trager einer gesellschaftlichen Detailfunktion, durch das allseitig entwickelte Individuum, für welches verschiedene gesellschaftliche Funktionen einander ablosende Betätigungsweisen sind" (p. 429). The French translation appears to be more literal than the English; Sorel demands a change in the first part of the sentence, but a change in the last phrase would be more appropriate.

83. Sorel, "La Science dans l'éducation," p. 438.

84. Ibid. Cf. Sorel, *Insegnamenti*, pp. 157-58, where he criticizes the Marxian illusion of "despecialization."

85. Ibid., p. 444.

86. Ibid., p. 454 (Sorel's italics).

87. Ibid., p. 444.

88. Sorel, *Matériaux*, p. 137.

89. Sorel, *De l'utilité du pragmatisme*, p. 427n (*FGS*, p. 369n).

90. Ibid., pp.426-27 (*FGS*, p. 290).

91. Sorel, *Matériaux*, p. 137.

92. For example, Marx says that limitation of the workday will be a primary agency to transcend alienation.

93. *FGS*, p. 173.

94. Sorel, *Matériaux*, p. 91 (*FGS*, p. 76). But Sorel denies that the skilled worker is simply a "multiple identity of the unskilled.": *Insegnamenti*, p. 160. (See below, pp. 119-23).

95. Ibid., p. 96 (*FGS*, p. 78).

96. Sorel, "La Science dans l'éducation," p. 350, citing Marx, *Capital*, French ed., p. 209 (see the Modern Library edition, pp. 529-530) (italics are Sorel's).

IV

THE DECOMPOSITION OF MARXISM, 1897–1901

The three great historical events in French socialism were the French Revolution, the Revolution of 1848, and the Paris Commune of 1871. The first revolution spawned Jacobinism, whose extreme form, "the conspiracy of equals" of Babeuf, reappeared in 1848 and in the 1871 Commune as the conspiratorial tactics of Auguste Blanqui. From Condorcet's writings of the revolutionary period developed Saint-Simonian and positivist socialism, the utopianism of a science of society. The Revolution of 1848 saw the appearance of Louis Blanc's National Workshops, a moderate form of state socialism; it also saw the appearance of both Marxism and the federalism of Proudhon. Both of the latter were to reappear, together with Blanquism, in the days of the Commune.

Despite the recurrent factionalism of its early period, the various currents of French socialism easily blended or became confused with one another. Sorel noted that there was a clearly Blanquist strain in Marx's diatribe against Proudhon, *The Poverty of Philosophy*, and that Marx and Engels "showed themselves over a long period to be quite favorable to Blanquist ideas."[1] On the other hand, as George Lichtheim notes, "Paradoxically, it was not the Blanquist majority but the Proudhonist minority of the Commune whose political outlook anticipated what, from the 1890's onward, came to be known as Marxism."[2] The Proudhonists opposed the terrorist tactics of the socialists and, as Sorel realized, Marx later came to share this point of view. Marx, in effect, synthesized Blanqui and Proudhon—a synthesis responsible for a great deal of ambiguity in Marxism. Furthermore, with its pretensions to science, it was easy for Marxism to become confused with the positivist revolutionary traditions in France; some who called themselves Marxists supported nationalism and the *Union sacrée* without seeming inconsistent. This often lent radicalism in its various forms a rather conservative air.

By virtue of this confusion in doctrinal heritage, Sorel viewed Marxism as having endured a "crisis" during the 1880s and 1890s, when socialist parties were being formed in France. To Sorel, each of the non-Proudhonian strains of socialism was wrong-headed and corrupt, either secretly or openly oppressive in doctrine and tactics. This corruption could be corrected and the "decomposition" of Marxism halted only if Marx's Blanquist elements, together with Engels's positivism, could be purged from socialist thought.

In attempting to attach Marxism to Proudhonism while severing it from the other socialist traditions, Sorel set himself a difficult enough task from a theoretical point of view, but it was downright herculean in practice, due to the historical development of Marxism in France. Despite the multitude of factions, pure Marxism (as opposed to Blanquist and other corruptions) was quite weakly represented in the Commune; it did not gain prominence until the 1880s. When it did appear, it took an extremely vulgar, deterministic form, somewhat positivistic in orientation.

Paul Lafargue (Marx's son-in-law) and Jules Guesde added a strong element of positivism to the mélange of Blanquism and Proudhonism when they formed the first Marxist socialist party, the Parti Ouvrier, in 1880. Lafargue, arguing out of the Saint-Simonian tradition, viewed Marxism as a sort of science; Guesde, regarded as more thoroughly Marxist, taught that workers' organizations should play second fiddle to party leadership, in imitation of the German Party. The Parti Ouvrier doctrine predicted the inevitable demise of capitalism through its own contradictions.[3] Eduard Vaillant, like Guesde a communard, but more Blanquist than Guesde, formed the Parti Socialiste Révolutionnaire in 1881. The party, often called the Parti Blanquiste, extolled the class struggle and was a natural ally of the Parti Ouvrier.[4] The doctrinal rigidity of both factions led to the formation in 1882 of the Fédération des Travailleurs Socialistes, the so-called "Possibilists," led by Paul Brousse. Brousse not only distrusted Marx's attempts to dominate the International but insisted that the solution to the political problem was to be found in elaborate schemes of public works.[5] (In this he was the heir to Louis Blanc's National Workshops, the disastrous failure of 1848.) Sorel notes, correctly, that although the Fédération declined in direct political importance, "little by little the French Marxists rallied to them. Their communism was transformed into an exploitation of industries by the state."[6] Sorel implies that the possibilism or opportunism of the doctrine of public works was due to the "facility of visualization which has caused such a success for this doctrine."[7]

Jean Allemane, originally an ally of Brousse's, rejected his opportunism and returned to Proudhon's doctrine of workers' action. On this basis the Parti Ouvrier Socialiste Révolutionnaire was formed in 1890 as a break-away faction of the Possibilists. This party absorbed that section of the Possibilists devoted to trade-union activity, and the class struggle became the center of its doctrine. The party accepted the general strike as the prime mode of action, expressing contempt for parliamentary activity. More than any other faction, Sorel admired the Allemanists, because, as he put it, by severing itself from political activity it had "been almost completely free from bourgeois influence"; it was the one group "in which the ethical idea had not lost its importance—at a time when the socialists who appeal to science are asking if law and morality are not words devoid of meaning."[8]

This emphasis on ethics led Sorel at the same time to a fleeting admiration for Jaurès, the head of the "integralist" group—a sort of Fabian society which attempted to find a middle ground between the Proudhonist tendencies of the Allemanists and the Blanquist Marxist traditions of the other parties. Despite his bourgeois origins, Jaurès had "shown that in the bourgeois classes there are always men capable of understanding the socialist movement. . . . The admirable conduct of Jaurès is the most beautiful proof that there is a socialist ethic."[9] Despite his admiration for the Allemanists, Sorel saw in Jaurès another Marx, but in this case a Marx who looked upon socialism as a genuinely moral rather than a purely ameliorative movement.

Sorel held these views until February 1898. In that year the Dreyfus Affair came to the fore. Integralists began to form electoral groups; to Sorel, then a Dreyfusard, they had abandoned their critical function and had taken up with the other Marxist parties. Indeed, by the sixteenth of October 1898, the Parti Ouvrier (the Guesdists) held a meeting in which all the aforementioned factions were represented, including Sorel's beloved Allemanists. A motion was adopted that proclaimed the common purpose and united action of revolutionary forces. Guesde, Vaillant, Brousse, Jaurès, Briand, Viviani, and Millerand were included in a permanent supervisory committee of the new socialist bloc.[10] It was a sad event for Sorel, who now despaired of socialist parties in general and Jaurès in particular. Party unity had signaled the triumph of both Blanquist and utopian ideas in the political realm.

Just a week prior to the French unity meeting, Eduard Bernstein had written a letter to the German Social Democratic Party assembled in Stuttgart. This letter of 3 October 1898 was the opening shot in the battle, known as the revisionist controversy, which was to rage in Marxist parties throughout Europe. Bernstein was to raise many of the same questions with regard to socialist doctrine that Sorel and Croce had begun to pose in France and in Italy. This "crisis" in socialism would further the ideas already advanced by Sorel and Croce, discouraged as they were by the sterility of the socialist movement.

The doctrinal innovations of the revisionists were appealing to Sorel. Furthermore, since he was cross-pressured into opposing both opportunism and doctrinal rigidity, he found in revisionism what he thought to be a refreshing disavowal of orthodoxy combined with sufficient moral insulation from electoral opportunism. It was with the formation in 1902 of Pelloutier's *bourses du travail* that Sorel finally gave up hope for any political party movement and adopted a direct-action syndicalism. For now, Sorel regarded the revisionists as opening a path for a new socialist culture, a culture the orthodox Marxists could not envision.

I

Until 1897, Sorel had seemed to find Marx's theory to be the answer to the need for an empirical and pluralistic social science. Marx, Sorel claimed, "did not regard society as a homogeneous whole which one can discuss as an entity: it is a multiform complexus of contradictory interests."[11] Therefore, it is simplistic to interpret Marx as proclaiming the automatic dependence of morals, art, religion, and science on economic factors alone.[12] To Sorel, Marx himself is being diremptive in his social science, and is attempting to clarify, by bringing into bold relief, certain phenomena heretofore ignored or underemphasized in historical and social analysis.

After 1897, however, Sorel was forced to come to grips with some of the ambiguities in Marxism. Before this, Sorel had done little direct explication of Marx. Discussions on Marx and Marxism appeared mostly as secondary questions in articles on various topics in *Le Devenir Social.* Gradually, however, as the scope of reviews and articles in that journal focused on Marx's theory itself, Sorel came to realize the unsatisfactory nature of most Marxist criticism. The more Sorel criticized Marxism, the more mediocre his colleagues on *Le Devenir Social* appeared to him. Eventually he resigned from that journal, convinced that the low level of its contributions could not be improved.[13]

The viewpoints many of his fellow Marxists had adopted seemed to Sorel as superstitiously scientistic as the opinions of the followers of Laplace: these men were looking toward a unified social science and, as a result, anticipating the utopian somnolence that had been the dream of the men of the eighteenth century. Many of these simplifications of Marx were due to elaborations of his doctrine by the large number of his followers who had not examined Marx carefully enough. Sorel felt that the social-democratic leaders of his time had taken Marx's writings as sacred texts which appeared all the more valuable to them because they could then be used to inculcate party discipline in the rank-and-file.

However, Sorel was constrained to admit that doctrinal interpretations of Marx were easy to construct, due to the lacunae and inconsistencies of Marx's works, as well as the assumptions that lay behind these inconsistencies. Ultimately, these conflicting aspects of Marx found a place in Sorel's own view of Marx, and he affirmed the insights of the Marxist analysis; but in October 1898 Sorel was telling Croce of his suspicion that Marx treated all phenomena as a unity.[14] Sorel later explained the origins of these new doubts about Marx: "In 1898, when I tried to account for the sources which had been utilized by Marx, I was quite impressed to see that the references of *Capital* indicate lacunae in the knowledge of the author. . . . Marx was not imbued with the scientific spirit of the nineteenth century." Instead, Marx had inherited certain rather backward views of the eighteenth-century "philosophy of nature" (*Naturwissenschaft*), prevalent in Germany in Marx's time, in which attempts were made to reconstruct the world by artistic intuition. "It does not appear that Marx devoted his attention to studies suitable for making the impressions of the old German teaching disappear."[15]

The upshot of this discovery was that Sorel found new holistic formulas in Marxism which appeared to be thoroughly in accord with eighteenth-century views on science—a new social astronomy—but these formulas did not seem to be applied consistently. There was in fact a two-value orientation in Marx's view of social phenomena—one rooted in old-fashioned German scientific thinking, the other grounded in the modern experimental view. In his adoption of the old-fashioned view, Marx appears to be statist—especially in the *Communist Manifesto*. On the other hand, in his later writings he appears to be a proponent of self-help, direct action, and pluralism; furthermore, at certain times he appears to take a brutally dichotomous view of class struggle, but in the *Eighteenth Brumaire* he depicts a variety of subtle class relationships. Finally, Sorel argues that in spite of Marx's Hegelian view of history, he does not always take a rigidly deterministic view of social development.

Sorel found it necessary to clarify Marx's work by separating it from its excessively doctrinal (i.e., party) elements. Therefore, it was incumbent upon Sorel to become the diremptive theorist vis-à-vis Marx. The result of this undertaking, of course, would be all the less attractive to the socialist parties because the total doctrine could not be reconstructed once the diremption had taken place, for this diremptive process was not confined merely to looking at certain angles of the theory itself. Rather, it demanded a wholesale reconsideration of the philosophical edifice of Marxism. As Sorel later expressed it:

> In what remains of the Marxist teaching it is necessary to establish a strict classification of formulas, for such formulas vary widely in the uses to which historians can put them: sometimes they can nearly always be used to lead us to the most important sources for elucidating discoveries; sometimes they can only be used cautiously for certain periods; and sometimes they reveal only quite secondary aspects of phenomena.[16]

Obviously, Sorel regarded still other formulas as useless.

Consequently, in the course of criticism Sorel had to attack not only orthodox Marxism but those men who had the greatest interest in upholding the doctrine and who reacted most strongly to Sorel's criticism—the political leaders of socialism. With this in mind, Sorel began publishing in 1897 a series of articles on Marxism in various journals, the best of which were later collected in Italian translation under the title *Saggi di critica del Marxismo*.[17] Sorel was inspired in many of his views by criticism from Italian writers, in particular Antonio Labriola, Benedetto Croce, and Serverio Merlino, as well as Eduard Bernstein, the father of German revisionism. These theorists caused Sorel to make explicit his formerly covert criticism of various Marxian tenets. From studying Labriola, Sorel was confirmed in his emphasis on the flexibility of Marx's theory and on a distrust of the state; from Croce, Sorel found support for his criticism of the theory of value and of history; from Merlino and Bernstein, he found a strong criticism of the theories of class and of action.

The relation of Sorel to Marxism in general and the nature of Sorel's recomposition of Marxist philosophy can perhaps best be demonstrated by his relationship to the Italian Marxist theoretician Antonio Labriola. Labriola rejected the same aspects of theory that Sorel did: both scorned the search for the essential nature of the first causes of social phenomena; both rejected anything in socialism that was not practical or based on everyday needs. As the acknowledged leader of the anti-positivist faction of Italian Marxism, Labriola was especially critical of figures such as Achille Loria, whose extreme positivist economic determinism dominated Italian socialism.[18]

In his appreciative introduction to the French edition of Labriola's *Essais sur la conception matérialiste de l'histoire*, Sorel sums up what he thought was the ground he shared with Labriola regarding the nature of Marx's teaching:

> Marx seems to have feared nothing so much as the idea of leaving behind a system of excessive rigidity and firmness. . . . Marx did not try to terminate a single theory. . . . He had not said the last word about value and on surplus value. Therefore, how blind are the critics who accuse the disciples of Marx of wishing to lock up human thought in a ring fence built by the master.[19]

After Sorel's departure from *Le Devenir Social*, his appreciation of Labriola did not sit well with the Italian philosopher; it was all too apparent that Sorel's understanding of Marx, however much it might dovetail with Labriola's, was going far beyond the bounds of criticism that the latter saw as useful for securing scientific socialism. Part of this estrangement derived from Sorel's own reading of some of Labriola's Italian colleagues, especially Croce, who were splitting from Labriola, criticizing him for his excessive orthodoxy. Frequent correspondence with Croce, commencing during the *Devenir Social* period, helped Sorel to clarify his views on Marx and to "denature" Marxism of the metaphysical assumptions adopted by so many of Marx's followers.

The thrust of this denaturing process had five basic components, all of which emerged at about the same time in his writings: the first component was an attack on the social-democratic view of the state and the utopianism and stagnation which almost invariably accompany it; the second attacked the Marxian theory of class; the third was an indictment of the Marxian theory of history; the fourth was an attack on the Marxian theory of value, which Sorel saw as containing a metaphysical view of justice; the fifth was a critique of the role of theory in Marxist movements.

II

Labriola condemned "the phantasmagoria of ever-recurring state socialism, the whole effect of which is to increase the economic means of oppression in the hands of the oppressing class."[20] Sorel and Labriola agreed almost completely on this point, although, as we shall see, their understanding of that idea led to differing conclusions. Basically, to Sorel, concepts of abstract justice rely on some fixed and unitary notion of the political good, which notions are ultimately utopian. Utopias easily materialize into actual policies undertaken by an existing order; however, there is thus a very thin line between utopianism and statism. Now, utopian thinking is, and must be, rejected by Marx because it "Socratizes" socialism. Because its abstractions fail to change and adapt to exigencies of constant economic transformations, utopian thinking may ultimately be regarded as reactionary; it is "fixed" and what is at one time avant-garde later gets out of touch with concrete economic development, requiring enforcement by a state apparatus. To Sorel, it is statist because utopias are the products of theorists who, "after having observed and discussed the facts, try to establish a model with which existing societies can be compared. . . . It is a composition . . . offering analogies close enough to real institutions that a lawyer can discuss it; it is a construction which can be broken down into parts and of which certain parts have been set up in such a way as . . . to be included in pending legislation."[21] It is therefore impossible for utopias to retain their oppositionist character.

Sorel's illustration of this is the Saint-Simonian vision of a rationally planned economy which developed into Louis Blanc's National Workshops in 1848.[22] What started as a unitary and authoritarian utopia based on new social principles ended in a more or less confused reformism in which "the most absolute intransigence is correlated with a well-tended understanding of immediate political interests by way of a subtle and facile casuistry."[23]

The upshot of this weakness in utopian thinking, its connecting link with the *status quo ante*, is, in Sorel's eyes, that utopians share with their more practical colleagues a superstitious respect for the state as the solution to all problems. A reliance on the state provides almost perfect continuity between present plans for reform and the statism of the old regime. Just as the kings had protected the factories of Colbert, the democratic state protects the workers. In both cases there is a triumph of what Sorel called a protectionist sentiment,[24] in which both capitalist protectionists and state socialists rely on the power of the state to enhance certain interests and suppress others. No wonder, then, that Marx should uphold the principle of free trade against a high tariff structure and protected industries. Under the aegis of free trade, economic development proceeds more rapidly; and, as Sorel insists, it is to *economic*, not political, solutions that real Marxists should turn for a transformation of the existing order. The true social revolution will take place through the productive processes, not through the state. Marxism must therefore be stripped of its lingering respect for the state in order to champion a regime of free producers.

In this economic realm, Sorel argues, we find an example of the two-value orientation that recurs in Marx's writings. Marx did not usually fall prey to statist solutions to economic problems, at least not to the degree that his followers did. By the time he wrote the *Gotha Programme* in 1879, his viewpoint had been stripped of its early utopianism and determinism and was focused instead on short-term and piecemeal solutions to workers' problems; he had abandoned the *dirigisme* so dear to the hearts of social democrats on the continent (and supported in the *Communist Manifesto*). Thus, Sorel argues that Marx's pursuit of children's education on the workshop floor and the educative tasks of the workers' movement in general is far more important than any doctrine on the capture of state power, the consequence of which would be the strengthening of parliamentary cliques, the stifling of any commitment to genuine renewal.[25]

Nowhere is the connection between utopianism and statism more apparent, according to Sorel, than in the German Social Democratic Party, whose chiefs he considered to be a "bourgeois oligarchy of demagogues who govern the working class, provide them with lectures, show which candidates to support in elections, and live off their profession as directors of the people."[26] Sorel views the social democracy in much the same way as Roberto Michels does in his formulation of the "iron law of oligarchy."[27] Leaders of the social democracy take care to preserve their power, and any assault on the ideology of the party is viewed as an assault on the leadership: "The sin against the hierarchy is, in all churches, much more grave than the sin against the Holy Spirit."[28] Bernstein's socialism, which speaks of gradually educating the masses to govern themselves, represents a theoretical maneuver to upset the Kautskyite leadership of the German party. For such a party leadership, any theoretical challenge is ultimately tactical; everything centers around "finding the sure and rapid means of attaining power."[29]

Ideological symbols used as underpinnings of party struggles are noted by Sorel; he contends that they are exemplified, in socialist history, by an event even more momentous than Louis Blanc's National Workshops. To Sorel, "the entire history of contemporary socialism is dominated by the legend of the Commune."[30] This legend enables the socialist party leaders to manipulate their followers by using the themes of class struggle, which emerged from the Commune, as programmatic and explanatory devices. Even Labriola accepted this conventional wisdom about the Commune, celebrating it as the dawn of a new era.[31] The Commune had in fact, according to Sorel, an effect on Marxism which lent it a particularly simplistic and brutal character. Sorel depicted the Commune as, in reality, a violent struggle between provincial France and the old bourgeoisie allied against the revolutionary workers' organizations.

The brutal defeat of the Commune pitted against a ruthless opposition, in a struggle "devoid of any ethical concerns," was transformed into a legend: "Proudhon's theories, so strongly imbued with juridical and moral concerns, were considered reactionary; there was nothing but mockery for the old socialists."[32] The new social-democratic propagandists consistently reminded their hearers of massacres and insisted that "it is necessary to use all the means of destruction which science places at your disposal in order to rule the whole bourgeoisie in a revolutionary way."[33] Hence, parliamentary socialists are among the most violent in their rhetoric; they proclaim that it might be necessary to cut off a hundred thousand heads. "After this little operation," sneers Sorel, "right could become a reality."[34] The bloodthirsty rhetoric of social democracy made manipulation all the easier, according to Sorel. It reminded him of the haranguing of Greek demagogues and of the "creative hatred"[35] martialed by leaders of angry mobs. The idea of class catastrophe enables social democracy to rule its followers, for it reduces the socialist program to simple fighting formulas easily understood by the voters.

III

The political logic emerging from the legend of the Commune was, to Sorel, quite fallacious. The particularly violent ideology of the social-democratic leadership led Sorel to his second revision of Marxism, based on Serverio Merlino's dictum that "society is not a closed arena in which only workers and bosses struggle."[36] To Sorel, this view typifies a catastrophic conception of socialism rooted in the simplistic Marxist interpretation of the struggle between social classes. The mistakes of class interpretation that are affirmed in Marx's *Communist Manifesto* and in his writings on the Paris Commune are also produced by certain interpretations of Marx's *Capital*. Here, we see only capitalist entrepreneurs and proletarians, transformed into abstractions, mechanisms in the economic system. This simple division has developed into the last word in Marxist sociology, in Sorel's view; it has reached a stage, recurrent in political thought, wherein "the less real and the more abstract ideas have a superiority over the real and concrete ones."[37] Sorel rejects this simplistic view in favor of a multi-class interpretation.

It is by virtue of this dichotomous class view that Marx, in his depiction of modern revolutionary upheavals, tends toward a rather melodramatic and "catastrophic" view of historical change. This view "introduces a paradoxical discontinuity into history, which prevents us from grasping the real developmental mechanism. It considers only *perfect states*, almost as would a physiologist going from the egg to the adult without trying to follow step-by-step development."[38] To Sorel, these catastrophic writings contain a "Blanquist (i.e., Babeuvist) odor." Citing Bernstein, Sorel even associates Marx with "proletarian terrorism," in which "a prodigious force which would precipitate economic development" would produce social transformation.[39] So, in 1877, we see Marx and Engels concerned with reviving the terrorist regime of the French Revolution.

Against this view of classes from the recesses of Marx's theory, Sorel sets the *application* of Marx's theories, especially in the *Eighteenth Brumaire* and *The Poverty of Philosophy*. In these works, Sorel notes a lack of precision in Marx's theoretical framework. In the *Eighteenth Brumaire*, Marx considers many classes and discusses various groupings—familial, political, and even national; in *The Poverty of Philosophy*, he discusses categories for clarifying the nature of an historical period: "needs, productive forces, their mode of production, the primary factors in production, and, finally, the relations among and between men which resulted from all these conditions of existence."[40] To Sorel, Marx is asking not who and what the men of a particular time were *in general*, but, rather, who they were in a very precise sense. Sorel concludes that the existence of these two contradictory understandings in Marx's writings demonstrate that he had only a somewhat confused notion of the word class.

According to Sorel, the false and incomplete theory of class struggle based on historical periods prior to our own produces quite grotesque results: "Even in our day it is rather difficult to believe that the struggle of the proletariat against capitalism engendered the policies of Louis-Philippe, Napoleon, Gambetta, or Jules Ferry, and I am not going to burden myself with maintaining these paradoxes."[41] If Marxism can be emancipated from this doctrinal baggage, it can help give the proletariat a new direction. If, as the social democrats insist, we are all the better for believing them, then socialism will be burdened with an erroneous view of history. The great problem attached to the Marxian understanding of classes in its more complex version—which conceives a multiplicity of classes—is that it could conceivably undermine the concept of ultimate cataclysmic struggle between two classes. It is possible that if class life remains as complex in our century as it was in Marx's, then the concept of class struggle will have little or no predictive value.

IV

Sorel has committed himself to the impossibility of predicting the future of society. It is therefore reasonable that he should cast further doubt on Marx's theories of history as they are applied to particular phenomena: the disappearance of small business, the end of the "idiocy of rural life," etc. If we accept the perpetual complexity of class life, then it is possible, according to Sorel, to foresee a similar complexity in economic relations, e.g., the possible continuation of small business and small agriculture. It is at this point that Sorel attacks what we today might call the postulate of resolution. Sorel, with Marx, perceives a host of economic conflicts throughout society. Their views diverge on the likelihood of universal resolution of conflicts; as we shall see, Sorel believes that it is this very conflict which sustains the action and critical tension necessary for social life.

Sorel does not consider conflict between socialist and capitalist institutions to be inevitable. Conflict may indeed exist, but no social law prevents cooperatives and capitalists from living side by side.[42] Put another way, some institutions clash, others coexist, and some displace others, but there is no historical postulate that militates in favor of any one outcome. The permutations of social life are so varied that it is impossible to predict the cataclysmic end of capitalist society with any degree of assurance. Furthermore, Sorel rejects Marx's law of "increasing misery": the struggle between capital and labor over wages should not be identified as an economic law and then further transformed into an immanent law of historical development. "It is not necessary to be a great scholar in economic science to discover that bosses want to have labor at the best possible bargain and to adorn this truism with the pompous name of the 'tendency' of the capitalist era!"[43]

Sorel sees in Marx's theory of history what is perhaps the root of the master's two-value orientation. According to Sorel, Marx attempted to establish a certain order among the various regions of social science and "naturally conceives this order according to deterministic Hegelian models,"[44] but he views Marx's determinism as limited.

Sorel blames Marx's Hegelian leanings for his admission that history advances under the existence of some mysterious *Weltgeist*. These same fatalistic Hegelian biases inspired in Marx the idea of technological and economic development in modern production, resulting in the disappearance of small enterprises which would be crushed by industrial giants. In Sorel's view, such historicist reconstructions lead back to the monist prejudices of the old utopians, wherein entire historical epochs are viewed *en bloc*.[45]

Sorel finds that some of Marx's texts support contrasting interpretations; thus, the *Communist Manifesto* appears to proclaim the inevitability of revolution, while the most deterministic of Marx's statements, according to Sorel, is found in the penultimate chapter of *Capital*, in which it is stated that "capitalist production begets its own negation with the inexorability of a law of nature."[46] With such bold assertions, it is not difficult to see how the social democrats, led by Engels himself, could deify history into some kind of moving force. Knowledge of the "essence" of this force, i.e., the relations of production, has become the key to the social democrats' certain knowledge "that the world is moving toward an unavoidable revolution, the general results of which they discern."[47] This formula enables German social democrats to justify party tactics on the grounds of knowledge of certain "final ends" which have been deduced from the Marxian theory of history. If this theory is taken seriously, according to Sorel, great errors are bound to occur. It is absurd to postulate long-range "socialist" solutions whose vagueness is admitted by their proponents and which are separated from our time by "many forms and intermediate societies." It is a short step from such long-range "solutions" to a view of society as a mechanism whose components "would be modified quantitatively in a uniform way according to empirical laws observed (in a partial way) at the beginning of large-scale industry." This assumption is, to Sorel, scientifically undemonstrable. "They have not yet observed that the social mechanism is extremely variable . . . because of rapid transformations that take place in industry."[48]

Such thinking leads to a social science based on extrapolation from existing phenomena. To Sorel, as we have noted in the previous chapter, "history is entirely in the past; there exists no means of transforming it into a logical combination, permitting us to predict the future."[49] It would be much more reasonable to think, however, "that a movement which is produced in one direction will not continue to follow very long; experience shows that predictions made by determining a so-called direction from the past have been contradicted by facts." Thus, Sorel did not think that it was paradoxical when he predicted that the proletarian revolution would be entirely different from past revolutions.[50]

Yet at times Sorel is inclined to defend Marx's ideas. In his textual analysis of Marx, Sorel argues that Marx did not go as far as his followers and that, at his best, Marx can be interpreted as taking stands that were at odds with what had come to be the social-democratic orthodoxy. One way to defend Marx, in Sorel's view, is to look at the circumstances under which he was writing. Sorel interprets Marx as rejecting utopian ends, and observes that the proximity of the Revolution of 1848 to the writing of the *Manifesto* may justify Marx's predictions of revolution. This was an "immediate palingenesis" rather than the "final end" of the social democrats. For Sorel, Marx's confident predictions of a revolution were put forth in an atmosphere so charged with revolution that predictions were of a tactical rather than a "strategic" nature.

But what of the statement in *Capital*, written more than twenty years later, in which Marx predicts the inevitable end of capitalism as conforming to a natural law? Sorel rather weakly characterizes this statement as a "fragment which, like so many other old sections, was introduced into *Capital*, and which Marx thought worth preserving because it presented the schema of the class struggle in a very lively manner."[51] This is a highly speculative and unprovable assertion, but does appear to mesh well with Marx's assertion that "the procedure of exposition ought *formally* to be distinguished from the process of investigation."[52] According to Sorel, Marx intended the idealism in his deterministic statements to be "only a rhetorical artifice, allowing the use of images which gave an especially clear impression of the social movement."[53]

In contrast to such assertions, the strongest defense of Marx made by Sorel has the most appeal and plausibility. Sorel distinguishes between two kinds of determinism. The first is found in the fatalism in which spontaneous and necessary natural forces dominate events, "the natural law" that seemed to be sweeping capitalism away through the forces of historical contradictions and which *seemed* to be the perspective at the end of *Capital.* The other determinism is one in which technological and social accidents merely average out to form historical tendencies so that, for example, life-insurance companies can create probability tables for longevity. Marx, according to Sorel, is closer to this second kind of determinism.

In Sorel's view, the Marx of *Capital* usually meant by *necessity* a blind unconscious force arising from a multitude of daily actions. Thus Marx does not necessarily refer to the order in which industrial processes succeed one another following an Hegelian world spirit. On the contrary, Marx stresses the importance of technological and historical accidents in the day-to-day decisions of industrialists.[54] Innovations such as new inventions do not "cause" other social phenomena in any simplistic way. Sorel stresses Marx's concern with the reciprocal dependence of social phenomena due to an infinity of causes. These causes, obscure and often extremely difficult to analyze, average out in what Sorel calls "sets" or groups of phenomena, whose development is necessary only insofar as the sets do not reveal "the free reaching-out to an end chosen by the will for reasons consistent with the result."[55] Social phenomena thus have intelligibility in an historical sense only in the way that the law of chance produces results capable of being averaged.[56] Sorel offers the example of the law of supply and demand, in which a host of individual decisions by buyers and sellers determines the price of a commodity. It did not surprise Sorel that Marx placed economic phenomena at the base of the social structure, since economics is the social science most capable of mathematical interpretation. The economy is subject to great change and wide variation, and economic laws are little more than the appearance of general trends which may not be applicable in any particular instance. Sorel notes that the actuarial tables of insurance companies speak of average life-spans but cannot predict the longevity of any individual. To Sorel, Marx's alleged determinism or fatalism need not be any more "deterministic" than these tables or than the price-system theory of *laissez-faire* economists.[57]

At the heart of Marx's two-value orientation is the fact that Marx, according to Sorel, "changed his method of exposition according to his needs and he knew that, because of the need for action, some imaginary correlations are substituted for *sociological reality* inaccessible to the understanding."[58]

V

After what Marx said about the precision of economics as a discipline, it is interesting to note that it is the economic branch of Marxian theory that Sorel rejects most thoroughly, invoking Bernstein's arguments in his disagreement with Marx. Here, according to Sorel, there is no two-value orientation in Marx's thought, and nothing can be salvaged from the theory of value. To Sorel, the Marxist theory of value and the theory of surplus value are entirely unnecessary to socialism because these theories impose upon Marxism a framework of abstractions concerning the just distribution of wealth in society.

Marx concluded that the term *value* meant "a particular social means of calculating labor employed in the production of an object," to be accomplished through the concept of labor time, that is, the time that is "socially necessary . . . to produce an article under the normal conditions of production, and with an average degree of skill and intensity prevalent at the time." Commodities produced in an equivalent amount of labor time must be of equal value. All commodities are "reduced to one and the same sort of labor, human labor in the abstract."[59] The product of a labor process in which the labor is no longer *necessary* labor creates no value for the worker himself. It creates "surplus value," which is a mere "congelation" of surplus labor-time. It creates exploitation, for the worker receives payment only for necessary labor-time; in order for the capitalist to withdraw more value from the process than he put into it, surplus value, or surplus labor-time, must be unpaid. "The rate of surplus value is therefore an exact expression for the degree of exploitation of labor paid by capital or of the laborer by the capitalist."[60]

Sorel questions the consequences of Marx's idea of normal conditions of production, "average" degree of intensity, necessary subsistence, etc. According to Sorel, Marx's theory of value assumes a "normal state" in the economy. Sorel maintains that Marx, like many other scientists and theorists he has discussed, is building a model—based on cotton mills—on which to elaborate a theory;[61] as with all branches of learning, of course, the model should not be confused with reality. The model implies the ability to define what a "normal" workday is and what "surplus" would be in real life. In short, the model assumes the ability to develop a kind of science of social pathology, the same assumption for which Sorel criticized Durkheim. In Sorel's view, Marx posits a simplified society and tries to proceed to a representation of economic phenomena by making use of the methods of the most abstract case. "He allows that a day's labor for a simple worker, after having reproduced the value of materials consumed in the mechanical process and the value corresponding to the existence of the worker, engenders a surplus value or net product which is the same in all industries."[62]

After reproaching Proudhon for, among other things, his "balance theory," Marx, according to Sorel, proceeds to a theory of economic equilibrium of his own:

> It is assumed that all industries are equivalent and all workers are reduced to a uniform type. An hour of work with a team of ten men will produce the same thing everywhere. In any and all fields it will create the same intensive scale of a kind that has its equivalent in merchandise of comparable value. Value is the ultimate factor on which differences in exchange are based; its quantum is proportional to the time employed. As a result of the perfect symmetry presented by *homogeneous capitalism*, values are also the rate of exchange.[63]

This simplification makes it difficult to pass from the abstract theory of value, with its gross-averaging procedure, into the real world of economic life; instead, we have a "rigid carcass" of theory which ignores instrumental differences of function, talent, or productivity and has little scientific explanatory value. As far as the theory of value is concerned, then, Marx was himself guilty of the penchant for unity and utopian metaphysics for which he criticized Fourier and Saint-Simon.[64]

Labriola was increasingly perplexed by Sorel's "premature lucubrations on the theory of value." Hostility was exacerbated by the defection of Labriola's most distinguished colleague in Marxist studies, Benedetto Croce, to Sorel's point of view. Croce, like Labriola, had begun his Marxism with a strongly anti-positivist bent; by 1897, however, Croce had broken with his early mentor and, inspired in part by Sorel's article, saw the theory of value as an instrument making economics into metaphysics. Marx had replaced the fetishism of commodities with the fetishism of labor.[65]

In his articles on the theory of value, Sorel does indeed come close to accusing Marx of reverting to the arbitrary constructions and metaphysical assumptions of rationalist natural-law theory. With its emphasis on social pathology, the Marxian theory of value assumes what a "normal" workday will be and thus gives rise to the term "unpaid labor." The concept of surplus value connotes the deprivation of the full price of one's labor. But if a normal workday and the full price of labor can be established, they can be so only in the most abstract sense; that is, one must affirm a sort of "natural right" to the "full product" of one's labor. Sorel insists that this claim harks back to the medieval English practice of legislating payment from master to servant according to the natural-law notion of "just price." When, during the industrial revolution, employers lengthened the workday without augmenting wages, it was perceived that the additional time was realized in wealth taken from labor by the master. This notion was elaborated by David Ricardo, "who had stressed the fact that capitalist profit would be a deduction of part of the product of the labor of the worker."[66] Sorel detects Marx's appropriation of the Ricardian theory of value—all wealth is the product of labor—as part of those "obscure formulas" which are equivocal and "should be banished from science."[67] The Marxist theory of value is generally framed in such a manner that it appears to prove that the laboring classes are increasingly dispossessed and that workers are "eternally robbed."[68]

Now if the "natural right" to one's labor were to become enshrined in the socialist pantheon, according to Sorel, the statist, reactionary, and idealist components of socialism would overtake the ethical ones. Laws would be passed limiting profits, and the autonomy of producers would be limited by "those who know" the laws of economics. These experts in the laws of economics would forge the ruination of industrial progress by managing industry through committees made up of an elite of intellectuals and politicians; this elite, separated from the life of work, would impose upon Marxist doctrine the canons of abstract justice, devoid of any concrete historical reference save that based on party advantage. According to Sorel, the attempt to make Marxism revolve, even in part, around a theory of distributive justice,

> to try to enclose the proletariat in the exclusive defense of material interests, would be to condemn the proletariat to remain eternally at the status of a subject class. This would be to give it as an ultimate goal an improved salary. These are the exclusively material concerns which brought the ancient poor to demagogues who were always ready to form an army of partisans ready for immediate gratification.[69]

It might be argued that Sorel's interpretation of Marx owes too much to Bernstein's own reading of *Capital*, which views the labor theory of value through the lens of classical political economy. Lucio Colletti says that Bernstein's view of economics owes more to Adam Smith than to Marx. Smith's law of value is based on the exchange of equivalents, which presupposes the equal value of commodities exchanged; thus, classical political economy abstracts the physical-natural or use value of highly diverse commodities in order to equalize them. Far from being a mere mental abstraction, as Bernstein, Sorel, and Croce contend, abstract labor takes place daily in the reality of exchange, but this exchange depends increasingly on the process of production. Marx's theory of alienated labor reflects the world of commodity fetishism, in which individual labor-powers are made abstract precisely because they are treated as separate from the real individuals to whom those powers belong.[70]

Colletti argues that Bernstein, in failing to recognize that this abstraction has its roots in the commodity fetishism essential to capitalist production, separates the process of production from the process of exchange. In so doing, he misconstrues the theory of value by concentrating his attention on the sphere of exchange itself rather than on productive relationships, "as though surplus value originated, in other words, in a violation of commutative justice, i.e., in a violation of the law of exchange based on equivalents."[71] Bernstein, not Marx, has thus reinstated the old mercantilist conception of alienation, in which the origin of profit lies in the difference between buying price and selling price. Colletti suggests that because he concentrates on these exchange relationships, Bernstein (and, we might infer, Sorel) places too much importance on consumer cooperatives.[72]

Colletti's argument against Bernstein can be interpreted also as a criticism of Sorel. It is generally maintained that the weakest part of Sorel's social criticism is his economics; yet it is unfair to argue that Sorel does not in some way anticipate this sort of criticism. Sorel does not necessarily accept the classical notion of equivalence. He acknowledges Marx's differences from classical economists on value; for the author of *Capital*, "average prices did not correspond to the value of merchandise, as Smith, Ricardo, and others believed."[73] On the other hand, he cites Marx's statement that the value form of the product of labor "is not only the most abstract but the most universal form taken by the product in bourgeois production."[74] Here Sorel recognizes Marx's assertion that such a form is not eternally fixed in nature for every state of society but is historically located in a period containing "*differentia specifica* of the value form, and consequently the commodity form, its further developments, money form, capital form, etc."[75] Sorel determines that in his doctrine of value Marx locates these various economic characteristics in a given period and connects them into a complete capitalist system, "remaining always faithful to this doctrine of uniformity"; Sorel himself decomposes them by isolating certain factors. He meets Marx head-on by maintaining even more strongly than Bernstein the essential heterogeneity of the capitalist system, especially among its manufacturing and exchange elements.[76] This distinction will be of enormous importance in Sorel's later writing, for, as we shall see, it is at this point that Sorel dispenses with an overall critique of capitalist production and concentrates his fire on what he regards as the relatively backward exchange capitalism characteristic of the emerging economies of Europe.

VI

Since the theory of value—that is, the theory of distributive justice—and the Hegelian philosophy of history have been pared from Marxism, Sorel insists that it is impossible to view what remains as an holistic theory that sees man as somehow seeking himself or affirming himself historically. What is left of Marxism is a partial theory, an experimental mode that entails both the "tight solidarity between theory and practice" and a plurality of phenomena that are "closely determined by practical concerns."[77] This unique restructuring of Marxism would later develop into a full-fledged pragmatism, but for the moment it only meant for Sorel that Marxism had sufficiently narrowed its scope to confine it to immediate tasks, shattering its unity to the point of having largely excluded ethical concerns from its method. Sorel had so constricted Marx that he had to call for a new doctrine rooted in the French economic system. Without that doctrine, socialism would be "suspended in the air,"[78] where Labriola leaves it.

The call for a new philosophy scandalized Elie Halévy, who accused Sorel (somewhat tongue-in-cheek) of having "betrayed" Marxism by allowing for mutual reciprocity of thought and action instead of viewing ideas as mere reflections of material interests. For Labriola, the problem was less academic. He insisted that the "complete elimination of the traditional distinction between science and philosophy is a tendency of our times."[79] Labriola thought that a consciousness of existing material relations seemed sufficient for social change, while Sorel saw the need for a new guiding principle which was not to be found in science itself. It was precisely this viewpoint which, to Labriola, shattered the unity of Marxist thought. Instead of unifying fact and value, science and action, past and future, Sorel made it necessary to interpret various fields of human activity with new methods of understanding peculiar to each field. Labriola was thus forced to dissociate himself from Sorel's view by citing *Anti-Dühring*:

> As soon as every individual science is confronted with the necessity of coming to a clear understanding of its position in the general interrelation of things and the knowledge of things, any special science of the general interrelation becomes superfluous. . . . If I had to give some sort of outline, it would not be out of place to say that the philosophy which historical materialism implies is the tendency toward monism.[80]

Labriola scores a point here: Sorel cannot consistently proclaim the plurality of various modes of thought, including the sciences, on the one hand, and proclaim the unity of theory and practice on the other, without converting Marxism to a partial theory akin to pragmatism.

Sorel was no more desirous than Labriola of leaving the dissociated elements of Marxism where they were. Since he wanted a new doctrine for French workers, it seemed to Labriola, as well as to many critics of Marx, that Sorel would have to introduce neo-Kantian rather than pragmatic moral elements into Marxian theory in order to make the theory square with the drastic reformulations undertaken at the hands of its critics. This introduction of moral criteria at first upset Labriola, because he felt that Marxism could stand on its own. Sorel, on the other hand, was one of the first to claim that Marxism could not possibly sustain itself, that it was only a starting point for social analysis but that, even if reduced to a series of general propositions about the nature of social investigation, it could be upheld as a contribution to the understanding of social life.

Further complexity is introduced by the fact that Sorel, in addition to rejecting Marx's theory of value, seemed to dispense with the Marxian theory of distributive justice. He scoffs at Jaurès's assertion that "the same sight of suffering and hope which comes from the mouth of the slave, the serf, and the proletarian . . . is the soul of the thing we call right."[81] Labriola, in an open letter to Sorel, protests:

> Aren't you going to preserve just a little corner of paradise for us? . . . For the present it would be a vain undertaking to try to make . . . people understand . . . a principle which declares that gratitude and admiration should come as a spontaneous gift from our fellow beings. Many of them would not care to reach out for progress when they are being told, in the words of Baruch Spinoza, that virtue is its own reward. . . . Has not morality taught us for centuries that we must give to each one his due?[82]

But then who is being the neo-Kantian, the idealist? On the one hand, Labriola wanted the unity of theory and practice but insisted on a categorical imperative of giving each man his "due"; Sorel, on the other hand, called for a unification of theory and practice, a new ethical doctrine *and* a plurality of methods. Since so many pages of *Devenir Social* had been devoted to attacking scientific monism, Sorel reduced Marxism to a series of propositions whose utility is both limited and varied in proportion to the primacy of economic phenomena in a given case; and in this he was confined to maintaining that the unity of Marxism, when viewed in a certain way, provides a mythical basis for a morality of the future. The new ethical doctrine needed fresh sources.

The results of Sorel's theorizing would not find a solution until late in the first decade of the twentieth century, but it is apparent even at this stage that Sorel has traveled some distance from Marxism toward pragmatism. Even before Sorel became a self-conscious pragmatist, he expressed the opinion that Marxism, insofar as it is a theory based on practice, is "essentially a doctrine of prudence which provides the means by which dangers can be recognized."[83] In a later essay, written when he had pragmatic criteria very much in mind, Sorel cites Marx's introduction to the *Critique of Political Economy*. Here, according to Sorel, the limited and immediate range of Marxian concerns is combined with three principles of social *praxis*: (1) social formations do not disappear until their productive forces can no longer develop; (2) new social relations do not replace the old ones until their material conditions have ripened in the womb of the old society; and (3) tasks do not really exist for mankind unless their material solutions already exist.[84]

Given such a viewpoint, no utopianism is possible. Marxism is a guide to action, a method for acting on and understanding events. Sorel sums up this useful part of Marx as follows:

> One should never speculate about law, political institutions, or the ideologies of art, religion, or philosophy without a clear picture of the economic life of the people under consideration in all its reality, with the historical division of classes, the development of technical processes, and the natural conditions of productivity. The connection thus established, between the infrastructure of society and its superstructure, illuminates the entities included in the latter and often leads into areas which allow us to interpret their history. In every type of question each historian ought to develop his own ingeniousness so as to show how the most interesting parts of the social structure relate to one another at a given time: No general rule can be established to guide such an inquiry.[85]

There are no means for defining or determining social culture or defining interdependence in a general way—only indications of movements.

In reducing Marxism to such analytical guidelines, Sorel has pointed out that there appears to be little or no moral agency in Marx, indeed, that "Marx had not spoken of morality." For Sorel, as for Marx, morality is social; it grows and develops in the context of concrete institutions. The thrust of Sorel's criticism of Marx is based on the fundamental proposition that Marx fails to discuss the juridical, familial, and community institutions on which the morality of the future must be based. It is incumbent upon Sorel—especially after his attacks on Marxism—to make constructive suggestions, especially in the light of his call for a moral renaissance. He must also take care to avoid neo-Kantian or Hegelian idealism, which Labriola accuses him (as he does Bernstein) of reviving. Sorel uses Marx's own precepts and general rules (but only as a starting point) for his discussion of new, socialist institutions. Since Marx prescribes that any change must take place within the material conditions already established (that is, within existing social forces), Sorel sees the basis of new socialist institutions as already existing within established organizations—cooperatives, unions, and labor exchanges.

Sorel is further supported by Marx's own assertion, in his address to the International, that workers must organize themselves in order to make their own revolution. For Sorel, the importance of socialism lies in its transformation of the life of the individual. Therefore, "everything which tends to diminish the spirit of responsibility, the value of personal dignity, and the energy of initiative ought to be condemned."[86] As a consequence, the socialist movement "depends entirely on the aptitude shown by the working classes in forming and instructing themselves and improving their virtue and their knowledge. The contemporary problem is much less a problem of force—as the political problems of the eighteenth century had been—than it is a question of education."[87] The end of this education should be "the moral formation of the working classes through personal experience and with a view toward *self-government*. . . . We ought to place our confidence in modest institutions, organized by the workers, institutions which have no pretensions to revolutionizing the whole world, but which are capable of changing the course of general opinion and which can *if we know how to use them* teach us to govern ourselves and make us worthy of freedom."[88]

Notes

1. Sorel, *La Décomposition du Marxisme, p. 31.*
2. George Lichtheim, *Marxism in Modern France* (New York: Columbia University Press, 1966), p. 13.
3. For a history of the development of socialist parties in France, see G. D. H. Cole, *A History of Socialist Thought*, vol. 3 (London: Macmillan, 1956), especially pp. 323-31, and Paul Louis, *Histoire du socialisme en France* (Paris: Rivière, 1946), pp. 222-25.
4. James Joll, *The Second International, 1889-1914* (New York: Harper and Row, 1966), pp. 16-17.
5. See Louis, *Histoire du socialisme*, p. 224.
6. *FGS*, p. 136.
7. Ibid.
8. Ibid., p. 110.
9. Ibid.
10. Louis, *Histoire du socialisme*, p. 238; G. D. H. Cole, *History*, p. 343.
11. Sorel, review of Antonio Labriola's *Del materialismo storico* in *Devenir Social* (Aug. 1896): 762.
12. Ibid., p. 761.
13. He expressed this opinion in a letter to Hubert Lagardelle, published in *Homme Réel* (Feb. 1934): 122.
14. Letter to Benedetto Croce, 19 October 1898, published in *Critica* 25 (1927): 173.
15. Sorel's Preface to Arturo Labriola's *Karl Marx: L'Economiste, le socialiste* (Paris: Rivière, 1910), pp. xix-xx. But see the letter to Paul Delesalle of 9 May 1918, in which Sorel refers to Marxist historicism as being upheld by the "pseudo-scientific fanaticism" which existed in Europe in the nineteenth century.
16. Sorel's preface to E. R. A. Seligman's *L'Interprétation économique de l'histoire*, pp. iii-iv.
17. (Palermo, Italy: Sandron, 1902).

18. For an elaboration of Labriola's relationship to Italian socialism, see Edmund E. Jacobitti, "Labriola, Croce, and Italian Marxism," *Journal of the History of Ideas* 36, no. 2 (1975): 300-320.
19. Labriola, *Socialism and Philosophy*, p. 193.
20. Antonio Labriola, *Essays in the Materialist Conception of History* (New York: Monthly Review Press, 1966), p. 17.
21. Sorel, *Réflexions*, p. 46 (*FGS*, p. 205).
22. Sorel's Preface to Pelloutier's *L'Histoire des bourses du travail*, p. 40.
23. Ibid., p. 47.
24. Ibid., p. 39.
25. *FGS*, pp. 80, 105-6, 157, 222, 311n22. See Sorel, *Matériaux*, pp. 61-150.
26. Sorel, "Les Dissensions de la social-démocratie allemande à propos des écrits de M. Bernstein," *Revue Politique et Parlementaire* (July 1900): 42.
27. See Roberto Michels, *Political Parties* (Glencoe: Free Press, 1960).
28. Sorel, "Les Dissensions de la social-démocratie," p. 44.
29. Ibid., p. 43.
30. Sorel, "La Crise du socialisme," *Revue Politique et Parlementaire* (Dec. 1898): 600.
31. Ibid., p. 601 and note.
32. Ibid., p. 601.
33. Ibid.
34. Ibid., p. 603.
35. See *FGS*, p. 305n38. For Sorel's remarks on creative hatred see *FGS*, p. 100, where he says that hatred "has become foreign to contemporary socialism" (by which Sorel means syndicalism).
36. Sorel, "Pro e contro il socialismo," *Devenir Social* 3, no. 7 (Oct. 1897): 869, citing Merlino's *Pro e contro il socialismo* (Milan: Treves, 1897), p. 27. See also Sorel's Preface to Serverio Merlino's *Formes et essence du socialisme*, p. xli.
37. Sorel, "Pro e contro il socialismo," p. 872.
38. *FGS*, p. 161.
39. Ibid., p. 164.
40. Sorel, "Pro e contro il socialismo," p. 870, citing Marx's *The Poverty of Philosophy* (French edition), p. 80.
41. Sorel, "Pro e contro il socialismo," p. 872n.
42. Sorel, "Economie et agriculture," p. 440.
43. *FGS*, p. 166.
44. Ibid., p. 139.
45. Cf. Sorel's *Illusions*, Appendix II; *Insegnamenti*, p. 9.
46. See Marx, *Capital*, vol. 1 (Modern Library ed.), p. 837.
47. *FGS*, p. 111.
48. Ibid., pp. 134-35.
49. Sorel, "Pro e contro il socialismo," p. 873.
50. Sorel, "Economie et agriculture," p. 292; *Insegnamenti*, p. 54.
51. *FGS*, p. 164.
52. Sorel's Preface to E. R. A. Seligman, *L'Interprétation*, p. xxii, citing Preface to second ed., *Capital* (see Modern Library ed., p. 24). Italics are Sorel's.
53. Sorel's Preface to Seligman's *L'Interprétation*, p. xxiii.
54. *FGS*, p. 122.
55. Ibid., p. 123.

56. Ibid., p. 121.
57. Sorel, "Idées socialistes et faits économiques au XIXe siècle," p. 520.
58. *FGS*, p. 116 (italics are Sorel's).
59. Marx, *Capital* (Modern Library ed.), pp. 45, 46.
60. Ibid., p. 241.
61. Cf. *Insegnamenti*, p. 155, where Sorel says that political economy was derived from examples in the cotton industry "as ancient physics was derived from the heavens."
62. *FGS*, p. 151.
63. Ibid.
64. Sorel, "Sur la théorie Marxiste de la valeur," *Journal des Economistes* (May 1897): 229.
65. Labriola, *Socialism and Philosophy*, pp. 164-70.
66. *FGS*, p. 152.
67. Ibid., p. 153.
68. Ibid., citing the work of Jules Guesde.
69. Sorel's Preface to Merlino's *Formes et essence du socialisme*, p. xvi.
70. Lucio Colletti, *From Rousseau to Lenin* (London: New Left Books, 1972), pp. 83-84.
71. Compare Bernstein in *Evolutionary Socialism*, trans. Edith C. Harvey (New York: Schocken, 1961): "By the simple fact that Marx applies the formula for the value of the whole of the commodities, it is already indicated that he makes the formation of surplus value fall exclusively in the sphere of production, where it is the industrial wage earner who produces it. All other active elements in the modern economic life are auxiliary agents to production" (pp. 36-37). It is not Bernstein's misinterpretation of Marx so much as his outright disagreement with him in regard to the relative autonomy of other aspects of economic life that plays an important role in the differences between Bernstein and orthodox Marxists.
72. Colletti, *From Rousseau to Lenin*, pp. 92-93.
73. Sorel, "Sur la théorie Marxiste de la valeur," p. 223.
74. Ibid., p. 224, citing Marx, *Capital* (see Modern Library ed., p. 93n).
75. Ibid. Sorel notes that Marx effected a transition in the theory of value in volume 3 of *Capital*, and cited Sombart's and Schmidt's criticisms of this late work. He adds that the criticisms of the theory of value were so telling that Engels, in the last months of his life, implicitly admitted its inapplicability to modern capitalist society: Sorel, "Sur la théorie Marxiste de la valeur," p. 222, citing *Devenir Social* (Nov. 1895). As Peter Gay points out, volume 3 of *Capital* abandons the assumption that values are expressed in actual prices and replaces it with the notion that competition among capitalists tends to bring the rate of profit into equilibrium. Prices no longer correspond to value—even in the last instance—but the total sum of values in a given society is equal to the total sum of prices. To this Böhm-Bawerk responds that "either products do actually exchange in the long run in proportion to the labor attaching to them—in which case an equalization of the gains of capital is impossible; or there is an equalization of gains of capital—in which case it is impossible that the products should continue to exchange in proportion to the labor attaching to them": Peter Gay, *The Dilemma of Democratic Socialism* (New York: Collier, 1962), pp. 177-78, citing Bohm-Bewark's *Karl Marx and the Close of His System* (New York: Augustus Kelly, 1949), p. 28.
76. Sorel, "Sur la théorie Marxiste de la valeur," pp. 225, 231.

77. Sorel, "Le Matérialisme historique," *Bulletin de la Société Française de Philosophie* 2 (20 Mar. 1902): 91-92. Cf. Sorel's Preface to Pelloutier's *Histoire des bourses du travail*, p. 31.

78. This is Labriola's paraphrase of Sorel in *Socialism and Philosophy*, p. 62. Neither Sorel nor Marx believed that socialism was a matter of distributive justice. Marx condemns equal right and fair distribution as "obsolete verbal rubbish." Robert Tucker rightly notes that the fundamental passion of Marx was not a passion for justice, because such a concern emphasizes consumption and distribution rather than production, and is, consequently, biased in favor of accommodation with the existing order. Tucker defines justice as a "rightful balance in a situation where two or more . . . are in conflict," and thus gives a Proudhonian definition to the term. This makes it easy to demonstrate Marx's opposition to the general notion. But Tucker goes on to argue that Marx, instead of being concerned with this sort of justice, was concerned instead with "the dehumanization of man," i.e., overcoming alienation: Robert Tucker, *The Marxian Revolutionary Idea* (New York: Norton, 1969), pp. 36 and 48.

As we have tried to show in the previous chapter, Sorel was pessimistic about the possibility of overcoming alienation. (In any event, resentment against alienation is certainly not entirely separate from a theory of justice, if *justice* is defined a bit more broadly than in Tucker.) Sorel is aware that there are moral concerns and residual vestiges of a theory of justice in Marx; he therefore felt it incumbent upon himself to reformulate Marxism with an eye to a moral philosophy, while denuding it of any vestiges of this theory of justice. He does this by replacing the concept of justice by the Proudhonian idea of struggle and overcoming, minus Proudhon's notion of "natural balance." Man attempts through effort to overcome relaxation, natural nature, and decay; this is the purpose of socialism.

79. Labriola, *Socialism and Philosophy*, p. 76.

80. Ibid., pp. 81, 84.

81. Ibid. (Sorel's Preface), pp. 193-94.

82. Ibid., pp. 10, 12.

83. Sorel, "Le Matérialisme historique," p. 92.

84. Sorel's Preface to E. R. A. Seligman's *L'Interprétation*, pp. xv-xvi.

85. Ibid., pp. xxxvii-xxxviii.

86. Sorel's Preface to Merlino's *Formes et essence du socialisme*, p. xxvi.

87. Sorel, "Les Facteurs moraux de l'évolution," *Questions de morale*, p. 92.

88. Ibid., p. 100 (italics are Sorel's).

V

THE CRITIQUE OF PSYCHOLOGICAL SPONTANEITY, 1900–1907

Many strains of rationalist thought and ideology support the notion that the very rationality of a concept renders its triumph inevitable. This notion has, as we have said, characterized Marxism in France, especially its Guesdist wing. George Lichtheim maintains that there was a pronounced tendency among French socialists to view Marxism as a socialist variant of the common evolutionist credo: "In this perspective, the difference between positivism and socialism reduced itself in the end to a simple matter of personal and political antagonism between Comte and Marx. This was more or less the view taken by Jaurès."[1]

There were two consequences of this confusion: it obscured the differences between the historicism of Marx and evolutionism; and it left unanswered a socialist theory of action, a theory of the will. In Sorelian terms, the first confusion consisted in a transposition of artificial and natural nature. To compare Marxism with evolutionism would reduce Marxism to a Feuerbachian natural nature, while "naturalism" (insofar as the word is found in Marx) really means—again to employ Sorel's terms—"artificial nature," the idea that the object that is perceived has already been affected by previous human action or contact. As we have seen, Sorel came increasingly to suspect that even Marx himself had not entirely dispensed with the old naturalistic metaphysics; instead, he had only moved from the holistic tenets of Feuerbach's natural nature to a new, holistic artificial nature. The critical tension necessary for creative activity may have existed in Marx's historical panoply, but his eventual goal was to overcome this tension.

Sorel had to do more than reaffirm the distinction between artificial and natural nature before he could be said to have overcome the problem of action. The quietism encouraged by the unidimensional positivist view of nature or of society could be overcome by adopting a stand against evolutionism and by siding with the partisans of spontaneity against the Cartesianism of the positivists, but, as we have seen in Chapter 3, Sorel was highly critical of the "spontaneity" school. It was only through a highly diremptive use of Henri Bergson, the chief spokesman of that school, that Sorel could mount an offensive against excessive reliance on the concept of evolution as applied to society, while at the same time distinguishing between the valid and invalid aspects of "spontaneity." This was to prove an ambitious undertaking, but one that helped Sorel overcome an outstanding difficulty in his own thought.

Sorel's theory of science argues that the environment discourages action and leads to routine. If, furthermore, a scientific decomposition of all thought by way of the concept of ideology encourages quietism, what theory of knowledge can we rely upon to rekindle the poetic dimension of our spirit in order to make action possible? Bergson would help Sorel answer these questions, but not until some transformations had been performed on Bergson's ideas that were almost as thoroughgoing as what had been done to Marxism. Sorel's view is that Bergson too is ideological, that one must uncover the ideological basis of his thought in order truly to benefit by it and to construct a social psychology that allows for a theory of action. Bergson's main contribution to Sorel was in helping him to express his theory of free action (including the action involved in the myth of the general strike). Sorel was always critical of Bergson and dealt with his ideas as "diremptively," that is, as partially and pluralistically, as he did those of Marx. Indeed, Sorel uses Bergson to fill in some of the lacunae in Marx's own theory—lacunae produced partly by Sorel's transformation of Marxism and partly by the skeletal nature of Marx's theory of action.

Sorel had first read Henri Bergson's *Essai sur les données immédiates de la conscience* in the early 1890s. It was this first work, plus Bergson's lectures at the Collège de France starting in 1901, which constituted the major Bergsonian contribution to Sorelian thought. Most of Sorel's understanding of Bergson in the *Reflections on Violence* is derived from these lectures as well as *Time and Free Will*, the *Essay on Metaphysics*, and, to a lesser extent, *Matter and Memory*.[2] However, it is Sorel's first extensive commentary on Bergson, his critique of *Creative Evolution* in 1907, that provides us with insights into their similarities and differences.[3] *Creative Evolution* contains Bergson's ideas on labor, views which Sorel criticizes because they are based on the misguided concept of "life" that Sorel regarded as ideological itself, that is, on hidden social causes.

Sorel's first reference to Bergson's thought is in his 1894 article in *Ere Nouvelle*, "L'Ancienne et la nouvelle métaphysique," in which he expresses admiration for Bergson's discussion of what Sorel terms "the invasion of emotions into the domain of representations" that has caused so much confusion in theories of perception.[4] Even at this early stage, Sorel criticizes Bergson for not uncovering the ideological assumptions by which our consciousness builds its constructions. In other words, Bergson is criticized for his inability to "concede the true constructions hidden beneath his argument. They are shadows having quantity, but in a vague way, and not paving the way for any scientific relationship."[5]

Sorel's ideological unmasking of Bergson is based on the assertion that Bergson, rather like Durkheim and other French and English sociologists, constructed a theory often built on analogies which prove untenable when applied to social and economic life; despite this fact, Bergson's thought secretly reflects the assumptions common to early capitalist society. That is, some of his biological analogies were themselves inspired by social models—and hence were twice removed from reality.

If the ideological nature of Bergson's thought was so pronounced, why did Sorel regard it as so fruitful in the first place? The answer is that Bergson's theory provides us with a way out of the ideology and action problems—it is itself a refuge from the world of continued unmasking once the essentials of its theory can be grasped in a "diremptive way."

I

Bergson distinguishes between two concepts, time and space. Space is the realm of geometric forms and measurement. Time cannot be entirely understood by the same intellectual faculties as those that grasp the spatial object. Basic to the concept of time is what Bergson calls *duration*. *Duration* is the world in time, a state of movement, becoming. As Bergson later expressed it, the intellect cannot perceive this motion or duration; the intellect can only perceive space. "When we say 'the child becomes the man,' . . . the reality, which is the transition from childhood to manhood, has slipped between our fingers. We have only the imaginary stops 'child' and 'man,' and we are very near to saying that one of these stops . . . is . . . at all points of the course."[6] The intellect can only perceive movement in terms which do not belong to the movement itself, but are successive "still" positions, as in a series of discrete frames in a motion-picture film. This, to Bergson, is not movement.

He reifies change into a reality that is more real than the successive stops through which change passes, something more genuine than the snapshots taken by the intellect in an attempt to depict movement.

Bergson is a philosopher of life or of the life force—the *élan vital*—which he depicts as movement:

> Life in general is mobility itself; particular manifestations of life accept this mobility reluctantly, and constantly lag behind. It is always going ahead; they want to mark time. . . . It might be said that life tends toward the utmost possible action, but that each species prefers to contribute the slightest possible effort. Regarded as what constitutes its true essence, namely, as a transition from species to species, life is continually growing action.[7]

This living entity, life as a manifestation of movement, must be apprehended by a set of faculties that go far beyond the intellect: "When the intellect undertakes the study of life, it necessarily treats the living like the inert, applying the same [geometrical] forms to this new object, carrying over into this new field the same habits that have succeeded so well in the old." If we leave biological and psychological facts to the intellect alone, to positive science, the intellect will "*a priori* accept the doctrine of the simple unity of knowledge and of the abstract unity of nature. The moment it does so, its fate is sealed. The philosopher no longer has any choice except between a metaphysical dogmatism and a metaphysical skepticism."[8] This dogmatism will impose an artificial unity on all things, while skepticism adds nothing to our knowledge.

From the point of view of a theory of knowledge, the intellect is more of an obstacle than an aid to a genuine understanding of life. Thus, if we view the world rationally, by way of the intellect, we distort the truth by filtering it through concepts; these concepts often throw an extra burden on our understanding of living reality because they arbitrarily weigh reality down with "dimension," with "height" or some other intellectually comprehensible notion that the reality of duration does not possess. As Bergson puts it, when we use intellectual concepts,

> we shall then soon discover that as we start from one concept to another, the meeting and combination of the concepts will take place in an altogether different way. [Whether] we start, for example, from unity or from multiplicity, we shall have to conceive differently the multiple unity of duration. Everything will depend on the weight we attribute to this or that concept, and this weight will always be arbitrary, since the concept extracted from the object itself has no weight, being only a shadow of a

> body. In this way, as many different systems will spring up as there are external points of view from which the reality can be examined.[9]

Thus concepts inconveniently divide philosophy into different schools "whose normal work is far from being disinterested. We do not aim generally at knowledge for the sake of knowledge, but in order to take sides, to draw profit—in short, to satisfy an interest."[10]

Science, which operates almost entirely within this rationalist framework, was the one area that Marx exempted from ideological thought, since it was confessedly and truly reflective of material relations and was conscious of the relationship between the subject of the investigation and the mode of inquiry. How, then, does science examine things that are active, vital? Bergson argues that even the realm of science itself is ideological if we are to examine living or moving things and insofar as our study is affected by concepts and categories. For Bergson, this means that, on the one hand, there is no genuine disinterested knowledge beyond either ideology or that of "still" geometric forms; that most knowledge is practical knowledge which is "aimed at the profit to be drawn"; or that, on the other hand, we must place ourselves beyond analytical thought, beyond intellection, in order to rise above interest.

How do we go beyond rational knowledge without sinking into emotionalism or vulgar sensuality? How do we transcend the boundaries of intellect in order to expand understanding, rather than distort it further? Bergson argues that the duty of philosophy must be to intervene actively, to examine the living things, things in motion, in duration, "without any reservation as to practical utility"; philosophy does this by freeing itself from strictly intellectual forms and habits.[11] Bergson would assign this role of transcendence to the animal instinct, as an alternative mode of understanding, except that the instinct is incapable of reflecting on itself and is therefore not really a means of understanding. The latter role Bergson assigns instead to intuition: "Instinct that has become disinterested, self-conscious, capable of reflecting upon its object and of enlarging upon it indefinitely."[12] It is intuition that makes us realize that neither mechanical causality nor teleological finality can give us an adequate knowledge of the living processes:

> By intuition is meant that kind of "intellectual sympathy" by which one places oneself within an object in order to coincide with what is unique in it and consequently inexpressible. Analysis, on the contrary, is the operation which reduces the object to elements already known, that is, to elements common both to it and to other objects.[13]

By placing oneself "within an object" through an intuitive act, one no longer sees points of view or perspectives: one obtains the absolute, the attribution to the object of, so to speak, certain "states of mind; I also imply that I am in sympathy with those states."[14]

The object of this knowledge, the "immediate data of consciousness," is our own consciousness itself; it is to become intimately acquainted with our own inner self or our "inner duration"—the one reality that we can seize from within. Since the object of our knowledge is living, we may begin the process of understanding by separating the living from the inert; the inert "enters naturally into the frames of the intellect, but the living is adapted to these frames only artificially, so that we may adopt a special attitude toward it and examine it with other eyes than those of positive science."[15] The separation of the living from the inert "allows us to emancipate ourselves from science and introduces us into that vast something out of which our understanding is cut, and from which it has detached itself . . . insofar as we compel ourselves to go beyond pure intelligence."[16]

The living entity most easily understood is the self. By penetrating through all the symbolism and objects of the material world and plunging downward into memories which have more or less adhered to these perceptions, we escape from spatiality into time. From memory we go to "the stir of tendencies and motor habits—a crowd of virtual actions, more or less firmly bound to these perceptions and memories."[17] If the elements of memory radiate from within outward, they tend to dissipate in the world. But if they are drawn inward, they create a continual flux which can be compared to the unrolling of a coil as well as a rolling up like a ball of thread, "for our past follows us, it swells incessantly with the present which it picks up on its way; and consciousness nears memory."[18]

Because of this flux of the inner being, Bergson maintains that we cannot pinpoint our consciousness on the scale of time, especially if that point is the so-called present instant. For Bergson, an "instant" does not really exist; what we call the present is "both a perception of the immediate past and a determination of the immediate future," i.e., a memory.[19] Although our consciousness cannot exist in the present, things and objects can do so: "To be present . . . and in a present which is always beginning again—this is the fundamental law of matter: herein consists necessity."[20]

For Bergson, freedom means an escape from the confines of matter, the present, the realm of necessity; it means reverting to memory or "plunging" into pure duration. This memory survives in two ways: (1) through motor mechanisms which connect it to the world of space through acting upon spatial objects; and (2) through independent recollections which are more proximate to the world of pure duration. The first form of memory connotes a rote lesson or the routine learned in industrial mechanics; the second connotes a unique event. The first memory is the acting out of our past, bringing it before us as if it were present; the second is pure representation evoking the past. The first is memory of a body—hence partly spatial—while the second is memory of the mind; the first issues from the spatial object, the second from pure subjectivity, duration.[21]

It is through memory that Bergson attempts to escape from the dilemmas involved in the concept of ideology; that is, from relativism and continual unmasking of motives. First, an escape from ideology is made in the idea that memory is self-validating. On the first level, I am assured of reality when I move from motor mechanisms, that is, when I am conscious of producing a movement from within or when I place myself in some way within a movement and "sympathize" with it. On the second level, where our consciousness is directly confronted with fewer intermediate symbols, I am duration, I am consciousness, that is, memory and liberty. By the discovery of this memory, the discovery of inner duration through intuition, we capture mind by an insight that cannot err because the mind, having had itself as its object, has grasped itself directly without the distortion of mediating symbolism. In this state, an unsurpassed objectivity can be obtained which makes disputation and argument over the state of consciousness superfluous.[22] In Bergson, pure objectivity is gained through pure subjectivity.

For Sorel, Bergsonian introspection was to have immense consequences for social science (and not merely in giving his myth of the general strike more complete expression). Sorel sees it as bridging the gap between religious and historical investigations, as confronting the unabashed relativism of the concept of ideology. How do we study morals when the underlying material conditions that produced those morals have vanished? Furthermore, if morals can be studied, how do we assume a moral position while at the same time insisting on the historical genesis and relativity of all morals?

Sorel argues that to study historical development one should employ the Bergsonian category of subjectivity. The historian does not place himself at an abstract vantage point. Rather, he always looks at things from within a phenomenon, that is, from "the point of view of internal principle":

> It is unreasonable to ask the historian to bring to his studies the superb indifference which the physicist can keep in his laboratory. . . . He is affected because he finds in the past moral

> values which enrapture or outrage him; he feels in the contact with ancient struggles, something of the ardor of modern social struggles. Thus, the past is not so dead that we cannot ask the historian to teach us what has happened to people who adopted certain ways of looking at life; it is not so lifeless that we cannot derive several moral teachings from what took place before. To make history into a science is not to explain all phenomena; it is to discover what is eternally alive in what at first appears to be an inextricable jumble of accidents. But moral feelings are like aesthetic feelings: they never age. Hasn't our century discovered how former civilization judged beauty? It is always possible to initiate ourselves in the same way into the moral sentiments of the past.[23]

Bergson had provided Sorel with an alternative to a one-dimensional positivism in the study of history. What remained, of course, was to transcend the other problem with which Sorel's philosophy of science confronts us: the problem of action. By plunging into pure duration, which is close to being pure subjectivity, Bergson is confronted with the criticism that he reduces his theory to pure mind. As soon as the body intervenes between consciousness and action in the world of objects, we are presented with a problem in the Bergsonian philosophy. Freedom to act is freedom to intervene in the material world, yet it is precisely this spatial world which is the world of "unfreedom." To revert to pure memory, pure detachment, is to become separated from the world of action: on the one hand, the subject who acts and lives amid the material world acts according to the logic of the automaton by virtue of the geometrical and predictable nature of his milieu; on the other hand, to resort to pure memory, pure recollection, means that we should end in a dream, a trance in which the body is only a sufficient condition. Here our tendency, much as in the spatial world, is to relax, to allow ourselves to float into passivity; the self is "scattered" and our past is "broken up into a thousand recollections made external to one another. They give up interpenetrating in proportion as they become fixed."[24] Thus, our personality veers away from time and inclines in the direction of space, its opposite. The movement away from time toward spatiality is the rule; the reverse is the exception. In Bergson's terms, "It coasts."[25] But if such relaxation were to triumph we would have neither memory nor will: something more than pure memory is needed in order for our introspective plunge to have meaning. Bergson shows that he realizes this when he says we cannot passively follow duration "as a sleepy shepherd watches the water flow."[26] To Bergson this would misconceive the unique character of duration and at the same time the essentially active and essentially violent character of metaphysical intuition. This active and intuitive mind-set is brought about by reversing the moral habits of thought. "The mind has to do violence to itself" by reversing all its categories. For this task a certain virtue is necessary—a virtue comparable to an overwhelming effort.[27]

Bergson would have us perform this reversal by an act of will. He argues that through intuition we coil up our will to a state of tension that avoids both the automatism of the spatial world and the passivity of the world of pure recollection. This act of will shatters pure reason and brings us to a realm of freedom:

> It is the essence of reasoning to shut us up in the circle of the given. But action breaks the circle. If we had never seen a man swim, we might say that swimming is impossible. . . . Reasoning, in fact, always nails us down to solid ground. But if I quite simply throw myself into the water . . . I may keep myself up enough at first merely struggling, and gradually adapt myself to the new environment.[28]

It is precisely through such intuited situations which at once transcend intellect and eschew passivity that

> we feel ourselves most intimately within our own life. It is into pure duration . . . in which our past, always moving on, is swelling unceasingly with a present that is absolutely new. [We are free during these unpredictable moments because] we feel the spring of our will strained to its utmost limit. We must, by a strong recoil of our personality upon itself, gather up a past which is slipping away in order to thrust it, compact and undivided, into a present which it will create by entering. Rare indeed are the moments when we are self-possessed to this extent: it is then that our actions are truly free.[29]

Now, this recoil is immensely creative. The more we succeed in making ourselves conscious of our progress in this action, this tightening of the spring of our will, "the more we feel the different parts of our being enter into each other, and our whole personality concentrates itself in a point, or rather a sharp edge, pressed against the future and cutting into it unceasingly."[30] Using contemporary terminology, Bergson's act of will is connected to our memory by an act of "implosion" rather than through the dissipated energy of an "explosion," through "fusion" rather than "fission."

Sorel's myth of the general strike is informed by many such passages from Bergson. The myth of the general strike is, as we shall see below, primarily an "expression of the will," and analogous to the creative movements set forth by Bergson. Bergson's act of will solves the problem which is posed when one is asked to choose between introspective passivity and mechanical automatism. Suffice it to say at this point, Sorel's act of will—the general strike—solves the problem of the disparity between the quietism of Marxist historicism on the one hand and the automatism of laboring man on the other. The common ground between Sorel and Bergson, despite differing aptitudes and solutions, is a concern for the automatism of "spatial" laboring man as well as concern for the nature of the inner man. Sorel, however, regarded Bergson as old-fashioned in his views on labor matters because he has reified inner duration into a reality rather than retaining it as an "expressive support," or, better, a handy diremptive device on which to relate our understanding. As we have seen, Sorel sees such symbolic models as necessary but easily distorted.

II

We noted earlier in this chapter that, for Bergson as for Sorel, science operates almost entirely within the rationalistic framework whose outlook is the geometric and the symbolic. That is why Bergson can so easily project what he calls the symbolic quality of rational thought into materiality itself; the materiality of things and the intellectuality of the mind are intimately connected. But because of this connection, Bergson associates the laboring process with the intellect and maintains that "intelligence, considered in what seems to be its original feature, is the faculty of manufacturing artificial objects, especially tools to make tools."[31] But if Bergson's metaphysical view were an adequate depiction of reality, how could one account for any movement, "duration," or creativity in the process of inventing tools or new scientific principles? Furthermore, how can it be said that Sorel owes so much to Bergson when Sorel lays such stress on the importance of the poetic motives of invention as a practical expression of civilizational vitality?

Sorel attempts to reconstruct Bergsonian metaphysics and uses as his starting point an idea that Sorel and Bergson have in common, one that has been omitted from the preceding analysis for the sake of clarity. It is a simplification of Bergson to say that he juxtaposes all science and intuitive thought. Although Bergson insists that the two areas of thinking are usually opposed to each other, there are occasional moments in which they intersect. Sorel would agree with Bergson that "modern science dates from the day when mobility was set up as an independent reality. It dates from the day when Galileo, setting a ball rolling down an inclined plane, firmly resolved to study this movement." Bergson insists that such path-breaking events in science, "those that have transformed the positive sciences or created new ones, have been so many soundings in the depths of pure duration."[32] That is, such moments in the history of science are not intellectual in character; they are epochal moments in the history of human creativity. For the most part, the ongoing processes of science are encased in logico-geometric forms and can continue on the same paths for centuries "whilst the act which creates the method lasts but for a moment. That is why we so often take the logical equipment of science for science itself, forgetting the metaphysical intuition from which the rest has sprung."[33] For Bergson, it is at such rare and creative moments that "science and metaphysics come together in intuition."[34]

This intuition, once attained, must find a means of expression and application which is "in the shape of well-defined concepts" of exactitude and precision. The discoveries of science are mediated by symbolism, transformed into laboratory models, or acted out in practical applications. Intuition of duration in science thus "quickly turns into fixed, distinct and immobile concepts," and that is why "men of science have fixed their attention mainly on the concepts with which they have marked out the pathway of intuition. The more they laid stress on these residual products, which have turned into symbols, the more they attributed a symbolic character to every kind of science."[35]

For Bergson, science, in order to be continuously creative, "must abstain from converting intuition into symbols." In order constantly to enlarge its domain, it must be "liberated from the obligation of working for practically useful results."[36] It is at this point that Sorel departs from Bergson, for the logical outcome of Bergson's view of science is to divorce practical industry from creative life. For Sorel, Bergson must avoid materiality in science since for Bergson all manufacturing, all practical invention is viewed as "a seizure of intelligence on matter"[37] or spatiality and is thus stagnant; it is the activity of automatons to shape and act upon the world of objects.

For Sorel, Bergson's connection of the materiality of things with the intellectuality of the mind is a translation of Maxwellian physics whereby, as we recall, scientific formulas are actualized in laboratory mechanical models; it is the laboring process that mediates between models (or practically manufactured objects) and the inventor's thought. Since this laboring process is so important for Sorel, he sees it as far more creative than Bergson does. It is therefore incumbent upon Sorel to criticize Bergson's view of labor.

In contrast to Bergson, Sorel describes the manufacturing process in the modern era as requiring a considerable amount of creativity; this creativity, in turn, demands an overcoming of points of resistance similar to those found in memory. First, there is the resistance of brute matter, which must be shaped into tools. This matter tends, as we stated earlier, toward immobility, the opposite of tension, creativity, or free activity; it operates (to revert to Bergsonian terminology) in the spatial realm. Then there is the need to overcome our own natural inclination to relax, to coast into passivity, the tendency toward repetitive tasks instead of free labor. Here, too, our personality descends in the direction of space. In the first case, the instance of the resistance of brute matter, solid and organized, becomes the vehicle whereby a finished product becomes the goal of the manufacturing process. To Bergson, this process of labor is naturally amenable to the idea of first or final causes, i.e., of teleology and hence of the intellection connected with spatiality. The causality that our intellect seeks and finds everywhere in the realm of space "expresses the very mechanism of our industry in which we go on recognizing the same whole with the same parts, repeating the same movements to obtain the same result." The finality that the intellect understands best is the finality of our industry, in which we work on a model given in advance, that is to say, old or composed elements already known.[38] As Bergson expresses it: "We are born artisans as we are born geometricians, and indeed we are geometricians only because we are artisans."[39]

The ramifications of this notion for Sorelian theory and for Marxism are considerable. Bergson's theory of labor, which operates in the realm of spatiality, is deterministic. As Bergson says, "Insofar as we are geometricians, then, we reject the unforeseeable. We might accept it, assuredly, insofar as we are artists, for art lives on creation and implies a latent belief in the spontaneity of nature. But disinterested art is a luxury like pure speculation. Long before being artists, we are artisans and all fabrication, however rudimentary, lives on likeness and repetition . . . on models which it sets out to reproduce. . . . All is given."[40] According to Sorel, Bergson connects the idea of causality with the idea of the spatial relation of the tool to the object being transformed. The relation of content to other content is a given in all labor that utilizes containers or receptacles of any kind.[41]

Sorel cannot accept Bergson's theory without altering it considerably. He agrees with Bergson's indictment of the idea of causality, as we noted in Chapter 3, but he complains that instead of linking labor with action and creativity, Bergson virtually divorces them. Precisely because it is always trying to reconstitute what is already given, "the intellect lets what is new in each moment of a history escape. It does not admit the unforeseeable. It rejects all creation. That . . . definite antecedents bring forth a definite consequent, calculable as a function of them, is what satisfies our intellect."[42] Sorel agrees that historical predictability is the presupposition of a strongly rationalist temperament, but Bergson goes on to deny the ability of *homo faber* even to contemplate future industrial development. To Bergson, labor is an anti-historical process; to Sorel, it can be creative and hence historical.

Bergson's "anti-historical" stance in respect to labor (and he must adopt it to respect his own distinction between living and inert, space and intellect) leads to a second difficulty for Sorel. If we admit that intelligence modeled on mechanical labor relates purely to materiality, hence to spatiality, then man *qua* worker—*homo faber*—remains trapped in automatism and determinism. Thus, Bergson views labor in an essentially opposite direction from that in Sorel's works. Instead of being potentially creative, Bergson links the act of making to the law of entropy (the fact that all physical changes have a tendency to be degraded into heat). Because the laboring process has what might be called a symbiotic relationship with the spatial matter on which it is working, labor represents an exhaustion of energy. That is why while Bergson can say that life tends to the utmost action, he also says that each species prefers to contribute the slightest possible effort aiming only at its own convenience.[43] Any organism has a natural tendency to coast in the direction of pure materiality.

Ever since his essay on "Science and Education," Sorel has modified this point of view. He agrees that man is inclined to automatism; indeed, he has based an entire theory of history on it. But he also insists that labor cannot simply relax; it must, rather, be associated with those great, if exceptional, periods of effort which Bergson claims to be characteristic of our plunges into pure duration. To Sorel, these plunges need not necessarily constitute a veering away from spatiality.

III

In order to connect his theory of intelligence to labor, Bergson, according to Sorel, must limit his demonstration to examples of workshops which deal entirely with hard bodies: metal, wood, or stone. Hence Bergson can argue that fabrication applies to brute matter, "solid and unorganized." To Sorel, this philosophy was acceptable in a period when most objects were manufactured by slaves or by workers without intelligence who submitted themselves to a regime of fragmented labor.[44] If we admit that intelligence is modeled on mechanical labor we must admit with Bergson that labor and the objects of manufacture are devoid of vitality.

Sorel claims that Bergson's notions correspond better to a previous stage of production which allowed men, operating with increasingly perfected machines, to coast into automatism as they performed increasingly repetitive and minute tasks; to become increasingly "insensitive to the insinuations of liberty."[45] This alienated condition is noted by Sorel, quoting Marx: men "are incorporated to a mechanism existing independent of them. . . . Facility of labor becomes a torture in the sense that the machine does not deliver the worker from labor—merely despoils it of all interest."[46] To Sorel, Bergsonianism reflects an outmoded, nineteenth-century view of industry in which the division of labor was carried to the extremes of alienation that Marx described in *Capital.*

Bergson fell prey to this outmoded attitude because he failed to make the distinction between the teleological idea of a "finished product" and the old-fashioned and repetitive *processes* of manufacture. It is not "products" that produce automatism, but processes. Modern mechanical rationalism, through constant improvement and transformation of tools and methods, can escape finalism and, hence, repetition and automatism.[47] Once we accept the viewpoint of mechanical rationalism, the prejudices arising from the old industry are no longer encountered "except in those vain and ignorant employers, of whom there are still so many today, who accuse the graduates of the technical schools of losing time by thinking instead of surrendering themselves to routine."[48] This very inventiveness and creativity annihilate these old prejudices and permit us to escape from finalism.

If Bergson's view of the simultaneous origin of matter and intelligence corresponds to outmoded historical and scientific traditions, the Marxian view of alienation as it has come down to us in twentieth-century scholarship has been rendered obsolete. Sorel asserts this: "In the past the worker would have drifted into automatism, but he now thinks about the operation of the machines, while recalling the lessons of his professional master, the instructions of his foremen, and his life experiences."[49] Since, as we saw in Chapter 3, the highly celebrated system of the division of labor "no longer corresponds to the needs of modern industry, which calls for qualities of observation, comparison, and decision,"[50] alienation, with its attendant boredom, has already been transcended, in Sorel's optimistic view, by a new and creative regime within the existing system.

Since Sorel thought that modern production methods entail more tension, due to the struggle between old and new methods as well as the increasing resistance of natural nature, reasoning must exist in production; insofar as a method of reasoning "that is concrete, individual, and therefore rapid does occur, [modern production methods] become true representatives of modern labor."[51] Thus, intelligence and creativity have increasingly come to coexist in modern industry. To Sorel, therefore, the political upheaval necessary to the Marxian solution to the problem of alienation has been rendered increasingly superfluous in proportion as alienation itself has become outmoded.

Sorel's rapprochement of the intellect and the vital means that routine does not disappear. The nature of the manufacturing process produces a tremendous psychological transformation in the worker. Rather than drifting into automatism, he is forced into greater and greater states of tension as he is required to master increasingly complex routines that no one in Marx's time would have thought possible.

We recall that Bergson distinguished between two types of memory: one, "pure" independent recollections, the other, motor mechanisms that connect memory to the world of space. Sorel implies that lessons learned do not drift into pure space but retain a semblance of creativity—in this case, the creativity of the artist who must master technique through repetition and surpass this routine by extending himself into the world of production. Sorel's workman has in fact become an artist. Just as the dancer must alternate between routine and fastidious attention to the details of execution, so the modern worker expresses his art by rising above the alienation of the old workshop and allowing both for the increasing creativity of production and for routinization.

Sorel refuses to accept the idea that routine and creativity are somehow mutually exclusive. Indeed, art and labor are united in one case, according to Sorel: "Savages execute agricultural labors as if they were veritable ballets"; therefore, they do not come to think of them as habitual, dull occupations. If soldiers derive great benefit from marching, it is because the rhythmic oscillations prevent them from thinking of the fatigues involved in walking. Here routine is actually opposed to pure intellectualism: "The aesthetic order manifests itself here through a sort of enrichment of the vital foundation at the expense of intellectualism and from this there results an exaltation of the organic virtualities."[52]

Furthermore, Sorel does not see an increase in routine as being inversely proportional to that tension which is essential to creative activity. On the contrary, the new methods bring on new tensions and new stresses which in turn demand further levels of routinization in order for the worker to be able to undergo new strains. Routine takes on a two-edged function: it enables workers to endure higher levels of technical productivity, and it inclines toward entropy; it must, therefore, be overcome. Contrary to Marx, the more the worker escapes into automatism and relaxation the more he is condemned to compensate for this and to struggle against this inclination by enduring "labor without a truce."[53]

The basis for Sorel's correction of Bergson's divorce between creativity and routine, the living and the inert, is provided in the psychological theories of Ribot, Wundt, and Hartmann. They show the path toward ending the Bergsonian dualism without either lapsing into mechanical utilitarianism or being tied to the yoke of metaphysics. To Wundt and to Bergson, Sorel owes the idea that it is difficult or impossible to explain psychology empirically, that is, to explain what is seen by what is not seen.[54] But the consequence of Bergson's alternative was to depict laboring activity—indeed, all social activity—as being so mechanical that it appears devoid of all moral content.

It was not Bergson, but Hartmann and, especially, Ribot who produced a psychology identifying physical and moral phenomena, and who enabled Sorel to expand his own moral theory using Bergsonian language. Sorel, like Bergson and Ribot, asks us to "descend so profoundly into our psychology that we can easily recognize in a clear way the sources of our psychology."[55] Like Bergson, Ribot argues that consciousness and feelings are prior to intellect; yet Sorel, employing Ribot's categories, argues that Bergson's thought errs in its view of the role of science in relation to the process of introspection. For Ribot, introspection requires us to examine pleasure and pain as part of our life force. Sorel, following Ribot, implies that Bergson accepts what he calls "scientific optimism" on its own terms: Bergson views the traditional interpretation of psychology against which he is reacting just as its practitioners did in regarding pleasure and pain as "two poles between which we move." Certainly, in such a case, argues Sorel, "We have thus been led to believe that we can spend all of our affective life on the pole of pleasure. . . . To change pain into pleasure is the problem that is posed when someone wants to realize the goal of attractive labor."[56]

Sorel and Bergson agree that this approach can only be self-defeating. Pleasure cannot be an index of attractive labor, because in seeking pleasure, Sorel says, "We separate ourselves from the world; we regard it as a toy made to amuse us."[57] To seek to abolish pain in favor of pleasure would only produce the ultimate alienation: our estrangement from the world is not even seen as estrangement, because pleasure is produced through our own powerlessness.

As long as Bergson interpreted contemporary psychology as basing itself on pleasure, as long as he dealt with it on its own terms, he was likely to look upon routinized labor as veering toward passivity and away from duration. But Sorel, following Ribot, argues that one can look upon pleasure and pain in another way. To isolate pleasure is not only to distort or alienate ourselves from the world but to distort our very understanding of it; pleasure must be reunited with the other senses. This cannot be done by isolating the life force from science; it must be done by having life mediate between science and understanding and thus "establish provisional rapprochements among beings."[58]

Ribot provides Sorel with a means of performing this mediating function when he argues that pain is produced under far more varied circumstances than pleasure: "It is with pain that Ribot begins his book, *The Psychology of Sentiments*, and it is here that we are led to ask if we do not finally have the long-searched-for contact between the domains of mind and matter." It is on this terrain that physical pain and moral pain are identified.[59]

Furthermore, Sorel—again following Ribot—does not argue that pain is antithetical to pleasure. Especially in our moral life, "the sentiments in which pleasure and pain are united in deep combination exert considerable influence." It is when these two aspects of our being unite that we experience "what Ribot puts in the category of the *sublime*, which is not only an aesthetic sentiment, and which everyone agrees comes very close to morals."[60] Indeed, as Sorel notes, Hartmann observes the same combination of pleasure and pain in the feelings of compassion.[61] It is in this sublime compassion that the social dimension of our psychology can be attained, but the social nature of the sublime inserts itself not only in compassion, but, Sorel adds, in the love between man and woman and in the love of the hero for the homeland,[62] as well as in the laboring process. Ribot provides a solution to the problem of relating routine and creativity in the laboring process—through "chemical modifications in the tissues and nerves, especially in the production of local or generalized toxins. Pain will thus become one of the manifestations and one of the forms of autointoxication of tissues under the influence of labor."[63] The feeling of fatigue attendant on all struggles is not without sweetness. It is accompanied by an indefinable voluptuousness, as if the muscles, formerly made taut by action, found in fatigue a desired relief. Modern labor, like the dance, "is capable of producing irresistible erotic impulses and of bringing about lessened tonality."[64]

In Ribot's theory of pain Sorel finds an explanation for his "psychoerotic law" uniting the sexual, martial, and laboring virtues. It is here that we find the basis for Sorel's reversal of Bergson's maxim that "the more consciousness is intellectualized, the more it is spatialized."[65] For Sorel, modern industry imposes increasing intellectuality on the worker. Instead of imposing a system whereby materiality and intellectuality are two poles of a psychological continuum which stretches from pure unattainable mathematico-geometric formulas to the imperfections of their attempted realization in workshops, why not, asks Sorel, "speak of the enormous differences between inventors and engineers?"[66] In this case, intellectuality is the constant state of attempting to overcome the materiality of the workshops constructed by engineers:

> The obsession of ideas exhausts and enervates. The inventor scarcely experiences rest. The night brings dreams of finished designs before his fitfully sleeping brain. . . . Anyone familiar with economic history knows the obstacles that must be overcome in order to introduce procedures that break with accepted usages; while inventors are elated by their ideas, knowledgeable and skillful experts oppose them with very strong objections, drawn from the exact knowledge of the difficulties encountered in production; methods that are readily employed today were perhaps long regarded as illusions of unbalanced minds.[67]

Here, inventors strongly resemble artists whom the academicians regard as mad. The struggle between inventors and engineers parallels the struggle between creativity and routine, but it transforms Bergson's connection between spatiality and intellectuality into an intense rivalry.

The routinized operative depicted in *Le Procès de Socrate* has been replaced in Sorel's theory by an artist who, triumphant in an industrial world, overcomes previous routines in recurrent waves: "Thanks to the spirit of invention, which is always on the alert, the arts of industrial mechanics extend their domain daily, and intelligence thus finds new means of representing phenomena which should escape it." Sorel can even say that "the current of materiality increases ceaselessly, thanks to its opposite, the current of invention."[68] If invention is this dynamic, then Bergson is wrong in viewing it merely as "a seizure of intelligence on matter." According to Sorel, this "denatures the poetic character of invention" and thus ignores the "fundamental identity among intuition, invention, and poetry."[69] This means, of course, that Bergson's distinction between intellect and intuition has been annihilated by Sorel. The inventor, like the artist, recomposes a model, but, in addition, "animates it with the bright fire of his own heart."[70] For both the artist and the inventor, the principal object is to illuminate something that matter obscures.

IV

Sorel is not content to transform Bergson's theory of labor; he also sets out to examine the ideological roots of Bergson's philosophy of life. As we have said, the myth of the general strike was inspired principally by Bergson's early ideas on the plunge into pure duration. *Creative Evolution*, published *after* the *Reflections*, elaborates some of the obscurities in Bergsonian theory. In *Creative Evolution* we find a theory of "life," the object of our intuition; but for Sorel, *Creative Evolution* obscures more than it illuminates.

Sorel goes beyond his assertion that Bergson's view of labor is inspired by primitive industrial techniques; it also comes from pre-capitalist analogies—analogies from which, according to Sorel, Bergson derives a fundamental assumption underlying most of his work: that we must return to the principle of unity in order to understand the laws of nature.

First of all, Bergson uses "life" and "life force" both as explanatory devices and as objects of a philosophy of action. In doing so he was led to attribute a general character as well as a purpose to life. Sorel's own discussion of vitalism denies this general character. According to Sorel, this viewpoint arises from the genetic fallacy, a reversion to primitive times when undifferentiated relations produced in the observer's eye a kind of harmony which was intellectually satisfying. A primitive harmony beginning at the origins of biological life is equally satisfying to sociologists, inspired by the placid life of ancient tribes, who are moved to use them to level indictments against the chaos of existing societies, as Durkheim and Marx (each in his own way) did.[71]

Sorel did not see Bergson's view of scientific knowledge as at all pluralistic. Bergson, in fact, seems not to abandon anything to contingency or to the chaos of accidents. In his hands, nature becomes almost a willed or conscious creation. More than once, Sorel suggests that Bergson's stance is inspired by a social theory—that is, by the "inner logic" of the unseen hand in free-market economics. Thus Bergson, despite his criticism of sciences for their "factitious unity," is led to reject the idea of disarray or disorder on what are practically pantheistic grounds.[72] For Bergson, disorder is no more absent in nature than it is in Adam Smith's marketplace. Just as the economists alternate one kind of order with another—the free market with, say, state socialism—so Bergson alternates the order of the inert and the automatic with that of the vital and willed. For Bergson, disorder really means the absence of one of these two orders and the presence of the other. There is no genuine disorder in Bergson; the idea of disorder is used to objectify "the deception of a mind which finds before it a different order from that which it needs."[73] This doctrine is opposed to everything in the history of art, according to Sorel: "Far from saying that the word 'disorder' exists only in language, artists affirm that disorder is the natural state of humanity; order is introduced only with great difficulty after a long civilizing process; he [the artist] is always menaced by arbitrariness and by academicism . . . which is a sort of arbitrariness."[74] Bergson's explanations "remain sterile" because they juxtapose the vital and the automatic; "we oppose the living and the academic."[75] But for Sorel, the living contains elements of the automatic and the rational, as well as the artistic or vital, parts of our psychology.

Finally, Sorel finds that the many brilliant insights, such as the concept of duration, that are found in Bergson are not just metaphors but are reified expressive supports, which perform the same distorting functions as Laplaceanism did for cosmology; Bergson "seemed to believe that the precepts of the biological philosophy contain more reality than the laws discovered by physicists in the course of their experiments."[76] The misplaced concreteness of the concept of vitality is the result of allowing biological and sociological phenomena to form two concordant series in which the causes suitable for explaining one explain the other.[77] Such a parallelism is responsible for Gustave Le Bon's "almost universally abandoned" social Darwinist doctrine that competition always results in the triumph of the most competent. For Sorel this doctrine confuses biological and historical phenomena.[78]

Notes

1. George Lichtheim, *Marxism in Modern France*, pp. 152-53.

2. Bergson lectured at the Collège de France after 1900. *Essai sur les données immédiates de la conscience* was published in 1889 and translated into English, under the title *Time and Free Will*, in 1910; *Matter and Memory* was published in 1897 (English translation, 1911); the essay "Introduction à la Métaphysique" was first published in *Revue de métaphysique et de Morale* in January 1903 and translated into English by T. E. Hulme in 1913. Since *Creative Evolution* was not published until 1907, Sorel's early writings on Bergson depend largely on Bergson's first book and on the public lectures.

3. This critique, entitled simply "Critique de 'L'Evolution créatrice,'"

appeared in five installments in the monthly *Mouvement Socialiste* (Oct., Nov., Dec. 1907, and Jan. and Feb. 1908). It was later revised for publication in the penultimate chapter of *De l'utilité du pragmatisme* (1921). "Critique," followed by the month and page of publication, refers to the original five-part essay; *De l'utilité* refers to the revised version.

4. Sorel, *D'Aristote*, p. 166.

5. Ibid., pp. 171-72.

6. Bergson, *L'Evolution créatrice* (Paris: Alcan, 1907), pp. 339-40, translated into English by Arthur Mitchell under the title *Creative Evolution*; citations here refer to the 1944 Modern Library edition. Most of Bergson's earlier ideas are contained in this work.

7. Bergson, *Creative Evolution*, pp. 141-42.

8. Ibid., pp. 214-15.

9. Bergson, *Introduction to Metaphysics*, (Indianapolis: Bobbs-Merrill, 1949), p. 29.

10. Ibid., pp. 38-39.

11. Bergson, *Creative Evolution*, p. 215.

12. Ibid., p. 194.

13. Bergson, *Introduction to Metaphysics*, pp. 23-24.

14. Ibid., p. 21.

15. Bergson, *Creative Evolution*, p. 217.

16. Ibid., p. 218.

17. Bergson, *Introduction to Metaphysics*, p. 25.

18. Ibid., p. 26.

19. Bergson, *Matter and Memory*, (London: Routledge and Kegan Paul, 1911), p. 177.

20. Ibid., p. 279.

21. Ibid., p. 87.

22. See Jacques Chevalier, *Henri Bergson* (New York: Macmillan, 1923), p. 89.

23. Sorel, *Questions de morale*, p. 79.

24. Bergson, *Creative Evolution*, p. 221.

25. Ibid., p. 221.

26. Bergson, *Introduction to Metaphysics*, p. 45, citing "Rolla," by Alfred de Musset.

27. Bergson, *Introduction to Metaphysics*, p. 51.

28. Bergson, *Creative Evolution*, p. 211.

29. Ibid., p. 219.

30. Ibid., p. 220.

31. Ibid., pp. 153-54.

32. Bergson, *Introduction to Metaphysics*, pp. 54-55.

33. Ibid., p. 53.

34. Ibid., pp. 53-54.

35. Ibid., p. 55.

36. Ibid., p. 52.

37. Sorel, "Critique de 'L'Evolution créatrice,'" (Dec. 1907): 52.

38. Ibid. (Nov.): 484, citing Bergson, *Creative Evolution*, p. 181.

39. Bergson, *Creative Evolution*, p. 51.

40. Ibid., p. 52.

41. Sorel, "Critique de 'L'Evolution créatrice,'" (Nov.): 486.

42. Bergson, *Creative Evolution*, p. 180.

43. Ibid., p. 142.

44. Sorel, "Critique de 'L'Evolution créatrice,'" (Nov.): 484.
45. *FGS*, p. 287.
46. See Marx, *Capital* (New York: Modern Library, n.d.), p. 389. This page is cited in Sorel, *De l'utilité*, p. 419 and note (*FGS*, pp. 287, 368n17).
47. Sorel, "Critique de 'L'Evolution créatrice,'" (Nov.): 484; cf. Bergson, *Creative Evolution*, p. 51.
48. *FGS*, p. 288.
49. Sorel, *De l'utilité*, pp. 420-21 (*FGS*, p. 288).
50. Ibid., pp. 419-20 (*FGS*, p. 287).
51. Ibid., p. 421 (*FGS*, p. 368n22).
52. Ibid., p. 431 and note.
53. *FGS*, p. 369n33.
54. Sorel, *Questions de morale*, p. 18.
55. Sorel's Preface to Georges Castex's *La Douleur physique* (Paris: Jacques, 1905), p. iii.
56. Sorel, *Questions de morale*, p. 17.
57. Ibid., p. 19.
58. Sorel, "Le Modernisme dans la religion et dans le socialisme," *Revue Critique des Livres et des Idées* (1908): 191.
59. Sorel's Preface to Castex's *La Douleur physique*, p. v.
60. Sorel, *Questions de morale*, p. 19, citing Ribot, *Psychologie des sentiments*, p. 43.
61. Sorel, *Questions de morale*, p. 19, citing Hartmann, *Philosophie de l'inconscient*, French trans., vol. 2, p. 395.
62. Sorel, *Questions de morale*, p. 19.
63. Sorel's Preface to Castex's *La Douleur physique*, p. v.; Sorel, *Questions de morale*, p. 18. Cf. Théodule Ribot, *La Psychologie des sentiments*, p. 41.
64. *De l'utilité*, p. 423 and note 2 (*FGS*, pp. 289, 369n25).
65. Ibid., p. 422 (*FGS*, p. 288).
66. Ibid.
67. Ibid.
68. Sorel, "Critique de 'L'Evolution créatrice,'" (Dec.): 43.
69. Ibid., p. 52.
70. Ibid., p. 50.
71. Ibid. (Oct.): 274-79.
72. See Sorel's letter to Croce, 11 April 1920: "In my view, it is quite likely that Bergson was heavily influenced by the writings of Schopenhauer; it is quite probable that *Creative Evolution*, in its first form, was more pantheist than it is now. Many theologians find in it much more 'pantheistic poison,' and we should not ignore the opinions of theologians, who are often shown to be quite subtle when criticizing 'dangerous books.'"
73. Sorel, *De l'utilité*, p. 428, citing *L'Evolution créatrice*, p. 242.
74. Sorel, *De l'utilité*, p. 429.
75. Ibid., p. 430.
76. Ibid., pp. 377-78.
77. Ibid., p. 390.
78. Sorel, review of Gustave Le Bon, "La Psychologie du socialisme," *Revue Internationale de Sociologie*, (Feb. 1899): 152, and in *Mouvement Socialiste* (15 March 1899): 316.

VI

THE CRITIQUE OF POSITIVISM, 1902–1906

We have seen that the greater part of Sorel's writings in the period between 1897 and 1902 were concerned with a redefinition of Marxism. These writings had taken on an anti-positivist tone; but they had largely omitted any explicit discussion of the role of science beyond that in his articles in *Devenir Social* published before 1897. In that early period Sorel had attempted to distinguish positivism from Marxism and psychological spontaneity, but after 1900 he made an extensive and concentrated attempt to deal with the question of positivism, especially the positivism of Renan.

It is hardly surprising that Sorel again raised the problem of science with special reference to the study of thought—particularly religious thought. The great Renan whom he so admired was best known as a religious historian. Furthermore, in *La Ruine du monde antique*, his early study of primitive Christianity, Sorel had, in a superficially positivist way, expressed the hopelessness of studying human thought scientifically. From 1902, when Sorel reissued *La Ruine* with many emendations, until 1906, with the publication of *Le Système historique de Renan*, the main focus of Sorel's writings concerned religious matters and the way they are interpreted.

The reasons for Sorel's concern with religion were not entirely intellectual, however. Sorel believed that the Catholic church was undergoing a "crisis of modernism" that was highly analogous to the modernism of the "official socialists." In both church and party there was a tendency to transform the old dogmas so as to put them in agreement with what were understood to be the methods of contemporary science; it was not entirely coincidental that both church and party tended to treat old notions of mysticism in a cavalier fashion, preferring popularity and political respectability to true devotion of followers; both favored a "liberal" interpretation of sacred texts in order to abolish the old barbarisms.[1] For Sorel, the practical effect of this modernism was superficiality both in socialist parties and in the church. For the socialists, anxious not to offend either anti-clericals or Catholic workingmen, a convenient "political solution" was found in ignoring religious questions altogether or in adopting the Anglo-Saxon solution of allowing each man to follow his conscience. "Socialism is an application of sociology," so the new modernism went; "sociology is a science; science is muddled by religious dogma; therefore free thought is essential to socialism."[2]

The *laissez-faire* policy of socialism was matched by the "liberal" policies of Pope Leo XIII (1878-1903), whom Sorel excoriated as "a bourgeois pope arrivé" and who, among other sins, attempted to co-opt both the money-changers and the working classes into a bland, bourgeois Catholicism that had replaced its old mysticism with a Jesuitical rationalism. There was indeed a strong desire on Sorel's part to debunk the pretensions of the modern Catholic church, not only by comparing it with socialism but also by insisting that it was "a fine subject of study for the Marxist." In Leo's papacy, particularly, Sorel found a "complete reflection of all the tendencies of an epoch in an ideology . . . classic in its regularity of patterns."[3]

Debunk the church as he might, Sorel was worried that further debunking might turn into the demystification of all social movements. Sorel detested Leo because he had brought on the loss of the "old heroic spirit" of Pius IX, and he wondered whether the Catholic church could ever engender "mystical forces comparable to those it had produced in the past." If it could be shown that the destiny of the church was at all comparable to socialism, would socialism be dragged down with the church further than it already had been? Sorel foresaw a time in which the same method of ideological unmasking used against the church could be used against his own type of socialism. Gustave Le Bon, for example, had in *The Psychology of Socialism* brought reason to bear on religious belief from a "scientific" point of view. As Sorel expressed it, such writing strongly influenced the fanatical admirers of progress among the bourgeoisie who "regard religion as old rubbish destined to disappear under the influence of scientific development." At the same time, the adversaries of socialism "hope to rob it of all its mystique by maintaining that it is nothing but a religious belief. The good people who sympathize with socialism in the hope of passing themselves off as members of the avant-garde will scorn socialism when they see it as a legacy of the past."[4]

Le Bon's approach implies a "higher positivism" that assumes the detachment and neutrality of the scientist. There is an implicit assumption in Le Bon's view that all ideologies (except Le Bon's) can be explained in terms of their mystical qualities. The corollary assumption is that rational logic is the only way in which such mystical ideologies are judged, but that is why Sorel is at pains to argue that we should "avoid all possibility of finding dialectically certain analogies between those profound psychological motives that explain socialism and those which motivate Christian belief."

On the other hand, if both the church with its mysticism and the "poetic spirit" of socialism—which Sorel had already discussed in the pages of *Devenir Social*—had anything in common, it was an heroic spirit. Why not, indeed, compare the ideological similarities of religion and socialism? In fact, in the pages of *Reflections on Violence*, Sorel does that very thing when he defines the myth of the general strike as an "expression of the will" analogous to "those which were constructed by primitive Christianity and by the Reformation."[5]

This apparent ambiguity in the ideological content of Sorel's thought is explained at least in part by the ambiguous nature of the church itself. Part of church doctrine was ideologically rooted in political practice; other aspects were mystical, with ties to our deepest psychology. The political practices of the church in the nineteenth century had blurred the distinction between philosophy and ideology, myth and politics. At the turn of the century, there was widespread controversy about the relationship between politics and theology, and between the French state and the Catholic church. The radicals and the left wanted a state educational monopoly; the church schools were under heavy attack. To Sorel, however, the church's educational institutions should have expected this situation. The church, through its alliance with the conservative forces in the state, was certain to gain the enmity of the more liberal and radical parties who had been suppressed at times during the Second Empire.[6] It was commonly postulated, especially by Marxists, that the church was a handmaiden of the conservative state, an ideological opiate whose function it was to bolster civic obedience. Sorel found some truth in these accusations when they were confined to the church at a given historical period. Supported within its own ranks by a class of professional ideologues whom Sorel calls a *classe pensante*—a thinking class similar to the professional rhetoricians of the Roman empire or to the old Socratics—the church failed to distinguish between civic obligation and its spiritual mission. To Sorel, it was quite easy for the people to make the same mistake. By confusing the church's civic function with its religious mission, people were unable adequately to distinguish religion per se from modern political phenomena such as socialism.[7] This confusion was strengthened by the tendency of some utopian socialists and positivists to manufacture a civic religion or to give their utopias religious allure.

According to Sorel, yet another confusion existed in the *fin de siècle* church: the confusion over religion vs. science. The *classe pensante* of the clergy justified its power on the grounds of superior knowledge, as does any sophist or intellectual class divorced from labor. Its knowledge is related to power, and its theology is used for the purpose of ruling. The temptation to employ magical formulas that strike terror into the hearts of the faithful will be overwhelming, and that is indeed what happened. But, argues Sorel, as soon as these magical formulas, whereby religious phenomena constantly reveal themselves in the physical world through retribution, lose their terror, the fear of the local curé will vanish and, with it, all respect for the church as a social authority. The church must dissociate itself from any such magical nonsense; it must become as mystical as it once was.[8] Failure to do this has resulted in a confusion of magical and religious belief. Magic produces pleasure and physical gratification; it attempts empirical proofs of God's presence. In doing this it has taken a most unfortunate step; it has entered the domain of science and competed with it. By competing with science, the church has attempted to undermine science—to debunk it.

Sorel looks upon his own time as one in which science (in the broad sense) and religion are experiencing malaise. Modern religious liberalism—especially Protestantism—and science have continually invaded each other's territory. Even the liberalized Catholic church, according to Sorel, insists on fighting not on the grounds of belief but of skepticism. Thus, in assuming that science is somehow the enemy, the church attacks the pride of modern science by deriding its claims to certitude. Using these "scientific" methods of attacking an opponent merely advances the "crisis" in Catholic thought by producing a kind of softness in both science and religion. People in the church attack science because the church is skeptical of scientific claims. Yet religion decries skepticism. By fighting against science on the latter's home ground, that of methodological doubt, the certainty of theology is replaced by the church's defense of its position through doubt rather than faith—an absurd position, bound to rebound unfavorably on the church.[9] On the other hand, science can only doubt and express itself skeptically. When functioning properly, it avoids religious questions. To Sorel, this resulted in a supreme irony, for the discoveries of Marxism were to him a large body of science, whose theory of ideological unmasking was rooted squarely in the tradition of radical doubt and skepticism. But, for Sorel, unless some areas of belief remained secure from refutation religion would subject itself to many of the same indignities to which Marxism itself had fallen prey. By incorporating the principle of doubt into one's dogma, the principle of certitude about one's own doctrine—hence one's ability to act—is shaken. Unless some areas of thought are secure from refutation, all dogmas will end by "unmasking" one another.

Religion (like socialism) had undergone a transformation from belief to science; from the mystical to the rational; from the mythic to the ideological. Religion had experienced a gradual decomposition from a set of tightly held beliefs to an ideology that was close to modern liberalism. Modern skepticism, to which the socialist tradition owes so much, comes from a rationalism which would unmask the historical sources of biblical accounts, and, in Sorel's time, culminated in Marx's "ideological method," the tearing away of metaphysical illusions. Bruno Bauer's rejection of the historicity of Jesus (because of the inadequacy of biblical sources) was to be radically extended by Marx into a universal historical method of unmasking the "real" (material) basis of all belief. Sorel felt that it was incumbent upon the social analyst to distinguish those elements of belief systems that are susceptible to scientific treatment from those which are not; to separate the heroic and mythical elements from the political and the rationalistic. In his early writings, he had made an attempt to do so which had proven unsatisfactory. His writings after the turn of the century consisted in no small part of an updating of the earlier efforts.

I

Sorel's first book, *Contribution à l'étude profane de la Bible* (1889), was written at a time when biblical scholarship was undergoing great transformations in the hands of men who were treating the Gospels as historical biographies of Jesus. This revolution in thought, which had commenced at the end of the eighteenth century and continued until Sorel's day, was highly influential on both liberal Protestant and skeptical thought. By constructing lives of Jesus, biographers could not avoid dealing with Jesus' personal motives or psychological drives; this attempt soon led to the question of whether Jesus' actions possessed any kind of "rational" explanation, whether the miracles could be "explained" through common sense. By accepting "lives" of Jesus, liberal Protestants saw their theology vindicated; by suppressing the supernatural aspects of religion, teaching would center on Jesus as a moral prophet at the expense of his miraculous and divine qualities. This perspective was attacked by conservative churchmen as sacrilege, and by radicals as bad history—referring to the Gospels' dubiousness as an historical source.

Central to the controversy were three overriding questions: (1) Was the concept of the "historical," or biographical, Jesus valid? (2) If it was acceptable, how should the inconsistencies among the Gospels, especially the Gospel according to St. John as opposed to the other three Gospels, the so-called "synoptic" Gospels, be explained? (3) If Jesus' motives can be deduced from the Gospels, was his intent primarily messianic, or did he view himself principally as a moral teacher?[10]

Among the many tendencies of Gospel scholarship, three are regarded as among the most historically significant, because they focus on the three questions outlined above. David Friedrich Strauss asserted that the controversy between the divine and the historical Jesus should be transcended by accepting as a synthesis of this conflict the idea of the Gospel as mythology. This Hegelian idea was transformed by Bruno Bauer of the Left Hegelians into a rejection of any possibility of deducing the historical Jesus because of the contradictions among the Gospels. Bauer's criticism, as we know, contributed greatly to Marx's theory of ideology, in which the father of scientific socialism not only criticized Bauer's exclusive concern with the world of thought but proclaimed the bankruptcy of the entire religious enterprise.[11]

Across the Rhine, Ernest Renan attempted to give the first French interpretation of *The Life of Jesus* by glossing over many of the problems of German scholarship. He presented an artistic portrait, dominated at times by "interpretations of taste," that at its best imitated an Impressionist painting; at its worst, vulgar St. Sulpice art. Renan attempted by means of his sentimental portrait to resolve some of these Germanic dilemmas and to fudge others. To Renan, the Book of John is different from the synoptic Gospels, but the conflicts are softened. Renan thought that a kind of "sympathy"[12] for religion, and a certain artistic sensitivity, permitted one to sense the teaching of the Gospels. But the nature of Renan's "sympathetic" treatment of Christianity meant that Renan himself was sometimes unclear or contradictory as to his intentions. He wanted to depict the exalted and sublime sentiments that underlie religious feeling; thus, he criticized liberal Christianity for its coldness and its rationalism. But despite this criticism, Renan thought a biography of Jesus could be written; and his methodology in writing the *Life of Jesus* is often close to that of the liberal Protestants or the skeptics whom he criticized. It is in this respect that Renan is significant. Renan often tries to reconcile the "liberal" or "teaching" side of Jesus with his own "romantic" understanding of Christianity. The vitality of the Christian life is undermined by the continuity of the rabbinical tradition.

Renan's interpretation of Christianity had an immense influence on Sorel's thought, which is suffused with references to Renan's works. Sorel at first praised Renan for his "learned exposition" of biblical history, for his "remarkable perspicacity in writing a criticism of liberal Christianity at a time when so many futile intellects were announcing the rebirth of idealism and foreseeing progressive tendencies in the church that had reconciled itself to the modern world."[13]

In his early years, Sorel paid far more attention to the "heroic" dimension of Renan's history of Christianity than to Renan's more "Protestant" characteristics. The unfolding of Sorel's thought is, in many respects, parallel to his increasing realization of the problems in Renan's scholarship: the latter's dulling of the sharper edges of religious and scholarly conflict; his failure to realize the difference between sentimentalism and heroism; the problems inherent in his desire to recognize the greatness of the founders of Christianity, on the one hand, and to debunk their supernatural qualities, on the other.

In his early work, Sorel blurred some of these problems; when he set down his first thoughts on biblical scholarship in his *Contribution à l'étude profane de la Bible* in 1889, he had not sufficiently differentiated his own perspective from Renan's. Like Renan, Sorel did not study the Bible with any purely theological end in view. "To present the Bible from the purely religious perspective would be folly," Sorel says; "the people would reject it." Instead, he thought that "it was necessary to enter into secular literature and introduce it as a classical work."[14] It is in this respect that Sorel wishes to emphasize the secular—even the political—nature of his biblical research. To what extent is the study of the Bible justified if it is not for purely religious purposes? Sorel argues that a "critique profane" is necessary because truth about the Bible has been distorted for "theological purposes," and in this he echoes Renan's *Life of Jesus*.[15] Rather than theological partisanship, Sorel says, "I have attempted to submit the Bible to a critical examination which is truly free of all prejudice." The results of this study, furthermore, mean to Sorel that his "conclusions are very close to orthodoxy."[16]

Sorel can say this because it is his understanding that the Bible, in its origins, performed a purpose that was partly political and educational: "The Bible is the only book which can be used for the education of the people, to initiate them in the heroic life, to combat the deleterious tendencies of utilitarianism and to arrest the propagation of the revolutionary idea."[17] It is apparent that Sorel, at this stage of his life, desired heroism but not discontinuity or revolution. His emphasis is placed on the moral transformation of the educated classes, and the *Contribution* is directed at "the university which teaches the people and the bourgeoisie who govern them."[18]

Sorel's political purpose in his first work is plain: the elite must be educated, not so much to scholarship but to the best life, which is the heroic life; this regime is sustained by a simple poetic education analogous to the biblical maxims learned by the old Jewish farmer-warriors. In the *Contribution*, Sorel attempts to demonstrate how the Bible performed this function for Hebrew culture and how this was transferred to Christian teaching. In doing so he takes a position on the controversy over the biographies of Jesus. The Bible provides us with an heroic education. First, it shows us the legend of David: the survival of this legend, the survival of the Bible, allowed the Jewish culture, and the Jewish people, to survive despite widespread persecution. Second, the Hebraic culture not only included legends, but was expressed in a language that was ideal for the poetic education for the heroic life. Sorel concludes the last third of the book with the idea that the Gospel according to St. John is the oldest, hence the most historically reliable, Gospel because, when examined textually, it shows itself to be the closest in mood and in expression to the old Hebraic culture. As such, it transmitted a quality of Judaism to early Christian culture.

Sorel's secularization of the Bible is most understandable through his interpretation of King David's conversion to Judaism. To Sorel, this conversion was due to political, not religious, reasons. King David was in constant struggle against hostile peoples, and Judaism provided a cementing force, a kind of civil religion, for his people. The legend of the messianic David was the necessary myth that held the scattered remnants of Judaism together in later times. "While others who were defeated by Rome were forced to abandon their language, their religion, and their moral existence, the Jews, dispersed and usually persecuted, attached themselves inseparably to the [Hebraic] law, because they always hoped for the coming of David, who would rebuild the Temple."[19] This hope "gave them courage to struggle, with immortal glory, against the Roman legions."[20]

It was the glory of David's reign, not the wisdom of Solomon, which produced this national myth, despite David's ruthlessness in politics and lack of severity in religion (which Sorel insists was produced by "necessity").[21] King David "merited this recognition of his country by his great qualities and because of the great results of his reign. If scholars have attributed to Solomon the Book of Wisdom, in which there is an excessively effete state of mind, the people have placed the Psalms, in which he breathed his entire soul, under David's name."[22] It is the hero, not the scholar or the man of wisdom, to whom Israel owes her survival.

For Sorel, too, national myths emerge not from scholarship but from a poetic language. Here, Sorel anticipates some of the concepts which later entered into his exposition of the myth of the general strike in the *Reflections on Violence* (1906). In the *Reflections*, Sorel says that the myth is identical with the convictions of a group, and its results "could not be produced by ordinary language; use must be made of a body of images which by intuition alone, and prior to any considered analysis, is capable of evoking as an undivided whole the mass of sentiments that correspond to the different manifestations of the war of modern socialism against modern society." The syndicalist myth is not a rational product; it develops from the ensemble of human impulses just as any true work of art does, and, like any true work of art, myth "flourishes best on mystery, half-shades, and indeterminate outlines; the more speech is methodical and perfect, the more likely it is to eliminate everything that distinguishes a masterpiece; it reduces the masterpiece to the proportions of an academic product."[23]

That 1906 statement is cited as one of the "Bergsonian" passages of Sorel's work. It is instructive to see Sorel in 1889—prior to his discovery of Bergson—attributing to the Hebraic language a facility in the construction of mythical thought that was later to appear somewhat characteristic of the myth of the general strike. By erasing the line between symbolism and philosophy, Hebrew infuses Judaic thought with an extraordinary creativity and freedom. In our modern rhetoric, we require that images be capable of being drawn. They must be sufficiently coordinated to correspond to something real. "The Jewish poet does not have to apply this rule, because he is not a designer: he has much more freedom in his choice of images and especially in the mode of arrangement."[24] In Hebrew, the images of lyric poetry are inevitably distorted, and this plays an important role in Jewish literature. "The image is never exact. When the poet compares a hero to a lion, he is obliged to create a fictional lion who is more than an animal."[25]

As a consequence of this lack of subtlety in Hebrew, it was extremely difficult, according to Sorel, to translate it accurately into the more refined Greek. This had ramifications for the world of labor. Unlike the Greeks, "the Jews were unable either to be painters or sculptors; it was impossible for them to give a precise form to poetic images." For this reason, says Sorel, outside of the myth of David, which was a special case, the Jews "never dreamed of the material realization of the images they invoked," when metaphors were based on arts that the Jews hadn't perfected.[26] In other words, as Sorel later expressed it, "Progress in the development of language was probably determined by the arts, especially the plastic arts, and man could not easily be led to express in his language the distinctions that he could not realize in his labor. The act must have preceded speech."[27] Sorel also notes the concurrent erotic content of poetry: "Eroticism requires a vaporous form; since lyric poetry does not need to be precise, it consequently lends itself to erotic sentiments."[28]

There is a deeper puzzle involved in the *Contribution*, however. Sorel's account of Old Testament myth is relatively easy to understand, but why should Sorel devote over a third of the book to what he calls "the problem of Jesus"? It appears that many of the questions plaguing the biblical scholarship of Sorel's time were to be connected to Sorel's treatment of Jewish myth. Sorel attempts in his argument to demonstrate, first, the greater "Jewishness" of the Fourth Gospel and, second, to show that its greater antiquity and proximity to the Hebraic tradition make it a more accurate document for discerning the true thought of the first Christians. The discussion is important because through an analysis of John, he argues that it is possible to discern the social and historical relevance of Christianity. To what extent is the great religion of the Occident infused with messianic intentions? To what degree is it merely a moral code? What is its relationship to action or to monastic quietism or to the validity of liberal Protestantism? It must be said that in the *Contribution* Sorel does not adequately come to grips with any of these problems, nor does he cope fully with the theological controversies over the biographies of Jesus. He does at least attempt to respond to these problems and most explicitly to the problem of the disparity among the Gospels.

Sorel attempts to show that, textually, the Fourth Gospel had gone the furthest in preserving the Hebraic traditions. To Sorel, John was the last of the Hebrew prophets and, like Ezekiel, was "very Jewish." As evidence of the antiquity of this Gospel, Sorel says that since there is no reference in John to the destruction of Jerusalem in 51 A.D., the Fourth Gospel must have been written prior to that event.[29] Conversely, the synoptic Gospels must have been written later, because their accounts of Jewish life were based on "fantasy" and were "closed to all Judaic culture."[30]

For his thesis, Sorel depends on the notion that there were vast differences between Greek mythology and the myths of the Jews. "The fundamental principle of Judaism prevented it from creating a mythology that was analogous to that of the pagans. Divinity, for the Hebrews, could not be decomposed in order to give birth to completely distinct persons," as is found in polytheistic religions.[31] The Greeks not only had a theology based on individual and distinct gods, but their gods had a personality and an "appearance." The Jews did not have such a religion. Sorel argues that the more specific and detailed an account of a religious event becomes, the more distant it is from Hebrew thought and language. The "vaguest" Gospel will be the one that is most proximate to Judaism.

Sorel proceeds to show that the synoptic Gospels have far more detailed accounts of the life of Christ; this detail, rather than proving their proximity to Jesus, proves that they are further removed from him. Sorel goes to extreme lengths to substantiate this claim of Johannine antiquity by showing that the "scientific" quality of the synoptics distances them from Hebraic lyricism: for instance, in Mark and in Luke, a woman who has lost blood for twelve years approaches Jesus amid a crowd, believing that she can be healed if she touches his garment. Despite the closeness of the throng, Jesus proclaims his awareness of someone touching his vestments, and the woman throws herself at his feet in confirmation. Luke attributes to Jesus the statement: "I felt a force leaving me."[32] According to Sorel, the materialization of the miracle of the woman's subsequent cure "corresponds well with the positivistic spirit of the [later] Greeks,"[33] and it demonstrates the non-Hebraic character of the synoptics.[34] Conversely, in the Book of John there are fewer miracles, because they are not inserted with any "dogmatic intention" as "proofs" of Christ's divinity.

Sorel's ambiguous view of positivism is apparent even in his early writing. That is why he finds the miracle especially helpful in dealing with both historical exegesis and social mythology. John is concerned less with the facts of the miracles and more with an affirmation of faith; thus, John is more vague and at the same time unabashed in his presentation of certain occurrences such as the miracle of Lazarus. The synoptics minimize the importance of this miracle, while for John it is central. Lazarus's story is embarrassing to orthodox Christians because it is easily "explained," and thus it undermines belief in the divine quality of miracles. For the rationalists, Sorel says, "the miracle is an example of legerdemain; the worker of miracles is a dexterous prestidigitator. Illness is apparent; death is only assumed; while the cure and the resurrection are fictions accepted by credulous and ignorant people. *If* one accepts these premises, he cannot study any religious phenomenon; there is no religion without miracles."[35]

To Sorel, however, the Jewish character of the Book of John obviated any problems with Lazarus: this Jewish character meant that the occurrences in the Fourth Gospel were meant to be taken symbolically and mythically, while, on the contrary, the synoptics "transformed elementary symbols into realities."[36] The "purely Jewish" symbolism of John contrasts with the bastardization of the ancient Jewish ethos in the synoptics—the result of grafting later Greek culture onto the ancient Hebrew tradition.

But if valid distinctions among the four Gospels can be made, Sorel should take a stand on the possibility of writing a biography of Jesus and, consequently, on whether Jesus' messianic intentions can be known. (Indeed, if the second question can be answered, an answer to the first question can be derived from it.) In proclaiming John to be the earliest Gospel, through the device of emphasizing the continuity between Christianity and Judaism, Sorel cannot proclaim that Jesus intended to announce even a new law, much less an apocalypse or a messianic return. Ironically, too, John becomes an historical source when Sorel maintains that "we do not see in John that Jesus presents himself as announcing a new law: on the contrary, he claims to have the sole legitimate interpretation of the tradition of Moses."[37] He cites the Johannine speech of Jesus that "he who believes in Moses believes in me."[38] That John was a valid historical source for Sorel at this time can also be inferred from his insistence "that the work of the synoptics has no historical value: the facts are arranged to suit dogmatic concerns."[39] Sorel implies here that Jesus' intention can be known; that he did not wish to found a church; that nothing new was intended in Christianity. The Jesus of the Book of John continues the Hebraic tradition.

Several problems are involved in Sorel's earliest attempt at biblical scholarship. If Sorel upholds the proximity of the Gospel according to St. John to ancient Hebrew culture, and claims that the Hebrew culture was symbolic rather than rational and historical, then how can he judge the content of the Fourth Gospel on historical grounds, that is, as an historical source? Indeed, this oscillation between respect for John as myth and John as an historical document recurs throughout Sorel's account here and even reappears in later writings. For example, while condemning the positivism of the synoptics, he extols the historical veracity of the Book of John because it "describes the great prophetic crisis of Mary Magdalene in a most detailed way."[40] The nature of the Gospel of John itself is not purely heroic even in Sorel's account. Many authorities today argue that John is not only the most philosophical of the Gospels, but that it was very likely written late by either a Greek or a Hebrew who knew Greek culture.[41] Sorel admits that John, at least from appearances, is "cold, incomplete, and insufficient" and adds that it has little in the way of moral teaching.[42]

What use, then, can be made of John? What is the purpose of attempting to establish the "Greek" character of the synoptics? Obviously, it is the established liberal Christianity that has assumed the conventional position of the primacy of the synoptics, but if John embodies Hebraic continuity, it is precisely the Gospel of John that emphasizes the teaching and moral nature of Christ rather than his messianic character, because messianism connotes something new in the world, a *ricorso.*

Finally, Sorel does not come adequately to grips with the changes in the Hebrew culture itself. He is at pains to explain how Christianity could wreak such changes in the Roman world when Judaism had become dominated and corrupt. But the entire brunt of this early Sorelian effort, inspired by Renan, centers on continuity between the two religions. In all likelihood, Sorel wrote the *Contribution*, prior to his extensive examination of the works of Giambattista Vico. It was from the Vicoian *ricorsi* that he derived the idea of a new beginning as the necessary element of moral reform.[43] The *Contribution* does not emphasize these *ricorsi* and shortly thereafter Sorel realized the inadequacy of the book.

II

Sorel underwent a considerable modification in his understanding of the historical value of the Fourth Gospel. First and foremost, it is apparent that by the turn of the century, Sorel denied that the Gospel of John possessed much historical value except as an expression of messianic spirit; consequently, he viewed the quest for the historical Jesus as a vain enterprise. Any attempt to understand Jesus' motives, to discover whether or not he intended to establish a new religion, or a new church, is a futile inquiry. Thus, Sorel undertook to establish his interpretation of Christian thought from the point of view of how early Christians reacted to it. That is, religious documents should henceforth be studied as expressions of opinion and belief of the writers of the documents rather than as raw material for the uncovering of the motives or intentions of the subjects of the documents; of how Christ was understood by the early Christians rather than what Jesus intended to do. This perspective allowed Sorel to treat the religious movements from a secular point of view but still to take the Bible seriously—almost, in a way, at face value.

In 1889, in the *Contribution*, Sorel blurred this distinction between accepting the "facticity" of the Bible and a more nineteenth-century "analysis" of it. Sorel came to refine his views in a quite understandable way. After accepting the idea of a *ricorso* and after his realization that continuity was not a sufficient ground on which to base an explanation of the relationship between Christianity and Judaism, Sorel was led to an extensive revision of his understanding of Renan's scholarship which culminated in his massive and scholarly *Le Système historique de Renan* (1905).

Renan used the psychology of religion to explain humanity, and he insisted that the study of society must include the study of the myths held by that society. Hence, to Renan, religion is relevant to science. Renan was thus a positivist in the larger sense of the word—the scientific study of humanity must include all of man's experiences and all his faculties.[44] The debt Sorel owes to Renan is obvious after a reading of the *Contribution*. There Sorel, too—despite his criticism of the positivist spirit—in his study of the Bible from a secular perspective echoes Renan's concerns. It is equally obvious that Sorel in the *Contribution* often made some of the same mistakes that Renan did.

By the turn of the century, however, it was apparent to Sorel that Renan was enough of a nineteenth-century positivist to want to "explain" religious phenomena from the perspective of outmoded nineteenth-century science. Thus, although Renan extols the sublime sentiments of religious feeling in discussing the miracle of Lazarus, he also says that Lazarus "simulated death, was placed in a family tomb, and emerged on the call of his master."[45] Sorel eventually came to the opinion that despite Renan's attack on liberal Protestantism, an attack that had great influence on Sorel, Renan was sufficiently affected by the German liberal Protestant scholars to want to "unmask the Pauline fabric of orthodox Protestantism, and to discover, beyond St. Paul, the 'true' teaching of Jesus [with] the intent of proving that the Founder of Christianity definitely did not wish to present himself as a god."[46] The practical outcome of such an endeavor, according to Sorel, was to write a layman's study with conclusions that were not merely secular but (despite Renan's pretensions of "sympathy" with religious phenomena) subtly hostile to religious sentiment. Thus Renan's discussions, acording to Sorel, are almost entirely devoid of the supernatural, despite the fact that the Resurrection is a central element in Christian belief.[47]

According to Sorel, Renan's "explanatory" approach to Christianity was at fault, in dealing with minute causes and great epochal historical forces; both are causal theories best left to theologians rather than historians. The miracle of Lazarus is explained by the use of minute causes and trivial incidents, but Sorel says that if history is presented as a series of accidents, then the most trivial cause may have had great influence. "We are party to an hypothesis in which it is necessary to know the totality of the present; we arrive at the point of seeing that great events could have depended on small accidents that are classified in the category of chance, and that no one dreamed of taking into consideration."[48] "Instinct rebels against the identification of history with mere chance: origins, containing much that is foreseen, seem to us to call for the intervention of superior forces."[49] To Sorel, however, causal "origins" of Christianity, trivial or great, are scarcely accessible to the scientific method, because they present great disorder; "we must accept an abyss when explaining the passage from one regime to another."[50]

The explanations offered by Renan for such events as the resurrection of Lazarus—accidents—or the monumental creation of a new religion—Jewish inheritance—are entirely hypothetical. As Sorel said, one does not *know* that fakery took place or that such and such an incident really did occur; these things can only be conjectured. The rational explanations of biblical miracles or of the foundation of Christianity must remain fictive because they remain unproven. If such fictional causes are reduced to mundane phenomena, the effect is to produce history, in this case the history of Christianity, in the form of a novel—that is, "to skillfully fashion a hypothetical cause for the effect that we must explain."[51] Sorel asks why we "must explain" such events in this way. For him, the problems involved in historical research are done away with, as they are in science, once we dispense altogether with the notion of causality: "As long as history is examined from the causal perspective it is impossible to ask what real facts could have given birth to the illusion of a miracle."[52] If an historian confines himself to the realm of what idealists would call "appearances" and relegates causal questions to theology, then the problem of historical fiction disappears. Only theologians need explain how such a mammoth event as the creation of Christianity could come about. Since such explanations must rely ultimately on supernatural causes (if they are to avoid ordinary fiction), theories of causation in such things are best left to theologians. Causes are ultimately the province of belief: God intervenes in the world in creating secondary causes. Scholars look only at quantitative determination; the miracle is outside their purview.

Now, in dealing with causality, that is, in conforming to old-fashioned canons of positivistic science that demanded attention to cause, Renan was presented with a great problem. How can a scholar adhere closely to the canons of scientific integrity set down by the positivists, while still taking religion and mythology seriously? Sorel argues that although Renan pretends to take religion at face value, his lack of seriousness combined with the peculiar methodological trap he set for himself result in his playing lightly with sacred things. Renan must explain the miracles and yet avoid calling them pious frauds—thus *explaining* away the glory of heroes and at the same time *preserving* their glory. Renan wants to have his cake and eat it too; to unmask ideology without debunking; to make something rational, and yet to preserve the heroic sense of the sublime. Renan sums up the ambiguity of his position: he is "a romantic protesting against romanticism."[53]

By recounting Christianity as would a novelist and insisting on scientific probity at the same time, Renan misses the point. One cannot, according to Sorel, fruitfully consider the origins of Christianity without engaging in highly unscientific forms of speculation. The methods of science are highly misleading when applied to religion. Renan failed to appreciate the radically different bases of analysis of religion on the one hand and science on the other. There should be a truce between theology and science. "There is a mystery in theology which science cannot try to deny"[54] and which theologians can claim as their domain. There are no valid scientific reasons to be put forth for or against the miracle. One accepts this for "*raison de conviction intime*."[55] History itself cannot be written to prove or disprove the Christian *idea* any more than Christianity can depart from its domain and methods in trying to prevent historical studies from clarifying *events* in its domain.

It is useless to try to discover what facts have been able to give birth to the illusion of a miracle; rather, "the question is of knowing if this belief has produced something in the history of Christianity."[56] In Chapter 3, we noted that Sorel projected poetic sensibilities into science while simultaneously separating the scientific study of the past from poetic projections into the future. In 1905, Sorel reconstitutes that separation by distinguishing between psychological knowledge of religious miracles whose origins are "mysterious and incommunicable" to the non-actor—knowledge that escapes all determinism—and the retrospective knowledge of the historian, who looks at the external whole of history without looking at particular causes.[57] As he says of historical knowledge, "We know in a certain way that Napoleon was defeated at Waterloo, but this sure knowledge applies only to the whole; when we come to the details of battle we are in the presence of innumerable contradictory accounts," which Sorel later relegates to the realm of poetry.[58] But Sorel had already limited looking at history *en bloc*, without diremption. On the one hand, Sorel's methodological individualism is reduced to an inaccessible psychology, while on the other he forecloses the ability of positive science to grasp the totality fully. Because of this uncertainty, the historian cannot do what Renan and other positivists did: predict the end of Christianity as Marxists did the end of capitalism. For by attaching Christianity to "sordid ghetto origins" Renan was vying for the honor of being one of Christianity's pallbearers.

III

It would be Sorel's new task to consider what is new and what has been inherited from Judaism in the body of Christian literature and thought. Sorel's new, clearer perspective on Renan led him to revise his ideas on the continuity between Christianity and Judaism and hence on the function of the various Gospels in Christian life.

In 1905, the Book of John was still viewed by Sorel as the oldest Gospel, but Sorel regarded it even more as a messianic document and less as a Gospel concerned with Judaic continuity than he had in the 1889 *Contribution*. Whereas in 1889 Sorel quoted Jesus, "Had ye believed in Moses, ye would have believed in me," in his 1905 work on Renan we see the disciples awaiting the imminent return of their master. The Fourth Gospel, according to Sorel, reflects this in a very "naive" way: "And if I go and prepare a place for you, I will come again, and receive you unto myself; that where I am, there may ye be also."[59]

Certainly much of Sorel's *explication du texte* of 1889 survives into the work on Renan; many of the differences are questions of emphasis, especially with regard to the antiquity of the Book of John. Nevertheless, Sorel's 1905 work shows a heightened appreciation of the remoteness of John as an historical document and, by virtue of their poetic nature, of all the four Gospels as a birth of a genuinely new development that can be intuited artistically and not schematized. "We must renounce the hope of ever knowing the entirety of origins, but it is much easier . . . to discover the paths by which morals, ideas, and institutions appeared in the state that is revealed to us at the end of the third century. We can thus acquire a partial knowledge of Christian life."[60] We can, by implication, also inquire what these ancient times can tell us about the nature of moral and ethical life today. Sorel tries to get round the dilemma in which Renan trapped himself—of treating the Gospels, and Christianity in general, as serious historical phenomena all the while he was explaining them away—by coming down firmly on the side of all the Gospels (not just John) as myth, as expressions of the will not wholly dissimilar to the myth of the general strike. He expresses himself in these Bergsonian terms: "If we compare the Gospels to luminous projections, we must add that these projections last a very short period of time in such a way that the spectator is unable to grasp the detail clearly and can keep only a memory of the feelings provoked by the whole. Such apparitions bear very little on the intellect and are susceptible to varied interpretations."[61] Biblical literature belongs more to poetry than to history and expresses very little objectivity. This poetry "springs forth from the popular spirit, strongly excited by hope, love, or terror, and expresses very primitive sentiments. Periods that are quite unsettled by war, by revolutions, beset by cataclysms, imbued with a lively sentiment of an impending rebirth, are quite favorable to a flowering of lyricism."[62]

The more one insists on the literary or lyrical value of the Gospels, the more their value as historical testimony is diminished. "Lyricism and history do not advance together. We know with what inexactness the various poets recount their lives; they never distinguish clearly between what actually existed and what they wish to have seen or done."[63] To Sorel, the synoptics are almost without historical value, and the unique character of the Fourth Gospel is that its messianism is "both vague and popular in such a way that we are led to look for the true 'historical origins' of the messianic doctrine in the apostolic period."[64] But the Fourth Gospel is a good source for historical origins only in the realm of the dogmas itself, not the actions of its subjects. Furthermore, for Sorel in 1905, there was far more to the myth of the early Christians than is contained in the Book of John. It is to the advantage of the "later" Gospels that we see a more highly complex myth evolve in tandem with the more sophisticated church organization.

It was apparent to Sorel that the solidity and militancy of the early church could not be due solely to the myth of the Book of John. Sorel notes that the early church "contained few members and did not have great solidity." Its leaders were content with rudimentary administrative duties and dominated by a "particularistic spirit."[65] The subsequent persecutions provided the church with the ideal cementing force that had been missing from the early stages. Under the influence of the persecutions, a climate of struggle and fear, present even in the earliest stages, was reinforced in the Christian movement. Sorel emphasizes that this mood is far from the feeling of extreme terror described in Renan's interpretation of early Christianity, for he says that "a regime of somewhat prolonged terror shakes profoundly the intelligence and morality of the people."[66] Instead, he says, there was a feeling which had a "remarkable analogy with that of the class struggle with which we have become acquainted in modern socialism."[67] The early Christians fought against the Romans, who, it seemed, waged a veritable theomachy against the Christian God. For Sorel, the function of the synoptic Gospels was plain: they provided a basis for explaining this struggle in terms of the anti-Christ as a cause of the persecutions. Even though Sorel thinks that the doctrine of the anti-Christ "probably developed at the same time as the messianic idea itself,"[68] the idea is expressed in the synoptics: "Many false prophets shall arise and shall deceive many. . . . But he that shall endure unto the end shall be saved. . . . And except those days should be shortened, there shall be no flesh saved; but for these elects' sake, those days shall be shortened."[69]

Sorel notes that continuity between Christianity and Judaism still exists through Christianity's borrowing many elements of detail from the Jewish apocalypses, but Christianity "well preserves its own unique character: the Jews awaited the great day of Jehovah with feelings of anger; now terror is imposed even on the just."[70] The inheritance of the old Jewish apocalypses had taken little directly from Hebrew literature and could thus accommodate Christian innovations, as Sorel is at pains to emphasize. Sorel notes that Christian messianism "derived a great deal from the concerns that dominated the milieu in which the apocalypses were read." The success of these apocalypses was due to the "terrible descriptions of the day of the Lord and the vengeance which menaced the enemies of Israel."[71] It was only gradually, after 155 A.D., according to Sorel, that Christian apocalypses separate from Jewish tradition began to emerge clearly.[72] Although the concerns of the two religions were similar—the preservation of the community—Sorel notes that Christian anxiety over persecutions was, in fact, greatly exaggerated. Following the research of Harnack, he says that "the language of the Christian authors was entirely disproportionate to the actual importance of the persecutions; there were very few martyrs before the third century."[73] But this does not matter to Sorel, for notwithstanding their exceptional nature, "the Christian ideology was based on these rather rare but very heroic events."[74] "The nobility of the attitude of the victims imposed respect and proved that they were worthy of liberty—the Spartan courage with which they died justified their belief in the triumph of the *Christian city*—their unbreakable solidarity produced the assumption of the living Christ."[75]

The synoptic literature of the anti-Christ dramatized the conflict between church and persecutors and explained the nature of the persecutions. Each persecution "became an incident of the war carried on by 'Satan prince of this world,' who was soon to reveal his anti-Christ. Thus the cleavage sprang simultaneously from the persecutions and from the feverish expectation of a decisive battle."[76] In short, it is apparent that this Christian mythology represents a false consciousness of a kind, but this matters very little to Sorel: the myth was ultimately linked in certain ways to property and to material conditions. During the persecutions, many rural peoples, according to Sorel, became Christian because Christianity opposed the official religion, despite the fact that many of these people did not know a single tenet of Christian dogma.[77] In Asia Minor, Christianity spread along with a strong textile industry because the conflicts with the rich transformed artisan cooperatives into Christian congregations; the militant Christian spirit, like all religious upheaval, possessed tension, and this was easily transposed from social tensions to religion. Eventually it was combined indissolubly with "a sentiment of imperial power that inspired the church in its conviction of forming the avant-garde of the army of the saints."[78] By linking Christianity too closely with Judaic culture, Renan, according to Sorel, failed to recognize the considerable discontinuity between the two religions.

Furthermore, Renan assumed that primitive Christian monarchy emerged almost spontaneously from the old Hebraic myths and free unions of piety. To Sorel, however, this monarchy was due in part to the defenses in a world of persecutions in which the monarchy of bishops could not confine itself to administrative duties. Here, too, according to Sorel, we must note the strong importance of ideological factors in the new Christian development. The episcopal monarchy emerged partly because of comparisons between it and the celestial monarchy. As Sorel says, "In primitive societies, each group views itself as being the center of a complete world; its God is the first god, . . . its prince the king of kings. One finds ideas of the same type in nascent Christianity. The great metropolises had preserved a strong sense of their autonomy."[79] The metropolises constituted their church as a free state modeled on Jerusalem: at its head was a sovereign, analogous to the brother of the Lord who had occupied the first bishopric; beside him were the elders that Saint Ignatius compared to the apostles and who shared with him the sovereignty.[80] In developing this sovereignty, the episcopate "would discipline the prophets from the point of view of making them rare or powerless. In this we see the presence not of an usurpation similar to that of the Greek tyrants in the democracies, but rather of a regular application of primitive monarchical power"[81] resembling the monarchy of an Algerian tribe more than that of a state.

It is in this context that Sorel, in 1905, attacks the problem of the disparity between John and the synoptic Gospels. It is Sorel's view that John was "written for a society which had not yet produced a fixed liturgy and which had an undeveloped dogma. Nothing is found in it which recalls this liturgical influence. In comparison with St. Paul, the author seems quite old-fashioned, because St. Paul argued much on questions of Baptism and the Eucharist."[82] On the other hand, the synoptics tell the story of the Eucharist without any great differences from St. Paul. Thus the synoptic Gospels are, to Sorel, "compilations of liturgical remnants to which several additions have been made. This explains how, therefore, there can be reciprocal influences and continual corrections which would not be expected in ordinary books."[83]

To Sorel, when fear of persecution declined, the Eucharist attained added forcefulness for the hierarchy. "The Eucharistic theory favored the concept of the ubiquitousness of the supreme power: all communities participated in the Body of Christ, received the same grace, and were inspired by the same spirit."[84] What Sorel calls the "Eucharistic cult" assured familiarity with Jesus through the offices of the hierarchy administering it. Viewing the synoptic Gospels, then, as the ideology of the hierarchy, Sorel says that church officials became all the more necessary as the Eucharist achieved greater importance. By the fifth century, millenarianism and the doctrine of the anti-Christ were dispensed with as mere circumstantial and temporary doctrines. The great upheavals expected by the first Christians and sustained by the social myth were replaced by an individualistic piety reified by highly detailed accounts in the synoptics.[85] The power of the synoptics compared to John was due to their dual function: first, of mythologizing messianism and the counter-doctrine of the anti-Christ; and, second, a later Eucharistic role in which the popular enthusiasm of the early days was greatly attenuated. To Sorel, the social and ideological transformation that occurs with the rise of the Eucharistic cult reflects the transformation of Christianity from a myth-bound social movement to an ideologically sustained organization based on individualistic piety; it was this transformation of Christianity, in which the synoptic Gospels played such a pivotal role, from a social to an individual basis which divorced it more and more from its Judaic antecedents.

IV

The importance of myth in the Sorelian interpretation of Christianity is shown in the relationship of the early Christians to Roman society. Christianity was not linked solely to the lower classes, according to Sorel: it was connected to the aristocracy as well—it was part of Roman society. Thus, Sorel regards as futile Renan's judgment that Christianity worked to destroy the Roman empire. Sorel asks, "What is the value of this judgment if we are interested above all in the ideal that he gives of the necessary victory of an ever-expanding Christianity over a continuously diminishing force?"[86] Sorel does not explicitly deny Renan's charge, and *La Ruine du monde antique* seems clearly to agree with it. What Sorel does say is that Christianity's relationship with the empire was highly ambiguous. At the same time that it "constituted a world apart, that the church formed a *politeia*,"[87] it was part and parcel of Roman society. "There is something paradoxical at first sight in the situation of the church, which had its followers in the upper classes, who were obliged to make many concessions to custom, and who yet could hold beliefs based on the idea of absolute cleavage."[88]

For Sorel, a similar phenomenon existed in the case of the English and American sectarians who were extremely rigorous in their religious severity, but quite practical and accomplished in their everyday business affairs.[89] In any event, to Sorel the importance of Christianity was not so much whether it worked for the decline of Rome, which Sorel viewed as inevitable, but whether Christianity would remain a vital force within the decline. To Sorel, so long as Christianity was dominated by the myth which reinforced the belief that it was a world apart, it would expand as a religion and become master of the hour. But when it began to share more and more the morals and attitudes of the general society, a society almost destined to decline anyway, according to Sorel, then Christianity would share in the general decadence.

Sorel, as an admirer of the classical city-state, had great respect for the Roman virtues that survived into the days of the empire. Christianity, according to Sorel, performed the task of revealing the "ideological dissociation" of the Roman empire of the decline, i.e., of showing the great gap between the professed virtues of the empire and its immoral practices.[90] At first Christianity performed this function merely by its everyday attitudes, by the fact that the Christian Romans of aristocratic lineage upheld the old virtues. "The families who had conserved respect for the old morals, who had believed in the classical culture and who did not despair of virtue were disgusted with the religious charlatanism, the ignorance, the immorality of the philosophers protected by Marcus Aurelius."[91] The Aurelius government was, however, for Sorel a government in full decline, a government of the philosophers—the most disastrous of all governments because it severed thought from the military and productive arts. It was a "coalition of government functionaries and swindlers" working on the ground of paganism while exploiting public credulity.[92] The virtuous practices of the Roman aristocrats who remained at once steadfastly Christian and culturally conservative showed them up for what they were.

On the other hand, the very fact that the Christians too acted in the realm of belief, according to Sorel, made their claims to virtue all the more dubious. For the church adopted more and more the conventions of Roman society and in doing so underwent a transformation in its moral structure.[93] In *La Ruine du monde antique*, Sorel discusses this problem and in doing so updates the sociology of virtue he outlined in *Le Procès de Socrate*. (Its republication in 1901 and the 1922 preface indicate Sorel's approval of the work despite qualifications.)

Military heroism had already been in decline in Rome, and Christianity did little to strengthen it. According to Sorel, once it was established, the church replaced military virtue with a mentality that was "hostile to the ancient concept of the heroic city."[94] By communing directly with the Deity, Christianity by-passed human respectability. The opinion of God was infinitely preferable to the esteem of fellow citizens. As long as the persecutions against the church continued, the church, in order to survive, had to conceive of itself as an army of saints battling against the prince of the world. "The Christians despaired when one of them faltered" and each member encouraged every other in "an unbreakable solidarity" to continue the battle.[95] This soon gave way to the notion that the opinion of one's fellows counted for little. Once the Eucharistic cult had replaced the social dimension of religion, the doctrine that "the Christian soldier should be humble" in the face of the Almighty surpassed pride in face-to-face relationships with fellow citizens.[96]

Sorel argues, then, that this affront to the pride of the Romans was the single most dangerous characteristic of Christianity. Respectability was important in antiquity, for "it was the principal means by which one gave men with whom one lived an advantageous idea of one's own character"[97] and personality. It was, in short, rather like a military uniform that identified the individual in his social role.[98] Christian mysticism had great contempt—to which the drama of the penance testified—for this respectability.[99] Moreover, emphasis on care of one's own spiritual interests led to quietism and a contempt for civic duties that helped to make Christianity responsible for the demise of the Roman empire. The military uniform that symbolized the most admired social role in antiquity was no longer held in high esteem. Accompanying this decline in prestige, the fighting virtues of the ancient soldier-warrior, which had been responsible for maintaining the freedom of the ancient city-state, were also weakened. "If," says Sorel, "the military spirit is weakened under the aegis of the bourgeois spirit, the social idea is also enfeebled."[100] The ancient ideal was given its *coup de grâce* by St. Augustine, who argued that, as with all other civic obligations, citizens owed military service as a necessary evil, but that it had no intrinsic virtue.[101] At this point it was the more militaristic barbarians who became "the true Romans."[102]

The second aspect of Sorelian morality is the Proudhon-like linkage between the will to resistance or the warlike virtues, on the one hand, and the steadfast virtues of an honorable family life, on the other. Clarifying his 1889 discussion on the vagaries of Hebrew, Sorel maintains that the same language that produces love poetry is

> very suitable for expressing the sentiments of absolute rebellion. If to the questions that constitute an infinity of nuances, the only solutions to which are replete with contradictions, modern men apply the archaic perspectives of the Hebrew prophets and, like them, divide everything into good and evil, they are led to call for the destruction of the established order with a savage enthusiasm. The Bible is thus highly suited to times of disruption and it provides, with unique forcefulness, texts which give hope for a catastrophic revolution.[103]

This is why the men of the Reformation saw in the Old Testament a prophetic expression of their passions, and, like amorous souls, knew only hatred or abandon. Eroticism and rebellion both divide the soul into armed camps.

The linkage of rebellion and eroticism also means that the preservation of Hebraic culture reinforced rather than weakened Jewish family life. As Sorel expresses it, "The difficulties that pharisaism created for entering into convenient relations with pagans produced excellent results, for they impeded extensive participation in the pleasures of Greek youth."[104] Sorel thinks that the relative sexual purity of Hebraic culture, which enclosed the Jew in the circle of his family, had as its direct consequence "the perpetuation in Israel of a type of [morals] that the Greeks and Romans admired in their own ancestors but which they no longer practiced." As war preserves the family, so the family preserves the old cultural heritage. "We cannot maintain, therefore," says Sorel, "that the precautions taken by the fanatics were lost to morality."[105]

The link between amorousness and rebellion means that the amorous soul need not be corrupt. Here, Sorel differs markedly from Renan, who had said that Talmudism was dangerous for a morality which "suffered slightly" from so many attacks projected on nature. While a morality is judged by its perspective on sexual relations, according to Renan, "the Talmud speaks too often of lewd things and assumes a rather vivid imagination in its readers. From the third to the fourth centuries, Jewish morality, and that of patriarchs and doctors above all, is presented as entirely permissive."[106]

Sorel concedes some truth to these accusations, but merely asserts that such claims are exaggerated (and hence distorted).[107] He admits that eroticism does recur in Jewish writings: if imprecise language can give rise to lyricism and poetic fancy, it can as easily include love as exclude it. But Sorel insists that this eroticism is not enough to corrupt Jewish life. Indeed, as noted above, in *Le Procès de Socrate* he insists that a healthy eroticism is necessary for a stable family life,[108] as is readily seen if the influence of Christianity on family life is compared to that of Judaism. If, to Sorel, a good society requires a healthy family life based on normal erotic instincts, Christianity, like Socratic philosophy before it, suppresses these instincts. Christianity's mystical contempt for the physical side of marriage deviated from normal sexuality and hence undermined the strength of the family. Sorel argues that Christian theology distinguishes the love of the divine presence of Jesus from human love: mysticism becomes a sort of catch-all category, in which all erotic expression, heterosexual or otherwise, is sublimated. Sorel reasons that "the faithful soul ended up by developing in his heart an extraordinary degree of love for Jesus, whom he conceived as being similar to him and of having a quality of humanity identical to his own." According to Sorel, this constituted a great discovery of Christianity, that is, of utilizing the factor of eroticism and redirecting it toward mysticism.[109] Love directed toward a divine figure debases the physical side of marriage. In this case Christ becomes the object of love, and as with the process of love, the faithful one consents to deprive himself, suffer, and favor the poor whom he loves; hence this love "is obviously masochistic."[110] As was true of Socrates' view of love, mystical insight into the Deity and the subsequent "purification" that occurs in human sexual relations mean that in practice "this intervention of the church in the most intimate of life's matters" has given an "entirely utilitarian meaning to love and has helped to debase the idea of marriage and the dignity of womankind."[111] Sorel's point here is that this kind of mysticism may succeed with a few monks, but it is obviously bound either to fail or to be perverted among the multitude, who are not subject to the same constant supervision as the mendicant orders.

The final aspect of Sorelian morality is his praise of the life of labor and the corollary teaching that intellectualism is subversive to this productive life. It is not necessary to view the Jewish tradition as a theoretical one; it is, rather, a highly materialistic religion. "The just will be rewarded by long life, prosperity in business, and the joys of family life; there is no ethic more useful," says Sorel. "This is the only moral principle worth the name since the dissolution of the old military Greek republics."[112] It is not the morality of literary men isolated from productive life (who are therefore decadent, according to Sorel); it is the ethic of the poor. Religious and ethical revivals do not spring from a work of reflection, subtle exegesis, or refinement of Greek intellectualism. "From the very beginning there must have been something passionate and mythological in it; that is why the Jewish apocalypses are of such great historic interest."[113] That is also why the Bible, according to Sorel, is written not for literary men but for workers: "It is a book of peasant democracy."[114] The Jews loved work more than any other people.

At first, Christianity cooperated with the empire in attenuating luxury and reviving the dignity of labor. But, for Sorel, the New Testament—especially the Four Gospels—is written for the mendicant orders. Unlike the Old Testament, the Gospels represent a utopia of consumption without labor. Sorel cites Matthew 6 in support of this notion: "Take no thought for your life, what ye shall eat, or what ye shall drink. . . . Behold the fowls of the air: for they sow not, neither do they reap or gather into barns; yet your heavenly Father feedeth them. . . . Therefore do not disturb yourselves with the question 'What shall we eat? What shall we drink?' or 'Wherewithal shall we be clothed?' For after all these things do the Gentiles seek."[115] Once one dreams of consuming without producing, as Sorel finds in this passage, "the principle of oligarchy is posed."[116] As was the case with Socratism, Christianity was based on the rule of an elect of rhetoricians and monks who could let God do their bidding—it was an ideology rooted primarily in the synoptic Gospels and bolstered by later Augustinianism.

Although certain Christian ascetics, notably St. Jerome and St. John Chrysostom, campaigned vigorously against luxury, the very excesses of this campaign undermined the positive aspects of property. The Romans were held to their land by the heavy civic obligations of the Roman seigneurs. These obligations were removed by Christianity, according to Sorel. As with sexual relations, the relations of property became a necessary evil. But as with eroticism, the lifting of restrictions on property allowed any aberration, including, in the case of property, unrestricted personal use. The Christian dogma that property was bad except in the service of God had the actual effect of debunking any positive civic value of property, and thus released it from civic restraints. The result was that the church's "rejection" of property in effect bolstered the worst Roman practices of exploitation, including glorification of the life of the parasitic consumer.[117] Perpetuation of exploitation meant that there was very little in the early church (aside from the earliest spirit of resistance) that Sorel was willing to call socialist.

It is Sorel's view that later Christianity and Christian discourse became dominated by theology and philosophy instead of by myth and were thus comparable to certain nineteenth-century utopian socialisms. The Jewish prophets aid an understanding of the heroic nature of early Judeo-Christian morals; canonical Christianity did not greatly change the corrupt morals of Roman society. Rather, it continued the decline of Roman morals by producing its own "ideological dissociation": "the attempt of philosophers to justify [things] by metaphysical reasons without accounting for the economic and historical infrastructure."[118] The old Roman schools of rhetoric were propagated for the use of the church. The church's end was to "form men of talent, capable of arguing in subtle ways against metaphysical errors; it could do no better than to follow the example of the Romans, who excelled in this genre."[119] In contrast to its mythical origins, the church in its maturity "posed as a rational juridical being" and contained resources that assured social services. In short, it took on more and more of the functions of the state. There was no other historical instance, argues Sorel, of such an "ideological somersault,"[120] in which ideas themselves were so important and ideological dissociation so complete as in the decline of Rome. It differed vastly from modern revolutions—especially from the French Revolution, in which material considerations were of such importance.

Because the church took on this abstract quality, its administration of social services, its assumption of many of the functions of the modern state, made its social practice comparable in ancient terms to the modern theories of Saint-Simonian positivism or planned societies. As a precedent for socialism, then, modern Christianity does not fit the needs of direct action which Sorel was later to spell out in his *Reflections on Violence*. The church is run on metaphysical abstractions, not according to the needs of men.

V

Sorel's writings on religion indicate a departure from the Marxian theory of ideology by preserving certain areas of human thought as immune from Marxist historical unmasking. Marx's assertion that "I hate all gods" stands in rigid contrast to Sorel's criticism of Renan for dealing lightly with sacred things. In the whole Sorelian critique, there is barely a hint of the Feuerbachian notion that Christianity is merely a kind of covert anthropomorphism.[121] Sorel takes religion much more seriously than orthodox Marxists did, but not because he was a believer; he insists that certain ideas are not only important but that they can be dealt with historically precisely because of their "imperviousness." Here Sorel foreshadows his depiction of the myth of the general strike which, because of its very mystery, vagueness, and basis in human impulse is outside of rational thought, is immune to all criticism. It is this imperviousness which makes it powerful and hence an historical force to contend with. Therefore Sorel does not deny the historicity of myths; they evolve from material and productive life. But these myths are, by virtue of their non-rational character, very much less likely to "come apart under fire," as it were. The very rationalist nature of liberal Christianity and the rationalist elements of socialism give them a vulnerability to Marxist unmasking that fervent religiosity and other myths lack. That is why Sorel can write a Marxist ideological analysis of "the illusions of progress" in which the historical roots of the concept of progress are set out with the express purpose of destroying that concept, while concurrently he can maintain that the myth of the general strike is secure from all refutation.[122] Because myths are historically rooted but irrefutable by history, Sorel can argue that myths are time-bound.

Certain parallels can be drawn between socialism and the thought of previous ages, but these are still limited in application. "Socialism returns to ancient thought; but the warrior of the city-state has become the worker in great industry; arms have been replaced by machines. Socialism is a philosophy of the producers; what can it learn from the Gospels, which are addressed to the mendicant orders?"[123] On the other hand, "Jewish thought," conserved by Christianity, gives an irresistible force to the movement that socialism conducts against modern society.[124] Sorel asks, "Why not return to the synagogue?" Today, he says, "Jewish thought has fallen into the public domain."[125] Socialism of the producers uses that portion of Jewish thought which is relevant and necessary to it and dispenses with the rest. Israel, argues Renan, has bequeathed to socialism "the protests of the poor, the call for justice, fraternity in brotherhood."[126]

Religion in general possesses elements which Sorel views as infused with the spirit of his own kind of syndicalist socialism. Sorel's own version of socialism is an ethic of self-sacrifice in which virtue and nobility surpass the call for justice and ease. It is a movement based on the finest impulses of man derived from ceaseless struggle, impulses that religion shares to some extent. Religious forces, when they are flourishing, provoke an enthusiasm which makes us understand the nobility of life and sacrifice based on love."[127] It is Sorel's view that the Christian church, despite its errors, possesses a genuine *faculté mystique* which "made an entirely new creation; it had discovered what Christianity called the Kingdom of God."[128] A genuinely new development occurred in Western civilization: the human spirit added to its domain. This domain may recede, as it has at the hands of both Catholic and Protestant liberal Christianity, but there is no foundation for Renan's prediction that it will be abolished or replaced by a new religion or that it will not enjoy a new flowering.

Unlike Marx, Sorel insists that religion in general and Christianity in particular are more than opiates, and that their interests and beliefs cannot always be reduced to a class or a sociological tendency. By its statist activity the church has invited a Marxist critique, and through its extreme laicization and politization (the founding of Catholic political parties and the like) it has invited scholars to analyze it by sociological reductionism. The church, according to Sorel, is more than that: "It is not merely an association, like so many societies created for a philanthropic, moral or educational end."[129] It is a community embodying the hopes and anticipations of the individuals composing it.

Despite their sharing of certain impulses, Sorel is wary of comparing socialism and Christianity. Though Sorel himself compared the myth of the general strike with the impulses of the early Christians, this was possible only "because the most noble aspects of socialism depend on activities of the free spirit." No form of socialism contemplates the afterlife, however; it will never give the "satisfaction to the spirit" that religion gives.[130] In comparing socialism to Christianity, certain abstract generalizations must be made about the quality of religious life that should not and cannot be made. To Sorel moral or *noumenal* experiences are at least as varied as scientific ones; indeed, the varieties of rationalism, whether in the form of socialism or liberal Christianity, appear to have more in common with one another than those experiences which remain inaccessible to our complete understanding. To compare socialism to religion is to trace its origins back to religious sentiments and to give it the same kind of continuity that obscured Christian origins when it was linked to Judaism by Renan. To Sorel, socialism in order to become a viable moral force must be as new and as fresh as Christianity was at its beginning. To him there is something insidiously ideological in the attempt to tie socialism to Christianity. It is done on behalf of certain "interests," just as the old biblical debates revolved around the propositions of dogmatic soothsayers.

The attempt to connect socialism and Christianity is either for the purpose of debunking socialism by attaching it to a "dying" religion, as Le Bon had done, or to bolstering a peculiar kind of state socialism in which state bureaucrats are seen as analogous to bishops. The latter was the goal of the Saint-Simonians; Sorel sees their version of socialism as having weaknesses similar to those of mature Christianity. This parallel, however, merely compares one religion at one stage of its development, manifested in a particular organizational form, with another kind of socialism subject to the same historical qualifications. There is nothing in the study of religion that entitles us to confuse religion with church or one sentiment with another; however, Sorel asserts, both religion and syndicalism possess myths. To uncover this common thread, Sorel must describe myth in a very broad and indiscriminate way. At one point he insists that myth is merely an ideology that has not been translated "into abstract forms."[131] The mythical component of religion depends on the latter's stage of development—its degree of rationalization—and the same is true of socialism.

Sorel's basic generalization, then, is that the vital stage of religious feeling, and of socialism, occurs when it is not made abstract, not intellectualized. The non-abstract, i.e., non-ideological qualities are the ones which infuse a movement with the qualities of the sublime; it is when these qualities are present that a movement achieves its greatest accomplishment, the transformation of morals.

In this way Sorel can praise the civil religion of the ancients and yet condemn the religions of the modern state as being debased by virtue of their official character. The former religions were quite different; they were thoroughly infused with mythic qualities, while the latter have accommodated themselves to the rationalism of the modern state. This does not forebode an ultimate decline in Christianity, however. As with sentiment in general and religion in particular, renewal is possible but can only be done under the right political and economic conditions.[132]

Notes

1. Sorel, "Le Modernisme dans la religion et dans le socialisme," pp. 179-81.

2. Sorel, "Léon XIII," p. 378; "A propos de l'anticlericalisme," *Etudes Socialistes* (1903): 241.

3. Sorel, "Léon XIII," p. 378.

4. Sorel, *Matériaux*, p. 311.

5. *FGS*, p. 200.

6. Sorel, *Essai sur l'église et l'état*, (Paris: Jacques, 1905), pp. 35-39.

7. Ibid., pp. 43-47.

8. Sorel, "Sur la magie moderne," p. 5.

9. Sorel, "La Crise de la pensée catholique," *Revue de Métaphysique et de Morale* (Sept. 1902): 548.

10. These are the central questions of Schweitzer's *Von Reimarus zu Werde*, which is still the definitive study of these questions, although it was published in 1906, a year after Sorel's book on Ernest Renan. See the translation by W. Montgomery, under the title *The Quest for the Historical Jesus* (New York: Macmillan, 1968). It is to this edition's excellent introduction by James M. Robinson that I am indebted for this paragraph and the one following.

11. Ibid., pp. 68-95, 137-60.

12. "If love of a subject can serve to give knowledge of it, I hope it will be recognized that I am not without this love. In order to write the history of a religion, it is necessary above all to have believed in it (for without this we will not understand how it has charmed and satisfied the human conscience)": Renan, *La Vie de Jésus* (59th ed., Paris: Calmann-Lévy, n.d.), p. civ, quoted in Sorel's *Le Système historique de Renan*, p. 51.

13. Sorel, *Réflexions*, p. 347 (American edition, p. 225).

14. Sorel, *Contribution*, p. viii.

15. Ibid., p. 261.

16. Ibid., p. 2.

17. Ibid., p. vii.

18. Ibid., p. viii.

19. Ibid., p. 93.

20. Ibid.

21. Ibid., p. 86.

22. Ibid., p. 92.

23. Sorel, *Reflections*, pp. 122-23, 144.

24. Sorel, *Contribution*, p. 149.

25. Ibid., p. 149.

26. Ibid., pp. 223, 226.

27. Sorel, *Le Système historique de Renan*, p. 204.

28. Sorel, *Contribution*, p. 148.

29. Ibid., p. 270; Sorel, *Le Système historique de Renan*, p. 453.

30. Sorel, *Contribution*, pp. 221, 198.

31. Ibid., p. 223.

32. Luke 8:48.

33. Sorel, *Contribution*, p. 244.

34. Cf. Sorel, *Le Système historique de Renan*, pp. 339, 449.

35. Sorel, *Contribution*, p. 279.

36. Ibid., p. 245; cf. p. 219.

37. Ibid., p. 270.

38. Ibid., p. 262, citing John 5:46-47.

39. Ibid., p. 278.

40. Ibid., p. 283.

41. For example, Raymond E. Brown, *The Gospel according to John* (Garden City: Doubleday, 1966), vol. 1, notes that older commentators "stressed Johannine borrowings from the schools of Greek philosophical thought" (p. lvii). Brown says that inevitably there were Hellenistic influences on Johannine thought. Furthermore, John contains fewer Old Testament citations than the other Gospels. On the other hand, "a large number of scholars are coming to agree that the principal background of Johannine thought was the Palestinian Judaism of Jesus' time" (p. lix). Sorel's view on the antiquity of the Fourth Gospel seems more eccentric today than it did in his time.

42. Sorel, *Contribution*, p. 269.

43. See Sorel, "Etude sur Vico."

44. D. G. Charlton, *French Positivist Thought in the Nineteenth Century* (Oxford: Clarendon, 1959), pp. 100-101.

45. Sorel, *Le Système historique de Renan*, p. 35, citing the first edition of Renan, *Vie de Jésus*, pp. 504-5. Sorel notes that this hypothesis disappeared from later editions, to be replaced by the speculation that Lazarus's family "fell into some excess of zeal" (Renan, *Vie de Jésus*, p. 374).

46. Sorel, *Le Système historique de Renan*, p. 12.

47. Ibid., p. 14.

48. Ibid., p. 9.

49. Ibid., p. 20.

50. Ibid.

51. Ibid., p. 14.

52. Ibid., p. 37.

53. Ibid., p. 32, citing Renan's *Souvenirs*.

54. Sorel, *Le Système historique de Renan*, p. 459.

55. Sorel, "La Crise de la pensée catholique."

56. Sorel, *Le Système historique de Renan*, p. 37. This view is remarkably similar to the one published by Albert Schweitzer a year later. "From . . . lack of conscience, Renan has not been scrupulous where he ought to have been so. There is a kind of insincerity in the book from beginning to end. Renan professes to depict the Christ of the Fourth Gospel, though he does not believe in the authenticity of the miracles of that Gospel. He professes to write a scientific work, and is always thinking of the great public and how to interest it. He has thus fused together two works of disparate character. The historian finds it hard to forgive him for not going more deeply into the problem of the development in the thought of Jesus, with which he was brought face to face by the emphasis which he laid on eschatology, and for offering in place of a solution the highly-colored phrases of the novelist": *The Quest for the Historical Jesus*, p. 191. Sorel, of course, saw no "solution."

57. Sorel, *Le Système historique de Renan*, pp. 5, 56. Cf Richard Vernon, *Commitment and Change: Georges Sorel and the Idea of Revolution* (Toronto: University of Toronto Press, 1978).

58. Sorel, review, *Le Miracle et la critique historique*, in *Revue Générale de Bibliographie* (April 1907): 148.

59. Cf. Sorel, *Contribution*, p. 262, citing John 5:46-47; *Le Système historique de Renan*, p. 375, citing John 14:3.

60. Sorel, *Le Système historique de Renan*, p. 211.
61. Ibid., p. 216.
62. Ibid.
63. Ibid., p. 217.
64. Ibid., p. 366.
65. Ibid., pp. 419, 423.
66. Ibid., p. 312.
67. Ibid., p. 315.
68. Ibid., p. 321.
69. Ibid., p. 378, citing Matthew 24:11, 13, 22; Mark 13:20.
70. Ibid., p. 378, citing I Peter 4:18.
71. Ibid., p. 188.
72. Sorel, *Reflections*, p. 185n.
73. Ibid., p. 183.
74. Ibid., p. 184.
75. Sorel, *Le Système historique de Renan*, p. 336 (Sorel's italics).
76. Sorel, *Reflections*, p. 185.
77. Sorel, *La Ruine du monde antique* (2nd ed., Paris: Rivière, 1925), pp. 14-15. This quote is from a preface written just before Sorel's death in 1922. Many long notes were added to the original 1894 work published in *Ere Nouvelle* for the first book edition of 1901. Dates of composition for each reference to *La Ruine* will appear in parentheses following the page number. I estimate that anything written after 1900 is included in Sorel's "mature" writing on this question, although he refined his view of the social myth several years after 1900.
78. Sorel, *Matériaux*, p. 12.
79. Sorel, *Le Système historique de Renan*, p. 423.
80. Ibid., p. 424.
81. Ibid., p. 425.
82. Ibid., p. 456.
83. Ibid., p. 223.
84. Ibid., p. 423.
85. Sorel, *Reflections*, p. 126 and note. Sorel refers to the early Christian beliefs as myths which quite naturally evolve into this piety.
86. Sorel, *Le Système historique de Renan*, p. 464.
87. Ibid., p. 464.
88. Sorel, *Reflections*, p. 184.
89. Ibid., p. 125n; *FGS*, p. 335n7. Sorel uses the latter example as evidence for the idea that the myth of the general strike will not interfere with practical concerns.
90. Sorel, *La Ruine*, p. 45 (1894).
91. Sorel, *Le Système historique de Renan*, p. 334.
92. Ibid., p. 332.
93. Thus, Sorel says that "Christianity did not greatly change the morals of Roman society": *La Ruine*, p. 57 (1894).
94. Sorel, *La Ruine*, p. 132 (1894), 251 (1901).
95. Sorel, *Le Système historique de Renan*, p. 336.
96. Sorel, *La Ruine*, p. 136 (1894).
97. Ibid., p. 254 (1901).
98. Ibid., pp. 254 and 144 (1894).
99. Ibid., p. 255 (1901).
100. Ibid., p. 133 (1894).

101. Ibid., p. 135 (1894). Compare Rousseau's *Social Contract* IV.viii, and Nietzsche's *Genealogy of Morals* I.10.
102. Sorel, *La Ruine*, p. 133 (1894).
103. Sorel, *Le Système historique de Renan*, p. 206.
104. Ibid., p. 158.
105. Ibid.
106. Renan, *L'Eglise chrétienne*, p. 254, cited in Sorel, *Le Système hitorique de Renan*, p. 159.
107. Sorel, *Le Système historique de Renan*, p. 160.
108. Sorel, *Le Procès de Socrate*, pp. 87-88, 99, 236.
109. Sorel, *La Ruine*, p. 294 (1901); cf. p. 258 (1901).
110. Ibid., pp. 255-56 (1901).
111. Ibid., p. 230 (1901); cf. *Le Procès de Socrate*, p. 95.
112. Sorel, *Le Système historique de Renan*, pp. 157-58.
113. Ibid., p. 187.
114. Sorel, *La Ruine*, p. 307 (1901).
115. Verses 25-32.
116. Sorel, *Le Procès de Socrate*, p. 198.
117. Sorel, *Matériaux*, pp. 321-25; *La Ruine*, p. 102 (1894).
118. Sorel, *La Ruine*, p. 46 (1894).
119. Ibid., pp. 82-83 (1894).
120. Ibid., p. 312 (1894).
121. "La Religion d'aujourd'hui," *Revue de Métaphysique et de Morale* (May 1909): pp. 542, 548.
122. Compare *Reflections*, p. 50, with the *Illusions*, passim.
123. Sorel, *La Ruine*, p. 311 (1901).
124. Ibid., p. 289 (1901).
125. Ibid.
126. Ibid., pp. 288-89 (1901).
127. Ibid., p. 310 (1901).
128. Sorel, *Essai sur l'église et l'état*, p. 40.
129. Ibid., pp. 36-37.
130. Sorel, *Matériaux*, pp. 313-14.
131. Ibid., p. 337.
132. Sorel, *La Ruine*, p. 314 (1901).

VII

THE FRENCH IDEOLOGY

The Third Republic was in no small part welded together by a consensus that centered on the Saint-Simonian idea which enabled Marxists and moderate Republicans to agree on the desirability of a rational industrial organization of society. As George Lichtheim notes, Saint-Simon and Marx, as well as Proudhon, "had accustomed their followers to regard the historical process as the final guarantor of those 'utopian' aims which the Enlightenment had formulated in an abstract manner"[1] and incorporated into the French revolutionary tradition. As we have noted in Chapter 4, this revolutionary tradition made it all the easier for French Marxists to side with the "radical" state in attacking the old traditions and social authorities. On the other hand, insofar as the workers found themselves confronting the bourgeoisie, the first bearers of the Revolution, they were pushed toward a wholesale rejection of the Jacobin heritage on which the Republic was supposedly based.

The exclusion of the syndicates from the Republican consensus culminated in the year 1906, when the unions commenced a series of strikes in favor of the eight-hour workday. It was at this juncture, 1 May, that the minister of the interior, Georges Clemenceau, developed his theory of a plot between the unions and various reactionary agents. Clemenceau was calling the bluff of the syndicalists. If the latter desired to declare their independence from the old political heritage, he helped them do it, and followed up his plot theory with exceedingly repressive measures, including imprisonment and even assassination of certain strikers.

The *Mouvement Socialiste* responded immediately with a strong campaign against Clemenceau, against the political and social system which he represented, and against the progressive ideology of that system. Spearheading the attack on the ideology of the Republic,

Sorel brought together many of his ideas on the Marxist theory of ideology in what is perhaps his most interesting book: *The Illusions of Progress*.

We have seen that Sorel spent the years from 1895 to the turn of the century primarily in criticizing Marx. From 1902 until about 1907, Sorel turned to examining in a more precise way the relationships between the economic "substructure"—the economic base that Sorel, despite his criticisms of Marx, still thought highly important—and moral and ideological activities. Sorel had criticized Marx for his vagueness on the relationship between thought and production, between material and psychological forces, between the superstructure of law, religion, art, and all the other expressions of what, for Sorel, were the ethical strivings of humanity, on the one hand, and the productive forces on the other. In Sorel's view, these relationships between thought and production could not be explained satisfactorily by Marx's term "reflection." This term, he says, "does not have a very precise meaning for [Marx] at all, since he applies it also to religion, and we know that for him religion was principally mystical nebulousness."[2] Obviously, the nature and variations of "reflected" mental phenomena are so vast that no precise scientific formula relating them to an economic base is possible. More importantly for Sorel, morality itself has only "an ephemeral existence" under Marxian formulas and it is therefore "impossible to determine what the ethical principles were for Marx."[3]

Sorel, like Marx, argues that ideas do not arise *in vacuo* but only in the flux of material life. An ideology to Marx is not simply a political idea but a rationalization, "reflection," or justification for a particular social group whose truth content is distorted by its social origin, its historical development, or its interested bias. Only the idea that accurately depicts historical reality is, in Marx's view, properly "scientific" and hence immune from being labeled an "ideology," an idol of the mind, a "phantom"—in a word, "false consciousness." The material bases for the existence of an ideology are perfectly understandable, given a proper understanding of material reality, but the ideology itself is an inaccurate depiction of the reality from which it has emerged. Thus, to use Marx's most noteworthy example, German idealism is an ideological reflection of its milieu; that is, there are material—hence scientific—bases for its existence. To Marx, however, it is still a false depiction of reality, and its true historic roots must be revealed to all; it was sufficient for a clear consciousness of the real ("scientific") bases of class relations to unmask the ideologies hiding them. Once social relations have been freed of mystical nebulousness, the proletariat will acquire a clear understanding of its own objectives. Placing an idea in historical context exposes the false elements of the idea, and class consciousness is thereby sharpened. Thus, the concept of ideology implies a tie to what we might call the ideological method, a sort of catharsis in which the very process of unmasking the "real" or material basis of an idea produces not only theoretical truth but the desired action to put the truth into effect. Sorel was eager to use the Marxian method of unmasking, though, as we shall see later, he was skeptical of the assumption of certain Marxists that it would produce automatic action.

In *The Illusions of Progress* (1906), Sorel deals with two interrelated concepts, the concept of ideology and the concept of history.[4] In undertaking to expose the social roots of the most important theory of history, i.e., the idea of progress, Sorel risks unmasking all historical thinking, including historical thinking about ideas themselves. Marx's theory of ideology, as well as his theory of history, may be convicted of being itself an ideology. Even Sorel's own attempt to replace the natural-law account of morals with an historical one was in danger. How could Sorel attack the Enlightenment view of progress while preserving the integrity of his own moral historiography? How could he debunk the ideology of progress, when he had so often referred to "progress" in moral, juridical, and productive relations? Labriola had criticized Sorel's concerns as neo-Kantian. In attacking the progressive edifice of the Enlightenment, Sorel could avoid constructing an updated categorical imperative; he was still enough of a Marxist to want to explain morals historically. But because he was a moralist, he had to go beyond debunking; he had to undertake a reapplication of his studies of ancient society, applying them in full force to the seventeenth- and eighteenth-century society that had produced the idea of progress.

This reconstruction entailed yet a further difficulty for Sorel. To what extent was his own moral system subject to the method of ideological unmasking that he, following Marx, used in uncovering the "illusions of progress"? Sorel knows only too well that the concept of ideology is a bottomless pit: a universal unmasking process can result in the complete degradation of all theories. But he had departed from Marx in two ways. As we have seen in the previous chapter, he had rendered certain ideas immune from debunking, but he also surpassed Marx by bringing science and the scientific method under the scrutiny of the ideological method, arguing that many scientific theories are not only historically situated but inspired by political phenomena. In Marx, the concept of ideology is opposed to that of science. In connecting the two concepts Sorel is suggesting that the Marxian edifice, taken as a whole, is ideological; that is, it is in the Marxian sense false consciousness. Since the concept of ideology owes its origin to the idea that all thoughts are historical data which can be partly "explained" by placing them in a social context, not only must Sorel be careful not to take abstract science as axiomatic, but the concept of ideology itself must be viewed as tentative. Marxism and science must not only be viewed diremptively, but the analytical tools Sorel employs in the diremptting process (in this case, ideological exposé of the idea of progress) must possess limits. The effect is paradoxical. Sorel started by outdoing Marx in his analysis of science; now he does not dare to follow Marx's *German Ideology*; instead he makes certain moral phenomena into convenient and implicitly pragmatic hypotheses by placing them outside the category of false consciousness through the method of a symbolic diremption from social science.

I

The problem of the interrelatedness of ideas and history is of course found in many philosophies of history. In his early "Study of Vico" Sorel had discussed ideas and their relation to history and had concluded that most philosophies of history possess a built-in paradox: by abstracting history into a perceivable pattern, these philosophies impart a direction and personality to history which transforms history into an ideal force.[5] This ideal force is at least one step removed from the way men actually behave, from actual history. The more ideal history becomes, the more ahistorical it becomes. It is, ironically, at its most ahistorical, its most ideological, when it takes the form of the most all-encompassing philosophy of history, the philosophy of progress.

In order to bring this idea out more clearly, we should first turn to Vico's philosophy of history, which, in Sorel's view, represents a halfway point between a completely ideal (hence pseudo-) history and an utterly realistic portrayal of historical data. In Vico we find that it is active men, in the complexity of their psychological states, who make history. This notion, with Hegel's historical Idea, inspired Marx's conception of ideology: that ideational states or sentiments are connected to certain types of social order. Vico rejected natural law and postulated the validity of knowledge as a conscious product of our own creation.

Sorel departs from Vico and, by extension, from Marx as well by distinguishing (at least for analytical purposes) the philosophy of history from the psychological sentiments motivating history. In his criticism of Vico, Sorel argues that the great Neapolitan failed adequately to come to grips with this distinction because he implied a coterminous relationship between psychology and society in a scheme of history which is itself predictable. Vico looks upon historical development as an organic growth in which thought and activity are brought together in an indissoluble whole, the development of which is, ultimately, guided by the will of God.[6] This view has much in common with primitive science and philosophy: it treats phenomena *en bloc*.

Vico imagines a pattern in history resembling the patterns one finds in philosophers and historians of classical antiquity such as Polybius and Livy—a pattern, in Sorel's view, "nourished by the study of Plato."[7] Plato and Polybius traced the succession and development of the various forms of government in an ordered way: monarchy, aristocracy, oligarchy, democracy, tyranny. In the *Republic* Plato correlated psychological and moral states with each successive regime: aristocracy was geared to bravery, oligarchy to acquisitiveness, democracy to a love for freedom. In Sorel's view, Vico undertook a similar enterprise: for example, Vico states that "citizens of a democracy no longer consider anything but their particular interests."[8] Vico attempts to order not only the regimes but the psychological states: "First men pay attention to necessity, then to utility, then to the search for commodities, next to pleasure and luxury," etc., according to the predetermined (and implicitly predictable) order of development of political forms.[9]

Sorel argues that if we could predict the direction of the development of peoples, we would repeat a fault of old-fashioned science: we would do as Vico did who "took as his base historically and empirically observed facts and attempted to account for their causes."[10] Just as modern science has suppressed finalism in nature, "in history we must no longer ask ourselves how order exists despite bad tendencies, since order exists only in our imagination." Science, Sorel adds, "is content with the sequence of things without feeling the need for anything to add to it, just as we cannot replace real historical movement by whatever law of development exists in the mind of the philosopher."[11] Not only does Vico, in Sorel's view, create confusion between stages of historical development and the moral sentiments which are presumed to predominate in them, but he infers a causal relationship between the two. In Sorel's opinion, such an inference develops into the circular argument that stages of moral development explain the system of morals, or at least explain the process that engenders the result.[12]

The real problem with this idealization of history is that it becomes ideological in the narrowest sense of the word: it is easily manipulated to justify the superiority of a certain regime and thus to legitimate that regime. According to Sorel, "Almost all creators of systems take their epoch as the one in which humanity has attained its progress or their own philosophic school as the ultimate expression of human thought."[13] Sorel notes that Vico, with Plato and Polybius, believed that certain periods of history embody political perfection. Polybius (and later Machiavelli) claimed that the Golden Age was that of the Roman republic; and Vico maintained just as arbitrarily that monarchy rather than republicanism was "the government which most conforms to human nature, to the periods in which reason is most highly developed."[14]

The union of "nature" and necessity in the theory of history provided the most powerful basis for its legitimizing function: Polybius's belief in the succession of various political forms led him to believe also that one could "trace their origins, development, and maturity according to a law of nature."[15] Like any natural phenomenon, old-fashioned science posited a necessity for these natural occurrences. According to Sorel, this historical concept reached its high point in Hegel, who argued for the superiority of the Prussian monarchy as the culmination of the historical Idea.[16]

Now, according to Sorel, Polybius and Vico (as well as Plato) never quite achieved the holistic or "oceanic" view of historical progress, wherein all phenomena become enmeshed to advance to higher and higher planes of achievement. Prior to the advent of the idea of progress, most theories of history, while idealizing it, permitted a critical tension whereby a regime could "step outside" the general trend of necessity. This tension is explained by the fact that ancient theories were almost entirely predicated on the assumption of ultimate decline and decay. Thus for Polybius, the superiority of the Roman constitution lies in its being placed, to a degree, outside history: for a time it was able to "cheat" the laws of historical decay.[17] Rome is deemed great both because it conformed to the natural cycle of rise and fall of civilizations and because through judicious statecraft it was able to combine a number of historical tendencies in a single "mixed constitution" and thus, for a while, defy the entropic tendency in history.

More importantly, Plato—to whom, according to Sorel, Polybius and Vico owe so much—"took pleasure in pointing out the improbability of his own utopia." The *Republic*, Sorel later asserted, was meant "to illustrate, through a particularly convenient form, [Plato's] ideas about good conduct, education, and the psychologies corresponding to various political regimes."[18] Most of the old utopias were not "historical" products at all. The etymology of the word *utopia* (noplace) underscores the character of the *Republic*, whose decline into known forms of government begins when history commences; the discussion of history begins only after the Republic itself is corrupted. "Far from believing that the natural movement of societies would give rise to his ideal city, Plato teaches that this movement would inevitably end in the known political forms of oligarchy, democracy, and tyranny, if it were abandoned to the play of temperaments as seen in the material world."[19]

In the ancient world, history contained traps: disaster and tragedy lay beyond triumph. Despite their faults, the old theories of historical entropy imply a struggle between what might be called the "natural nature" of historical entropy and "artificial nature," in which energy and virtue "force" history in a direction different from its natural bent. There is no doubt that the superior regimes would eventually succumb. Sorel notes that even Polybius "considered the Roman constitution as having lost, in Polybius's own time, its old force and, despite its perfection and complexity, as having to be brought into the cyclical movement" of constitutions.[20] But this tendency limits the usefulness of historical philosophy as a political ideology. Historical thought was normally pessimistic, and history lacked the quality of beneficence, of bounty, that theories of political legitimacy possess—the theory that a regime is lawful because it produces good. Beneficence could not be attributed to history until history became an independent object of study rather than a method of studying events, and this independent quality was given a remarkable boost when the cyclical theory of history was replaced by the ideology of progress. At this point history came to possess a quality of infinite beneficence, and it dominated political discourse to an extent undreamed-of by the ancients.

The underlying political premise of Sorel's discussion of history is that if a government and a society are viewed as historical products, and if historical development is benign—as the ideology of progress suggests—then the regime that is the product of historical development shares the beneficence of the progressive force that moves it. According to Sorel, as long as history remains cyclical there is a complicated clash of motives and events, implying a plurality in human affairs. The implicit tension between what is and what ought to be exists in what history is and what it is not, that is, between the best regime of the old utopias, and the best possible regime, the accommodation of ideals to the dreary realities of history.

When in the seventeenth and eighteenth centuries the idea of history became linear, coupled with a concept of indefinite improvement in all fields, pessimism was replaced by the belief that a series of minor setbacks on the path to perfection could be set right after some refinements in our way of thought. Under this new view, tragedy could be explained away as a reasonable and necessary part of the greater plan for historical fulfillment. Fate, which had an aura of mystery, was replaced by a "history" in which everything is either explained or explicable.[21]

In a world in which tragedy becomes rational and everything can be explained, truth, in Sorel's view, assumes a broad unitary character. If everything is an historical development, truth becomes part of a broad continuum; the difference between what is and what ought to be is obscured by placing everything on the same line extending between past and future. If perfection is possible in this world, events can attain the unity heretofore characteristic only of utopias which, like Plato's, were explicitly ahistorical. Marx brought Plato's heavenly city down to earth.

> Marx must have established more than once a connection between the warriors of Plato's *Republic* and the workers of large industry whom socialism is organizing. . . . He evidently believed that modern workers, dispossessed of property, deprived of a family establishment, and reduced to a salary that forbids any accumulation of money which would permit joining the ranks of the employers, are as well prepared for communism as the Platonic guardians to whom the philosopher denied the right of having lands, a family, and any monetary resources. But if we abandon these abstract analogies and face reality, we perceive that the nature of Plato's book discourages those who, on the faith of Marx and Engels, believe that history is in the process of preparing for communism.[22]

In the *Illusions* and in later essays, Sorel places Marx in a category with other nineteenth-century utopians who started with history and ended by denying it, and who, claiming to start with the material to explain the ideal, ended in an ideological never-never-land:

> The *Idea* that, according to Hegel, carries man toward reason will indeed, according to Marx, achieve its beneficent work in imposing the unity required by rationalism, where only plurality—the detestable fruit of chance, immoderate desires, and general ignorance—reigned before. Marx understood that this passage from heterogeneity to homogeneity is not the same type of movement as that produced by a mechanism of antagonistic forces similar to those which he had recommended considering for a full understanding of the past. Transformations will result henceforth from ideological causes. The materialist

> theory of history is applicable only for the time which Marx called "prehistoric."[23]

This transformation in Marx, which Sorel presents here in far more pronounced terms than he did in the late 1890s, is due, according to Sorel, to the heritage of the idea of progress.

The ultimate pessimism of the ancients did not mean, in Sorel's interpretation, that no improvement was then anticipated or attempted in human affairs: his attack on Socrates is rooted in the contrary assumption. What Sorel does argue is that the idea of progress transformed the anticipation of piecemeal improvement into a "science of the world" which was far more total and complete than anything anticipated by the Socratics,[24] a doctrine in which all aspects of human endeavor are grouped together to advance, in Condorcet's terms, to "infinite perfectability."[25] Thus Sorel commences the *Illusions of Progress* by noting that the progressive idea begins with the argument for artistic progress; that literature, along with morals, science, and statecraft, can eventually be subsumed into the giant science that so inspired pre-modern philosophies of unitary knowledge.

The ancient dualism between the ideal and the corporeal which was part of even the Platonic system was replaced by a more monistic construction, in which the complete historicization of all activity was assumed to go hand-in-hand with the accumulation of knowledge. The Enlightenment view that knowledge, once disseminated, would make truth and error almost impossible led Condorcet to argue that the Lockean philosophy of knowledge was valid in morals, politics, and economics, and insured "almost as sure a development in these sciences as we find in the natural sciences."[26]

Ironically, in Sorel's view, this historicization, based on a pseudo-history, was to assume a freedom and a manipulability that made it the most useful of all ideological guises. It was the ideology most easily linked to other eighteenth- and nineteenth-century ideologies, the one ideology that preferred to open new paths in social science and, more than coincidentally, led to new methods of domination. It was, to Sorel, part of the array of philosophic weaponry used by certain avant-garde segments of the seventeenth-century French ruling class.

There is little doubt, indeed, about the conventionally Marxist approach he appears to take in thus associating an ideology with the powerful class. Sorel commences his book by asking Marx's question:

> Does it require deep insight to understand that man's ideas, concrete observations, and abstract conceptions (*Vorstellungen,*

> *Anschaungen und Begriffe*), in a word, man's consciousness (*Bewustsein*), change (*sich andert*) with every change in the conditions of material existence, in his social relations, and in his life in society? What else does the history of ideas prove if not that intellectual activity changes as material activity changes? The ruling ideas of each age have ever been those of its ruling class.[27]

Sorel presents the concept of progress as arising not solely from brutish material forces or from any deep-rooted social instincts, but from the philosophical and literary world itself. There is an implicit parallel between the uses to which the idea of progress has been put and Sorel's early portrayal of the uses of Socratism in the hands of Athenian aristocratic clubs. In both cases, what originated in a netherworld of theory—the most ideological of all worlds—later came to be used for political purposes far from the intentions of the creators of the idea.

According to Sorel, the milieu in which the idea of progress first developed was the world of the "*gens du monde*," habitués of the salons. These *gens du monde* were, in Sorel's eyes, dissociated from their economic roots. Aristocrats who had abandoned their estates in favor of the livelier (and unproductive) court life, parasitic philosophical showmen, salon ladies, and literary clowns:[28] all came together to compose, in Sorel's eyes, an exquisite portrait of a society contemptuous of production and scornful of the old morals, a society devoted principally to novelty for its own sake, to literary adornments which appeared profound but demanded little discipline or work.

The milieu consisted very much in an alliance among aristocrats, literary men, and orators, which, again, was not entirely dissimilar to Sorel's portrait of ancient Athens. There was in the eighteenth century a continuation of the "old tradition that a court needed skillful orators who pleased people with brilliant conversation and who were capable of shedding luster on the prince who patronized them. . . . Every great household had a small court abundantly provided with its exceptional persons."[29] Sorel repeats Taine's description of the setting:

> Among the houses in which society people dine, there is not one that does not have its house philosopher. . . . Their paths can be followed from salon to salon, from chateau to chateau. . . . [It was] a kind of superior opera in which all great ideas capable of interesting a thinking person march in procession and collide, sometimes in serious costume, sometimes in comic disguise. . . . Every possible bold idea in the political or religious

> realm was brought forward and discussed pro and con. . . . How could one prevent the nobility, which spends its life talking, from seeking out men who talk so well?[30]

The idea of progress made its first appearance as "the quarrel between the ancients and moderns," an ideology of the literary men of the salons, taken up by their patrons as a justification for supporting these figures. Thus one of the most outstanding salon disputes was the one that began, in the lively era of the late seventeenth century, between the partisans of the ancients and those who insisted that, for example, the artistic works of the frequenters of the salons were superior to the relatively primitive products of a Raphael or a Leonardo. Sorel argues that the lions of the day—the great creators of the idea of the superiority of the moderns, Perrault and Fontenelle—could claim their contemporaries' (and their own) superiority over their predecessors because of the historical tendency of knowledge to accumulate over the ages. As Sorel implies in the opening pages of his work, the idea of the superiority of the moderns is little more than self-promotion on the part of some second-rate literary figures who used the somewhat dubious proposition that since the Renaissance had benefited from studying the men of the classical period, the men of the seventeenth century would benefit still more by studying the accumulated wisdom of the Renaissance. The assumption that the men of the Renaissance must have been superior to the ancients was extrapolated into a claim that the practitioners of modern literature have benefited by the general accumulation of knowledge based on experience.[31] What better justification could a literary man use in support of his credentials as harbinger of the highest expression of art, and as a qualification for being hired on as a court philosopher?

If the doctrine of the superiority of the moderns bolstered artists' and writers' self-esteem, to Sorel the moral consequence of the doctrine in respect to aristocratic patrons was even greater. The era in which the idea of the superiority of the moderns flourished was the beginning of a period of great merriment and jollity: "Fear of sin, respect for chastity and pessimism had all but disappeared." According to Sorel:

> Such a society could not abandon itself to happiness without justifying its conduct; it had to prove that it had a right not to follow the old maxims. For if a society was not able to give this proof, was it not liable to be compared to the son who is in such a hurry to enjoy the paternal inheritance that he devours resources for the future? Hence they were very happy to find able apologists who could solemnly establish that it was all right

> to amuse oneself without fear of the consequences: this was the origin of the doctrine of progress.[32]

Here was the driving force that transformed a literary doctrine into an all-encompassing historical one.

This transformation was assisted heavily by the concurrent introduction of Cartesian philosophy into the salons. Cartesianism gave the doctrine of progress its malleability by enabling its proponents to deal with all subjects. By introducing his famous rule of methodical doubt into philosophy, Descartes, according to Sorel, "was able to introduce aristocratic modes of thought into philosophy."[33] The rampant skepticism encouraged by this method, as well as Descartes's reduction of God to a mere trifle, gave a philosophical legitimation to the general passion for disputation, and confirmed the right of the men of the salons "to speak with an imperturbable assurance of things they have not studied."[34] Cartesianism paved the way for a "complete science of the world" that enabled the *gens du monde* to put forth opinions on everything without having any special instruction.[35] It was an "ornament of the mind, which, freed of prejudice, sure of itself, and confident of the future, made a philosophy assuring the good life to all those who possessed the means of living well."[36]

The extraordinary malleability of this idea of progress was due, in large part, to the Cartesian tendency to abstraction—to what Sorel called a contempt for the empirical side of things.[37] He notes that the more abstract a doctrine is, the more divorced it is from empirical reality and the easier it becomes to transform the doctrine out of all recognition. In the eighteenth century, according to Sorel, this predominance of the rootless idea found its quintessential expression in Rousseau's plea, in the beginning of his *Second Discourse*, to "put aside all the facts."[38] Such ideas as the social contract found a ready audience in the literary aristocracy, who took liberties with experience and who "were not far from admitting that in order to reason on the true principles of nature one must not linger too long over data furnished by observation."[39]

To be sure, Sorel sees the creator of an idea as being as free as an artist working with new materials. Ideas, once formed, establish links with other current ideas and thereby become part of the predominant doctrine of a given period. A later period will find in that doctrine certain meanings and interpretations which may well be quite different from the initial intention of the author.[40] Sorel is at pains to demonstrate not only the malleability of the concept of progress itself but how the concept, in establishing links with other ideologies of the period, was able to transmute the edifice of European philosophy from literary diversions, meant for a class of aristocratic fops, into powerful revolutionary instruments.

The idea of progress derived its special power and influence from two qualities: predictability and a matchless assurance; a claim to what Sorel calls "historical scientism," on the one hand, and an utter contempt for its own historical roots, on the other. Sorel argues that the idea of progress is a diremption, at times a tool of limited value in providing us with a symbolic understanding of the cumulative force in science and of certainty in social movements. This "symbol" of progress has been hypostacized into a conviction "that it is possible to ascertain scientifically the general drift of the things which most interest civilization."[41] Thus the *gens du monde* and their sociological successors "firmly believe that a good understanding of the totality of the past would allow . . . perceptions of future totalities."[42] Had the origins of this ideology been carefully preserved and remembered, such a hypostatization would have been unlikely. However, progress, according to Sorel, became a "rationalist symbol" which had been pushed "far enough along the path of antinomies" that it was easy to forget its historical roots.[43] Hence it became as axiomatic as the fundamental concepts of the sciences, of whose origins very few people are aware. Both historical scientists and science properly so-called "pass for ideals produced by our minds when they are excited by prolonged contact with experience. As philosophers are generally much more interested in the method used in the teaching of a doctrine than in the true essence of the doctrine, they have often believed that a system would merit an absolute confidence if it were capable of being presented as an imitation of ancient geometry."[44] If humanity were someday to become enlightened, it would submit itself to the leadership of master philosophers. "It could then replace the miserable world of history by a world which, adapting itself perfectly to the scholarly disciplines, could be regarded as elevated to the level of the mind."[45]

II

It was the equation of historical and scientific knowledge, an alliance between nature and history, which finally transformed the idea of progress from a moral to a political doctrine. "Fontenelle's contemporaries were impressed by seeing to what extent royal majesty was able to rise above mere chance in a seemingly definitive way."[46] Following Tocqueville's and Taine's views on the rise of centralized administrative monarchy in France, Sorel notes that the men of the late seventeenth and early eighteenth centuries were inclined "to relate all social movements to the impetus society received from central authority." By virtue of the regularity and constancy of the royal administration, they regarded royal institutions in general as being a sort of constant force that added some new improvement each day to those that were already acquired. These improvements seemed to follow in a clear-cut and necessary way. Since life had indeed become softer for the aristocracy and upper classes under Louis XIV, "could it not be assumed that the forces that had produced this improvement of life resulted from the new constitution of societies by a sequence of events as natural as those found in the physical world? If these forces continued to operate, could it not be assumed that the social world had an accelerated momentum similar to that of a falling weight obeying the laws of gravity?"[47]

The immense boost in prestige the centralized monarchy was to receive at the hands of the idea of progress meant that the ideology of sovereignty, the idea that it was preferable to have a single, all-powerful source of authority, became the adopted political theory of progress. Sovereignty was legitimized because it was progressive; progress was guaranteed because there was an immense, all-powerful, central power whose increasing successes ensured continued benefits from perpetual social experimentation. When the power of the monarchy was displaced by the republic, a hidden continuity lay beneath the surface of apparent social change, for when the doctrine of sovereignty was attached to the doctrine of progress, it assured that even the most cataclysmic change of modern times would and must end in the reestablishment of order and stability.

The concept of a single sovereign power was legitimized in English political thought by the concept of the social contract. When Locke's theory of contract was imported into France, according to Sorel, it was grafted onto Rousseau's doctrine of the general will, which was in turn misinterpreted by the general public into a justification for democratic absolutism. According to Sorel, Rousseau, by "putting aside all the facts," made of Locke's theory a "marvelously obscure masterpiece of literary exposition" which greatly appealed to the speculative tastes of the *gens du monde* and the aristocracy.[48] Rousseau's simplification of society encouraged a sweeping aside of outmoded traditions and historical remnants, while the state was regarded as a sort of hypothesis which serves to formulate principles:

> Like physics, society can also be simplified and can be found to contain atomistic clarity if national traditions and the genesis of law and the organization of production are disregarded in order to consider nothing but the people who come to the marketplace

> to exchange their products. . . . By so idealizing commercial law, social atoms are indeed obtained. In the eighteenth century men had such a high regard for commerce that they were very much inclined to think that natural law, thus arrived at by an abstraction of commercial law, must prevail over existing law, as the latter was full of traces of historical influences.[49]

These social atoms, according to Sorel's interpretation, are likened either to prudent merchants or to nomadic artisans selling their skills to the highest bidder: the citizens are cognizant of their own interests. Therefore, in Sorel's view, Rousseau thought he could assert that "if, when a sufficiently informed body of people deliberates, the citizens have had no communication among themselves, the general will will always result from the great number of little differences, and the deliberation will always be good."[50]

According to Sorel, Rousseau's view was highly ambiguous. He thought of the general will as analogous to prices in the market. Now, as long as the atomistic model prevailed, as long as citizens were likened to merchants or artisans who are close to the abstract model of man one finds in the contract theory, great limitations are placed on government. Sorel quotes Rousseau, who said that an artisan "is as free as a farm laborer is a slave: for the latter depends on his field, whose harvest is at the discretion of others. . . . Whenever someone tries to plague an artisan, his bags are soon packed; he takes his tools and moves on."[51] Sorel says that such an individual retains the complete liberty of action possessed by men who exchange their skills or their goods in the marketplace. If the general will established a state religion to which adherence would be compulsory (and Rousseau wanted such a religion), the banishment of men who refused to obey the religion "would hardly be a rigorous measure for nomadic artisans."[52]

On the other hand, the doctrine of the infallible general will allowed for a much more absolutist interpretation, a democratic despotism, in which the assembly possesses absolute power over the lives of the citizens based on the fundamental legitimizing principle of the general will, "the total alienation of each member together with all his rights to the community."[53] Sorel points out the intrinsic danger of such a concept of sovereignty:

> Whatever the power of the collective body is, it does not constitute sovereignty in the view of the citizen; that would almost be like saying that a machine in which 100,000 spindles are turning is the sovereignty of the 100,000 spinners which it represents.

> . . . Between power and the individual there is only law; all sovereignty is repugnant, it is the denial of justice, it is religion.[54]

This criticism is of course partly answered in Rousseau's own insistence that the general will is greatly enfeebled or obscured in a large country or one with representative (as opposed to direct) government. Although Sorel does not explicitly say this, he does regard Rousseau's system as having been greatly abused and subject to great misinterpretation. Thus, in Sorel's eyes, the vagueness of the doctrine meant that "when the circle of Rousseau's readers grew, the meaning of his doctrines changed; founded on the hypothesis of a society of self-governing artisans, they were taken literally by the people when the latter were called upon to play an important role in the formation of opinion."[55] Thus the people reproduced, in a democratic form, the absolutism that certain theorists of the *ancien régime* had created for the kings of France. "The heritage bequeathed by Rousseau to modern times consists in the idea of an omnipotent democratic state."[56] The idea of progress cemented this ideology of democracy to the state by means of a vision of ever-increasing power whose ability to reform and improve society was limitless. To Sorel, such a social and ideological system could only enable the boldest projects to assume an increasing aspect of reality. Anything could be tried if progress could assure a minimum of harmful consequences.

The ultimate paradox of the idea of progress, in Sorel's view, follows from this boldness. What started as the ultimate historical viewpoint has ended in an entirely future-oriented system of ideas whereby no lessons need be taken from the past. The *gens du monde*, the bourgeoisie and the aristocrats, freed from their feudal ties (and obligations), could easily call for the abolition of all existing laws and customs of France. To all of them, "France appeared to be much better prepared than any other country for a faultless application of political theory, for it had the most truly enlightened philosophers . . . who held forth in salons and were lionized by the ladies for their original or startling ideas. . . . To gain this reputation there is no need of legal, historical, or social knowledge."[57]

Sorel tries to show that the idea of progress embraces the various institutions of bourgeois society and enables those institutions to encompass and thereby to dominate all the disparate elements in society and forge them into an apparent unity. For Sorel, the progressive doctrine does not represent the natural order of things but is, rather, the basis of the ideology of the modern institutions of domination. The idea of progress has as its principal function the papering over of genuine differences, obscuring the sharp coloration between good and bad institutions, stifling the conflict which was necessary to bring new proletarian institutions into full emergence.

For Sorel, the idea of progress represented a kind of grand strategy of optimism which had several principal thrusts. The first of these tendencies is contained in the "progressive" principle of continuity. Sorel accepts Tocqueville's and Cournot's assertion that the French Revolution commenced long before 1789. In destroying most feudal institutions in order to aggrandize his own power, Louis XIV erected a huge centralized bureaucracy whose immense prestige, as we have noted, helped to foster the idea of progress. But, as Cournot points out: "Once the prestige of the monarchy had been destroyed, all the other truly governmental institutions were also dealt a mortal blow, and there remained only an administrative machine which could be used by the government. In trying to make the monarchy divine or to model it on more Asiatic than European examples [Louis XIV] made it a symbol that was exposed to the contempt of the people from the moment it ceased to be the object of genuine veneration."[58]

Sorel says (and most historians agree with him) that Louis XIV had permanently stamped French political culture with the traditions of what is today called *dirigisme*: the control of economic and political decisions by the central governmental bureaucracy. This administrative monarchy continues to this day, according to Sorel (and most authorities on French history would again agree). Once the monarchy had been deposed, only the administration, which could be used by any government, remained. This administrative continuity had as its chief ideological support the very notions of progress which had developed with it. Each time the state changed hands, the administration gained strength, and so did the ideology of progress. The *ancien régime*, bourgeois liberal democracy, and modern social democracy were all part of the growing strength of the national state. All the beliefs held by the old regime are retained by democracy, which is a "corrupted caricature of the *ancien régime.*"[59]

This continuity leads to a second aspect of domination: the elite of one era has survived and strengthened itself in another. Progress is the ideology of the "victors" of an epoch[60] —the dominant class that inherits power. Not only is the civil-service administration as important in the modern state as it was in the *ancien regime*,[61] but so are the *gens du monde* and aristocracy who try "to continue this exploitation of the producing masses by an oligarchy of intellectual and political professionals."[62] The clever conversation of the salons has now been incorporated into the official curriculum of écoles centrales, lycées, and the Sorbonne, which popularize knowledge "in such a way as to put young republicans in a position to hold an honorable place in a society based on the ideas of the *ancien régime* . . . to want democracy to model itself on the defunct aristocratic society . . . to place the new masters on the same social level as their predecessors."[63]

Sorel argues that modern liberal education is elitist: "Contemporary experience shows that vulgarization of knowledge does not make the people capable of choosing and supervising their so-called representatives, and it is hardly paradoxical to assert that the more we march with the wave of democracy, the less efficient this supervision will be."[64] Nothing, Sorel therefore asserts, "is more aristocratic than democracy."[65] In place of the aristocrats of the salons is the current press, along with contemporary politicians: in both, one finds satisfaction with superficial reasoning, a great show of noble sentiments, and an admiration for science.[66] In place of the royal functionaries, we have a modern civil service, and the politicians flatter the sensibilities of their constituents with a deftness that would have made the eighteenth-century man of letters chortle with approval. The main difference, according to Sorel, between the two periods is that in the stead of the king are the people: both proclaimed themselves sovereign, while in reality being totally dominated by those ostensibly their servants.

Associated with the ideas of continuity and elitism is Sorel's third idea, that the concept of progress is essentially a conservative force in society. Despite its revolutionary pretensions, there is an underlying conservatism in the notion that each change in society, legitimized by the idea of progress, implies an improvement. Such a view leads to the belief that this is the best of all possible worlds and if only we tinker about a little more, it will be better still. What else can be believed if any regime is legitimized by history as the product of progressive development? In Sorel's eyes, the idea of progress does not discourage change; it merely allows any change to satisfy our desire for more thoroughgoing transformation. Under such a view, any change that does occur serves only to strengthen existing forces. Change—even revolutionary change—becomes like scar tissue: the new skin becomes part of the old one, only stronger. Such institutionalized change discourages revolutionary activity, replacing it with a kind of social quietism in which the practitioners of revolution, like the social democrats, cross their arms and smile cynically to the refrain: *plus ça change, plus c'est la même chose.*

Sorel believes that such a perspective can only produce a geometric increase in the powers of centralized government insofar as it has assisted, embodied, or fostered this progressive change. The social democrats advocating state-run industries and a stable social order are the heirs of that royal bureaucrat and progressive ideologue Turgot, whose boldness was modified when he advised the king: "As long as your majesty does not stray from the path of justice, he may consider himself absolute legislator, and he may count on his good nation for the execution of his orders."[67]

It is not difficult to see why Sorel regarded the ideology of progress as a camouflage for allowing history to relax, for allowing men to abandon their vitality and to enjoy the benefits of accumulated human wisdom. In Sorel's view, the progressive idea is associated with the doctrines of both democracy and centralized government, and is hence indissolubly linked to decline—in a word, to historical entropy. Democracy, social democracy, centralism, and rationalism are all part of a unified tradition that has lulled Western society into somnolence, passivity, acquiescent optimism, and decay.

It is of course shocking for liberal democrats to read what is perhaps one of the most spirited attacks mounted since Rousseau's *Social Contract* against the idea of representative government. It is important to keep in mind that it is continental democracy with its associated *dirigisme* that Sorel is attacking, for in linking democracy with ever-increasing central government, demagogy, opportunism, and the rule of mass man he is of course the representative of a venerable tradition in political thought (going back to Plato) which sees democracy as akin to tyranny. We must be cautious in attributing to him those "fascist" sentiments by which modern democratic writers all too readily label those who do not agree with them. In criticizing democracy, Sorel is not thereby justifying authoritarian force; rather, he opposes democracy because in his view it is associated with centralism as against local liberties, with equality at any price, with force in place of law, with unity against plurality. Sorel adopts Proudhon's viewpoint: "So long as democracy does not rise to the true conception of power, it can only be, as it has only been until now, a lie. . . . The Revolution consecrated the word 'democracy' as a lodestar; for sixty-six years we have been making a scandal out of it. . . . As opposed to divine right, the Revolution poses the sovereignty of the people, the unity and indivisibility of the Republic; words devoid of meaning, suitable and useful only for masking the most horrible tyranny."[68]

III

Sorel's condemnation of democracy is concentrated on the Continental tradition of sovereign majoritarianism. However, he is aware of another tradition of Western thought whose origins lie within liberalism. This is the tradition of Montesquieu, Tocqueville, and Madison, whose purpose was to divide sovereignty rather than to concentrate it. (Sorel takes care to emphasize that Rousseau's thought can be interpreted as belonging to either one of these schools.) Sorel's respect for this latter tradition derives from his concern for the idea that true popular power lies in plurality, that pluralism in politics parallels, in a general way, pluralism in science, and it is only through political pluralism that the freedoms of the individual can be preserved. This is Proudhon's true conception of power. "*Demo-paideia*, not democracy, is my party," said Proudhon, meaning that the culture of the people is more important than the rule of the people.[69]

Sorel's awareness that there are two traditions of Western thought commonly associated with the words *liberalism* and *democracy* later led him to ruminate on the difficulty that besets the theorist undertaking to define the two terms.

> With regard to liberalism one must take care in using the meanings of the word employed by contemporary political theorists. One of the meanings is: the organization of a juridical system which permits the citizen to defend his intellectual, moral, and civic independence in as sure a way as he defends the rights of property. Democratic parliaments have been supposed to be capable of guaranteeing the existence of this system, but experience has not been favorable to the parliamentary regime: it always develops into an exploitation of the country by politicians and, in fact, tends increasingly to resemble a Greek tyranny. The Americans, by a series of quite bizarre circumstances, have preserved several fragments of institutions that occasionally allow citizens to oppose parliamentary sovereignty. . . . There is a great deal of the *Roman ideal* in such a liberalism which we should see vanish only with infinite regrets.[70]

Part of the purpose of the *Illusions of Progress* is to show that moral superiority and respect for juridical institutions are not to be found in a centralized democracy. Nor are they to be found in a mere warming-over of those "American" institutions of interest-group liberalism that Sorel sees as "probably destined to disappear."[71] Sorel would, instead, hark back to something like the "Roman ideal" which, according to Sorel, inspired these "liberal" views.

These ideals are, in Sorel's understanding, reconstructed with modern conditions in mind by Proudhon, who also refers to antiquity. Proudhon's mutualist or federalist version of liberalism envisions the fragmentation of sovereignty. "In order to save the freedom of the nation, emancipate the populace, create peace, and develop the principles of the Revolution in Europe, I see only one means: divide France into a dozen independent states and suppress Paris."[72] The economy would be run by agricultural and industrial cooperatives so that "any interest, idea, or social and political element can be introduced into it."[73] Such an arrangement, however, in both Sorel's and Proudhon's understanding, requires responsibility in public administration and a respect for the law strong in proportion as sovereignty weakens: "Good public administration is only possible if it is greatly inspired by juridical practices, which makes the plurality of interests conspicuous."[74] By juxtaposing good juridical practices and the exercise of sovereignty, Proudhon identifies the exercise of law with the exercise of authority, while the exercise of sovereignty is identified with repression and policing. The former is "legitimate" in the deepest sense of the word, while the latter is illegitimate, fraudulent, repressive.

The cutting edge of this legitimacy lies in the solidity with which the juridical system defends property. As an institution, property functions as a bastion of autonomous regulation. To Sorel, as well as to Proudhon, the rights of property are narrowly attached to the federative principle uniting the two conflicting tendencies of self-interest and politization: as a principle of self-interest, it encourages the concern for what is one's own; as a social institution, it encourages the possessor to take care that his property is not detrimental to the public interest—he is constituted policeman and overseer of himself. "This double quality is essential to the constitution of liberty; without it the entire social edifice collapses and it becomes necessary to return to a policy of policing and authoritarianism."[75]

Relegating notions of primitive communism to the same category as Platonic utopias, Sorel insists that law does not come into being before the emergence of private property. Again with Proudhon, he asserts that private law appears for the first time when heads of families, inheriting property through the addition of numerous productive forces, bequeath improvements to their successors. The relation of landed property to a strong legal system is noted by Sorel: everyone knows that agricultural cultivations, of which the masters keep exact day-to-day records, have an economic value much superior to properties which are less carefully recorded. Sorel notes that Ihring greatly admired the early Romans for having admitted no other disruptions of property than those needed for good cultivation. The future of the domain was thus protected against errors and caprices.[76] In such a system too, in Sorel's view, direction by the head of the family meant that his own responsibility in managing the property was paramount. The Roman *pater familias* assumed the role of private king, placed in a position of obeying the law of property strictly while at the same time governing the property. Being governed by laws, his kingship was the opposite of tyranny by virtue of the example of obedience to authority he set for his children and servants.[77]

For Sorel and for Proudhon, this Roman system of stable law, like all strong systems of law, was inextricably linked with the Romans' actions as creative and productive beings. What Sorel calls the juridical sentiment is formed when man reflects not on law itself but on the conditions of production. Law becomes all the more stable "insofar as man's life is more strongly taken up in his work."[78] Once the relations between man and his work have been severed, respect for the law is weakened, and direct authoritarian policing must inevitably take its place. The emperor replaces the senate, the Hobbesian sovereign replaces assemblies.

When an economic system leads to a severing of relations between man and his work, Sorel says that the resulting system is based upon "abstract" property,[79] and we could indeed read into this idea a sort of syndicalist view of Marx's "alienation." But whereas Marx saw the increasingly abstract relations of property as progressive—that is, as leading more or less inexorably to the social revolution—and whereas even Proudhon (in his early days) saw the development of abstract relations (which he criticized) as leading to a federalist system,[80] Sorel regards these abstract relations as leading to the decay of law and toward its concomitant, authoritarianism.

It is at this point that Sorel connects the idea of progress to his own view of historical entropy by using Rome's decline to exemplify the problems involved with abstract property. According to Sorel, the weakening of the landed (and aristocratic) system of property and its replacement by a more "liquid" or commercial economic system eventually undermined the republican virtues of the Romans and opened the system for the empire. Landed property is for Sorel less abstract than commercial property. Under the private law of the Roman family, "the collective sovereignty which is so exorbitant and so redoubtable is broken. Against this sovereignty is erected the domain of property. . . . Allodial property is a dismemberment of sovereignty and in this respect is particularly odious to the power of democracy. It is not pleasing to democrats inflamed with the ideas of unity, centralization, and absolutism."[81]

Sorel notes that there was established in Rome a marked distinction between *res mancipi* (productive forces) and other forms of wealth.[82] Land was productive and no dismemberments of such properties were allowed; land was virtually inalienable. When the Roman lower classes made claims against the land-holding aristocracy a weakening of the law resulted. To Sorel, commercial law, in legitimating the ambitions of the new Roman capitalists—capitalists who were almost entirely speculative rather than productive—created a new class of men. This new class, wanting honors and riches, was obliged to buy protection from the demagogues, who drove the consequences of the new "egalitarian" laws to the logical extreme of demanding a distribution of wealth. All standards became commercial standards: soldiers were treated as well-paid mercenaries rather than as citizens; Caesar regarded the capture of Persia as a capture of the Persian treasury. "The true character of the Roman economy was that of a state capitalism which would have made Bismarck envious." In such an atmosphere it was, for Sorel, not surprising that in the last days of the republic and in the first days of the empire, "the majority of senators dreamed only of honors, of money, and of power; they joined ranks with the most powerful and put a distance between themselves and the small faction of conservative intransigents led by Cato."[83] The military and social realms became increasingly enfeebled; the new men, lacking real estate, claimed equality for their commercial property, thus undermining Roman property relations.[84]

A new system of law emerged, based on the relations of "abstract property" and paralleling the separation of man from the earth.[85] This system of abstract law implied an almost complete change from the civil law of the old aristocracy to the commercial law of the new men, which dealt with what Sorel calls "occult associations of corporate groups." Inheritance taxes and other state interference were obviously more acceptable and less disruptive to such groups than they were to landed proprietors; this kind of abstract law is far more administrative, because commercial relationships are far more political. Under such a system, according to Sorel, "private rights are destined gradually to lose their authority. . . . The prestige of private law would obviously follow the same descending path as the prestige of private production."[86]

According to Sorel, this same pattern can be found in modern capitalism:

> The rich bourgeoisie is losing more and more respect for the principles of civil law. . . . In the new economy that the rich

> bourgeoisie considers the noblest, direction by the head of the family has completely disappeared. Having become a stockholder, he is content to hold a certificate giving him the right to a variable revenue. . . . In the formation of the large fortunes of today, speculations on the stock market have played a far more considerable role than have the beneficent innovations introduced into production by able heads of industry. Thus, wealth increasingly tends to appear detached from the economy of progressive production, and it then loses all contact with the principles of civil law.[87]

This situation, according to Sorel, imparts a character to capital which Marx defined as "commercial" rather than "industrial."[88]

The "progressive ideology" that supports expanding productive giantism, together with the increasing commercialism of capitalism, will lead to indefinite extension of the economic powers of the state. The economy, especially commercial capitalism, lacks those fixed and continuing qualities possessed by the agricultural domain. Commercial capitalism requires quick decisions and speculative daring that entail a vast amount of arbitrary decision-making. As the state becomes increasingly involved in such a system, in Sorel's view, we risk increasing arbitrariness on the part of the state. But for Sorel, it is "the moral authority acquired by judicial bodies that makes administrative bodies fearful of committing arbitrary acts."[89] If the state intervenes with increasing arbitrariness in an economy dominated by commercial capitalism, private rights will gradually lose their authority.

Sorel's historical sense is too sophisticated to call for a return to the Roman system of historical law, but he seems to be unable to attribute the laudable productivity of the modern capitalist system, a system he admires, to the very abstract nature of modern productive relationships. The occult associations of corporate groups which he condemns find their modern equivalent in the limited liability corporation, a juridical institution necessary to modern capitalist productivity and grounded in the limited legal responsibility of its shareholders.

Sorel seems dimly aware of this problem of defining abstraction, but he narrows the area of controversy by condemning modern capitalism for its excessive reliance on financial dealings as a distinct realm of activity and by separating these dealings from productive relationships. In proclaiming that modern capitalism is dominated by commercial (or exchange) capitalism rather than industrial capitalism, Sorel can avoid the onus of transforming the entire industrial system and thus reduce the risk of attacking the sacred principle of productivity. He thus focuses his proposals for reform solely on the principle of exchange, which is, in his view, a mere "mechanical attachment" to the productive process. "In production, the parts exist only through the whole; in exchange, the whole is a mathematical addition of separate parts."[90]

Sorel must go further than this, of course: he must later argue that modern syndicalism as a workers' organization of production should dispense with the capitalist directors of industry. The worker in the factory is the new *pater familias*. But the factory worker is not working on the land; he is working in the more "abstract" milieu of industrial production. Furthermore, isn't the collective ownership by the workers of industrial cooperatives still a sort of abstraction? To Sorel, the overcoming (partial overcoming, in his case) of alienation can only occur in a society in which authority is restored and a new juridical system arises from the milieu of the workers. To Sorel, the capitalist class or the state is the most abstract institution; when this abstraction has been displaced by a new juridical system, alienation will be partly overcome.

Sorel's discussion of the form the new juridical system will take is scanty, but the advocate of "violence" also envisions a new array of "social authorities" whose direct involvement in production compels the practitioners of the industrial art to think directly about the authority of the juridical system. In only one early essay, "The Socialist Future of the Syndicates," is this authority-function of the trade unions discussed. There Sorel sees examples of trade unions of various countries performing an authority-function vastly superior to that of the police. The one concrete example he gives is that experience has shown that the police appear to be powerless in combating alcoholism, while union leaders appear to be much more effective in doing so.[91]

The *Illusions of Progress* is a depiction not just of the decay of an ideology but of the social regime that employs the ideology. The ideology of the national state has so eroded local energies and so undermined the respect for institutions—especially juridical institutions—that only workers' organizations are seen as an alternative. As Sorel says, the administrative spirit of the modern state is inferior to the union in which are grouped workers who have given proof, to a particularly high degree, of productive capacities, of intellectual energies, and of devotion to comrades. In such a syndicate, liberty is encouraged and, by reason of the necessity for economic struggles, the will to solidarity is always firm.[92] "By this constant tension of the will," the syndicates, experienced in economic struggles, Sorel argues, "strongly approximate *social authorities*, which do not fulfill their censorial functions well unless they are dominated by a passionate feeling for the duties imposed by tradition. When this psychological state degenerates, these authorities are transformed into an oligarchy against which the men whom they were supposed to protect revolt."[93]

Sorel tells us that the new society must be backed by a strong juridical system, respect for law, and a highly responsible administrative apparatus. Furthermore, this system can be sustained only by the "tension of the will" attained in economic struggles. Beyond this he tells us little, lest he be open to charges of utopianism. He thus prefers to call the entire federative system an "hypothesis." This hypothesis, he says, "constitutes perfectly a convenient means of representing *mythically* the realization of this program of public law. . . . The reality of federalism is not absolutely necessary for the realization of federalist tendencies. The difference between the ready-made ideal, which is the model of the political idea, and real historical development is found again and again at every stage of social science."[94]

How extensive this system of myth is in Sorel is a question that is frequently raised. It is certainly, as we shall see, at the basis of the tension of the will which sustains the proletariat in its economic struggles, but we do not know if these struggles are leading to any really new concrete institutions. Sorel notes that the "regime of which Proudhon dreamed will perhaps never be realized."[95] In his pessimistic response to Proudhon—that democracy will not necessarily be a prelude to federalism—Sorel goes so far as to say that "the federative government can only be a myth, which functions as a device to incarnate quite essential principles."[96]

The nature of this myth can only be proved by an extensive study of social myths in history, and this Sorel does first in his discussions of the myth of the general strike in *Reflections on Violence*, to be considered in the next chapter.

Notes

1. George Lichtheim, *Marxism in Modern France*, p. 157. See also Zev Sternhell, *La Droite révolutionnaire 1885-1914* (Paris: Editions du Seuil, 1978), pp. 324-25.

2. Sorel, *Saggi di critica del marxismo*, p. 192.

3. Ibid., p. 189.

4. This work first appeared in *Mouvement Socialiste* (Aug.-Dec. 1906) and was published in book form by Marcel Rivière in 1908, with four subsequent editions. An American edition, *The Illusions of Progress* (Berkeley, Los Angeles, London: University of California Press, 1969) was translated by John and Charlotte Stanley; all references are to this edition.

5. Sorel, "Etude sur Vico."

6. Ibid., pp. 794-95.
7. Ibid., p. 788.
8. Ibid., p. 792, citing Michelet's translation of Giambattista Vico, *La Science nouvelle*, 4.6.2, p. 595.
9. Sorel, "Etude sur Vico," p. 916.
10. Ibid.
11. Ibid., p. 808.
12. Ibid., p. 919.
13. Ibid., p. 805.
14. Ibid., p. 806, citing Vico, *La Science nouvelle*, 4.6, p. 597.
15. Sorel, "Etude sur Vico," p. 787, citing Polybius 6.9.
16. Sorel, "Etude sur Vico," p. 805. Sorel cites Engels's discussion of Hegel: "According to all conventions, a philosophical system in order to be respected must cling to some absolute philosophical truth. Also, while proclaiming that this absolute truth is nothing short of the logical process, the historical process itself, it sees itself forced to place a limit on this process, because it is quite necessary, in the end, to place limits on its own system. What philosophical knowledge can do, so can historical practice. Humanity which, in the person of Hegel, has arrived at elaborating the absolute idea, would be advanced enough to realize this idea in practice." Sorel notes Engels's further comment on Hegel's *Philosophy of Right*, that Hegel was led to proclaim the excellence of the Prussian monarchy limited by the "Estates General of the sort found in the *ancien régime* that Frederick William III promised his subjects," and to "demonstrate, through speculation, the necessity of an aristocracy": *Ludwig Feuerbach and the End of Classical German Philosophy*, English translation in Karl Marx and Frederick Engels, *Selected Works* (Moscow: Foreign Languages Publishers, 1958), vol. 2, p. 364.
17. Sorel, "Etude sur Vico," p. 787. Cf. p. 934: "Vico is not so deceived by the sophism of ideal history that he does not see that Rome presents, from this viewpoint, an exceptional character."
18. *FGS*, pp. 243-44.
19. Ibid., p. 243.
20. Sorel, "Etude sur Vico," p. 787.
21. Compare Sorel on Socrates: "[Socrates says that] tragedy is a form of popular rhetoric intended to flatter without edifying. We might think that this senseless statement belongs to Plato himself. One could not be more unjust toward the most marvelous product of Greek civilization" (*FGS*, p. 69). According to Sorel, Socrates also shared the optimism of the idea of progress without its holistic view of science. (Compare *Reflections*, p. 30, to *Le Procès de Socrate*, pp. 303-4.)
22. *FGS*, p. 243. Shlomo Avineri has pointed out that Marx's Philosophical Manuscripts, which are, by his and every other account, the most "humanistic" of Marx's writings, assert the necessity of a kind of "barracks communism" not wholly unlike that depicted by Plato. Avineri relegates this condition to an early "socialist" stage in historical thought that gives way to communism at a later stage: *The Social and Political Thought of Karl Marx* (Cambridge: Cambridge University Press, 1970), p. 224, citing the *Manuscripts*, 3, chap. 3.
23. *FGS*, p. 241. Sorel argues that Marxian holism reached its high point in *Anti-Dühring*, in which "Engels likened his communist ideal with social monism in a way which leaves no room for difficulty of interpretation. In

the future society there will no longer be this anarchy of wills which makes economic phenomena similar to natural phenomena, regulated by necessity; no more practical causes coming to interfere; no more chance; all is subject to reason alone. . . . The world is reduced to one man: to Engels" (*FGS*, p. 347n79). For an affirmation of Marx's holistic and monist tendencies, see Bertell Ollman, *Alienation: Marx's Conception of Man in Capitalist Society* (Cambridge: Cambridge University Press, 1976).

24. To Sorel, Socrates was still somewhat of a pluralist: see *Le Procès de Socrate*, p. 313.

25. Condorcet's optimism is not shared by any known thinker in antiquity. It is found in *Outlines of an Historical View of the Progress of the Human Mind* (p. 346 of the anonymous English translation published in London in 1795).

26. Sorel, *Illusions*, p. 23, citing Condorcet, 9th epoch.

27. Ibid., p. xlii, citing Marx's *Communist Manifesto*.

28. In addition to the other functions performed by the inhabitants of the salons, Sorel says, "We must recall the role of the court jesters of the Middle Ages. In the eighteenth century there were true clowns in the salons, such as 'Galiani, who was a clever dwarf or genius—a kind of Plato or Machiavelli with the zest and mannerisms of a harlequin'" (*Illusions*, p. 67, citing Taine's *Ancien régime*).

29. Sorel, *Illusions*, pp. 64-65.

30. Ibid., p. 65, citing Taine's *Ancien régime*.

31. Sorel, *Illusions*, p. 4.

32. Ibid., pp. 11-12; cf. p. 21.

33. Ibid., p. 19.

34. Ibid.

35. Ibid., p. 21.

36. Ibid., p. 22.

37. *FGS*, pp. 234-35.

38. Sorel, *Illusions*, p. 49, citing Rousseau's *Discourse on the Origins of Inequality among Men*.

39. Sorel, *Illusions*, p. 48.

40. Ibid., p. 14.

41. *FGS*, p. 231.

42. Ibid.

43. Ibid., p. 235.

44. Ibid., pp. 235-36.

45. Ibid.

46. Sorel, *Illusions*, p. 12.

47. Ibid., p. 12.

48. Ibid., p. 47.

49. Ibid., p. 49.

50. Ibid., p. 54, citing Rousseau's *Social Contract*, chap 2, sec. 3.

51. Sorel, *Illusions*, p. 50, citing Rousseau's *Emile*, chap. 3.

52. Sorel, *Illusions*, pp. 51-52.

53. Ibid., p. 48, citing Rousseau's *Social Contract*, chap. 1, secs. 6 and 9. Sorel emphasizes that this is the way in which the statement was interpreted. Rousseau himself was inspired, according to Sorel, by the feudal communal system and the Swiss democracies: "This 'alienation' is the submission to the 'collective domain' of the city." He notes, further, Rousseau's statement that the members of the community are, in fact, not

despoiled.

54. *FGS*, p. 350n18, citing Proudhon's *De la justice dans la révolution et dans l'église*, vol. 2, pp. 120-21.

55. Sorel, *Illusions*, p. 54.

56. Ibid., p. 53. But Sorel insists that Rousseau's intention was not to provide a justification for terrorism: "Jean-Jacques Rousseau," *Mouvement Socialiste* (June 1907): 527.

57. Sorel, *Illusions*, p. 98.

58. Ibid., p. 31; cf. *Insegnamenti*, p. 311.

59. Letter to Mario Missiroli, 19 June 1916, in Sorel's *'Da Proudhon a Lenin' e 'L'Europa sotto la tormenta'*, p. 601.

60. Sorel, *Illusions*, p. xliv.

61. Ibid., p. 35.

62. Ibid., p. 150; cf. *Insegnamenti*, p. 48.

63. Ibid., p. 25.

64. Ibid., p. 27.

65. Ibid., p. 150.

66. Ibid., p. 27.

67. Ibid., p. 95.

68. *FGS*, pp. 249-50, citing Proudhon's *De la justice*, vol. 2, pp. 116, 120-21.

69. Sorel, "Trois problèmes," *Indépendance* (Dec. 1911): 262, citing Daniel Halévy's *Apologie pour notre passé* (Paris: Cahiers de la Quinzaine, series 11, no. 10, 1908), pp. 92-94. The French is *la démopédie.* In terms of power, it is the people speaking with a number of voices rather than as a single unit; the latter constitutes the theory of sovereignty and is based on force. There is an implicit juxtaposition here between power and force. Thus Proudhon asks "that the collectivity in question does not vote as one, by virtue of a particular feeling in common, which would only lead to an immense swindle, as can be seen in the majority of popular judgments. To fight as one is the law of battle; to vote as one is the opposite of reason": Proudhon, *De la justice*, vol. 3, p. 119, cited in *FGS*, p. 249. But how different is Proudhon's notion of the "collective reason" from Rousseau's general will? We read in Proudhon: "Respect only the decisions of your common reason, whose judgments cannot be yours, freed as it is from that individual sovereignty without which you would only be shadows" (*De la justice*, vol. 3, p. 102). The difference probably lies in Rousseau's idea that the general will is sovereign and emerges from the silence of the heart. However, it is also discovered by counting the pluses and minuses of votes.

70. Letter to Missiroli, 24 October 1914; *'Da Proudhon a Lenin'*, p. 516.

71. Sorel, *'Da Proudhon a Lenin'*, p. 516.

72. *FGS*, p. 252, citing Proudhon's *Correspondance*, vol. 14, pp. 218-19.

73. *FGS*, pp. 249-50, citing Proudhon's *Contradictions politiques*, pp. 190-91.

74. *FGS*, p. 248.

75. Sorel, *Introduction à l'économie moderne* (Paris: Rivière, 1922), p. 160.

76. Sorel, *Illusions*, p. 172.

77. Ibid., p. 173.

78. Sorel, *Introduction à l'économie moderne*, pp. 71, 67.

79. Ibid., pp. 153-54.

80. It must be remembered that one of Sorel's main criticisms of Proudhon is that Proudhon himself was an ideologist of progress.

"Proudhon regards democracy as a preparation for the republican regime. . . . I believe that is why he did not dare to complete his *Contradictions politiques*. . . . It would have been very painful for him to admit that he was wrong to hope for so long for a republican transmutation of democratic life" (*FGS*, pp. 250-51). Sorel is more pessimistic, but he does argue, as we shall see, that the centralized and democratic regime of capitalism has opened up the opportunity for a newer and decentralized regime of syndicalism; and this regime is inspired by Proudhon's republic. Sorel argues that the young Proudhon adopted progressive views which he later dropped. These views were accepted on authority rather than through reflection. That is why Sorel excuses Proudhon's metaphysics. "I think *Democracy in America* had a considerable and perhaps decisive influence on Proudhon's early works." Sorel notes that Tocqueville's writings anticipate the inevitable arrival of democratic conditions and that, for Tocqueville, to resist this movement would be to "resist the will of God." Sorel maintains that Proudhon's *Contradictions économiques* "was written in order to develop the same egalitarian theme by showing that equality arises out of economic development like a hidden law. It seems . . . he had been struck by the great effect produced by Tocqueville's concepts" (*Illusions*, p. 141). But Sorel adds that Proudhon did not intend to *demonstrate* the existence of an historical movement toward equality of conditions. Instead "he received this fact from Tocqueville and he wanted to find a metaphysics in it by establishing a philosophical order in economics. He took the world as whole and tried to extricate from it an order that could take account of the law proclaimed by Tocqueville" (*Illusions*, p. 142). The coup d'état of 1851 made Proudhon much more pessimistic and permitted him "to understand much better his vocation as a moralist" (*Illusions*, p. 144). Sorel regards Marx's criticism of even the more optimistic Proudhon as careless and superficial: "For Proudhon rejected as clearly as possible 'the providential government whose non-existence is sufficiently established . . .'" (*Illusions*, p. 141, citing Proudhon's *Contradictions économiques*, vol. 1, pp. 360-61). But this appears to be a rather weak defense of Proudhon if it is admitted that he accepted Tocqueville's authority. Sorel appears to be using the cause of Proudhon's errors as a plea that they were not errors.

81. Sorel, *Introduction à l'économie moderne*, p. 159.

82. Sorel, *Illusions*, p. 172.

83. Sorel, "Grandeur et décadence de Rome," *Mouvement Socialiste* (July 1906, Feb. 1907): p. 256.

84. Sorel cites Renan: "The Roman empire, in humbling the nobility and reducing the privilege of birth to almost nothing, increases, on the other hand, the advantages of fortune. Far from establishing the effective equality of its citizens, the Roman empire, opening wide the gates of the city, created a great division between the *honestiores*, the notables (the wealthy), and the *humiliores* or *tenuiores* (the poor). By proclamation of the political equality of all, the inequality of the law was introduced, especially in penal law" (*Illusions*, p. 164, citing Renan's *Marc-Aurèle*). Sorel argues that this process took place during the transition from republic to empire through the claims of capitalists. Cf. "Grandeur et décadence de Rome."

85. Sorel, *Introduction à l'économie moderne*, pp. 153-55.

86. Sorel, *Illusions*, p. 162.

87. Ibid., p. 169.

88. Cf. ibid., p. 188: "According to Marx, there are three types of

capitalism. Usury and commercial capital are secondary forms [that were] present in history before capital in its fundamental form, which determines the economic organization of modern society. . . . In precapitalist society the usurer can take possession . . . of the total surplus value; the result is that usury capital paralyzes the productive forces instead of developing them" (citing *Capital*, vol. 3, pt. 2, pp. 164-67). To Sorel as well as to Marx, commercial capital has many of the same characteristics. Thus, he says that "the trust is related to usury capitalism and the cartels to commercial capitalism" (*Illusions*, p. 202).

89. Sorel, *Illusions*, p. 162.
90. Sorel, *Introduction à l'économie moderne*, pp. 143-44.
91. *FGS*, pp. 91-92.
92. Ibid., p. 91.
93. Ibid., p. 309n88 (Sorel's italics).
94. Sorel, *Introduction à l'économie moderne*, p. 161.
95. *FGS*, p. 250.
96. Sorel, *Introduction à l'économie moderne*, p. 160.

VIII
THE SYNDICALIST EPIC

Syndicalism emerged in France at about the same time that the first Marxist and socialist parties were being formed. In 1884 a law was passed making it legal to form trade unions, and in that year a central trade union, La Fédération Nationale des Syndicats, was formed at Lyons. From the very first, the Guesdist socialists dominated the Fédération. By the turn of the century, unions had put their mark on the industrial life of France. By 1899, 55 percent of all strikes involved union members, and the figure reached 80 percent by the middle of the first decade of the century, when Sorel was writing the *Reflections on Violence*. As a sequel to the freedom given to unions, the first *bourses du travail* (labor exchanges or employment and educational bureaux) were set up in 1888. These *bourses*, federations of local trade unions, established a national organization in 1892, under the leadership of Fernand Pelloutier.

The syndicalist movement's relationship with the political wing of socialism was strained from the very beginning. The Marxist parties in France, especially those dominated by the Guesdists, were deeply distrustful of strikes. In the 1880s, in reaction to Guesdist control of labor congresses and the increasingly frequent political attempts to take over the union movement, repeated resolutions in favor of the general strike were introduced. The Confédération Générale du Travail was founded when a general-strike resolution of 1894 led to the collapse of the Guesdist-dominated Fédération des Syndicats. Furthermore, the entry of the socialist Millerand into the "bourgeois" cabinet of 1899, a government which did not change its attitude toward the working class, shocked the unionists. The repression of the unions by the state appeared to be as great as it had ever been.

This repression was considerable. Although the 1884 law made it as easy to organize unions in France as in Britain or Germany, Peter

Stearns points out that in terms of enforcement of order, it is probable that French police and militia were rather more severe than were those in the other industrial countries. France was also the only industrial country that regularly sent military troops into mining and dock strikes.[1] This heavy-handedness, together with a relative lag in social legislation, made it easy for unionists to turn against all state activity and to scorn "socialist" governments along with conservative ones.

Of the three major European powers, France had the most "advanced" political system in terms of centralization and bureaucratization, but her industrial mechanism was the weakest and appeared most dependent on the state. This relative underdevelopment of French capitalism permitted continued encouragement of the Proudhonian craft-and-artisan ideology of French production. Stearns argues that the relatively small size of French firms would have enabled relatively easy victories on the part of trade unions without state force.[2] The small size of business reflected a correspondingly small size in the average union (only 170 members in 1905). The entire picture gave Sorel the false impression that France had somehow cheated the capitalist tendency toward economy of scale, that she was the harbinger of a new historical tendency toward decentralization and local control rather than centralization. It was on this assumption that the *Reflections on Violence* was written in 1905-1906.

The *Reflections on Violence* is a strange work. Published in *Mouvement Socialiste* in 1906, the same year as the *Illusions*, it was to be Sorel's *livre standard*, the book which spread his fame more than any other and which probably would have insured his fame had he not written anything else. The conventional attitude toward the *Reflections* is that it is a book about myths and about violence, especially about the myth of the general strike, an idea which was very much in the air in the French labor movement at the time. However, the book is a bit of a disappointment in this respect, for in many ways the *Reflections* is far more a *livre de circonstance* than the *Illusions*: in it, one finds constant references to political movements of the day; discussions of personalities abound. Interspersed are theoretical statements which when taken either individually or collectively might form the corpus of Sorel's political theory, but that theory is curiously skeletal. This is why most of the many articles and books written on Sorel have as their goal the explanation of the *Reflections*, using other writings as a vehicle for their analyses. One recent work concluded with a chapter on the *Reflections*, as if Sorel had written virtually nothing after 1906 (ignoring the fact that Sorel wrote about a third of his output after that date).[3]

I prefer to look upon the *Reflections* in a slightly different way; instead of viewing it as the one book worth explaining (for it is obvious that Sorel had already created a "system" before it was written), we should accept it as the work which attempts to pinpoint and resolve the ambiguities and loose threads that were still obvious in Sorel's political theory. Instead of the one book to be explained, we can argue that it is the one book which tries to explain, to gather up the loose ends. Although the results are similar, our approach should be that the theory of myths for which Sorel is most famous performs specific functions in Sorel's thought and that these functions are in some respects a *deus ex machina* helping him to avoid certain problems.

The first of these problems is the problem of sovereignty. Sorel had not dealt satisfactorily with his desire for a new social and legal system because for him to do so would render him liable to charges of utopianism. But what kind of organization could Sorel advocate that would be immune to these charges? The answer was found in the socialist movement itself. If Sorel was to avoid constructing a nonexistent utopia, he could only search for the alternative in the ongoing workers' movement, which had the advantages of being outside the state and of actually possessing a new ordering principle.

Yet to sustain itself, this workers' movement needed more than a new juridical system. It required impetus (a series of impulses, in Sorel's terminology) which would enable the workers' movement, embodied in syndicates and *bourses du travail*, to sustain the constant battle necessary to overcome its own inertia, its natural nature, as well as outside resistance. Thus, the second problem Sorel had to face in his critique of Marx was how to envision social conflict without clinging to one or another of the old ideologies based on historical "scientism." Sorel saw the absolute necessity of the feeling for certainty in the workers' movement. Whatever Sorel's proclamations against the optimism of the progressive philosophy might have been, he knew that a feeling of hope and anticipation preceded any social transformation. How is this feeling transmitted without a theory of history and the continuity and passivity that appear to accompany it? To Sorel the myth of the general strike provided this certainty without determinism.

Third, Sorel criticized Marx's catastrophic revolution. Yet how can a social revolution avoid the brutality of the French Revolution and the Paris Commune, a brutality Sorel consistently abhorred? By transforming Marx's catastrophic revolution, along with all the other great social movements, into a myth, Sorel could envision a series of revolutionary impulses whose very nature would be to limit the brutality of the revolutionary movement, impulses that would set ethical limits to what we commonly call violence.

What surprises the students to whom *Reflections on Violence* is assigned in classes in political theory is the comparative lack of violence in the book, provided we look upon violence in the conventional way. No one would accuse Sorel of being a pacifist, but much of the *Reflections* is devoted to a study of the limits of violence, the suppression of hatred, the minimization of brutality and brigandage, and the ethics of war, which, for Sorel, had its own Proudhonian rules. By conventional terminology, the most violent thing about the *Reflections on Violence* is the title. As we shall see, a more appropriate title might be *Reflections on the Morality of Social Conflict* or *The Ethics of Rebellion*. Speaking frankly and perhaps rashly, had the book been titled more appropriately it might not have been so controversial.

The problems considered in the *Reflections on Violence* may be "solved" by the myth of the general strike, but the "solution" has its own difficulties. How, we might ask, can a myth based on the activity of the strike possibly conform to Sorel's own criteria of virtue—productivity in place of relaxation, struggle against natural nature, and self-sacrifice instead of distributive justice? The goals of the unions appear to be increased leisure, less labor time, and more justice—all of which are to be gained through strikes stopping the very production the virtues of which Sorel extols. Here the hypothesis is that the general-strike myth will transform the morals of the workers and sustain the syndicalist movement's independence, which is what gives the myth its "real" or institutional basis.

Finally Sorel had noted the problem of upholding the absolute separation of classes created by the bourgeoisie's corrupting policy of "social continuity through philanthropy." Yet he warned of the "danger" of presenting to the proletariat "everything which comes from the bourgeoisie as stupid and ridiculous." For certain bourgeois institutions had upheld the laudable concept of liberty. The myth of the general strike "juxtaposed violence to beneficence in order to repudiate and ridicule paternalism in the ruling classes" without casting nihilistic aspersions on the concept of liberty (or, indeed, "on all ethics") and, conversely, without lapsing into democratic adulation of the "wisdom of the people."[4]

In this chapter we will discuss: (1) how syndicalism in France could be seen by Sorel to provide this institutional base of resistance; (2) how the myth of the general strike seemed to embody Sorel's standards of moral virtue; (3) how this myth provided Marxism with the certainty necessary for activism without the quietism found in the dialectic or the theory of progress; (4) how it sustained the class struggle without brutality; and (5) how it sustained a revolt against liberal humanitarianism while retaining liberty.

I

Sorel revised Marxist theory by proclaiming the class struggle to be brutal and by rejecting sovereignty. The departure from Marx in Sorel's political thought consisted in treating the state and the economy as separate entities, in taking the state seriously. The "seriousness" with which Sorel takes the state is odd; old-line Marxists set out to capture the state and to make it do the bidding of the new proletarians, but, paradoxically, Sorel ignores it, preferring to avoid the jealousy and strife that invariably attend the capture of state machinery. In doing so he avoids the catastrophe of capturing the state and also avoids any political continuity (outlined in the *Illusions of Progress*) between the old ruling class and the new. There is indeed a formidable irony in Sorel's depiction of the historical and "progressive" displacement of one ruling class by another, especially if the French Revolution is taken as the model: it is extremely brutal, and it accomplishes little in the way of change. The Sorelian solution is that the proletariat "walks away" from the state by concentrating its energies on entirely new institutions. These institutions in turn preserve the hard-won economic gains of the capitalist era but radically decentralize the authority structure—a continuity in economic matters which replaces the political one. This continuity in economics allows a permanent revolution in productivity, a revolution that takes place in the hearts of the members of the new proletarian institutions. No longer dependent on the state, filled with the ebullience of a newly gained self-reliance, a new order of innovation and creativity occurs in the economy which constantly re-makes itself and constantly revolutionizes its bases. Sorel therefore gives us a new paradox to replace the old progressive irony. The greatest of all social revolutions occurs by ignoring the state, and the greatest of all economic revolutions is obtained through economic continuity.

As we noted in Chapter 4, Sorel critized Marx's view of the state as ambiguous: on the one hand, it encouraged workers' self-management, while on the other hand—especially in the *Communist Manifesto*—it encouraged state ownership and centralization. To Sorel, this ambiguity resulted from Marx's failure to pay sufficient attention to the state, from his treatment of political phenomena as a sort of "dependent variable" of the economy. Despite Marx's subtle appreciation of reciprocal dependence between the realm of politics and that of economics, Sorel felt that, by virtue of this passive view of the state, Marx failed adequately to separate economic organization and political organization; that syndicalism together with the general strike clarifies this separation.

Sorel notes that Marx does recognize that increased centralization has occurred under capitalism. Sorel agrees that capitalism and the state go hand-in-hand, and cites Marx to the effect that the emerging bourgeoisie could not do without the constant domination of the state. That is why Sorel himself can maintain that the thinking of democratic socialists is dominated by the statist prejudices of the bourgeoisie. But the relationship between the state and the economy in Marx's thought is, according to Sorel, simplistic. Since Marx took England as his economic model and generalized on it, he regarded the state under capitalism ultimately as a creature of business interests. According to Sorel, in such a case it was easy for Marx to envision the transformation of proletarian consciousness "under adhesion to an agitation led by politicians,"[5] for these politicians, like those of the bourgeoisie, were to be loyal servants of the new ruling class after the revolution. Sorel saw Marx as extrapolating into the revolutionary era the relationship between the state and the dominant economic class that had prevailed under the bourgeoisie.

Marx did not envision the development of a separate political class because, in his transitional scheme, politicians represented—almost reflected—the interests of either capitalists or workers. Thus, in Sorel's view, even when Marx did discuss workers' control of industry, it was because Marx could not bring himself to believe that a social-democratic state could have interests that were actively hostile to those of the working class. In short, Sorel asserts that Marx "took no account of the continuous development of the modern state. . . . He spoke and acted as if the socialist world, falling amid the workers engaged in corporate conflicts, were enough to organize the proletariat."[6] Just as the economy advanced under the fatalistic laws of economics, so the state would follow, and with it the march of statist socialist propaganda.

We have seen that, for Sorel, the consequence of this Marxist simplicity was an inclination toward unity. Marx (and, even more, Engels) was inclined toward free trade, because then the almost automatic laws of capitalist development (concentrating the economy in a few firms, after the elimination of the weak ones) would hasten the progress of nationalization and state socialism.[7] Sooner or later, so the thinking went, trusts and monopolies would dominate capitalist economics. Sorel rebelled against the doctrine that such a tendency was progressive; he viewed monopolies as "backward forms of organization."[8] For Sorel, the centrifugal force of independent enterprises is the forward-moving element of the society, and the centripetal "economies of scale" retard development. Such immense enterprises wish to eliminate market forces in favor of their own arbitrary decisions. "They have a fear of throwing themselves into the unknown,"[9] and are thus similar to the administered economies of the modern state. In Marxist theory, the centralization of the economy and that of the state go hand-in-hand. We have noted in Chapter 4 Sorel's appreciation of Marx's "syndicalism"; after 1901 or so, Sorel became more firmly convinced that the philosophical presuppositions of Marxism militate heavily in favor of statism and parliamentarianism. Marx is seen ever more intensely as the rationalist rather than the empiricist, as soft-headed rather than hard-headed. Sorel's renewed criticism of Marx is that his schema is lifeless and his research imperfect: "Living in a country [England] saturated with Christianity, he did not seem to have dreamed of asking about the influence of moral education on the English working classes. . . . He did not ask what relations exist between his concept of the class struggle and national traditions."[10]

Sorel himself intended to take national traditions into account. This, in fact, was exactly what Fernand Pelloutier, the general secretary of the Fédération des Bourses du Travail, did in his *Histoire des bourses du travail* (1902).[11] Sorel wrote a preface for this work in which he praised Pelloutier for dealing squarely with the French national tradition of centralization. It was Sorel's view, as well as Pelloutier's, that the tradition of centralization and national sovereignty started by Louis XIV had confirmed in the French socialist tradition the ideas of philanthropy and unity which help transform socialism into pure and simple democracy when it is governing.

In Pelloutier's view (as well as in Sorel's) continuity between the old elites and the new ones meant that working-class organizations that participated in political action risked being swallowed up by the dissoluteness of fashionably morbid humanitarianism. This pessimism was diminished, however, by both Sorel's and Pelloutier's awareness of a second tradition in French society: against the predominant tradition of a centralized administration, there existed in France a highly decentralized economy. France had defied the parallel vision of Marx because its economy had gone in an opposite direction to that of its politics. Furthermore, according to Sorel, as a consequence of the decentralized economy, local community spirit was strong in France.

In Pelloutier's and in Sorel's view, this split personality in French society saw a corresponding division in the French socialist movement itself, between on the one hand partisans of political action (participation, parties, propaganda, and parliamentary activity), and on the other hand the advocates of direct economic action, workers' education, and the general strike. In Pelloutier's words:

> Two conceptions divided the ideas bearing upon the mode of organization and the struggle of the socialist collectivity. One, professed by ignorant and routinized men (despite their economic knowledge), was inspired solely by visible phenomena and, viewing the state as the artisan of social organization whereas it was merely the instrument, regarded the state as being indispensable to the perfecting of societies; and, consequently, tended to augment its characteristics by adding to it those of producer and distributor of the public riches. The other conception, coming from men whose intuition makes up for the shortcomings of economic science, thought (with Proudhon) that the social functions can and ought to be limited to the satisfaction of human needs of every kind and, maintaining that the state has as its reason for being only the security of superfluous or harmful political interests, concluded with its replacement by the free association of producers.[12]

For Sorel, Pelloutier and his organization, the Fédération des Bourses du Travail, embodied what was best in the second of these national traditions. The *bourses* were labor exchanges or employment agencies, run by the workers themselves in a given locality, and having as other functions workers' education and certain trade-union activities, including the organization of strikes.[13] For Sorel, one of their principal advantages was in their local character: "The organization of the *bourses du travail* has as its primary basis the existence of relations which unfold among workers, belonging to the various professions, who live in the same locale." In Sorel's view:

> Workers in the same city have more common interests than workers in the same profession in towns that are far apart. . . . France is one of the countries where the blending of local interests is most complete and where, consequently, the concrete unity of the working class is most easily realized. Industry in our country is old and remains dispersed much more than in England, because the old factories have been centers of attraction almost everywhere.[14]

To Sorel, then, the autonomous workers' movement of the *bourses* embodied a countervailing historical tendency, opposed to the progressive norm of centralization. In fact, it was contrary to virtually every non-anarchistic tendency in modern political thought.

Sorel sees the syndicalist organizations as heading in the opposite direction from Tocqueville's visions of nearly inevitable centralization and leveling: "Among the remarkable phenomena of the present workers' movement, we should note the tendency of workers' organizations toward local groups that leads necessarily to a federalist [i.e., Proudhonian] point of view. As much as any sociological formula can be exact, we can say that *if capitalist society was characterized by the advance toward unity, the present workers' movement tends toward local division*."[15] The *bourses du travail* Sorel sees as

> associations of comrades, true socialist companions, into which one enters in order to do something without outside direction, in order to cooperate effectively in works whose usefulness one understands. We thus come to understand that social questions are not resolved by the science of a few doctors and through the able tactics of party chiefs, but that they are resolved every day insofar as the morality of the workers increases. The old authoritarian formula of state socialism is tempered because the sentiment of *self-government* is developed in the masses; indeed, whoever says federalism also says liberalism, the limitation of authority through public opinion and the balancing of powers.[16]

This remarkable restatement of the liberal concept of checked and divided power would be realized, according to Sorel, only if a mode of thought were to become predominant that is far more powerful than bourgeois liberalism, with its necessarily statist ideology of progress. What was necessary was the constitution of syndicates as counter-entropic "societies of resistance" whose goal would be not only to establish a mode of action which would galvanize the will of its potential participants but to create a new moral system as well.

According to Pelloutier, the process of removing oneself from the omnipresent political system required activity beyond mere workers' education, even if it did not extend to political action or to violence per se; indeed, at their congress held at Tours in 1892, the *bourses* resolved that there "was no advantage to bloody revolutions of which the bourgeoisie were the sole beneficiaries . . . offering to ruling classes a new opportunity to drown social demands in the blood of the workers."[17] The alternative posed by the congress was the idea of a great refusal, a mass turning of backs to the established powers, "the universal and simultaneous suspension of the productive force, i.e., the general strike, which, even limited to a relatively restricted period, leads the workers infallibly to the claims formulated in its program."[18] To Pelloutier such a strike, in which all workers would lay down their tools, was a purely economic device that avoided all political activity. The continued harassment the *bourses* experienced at the hands of the government only exacerbated their antagonism to political institutions. Thus, by the next congress, at Toulouse in 1893, "the irritation of the syndicates against the government was so great that an enthusiasm much greater than the preceding year welcomed the proposition of the general strike."[19]

Although the virtual unanimity with which the idea was accepted was, in Pelloutier's view, "the effect of anger, the unreflected manifestation of a momentary desire for revolt,"[20] the concept nevertheless possessed one overwhelming, potentially positive, function: it could mobilize mass sentiment and enable the decentralized organization of the syndicates to attain unified action without central direction. Pelloutier himself confessed that one of the major weaknesses in early working-class organization was that "each member organization was the sole judge of the opportunity for a strike."[21] Didn't the general strike, as an agency for uniting the various aspects of local syndicates into a united and coherent movement, pose the problem of self-negation of local autonomy? To Pelloutier, this was not a serious problem so long as politicians themselves were excluded from all decision-making: "By means of a purely economic order, excluding the possibility that collaboration with parliamentary socialists would enable the latter to exploit the syndicalist effort for its own ends, the general strike should necessarily respond to the secret desire of corporate groups."[22]

Pelloutier did not elaborate on the importance of this "secret desire," but it is safe to say that the phrase so impressed Sorel that, for him, this secret impulse became one of the single most important aspects of the general strike itself. In Sorel's eyes, these secret desires sustained the general strike while the latter sustained the *bourses* and unions in the struggle between classes.

This class struggle created a further series of questions for Sorel. Had he not previously rejected the catastrophic conception of Marxism? Sorel abhorred a blood-bath, a repetition of 1793 engendered by political revolution. Can the class struggle avoid this? Syndicalism and the myth of the general strike solve this difficulty for Sorel. When Marx committed the error of thinking that the social revolution would follow the economic revolution, according to Sorel, he saw all institutions in society shattered in a catastrophe *en bloc*. However, with the establishment of the *bourses* the social revolution has, in one sense, already occurred. By continuing the good usages of the workshop inherited from capitalism, workers do not have to carry out a blood-bath. It is true that Marx envisioned the mechanistic means of production under socialism as having already been established under capitalism, but Sorel goes one step further by arguing that a socialist society has already been created *within* the *bourses*. Furthermore, for Sorel this system of social relations consists partly in the apparatus of the workshop: the good usages of the workshop are obviously the source of the tools of the future. As Sorel says, "Socialism will not only inherit the tools which will have been created by capitalism and from the science that has emerged from technical development, but also the procedure of cooperation which will be constituted at length in the factories."[23] In short, the class struggle occurs amid a kind of productive continuity, whereby the organization of the workshop under socialism is not modified to the point of causing to disappear what had been viewed as essential in the productive process. As long as there is no *economic* catastrophe, the catastrophe of the myth of the general strike is bound to be dissimilar to the blood-bath of 1793, when the economic and political revolutions were intertwined. With the creation of socialist institutions with no political parallels, it is possible simply to turn one's back on the political system. Sorel's socialism signals the end of political revolutions. As Sorel states it, Marxism wouldn't be shattered in the least by the error it committed of envisioning a revolutionary catastrophe, provided that the French Revolution is expelled from any role in socialist thought. "The proletarian revolution, for the convenience of exposition, can thus be conceived under a catastrophic form . . . as a social myth to which is joined the ideal of the general strike."[24]

By replacing the political continuity that he had so strongly criticized in the *Illusions* with economic continuity, Sorel can avoid political activity altogether. In this respect Sorel might be claiming to be more of a Marxist than Marx. If Marx can claim that economic institutions have already made the world ripe for revolution, then we need no longer depend on the state for the enforcement of our new claims, for new socialist institutions have already been created by the movement of the economy. For Sorel, socialism consists in the actual operation of the productive institutions. The socialist movement which eschews party politics must focus instead on the day-to-day operation of alternative institutions, that is, on the *real* socialist movement. Sorel sees support for this perspective in the words of Eduard Bernstein, who said that "the movement is everything, the end is nothing."[25] For Sorel, socialism is "the workers' movement, the revolt of the proletariat against ruling institutions. It is the organization, both economic and ethical, that we see taking place before our eyes to struggle against bourgeois traditions."[26] Thus, although socialism is rooted in actual institutions, it should not be considered as a predictable political or material transformation. Teleological considerations have been effectively reduced in this respect:

> It is of small importance whether communism arrives sooner or later, or whether it ought to be preceded by more or less numerous stages: what is essential is that we can account for our own conduct. The "final end" exists only in regard to our internal life. . . . The final regime imagined by socialists cannot be fixed at a precise date by sociological prediction; it is in the present. It is not outside us; it is in our hearts. Socialism is being realized every day, under our very eyes, to the extent that we know how to direct institutions, and, consequently, to the extent that the socialist ethic is formed in our consciousness and in life.[27]

The difficulties in the path of socialist reconstruction can be seen in the operation and activities of workers in those socialist institutions. It is not enough for Sorel to claim that because the economic and scientific basis for the creation of socialist institutions has been established, a socialist mentality of the love for creative labor will automatically be created. The whole purpose of Sorel's writing is to argue that since our nature inclines us away from creative labor because of the effort needed to resist the encroachments of natural nature (see Chapter 3), a thoroughgoing moral transformation is needed in order to reintroduce creativity into our daily lives. The creation of socialist institutions requires a battle on many fronts: not only must we struggle against natural nature, but we must fight the ever-encroaching threats of established institutions, as well as the parasitic aspects of capitalism (implicitly, finance or commercial capitalism). To Sorel, such constant warfare does indeed require an apocalyptic transformation, but not in the way he claims Marx envisioned. The change Sorel demands is a change in our own outlook on life:

> Socialism is a moral question in the sense that it brings to the world a new manner of judging all human acts and, to employ Nietzsche's celebrated term, a new evaluation of all values. . . . Like Christianity before Constantine, socialism does not accept any solution given by official civilization; it knows neither if it can nor when it can realize its actual aspirations, for the future changes our economic conditions as well as our moral ideas. It passes itself before the bourgeoisie as an irreconcilable enemy and menaces it with a moral catastrophe still greater than a material one.[28]

Sorel envisions this transvaluation of values as a Vicoian *ricorso* in which the philosophical underbrush of developed society has been cleared away and replaced by the profoundest feelings of the poetic sense. To Vico, primitive peoples "animated nature without decomposing it."[29] In such poetic periods, "the logic of imagination replaces the logic of philosophy."[30] For Vico as well as for Sorel, the high Middle Ages exemplified these epochs because then heroism was far more important than a mere rivalry of material interests.[31]

Sorel admits that in our time it would be impossible to reproduce a medieval natural mythology, even a barbarous one, "without soon ending in the flat mythology of our classics."[32] He envisions a sort of mythology of artificial nature that makes the modern proletarian somewhat analogous to the mythic hero, adding, however, that although the myth itself obscures distinctions it must necessarily be partial. "If the new beginnings can be reproduced only *en bloc*, as Vico thought, there would be few chances for a durable renaissance of Marxism; but each strike, however minor, can become a partial *ricorso*; this little socialist current that is produced can be conserved and accumulated with the others if the socialists know how to direct them conveniently."[33] That is why Sorel sees efforts on behalf of the *bourses du travail* and trade unions as important for maintaining these institutions as "societies of resistance."[34]

The myth of the general strike is based on the accumulated vision of these actions. It assumes that any revolution which is not accompanied by these partial *ricorsi* is a fraudulent revolution and that the success of any revolution in producing such *ricorsi* makes discussion of the material consequences of that revolution of secondary importance. Furthermore, such a myth ties together material and ideological elements by uniting the class struggle, the creative act, and the laboring process.

II

Sorel's notion of heroism is, as we have seen, rooted in the process of labor; in the *Reflections* he links this doctrine to the class struggle by transmuting both labor and struggle into creative acts. This is done through a psychological preparation which anticipates constant improvement in the workshop, a struggle against entropic natural nature, and a preparation for the social battle which is "bound" to come. This certain expectation of the battle is produced by the social myth: it reaps the benefit of the idea of certainty that the notion of the dialectic produces, without accepting any theory of the dialectic itself and without falling heir to the quietism of the social democrats, who have elevated the inevitability of the revolution into an excuse for inaction. Sorel attempts to depict a junction of the psychological and material dimensions of revolutionary action by means of the world of fabrication as the common denominator. We should therefore discuss this idea of labor before turning to the myth itself.

By joining together the principles of struggle, creativity, and industrial production, Sorel can unite the professions which embody the moral structure of the modern world: warriors, artists, inventors, and producers all act in areas whose characteristics have progressively approached congruence with the finest characteristics of contemporary industrial life. The world of art has become increasingly similar to the world of productivity, and art and production unite in a never-ending war against natural nature. Thus, artists, warriors, inventors, and producers have four characteristics in common: all four activities are creative; all are based on direct experience uniting subject and object; all are somewhat mysterious; and all entail great struggle and self-overcoming.

One normally looks upon creativity and individualism as the preserves of artistic life, while military and industrial activities are viewed as conformist and regimented. However, as we have seen, Sorel thinks (and here he is in apparent agreement with some of Marx's vague statements on the subject) that art will be in some way the means by which the workers join intelligence and manual work. Artistic education, instead of being intended to give pleasure to the leisure class, serves to make work attractive. This attractiveness, in Sorel's view, insures the material progress and the certainty of man's greatness, "without which there would undoubtedly be no solid realizable moral progress today."[35] For this love of work to be attained, according to Sorel, one must give the machines with which the laborer works aesthetic charm: "fullness, good proportions, and dignity."[36] The new purpose of art is to place manual work on the same level as scientific work, to give dignity to a laboring process which the ancients considered servile, "to find a proud joy in conquered difficulty and to feel free in accomplishing our task."[37] This feeling of freedom means that "the modern industrial tools have as their equivalent in the Greek city not the tools of slaves but the armaments of free men: we should build our machines and our factories as the ancients built their triremes, fortifications, and temples."[38] The ancient builders of military equipment should inspire us, but masterpieces of antiquity, in Sorel's view, whether statues or paintings or military equipment, should not be studied with a view to imitating them. On the contrary, there is "a need to form a strong individuality in oneself and to render more sound the inspirations which spring from the very root of our being. . . . If all men become workers and work with art, one can hope that the aesthetic education that will be given to them will have the effect of developing individualism in the world; and that is good."[39]

If the ancient builders of military equipment should be imitated for the spirit of individualism in their creations, then Sorel seems to have departed somewhat from the early pronouncements he made in *Le Procès de Socrate* to the effect that "obedience is the school of command." Instead of extolling the marching phalanx, Sorel emphasizes the individual and liberating qualities of war and is impressed by the lack of obedience in the old armies.

> During the wars of liberty, each soldier considered himself an important person with something very important to do in battle, rather than regarding himself as only a cog in a military machine entrusted to the supreme direction of the master. In the literature of that time, the free men of the republican armies are continually contrasted to the *automatons* of the royalist armies. . . . Battles could therefore no longer be put in the framework of a chess game, with man comparable to a pawn; they became compilations of heroic exploits accomplished by individuals who drew the motives of their conduct from their own enthusiasm.[40]

Sorel attributes the extraordinary French victories to "intelligent bayonets."[41]

The similarities among productivity, art, and war not only imply individualism in war, but warlike struggle and tension within art and production. As we have noted repeatedly, for Sorel an artistic approach to production does not lessen struggle and fatigue but merely enables us to withstand it better so as to endure more of it. In overcoming natural nature, we will never be able to escape from the necessity of fatigue in the productive process; "production will never become a sport."[42] Work is steadily becoming more intense and more absorbing. "All our capacities of attention must be strained with an application that no one suspected in the past."[43] The elimination of dull routine from the productive process means only that the worker, transformed into a creator, is increasingly proximate to an inventor as well as a scientist, and as an inventor, he "wears himself out in pursuing the accomplishment of ends which practical people often declare absurd."[44]

To Sorel, the consequence of this struggle against nature is that production becomes increasingly important in our lives and informs the world of art itself. In fact, art and productivity become at the same time increasingly aesthetic and utilitarian. The delicacy of the luxury arts is rejected:

> There is no longer any place for the importance of the minutiae of work. In the beautiful ironwork that the German government had so proliferated at the Exposition, there was no studied refinement of this sort; the roughness of the work of the forge with its hammer-blows and its robust solderings was not hidden by any artifice or any mending: it was *art truly understood by men who feel strong.*[45]

For Sorel, even the more delicate arts of antiquity required a demonstration of this same robustness, the same overcoming of resistance, of an inner tension. Most paintings and statues are bad because they do not reveal a Bergsonian sympathy with the subject of the art on the part of the artist. Such a sympathy can be experienced only through the presentation of the subject of art in a state of movement, in a state in which "the tension of immobility is transformed into a clear idea of mobility."[46] This movement is expressed by an impression of tension found in the statue or in the canvas itself. Good art is for Sorel "the result of an explosion of latent forces which have slowly been built up in the soul of the author."[47]

This sympathy for the subject coupled with the greater practicality of art itself means, in a world increasingly characterized by the importance of manual labor, that artistic sensibility is becoming more universalized and is being experienced directly. There is progressively less distance between the artist as producer and the artist as consumer, a unity causing a corresponding decline in the distance between the subject and the object in the productive process. Sorel juxtaposes the old aristocratic arts, in which society was divided between passive spectators and active participants (mainly for the benefit of the privileged spectators), to the new art, in which the public participates actively in both the production and the consumption of art. In one of his more Rousseauian statements against *luxe*, Sorel says:

> In the Golden Age of antiquity, art involved very many citizens. The great importance of sacred dances was in part due to the fact that they joined together all citizens as participants. The choirs of singers and the public celebrations derived their value from the same cause. Aristocratic art, by tending to hand over the roles of participants to mercenaries, broke the unity which seems to be in the process of being recreated. . . . There are many arts which require an active intervention of citizens, and these arts are now progressing.[48]

The cerebral quality of decadent art is replaced by a laboring process that synthesizes the intellectual and emotional faculties with those instincts which move us to forge natural nature's materials into products. The result of this newer unity is a Proudhonian equivalent of *praxis*:

> The old dualism of the mind and the body, the head and the hand, on which the old economy was based, is tending to disappear. . . . Proudhon has explained this. . . . "The idea is born of action and must return to action, under pain of failure for the actor." All that would remain in the domain of pure speculation and which is not translated into any practical result seemed to him the result of the intellectual amputation of man. Subject to the harsh law of work, man is incapable of freeing himself to live as a pure spirit.[49]

In the eyes of Proudhon and Sorel, industry is strongest when it is directly acted on by workers, and least effective when planned by university graduates, civil servants, or social-democratic politicians. For Sorel, the capitalist in France plays a role analogous to that of the passive consumer in the realm of art. As we noted in Chapter 3, Sorel regarded the French capitalist class as unproductive, as relying on their privileges as intellectuals rather than as producers. "Experience shows that there is nothing exceptional in qualities of leadership and that they are found very commonly among manual workers, perhaps even more than among intellectuals." According to Sorel, the leaders of the French syndicates "have seen that the domination of the public powers was founded on the supposed superiority of the intellectuals."[50] But "as the character and intelligence of the workers improve, the majority of the overseers can be eliminated."[51] Sorel is not hostile to—indeed, he admires—the capitalists who are directly concerned with productivity; that is why he can applaud Andrew Carnegie's condemnation of the practice of wasting money on the support of incompetents.[52]

In war, too, Sorel distrusts the separation of the role of actor from that of planner. According to Sorel, it is not the generals who run the war but the soldiers on the line.

> Until the time Napoleon appeared, war did not have the scientific character that later strategic theorists sometimes believed would be attributed to it. . . . Historians imagined that the generals before Napoleon made great campaign plans; such plans did not exist or had but a minute influence on the progress of operations. The best officers of that time realized that their talent consisted in furnishing their troops with the material means of expressing their enthusiastic outburst; victory was assured each time the soldiers could give free reign to all their

> spirit without being hindered by the bad administration of supplies.[53]

The obscuring of the line between subject and object makes rationalistic analysis of art, war, and the productive process extremely difficult. These activities, in Sorel's terms, "live especially on mysteries, shadows, and indeterminate nuances."[54] Production, Sorel says, is "the most mysterious aspect of human activity."[55] If we reject this mysterious dimension of experience, we reduce all activity to the common denominator of a superficial rationalism that places very different matters on the same level through love of logical simplicity. "Economic relations are not exactly reducible to quantitative ones; life is not equivalent to mathematical calculations and . . . the law of cost accounting does not govern the world rigorously."[56]

So too with art. Sorel says that the artist possesses genius only insofar as he does not analyze the substance of his own creativity too closely: "He himself has genius only insofar as he does not know himself."[57] That is one reason why Sorel insists that it is as impossible to draw up canons of artistic excellence as it is to depict the psychological characteristics of military bravery. These activities begin mysteriously and end mysteriously:

> [Adventures in battle] easily lend themselves to the work of the imagination, because it is always impossible to know what occurred in battle. Two visual accounts are not in agreement. Although the wars of the Revolution and Empire are quite close to us, it seems difficult to know just what has occurred in these great events; in the cases in which it is possible to grasp the formation of modern legends, we find that they hardly depend on a slow transformation of things, but they are formed above all by a fantastic representation, provoked in the first instant by violent emotions.[58]

For Sorel such manifestations of emotion are not histories in the usual sense.

By depicting the economic myth of the general strike in terms of the emotions which accompany adventures in battle, Sorel can maintain that the four attributes of creativity, mystery, struggle, and direct experience impart to the souls of the workers a sense of the sublime, analogous to the poetic spirit of those periods in history which have experienced a return to barbarism. This feeling of the sublime cannot be analyzed or broken down; separating it into its component parts denatures it. That is why the quality of mystery constitutes perhaps the most important aspect of the general strike myth. The picture the proletarian has in mind is of some sort of catastrophe which "defies description."[59]

> The barbarians felt awesomeness which seems quite puerile to us when we frequent the places they had peopled with fantastic beings; the literature of the classical period would concern itself with describing the places that tradition had consecrated, and it was unable to produce any emotion. In order to rediscover the sublime, it is necessary to transport ourselves into entirely different milieux—but into milieux which are capable of arousing in our souls emotions analogous to those that were experienced by the primitives. The sea, the mountains, great solitude are capable of giving this impression of inner awe (if we can use that barbarous expression) without which there is no sublime.[60]

When we transform our souls back to primitive states, "we must obviously set aside all those things which belong to prejudices, literary modes, and academic rules and consider only what is truly living." In Vico's words, such a transformation allows "the impossible to be nonetheless believable,"[61] because in such cases men have great difficulty in separating poetic descriptions from historical ones.

Sorel therefore commences his discussion of the myth by asserting a proposition that he claims is "so simple that I did not believe it had to be emphasized: men who participate in great social movements represent their immediate action in the form of images of battles assuring the triumph of their cause. I propose calling these constructions myths: the syndicalist general strike and Marx's catastrophic revolution are myths."[62] In particular, the myth of the general strike is described as "an organization of images capable of evolving, *as a whole and solely by intuition*, prior to any deliberate analysis, the mass of sentiments that correspond to the various manifestations of war entered into by socialism against modern society."[63]

Whether the content of the myth in its mystery actually materializes is as irrelevant for Sorel as whether the second coming of Christ actually occurs is for the movements of messianic Christianity. "Any attempt to discuss how far the myth can be taken literally is devoid of sense. . . . It is only the myth as a whole that counts."[64] Thus, Sorel finds it easy to say that "no progress of knowledge, no rational induction will ever make the mystery that envelops socialism disappear."[65] It is the beginning or epic stages of a revolution in which new doctrines are presented in shades of mystery—incomplete, paradoxical, and symbolic—that finally end in being dissolved into "the ensemble of our knowledge."[66]

The mystery of the myth is linked to its individualistic and creative qualities; the myth is non-scientific. At this point Sorel invokes Bergson to help him convey the aspect of the myth that is revealed in the hearts of the proletarians. Just as the artist who communicates through symbolic signs wishes to create a fully unified ensemble for himself, so the "social poetry" of the general strike may vary with each individual: the revolutionary impulses the myth conveys to each individual are based on deeply personal experiences as well as social ones. Invoking Bergson's doctrine of memory, Sorel asks us to consider our "inner states" and what happens to us during a creative moment. The periods of "deep introspection" required to reach the inner self, moments when we "grasp ourselves," the rare moments when we are truly free (to use Bergsonian terminology) occur when we "carry ourselves back in thought to those moments of our existence when we made some serious decision, moments unique of their kind and which will never be repeated."[67] Such "new" decisions break the bond of reason that encloses us in the "circle of the given." Just as one learns swimming, not from textbooks, but by being thrust into the new milieu and adapting to it, so "we enjoy liberty above all when we try to create a new man in ourselves for the purpose of shattering the historical framework that encloses us. . . . When we act, it is because we have created an entirely artificial world."[68] At such moments we are dominated by an overwhelming emotion characterized by inner turmoil—a psychological movement.

In order to create this artificial world, according to Sorel, we must have myths: these myths foster the "individualist strength in the aroused masses"[69] which "leads men to prepare themselves for a battle to destroy what exists."[70] This enthusiasm for battle is a replication of the one found in the revolutionary armies. Workers "envisage an immense uprising that can again be called individualistic: each one marching with as much ardor as possible, operating on his own account, scarcely concerning himself with subordinating his behavior to a carefully constructed overall plan."[71]

Furthermore, this unmediated quality of the general-strike myth enhances a sense of personal and productive worth. The myth is experienced directly, Sorel tells us:

> The great advantage the strike offers us when conducted solely by the workers without interference from politicians is that the worker learns from it to count on the value of his own personal effort, on his responsibility, and on the influences these sacrifices have on future events. In changing the conditions of his work, he knows that he obtained results gained by his intelligently employed efforts; he resembles a peasant who creates a

> better domain for his family through a better cultivation of a heretofore neglected field.[72]

Finally, the sense of tension necessary for creative and productive work is inherent in the general-strike myth. Again in Bergsonian terms, the creative soul is like a coiled-up spring, but Sorel seems to be of the opinion that a *détente*, a release, of this spring must occur in a sublimated form as the release of positive creative energies. The fundamental question for Sorel is to what extent the *myth* of the general strike replaces the *actual* general strike, in the way modern productivity has replaced the wars of antiquity. Sorel seems hesitant to resolve the conflict between bourgeoisie and proletariat. To do so might, according to Sorel, repeat the mistakes of 1789 that ended in lax morality and in terroristic despotism. Sorel can maintain that the great difference between the general-strike myth as a projection of class war, on the one hand, and modern conventional war, on the other, lies in the fact that political wars "end in accords," in resolution of some kind.[73] Sorel has in effect replaced the Marxist doctrine by which the class war is resolved in fact with a mythical struggle. Marx's catastrophic revolution "should not be taken as materially established, directed and determined in time. It is the ensemble [of strike images] alone which should impress us, and this ensemble is perfectly clear."[74] Sorel gives us a Proudhonian balance between two strong forces—each certain of victory, each anticipating triumph. The virile American capitalist should replace the decadent European one and the proletariat replace the heroic soldier in the industrial equivalent of war. That is why Sorel employs such terms as *preparation* and *anticipation* in his analysis of the general-strike myth. The sense of expectancy of the forthcoming battle enhances the tension, the mystery, and the creativity of the subject, and leads Sorel to argue that the materialization of the myth is of secondary importance.

III

In order to make this point clearer, we should now turn to the first of two functions the myth of the general strike performs in extricating Sorel from his difficulties in regard to his criticism of Marxism and of socialist utopianism. This consists in providing a motor image of the future, an image necessary for action, without making that image utopian.

Sorel criticizes Marxism in its social-democratic form as deterministic, as providing us with a pseudo-science of predictive history. This science is, in Sorel's view, necessarily utopian as well, for it led many social democrats to depict the city of the future that lay at the culmination of the historical process. This mixture of historicism and utopianism should not be mistaken for science.

On the other hand, Sorel recognizes the need for motor images to be viewed *en bloc* if they are to move people to act. There is, in short, a clash between criticism of Marxism as a science of predictive history, on the one hand, and acknowledgment of the need for men to think holistically, on the other. The theory of the myth reconciles this apparent conflict by asserting that if the integrative and holistic character of thought is viewed in a certain way, it produces the opposite of the quietism found in the theory of progress or the dialectic; it produces action. Although we must reject predictive and fatalistic historicism, we can, in Sorel's view, reap the benefits of the idea of certainty found in the dialectic by the simple device of not thinking about the future in a utopian way. Some sort of vision of the future is needed:

> We are not able to act without leaving the present, without thinking about the future, which always seems condemned to escape our reason. Experience proves that some *constructions of a future, undetermined in time*, can possess great effectiveness and have very few disadvantages when they are of a certain nature; this occurs when it is a question of myths, in which are found the strongest inclinations of a people, a party, or a class, tendencies which present themselves to the mind with the insistence of instincts in all of life's circumstances, giving an appearance of complete reality to the hope of imminent action on which the reform of the will is based.[75]

Science cannot calculate the future the way an astronomer calculates the phases of the moon. Though the myth of the general strike must deny the accuracy of historical predictions, the device allows the workers to feel that their cause is "assured of triumph,"[76] to reject belief in utopia and yet have some picture of the future. Such feelings or visions of future triumph Sorel calls myths; primitive Christianity, the Reformation, the French Revolution and, of course, Marx's catastrophic revolution itself are examples of myths.[77]

How can the myth of the general strike inculcate conviction and still view historical science with suspicion? Sorel says that the myth must depict the great epic as occurring in the *near* future, for it is in the nature of epic to deal with the future and not the past. Myths are, therefore, not descriptions of things but "expressions of the will."[78] He takes as a prime example of the phenomenon the French Revolution, which appeared to many at the time as a series of glorious wars whose historical consequences could not be predicted; it was "the epic of the wars which had filled the French soul with an enthusiasm analogous to that provoked by religions" and which rendered all criticism impossible.[79] When the masses are deeply moved in such a way, they are thrown into an entirely Homeric or epic state of mind in which the "social poetry"[80] of the general strike becomes a phenomenon of war. As such a "state of mind," the myth can be viewed as a psychological surrogate for the law of historical development. That the cause of the people is "assured of triumph" is not inconsistent with the failures of a science of historical prediction, for they no longer search for unity in the imminent developments of man that seem to give order and appearance to history, but in psychological developments hidden beneath them. It is what takes place in our own minds or souls that is important; that is where the myth is. Nowhere is the essential nature of the myth more succinctly stated than in Sorel's assertion that it is not the "socialism of things" with which he is concerned but the "socialism of socialists."

IV

Since the first principal function of the myth is to give us certainty without a rationalistic ideology—improvement without the ideology of progress—the second function the myth performs in Sorel's thought is more easily depicted: Sorel can retain his criticism of the brutality of Marx's catastrophic revolution and yet depict a vision of catastrophe which entails "a minimum of brutality."[81] The myth of the general strike, while proclaiming the creativity of violence, places strict limits on the excesses one usually associates with it. Sorel does this by emphasizing creativity in place of hatred, production in place of distributive justice.

How, it has been asked, can the idea of a strike whose purpose is to halt production be reconciled with the idea of improved production? According to Sorel, if jealousy causes us to destroy fruitful productive methods and hatred produces needless killing, worthwhile production is impossible. By depicting the revolution mythically, that is, by appealing to our best instincts, the drama of the general strike acts as an ethical restraint on brutality and even on physical damage to property.

In his attitude toward violence in the realm of economic productivity, it would be a grave mistake to assume that Sorel is an heir of the Luddites or the saboteurs of early capitalism. We know enough about Sorel's concern with the creative role of industry to understand why he says that "sabotage is a reactionary vestige of the *ancien régime* which society should abolish."[82] His criticism of the capitalist class is not based on the idea of economic injustice in the distributive sense, but on the view that the capitalist class inhibits productivity—that it is parasitic. The allies of the capitalists, the democratic politicians, are even less productive and hence are incapable of producing any genuine social change. Since the myth of the general strike is indissolubly connected with a love for production, the myth possesses self-contained limits to impeding that productive process. In this respect, Sorel proclaims himself the heir of Marx, whom Sorel interprets as arguing that "on the day of the revolution, the proletariat will be disciplined, united, organized by the very mechanism of production."[83] Therefore they cannot, according to Sorel's interpretation of Marxism, destroy the basis of this discipline. If the productive methods and organization of workers are already in place, Sorel envisages revolutionary activity as ridding the productive process of those more parasitic elements of the capitalist class who are not essential to modern production. Commercial capitalists, allied with intellectuals and bureaucrats, remain the enemy, Sorel says: "In big industry many high-level employees could be eliminated if large stockholders did not need to place clients. A better division of labor would allow, as in England, the concentration of work (now done badly by too many engineers) in a small group of very learned and very experienced technicians . . . and . . . the majority of bosses done away with. . . . This says, then, that the socialization of the means of production would require a huge lock-out."[84] If the revolution ever does occur, the financial and intellectual classes would constitute that section of the superstructure on whom the workers simply turn their backs.

According to Sorel, such a lock-out demands an efficient organization of production in a period of great economic prosperity. Workers do not rebel against poverty so much as against the failure of the economic system to live up to its potential. Thus Sorel reminds his readers that the "economic crises" of which Marx spoke were different from periods of economic decadence. Crises should be distinguished from a general economic decline. A crisis is a short-range maladjustment in a dynamic economy; an economic decline is a long-term, general loss of productive vigor.[85]

Sorel proclaims the "danger for the future of civilization produced by revolutions which take place in a period of economic decadence."[86] According to Sorel, the myth looks upon the future with "bright hope," and it is essential that the future of productive forces be presented in the same light:

> It is important to lay stress on the high degree of prosperity industry must possess in order that the realization of socialism

> may be possible, for experience shows us that it is by seeking to *stop the progress of capitalism* and to preserve the means of existence of social classes which are on the downgrade that the prophets of social peace chiefly endeavor to capture popular favor. The dependence of the revolution on the constant and rapid progress of industry must be demonstrated in a striking manner.[87]

Sorel's concern with decadent or declining classes, that is, with those which are severing themselves from production, implies a vague theory of authority. Sorel does not discuss authority explicitly in the *Reflections*, but implicit in its pages is the assumption, later outlined explicitly in *De l'Utilité du pragmatisme*, that a decline in the authority of the ruling classes produces a corresponding increase in the force employed by those authorities to sustain their position in society. By *force* is meant repression by the agents of the state and its ruling classes.

This partly explains the extraordinary importance attributed to demagogy and ruling-class ideologies in Sorel's thought. Throughout his writings Sorel has asserted that a state maintains its supremacy through ideological eyewash (e.g., progress) and, when this fails, by force. As we have seen, according to Sorel part of the ideology of any modern ruling class consists, in addition to the ideology of progress, in the ideology of distributive justice attained through equal shares (the theory of surplus value is the equivalent of this ideology in Marxism).[88] Demagogic leaders easily persuade the masses to believe that the best way to improve their lot is to make claims on the rich for equal distribution, but these sentiments of justice are only sustained through arousing feelings of jealousy.

According to Sorel, this jealousy is not a stable sentiment; it transforms itself into something much worse. Jealousy is a sentiment of weak and passive (and, by implication, unproductive) beings. Leaders, on the other hand, have active sentiments. Once the sentiment of jealousy is wielded by them for their own purposes, "jealousy is transformed into a thirst to obtain, at whatever cost, the most coveted situations, and they employ to this end any means which enables them to set aside people who stand in the way of their onward march."[89] Once the "masses who are led" are convinced of the utility of employing the state to pester the rich, "we pass from jealousy to vengeance, and it is well known that vengeance is a sentiment of extraordinary power, especially with the weak."[90] The root emotion of vengeance is the "creative hatred" advocated by Jaurès. Such hatred Sorel regards as a "caricature of the class struggle."[91] Sorel said in an earlier essay that "hatred can unleash upheavals, destroy social organization, and throw a country into an era of bloody revolutions; but it produces nothing. . . . Tyranny quickly succeeds tyranny."[92]

Upheavals are directly connected to what we ordinarily call violence; Sorel's understanding of "violence" against the ruling classes must therefore be rather different from the usual meaning of the word. Working-class violence must be relatively free from vengeance, jealousy, hatred, and tyrannical bloodletting. If violence on the part of the working classes does in fact contain these elements, it is no different from the force and brutality employed by the old rulers. Thus Sorel says that "the term *violence* should be used solely for acts of rebellion; we should say therefore that the object of *force* is to impose a particular social system of minority rule, while *violence* aims at the destruction of that order. The bourgeoisie has used *force* since the beginning of modernity, while the proletariat now reacts against the middle classes and against the state through *violence*."[93] However, if the revolt is to be free of hatred and tyranny, the distinction that Sorel draws between violence and force is more than a terminological refinement; it means that "violence had a completely different meaning in the old revolutions. . . . The future revolution will not be comparable to that of the eighteenth century."[94] Indeed, it appears that Sorel equates force with brutality and redefines violence as a negation of brutality (where brutality is violence in the commonly understood meaning of the term). In order to clarify this distinction between force and violence in qualitative terms, it would be fruitful to make comparisons between Sorel's thought and that of Albert Camus. In *The Rebel*, Camus distinguishes *rebellion*, an act of refusal of existing repression, from *revolution*, which attacks the existing order with both a plan for the future organization and a worked-out theory of historical destiny—usually rooted in the ideology of progress. Rebellion can be compared with the "violence" of the myth of the general strike because, unlike revolution, it is non-utopian and eschews the repressive "force" of the state. Most importantly, to Camus, because of its very nature rebellion possesses built-in limits to its own force (brutality). By confining itself to an act of refusal, it negates the existing authority through establishing limits to power itself—hence to its own power.

There are of course considerable differences between Camus and Sorel, despite the former's expressed indebtedness to the latter. Camus has no myth and at times seems to be more inclined than Sorel to reject any violence or struggle. Sorel, at any rate, does not reject material conflict altogether. He is not a pacifist. What he has tried to do is to emphasize the importance of the content of feelings or sentiments in determining the content of revolutionary acts; that is, whether the struggle will, when dominated by feelings of hatred or personal gain, degenerate into what he calls a "politico-criminal association" exploiting society from the outside or whether action, motivated by the feeling of the sublime, will thrust brutality into the background and remake society from the inside. This "inside," this noble side, that is, the side considered by poets in social conflict, consists in the striving for immortality, "the sentiment of glory which Renan so justly looked upon as one of the most singular and most powerful creations of human genius, and which has been of such incomparable value in history." For Sorel, to "conquer glory at the peril of one's life" leads to "the idea that the profession of arms cannot be compared to any other profession . . . that history is based entirely on the adventures of warriors."[95]

War fails to perform these functions when "the object of war is no longer war itself," when "its object is to allow politicians to satisfy their ambition."[96] In this category of demagogic or democratic wars, Sorel includes those wars fought on behalf of imperialism. He defines the latter as wars which are fought so that "the foreigner must be conquered in order that politicians obtain great and immediate advantages. . . . Under the influence of the desire for gain, the people permit the government to develop its authority in an improper manner without any protest so that every conquest abroad may be viewed as having its inevitable corollary, a conquest at home by the party in office." For politicians, "the proletariat is their army, which they love in the same way that a colonial administrator loves the troops which enable him to bring large numbers of Negroes under his authority. . . . They keep up the ardor of their men as the ardor of troops of mercenaries has always been kept up by promises of pillage."[97] Sorel scorned the Moroccan intervention which was justified in terms of democratic rhetoric and on the grounds of universal justice.[98]

But what of Sorel's views when plunder and politics play little or no role in imperialism? Does war for its own sake mean power for its own sake, or a Nietzschean "will to power"? Pierre Lasserre argues that Sorel is a "theorist of imperialism" and refers to Sorel's admiration for Nietzsche's "superb blond beast prowling in search of prey and bloodshed."[99] It is Lasserre's view that Sorel "depended" on Nietzsche by admitting only aristocratic right, except that it is the working class which is the aristocracy today. For Nietzsche the true law and the only possible law is an aristocratic right which is "conceived as the imperious decree which organizes relations among men for the benefit of its sovereignty."[100] Victoriously installed in the bastions of the old social powers, the workers' army will impose its will imperiously, in a "pure expression" of the morality of force.[101] "Everything that it will establish in law henceforth will emanate from it. If our epoch is the epoch of imperialism, Sorel invented working-class imperialism."[102] To this Geneviève Bianquis adds that Sorel, relying on a theory of "Nietzschean imperialism," extols a morality in which "the strongest triumph."[103]

Sorel scorns comparing the proletariat with the superman of Nietzsche, whom Sorel used primarily for illustrative purposes.[104] Lasserre and Bianquis mistakenly attribute to Sorel a theory of sovereign power which he had spent a good portion of the *Illusions of Progress* denouncing. That is to say, a theory of imperium, as Lasserre states it, relies on a single, centralized source. It ignores the Proudhonian (and perhaps the Nietzschean) idea of balance that is essential to Sorel's view of power. This idea of balance, as we have seen in regard to Proudhon, goes beyond the warrior ethic. Sorel does not confine himself to the poetic view of violence for which he invoked Nietzsche's authority, but juxtaposes it to a "sacerdotal"[105] morality that Nietzsche scorned; following Proudhon, Sorel transforms this priestly morality into an ethic of "sexual fidelity and devotion to the weak" based on family love.[106] To Sorel freedom is possible only when these two viewpoints are balanced with one another and also with the ethic of labor which "escapes Nietzsche's classification."[107] This proximity of freedom and conflict indicates why Sorel insists that this concept of balance should be part of the warrior ethic itself. Proletarian violence should strengthen the bourgeoisie and vice versa. Only when the two warring classes achieve a kind of equilibrium will capitalist society have reached its "historical perfection"; to Sorel, this perfection has been reached in the United States, where Andrew Carnegie and others did so much to combine virtue and liberty.[108]

V

This leads to the final function of Sorel's myth of the general strike: to provide a coherence and unity to the syndicalist movement while at the same time preserving social plurality and individual liberty. Sorel is partly inspired by the traditions of the liberty-loving English Yeoman of the sixteenth century whose heirs are responsible for the "extraordinary greatness of the United States."[109] On the one hand, this class produced energetic adventurers such as Theodore Roosevelt, that is, "the Yankee ready for any kind of enterprise." Sorel asserts that "if the professor of philology had not been continually cropping up in Nietzsche he would . . . above all . . . have established a parallel between the ancient heroes and the man who sets out to conquer the Far West."[110] Sorel denounces the European mentality described by Tocqueville, in which the spirit of association is based on the imitation of the military corps, and extols the American spirit "in which the warrior type is pushed to its extreme form in the cowboy" who loves drinking, playing, and the boisterous pleasures. Admirable in the face of danger, insouciant, intemperate, and improvident, this figure is "animated with the spirit of liberty."[111] Sorel's doctrine of individualism is guided partly by the myth of the American West. Informed not a little by the writings of Paul de Rousiers, a disciple of Frederic Le Play, Sorel noted that the English Yeomanry not only produced adventurers but produced a new social authority, the social basis for the sectarians who settled America. These sectarians were the bearers of "apocalyptic myths" which possessed qualities similar to those found in the general-strike myth of the syndicalists. And as the Yankee adventurer was the carrier of a culture devoted to freedom, so the religious sentiments of these descendants of the Yeomen upheld values of liberty analogous to those found in syndicalism. Both Yankee Protestantism and syndicalism possessed apocalyptic myths which in no way impinged upon the liberty of the citizen to engage in secular causes or to pursue practical ends. "Revolutionary syndicalism is the equivalent of the Protestant sects which in America are so autonomous and so young."[112]

Sorel noted, first of all, that the English and American sectarians were, despite their religious exaltation, very practical men. "Social myths do not prevent any man from learning to profit from all the observations he makes in the course of his life and . . . they are no obstacle to the fulfillment of normal business."[113]

More importantly, Sorel thought that just as with the Protestant sects, there is no reason why society should be limited to specifically socialist institutions. Nothing should prevent socialists from entering into other groups devoted to temperance, art, or science, and socialists needn't concern themselves with whether the founders of these institutions are socialist. He opposes the "splendid isolation" of modern totalitarian movements in which all activities are connected within party organizations or front groups. "Just as the most zealous members of the American sects follow their own paths, syndicalists can participate in the common political life without abandoning their principles."[114]

He even went so far as to suggest that syndicalists can work with political parties in anti-clerical battles, although he objected to the discipline and party-line voting of the organized political parties, and insisted that "each one should act in his own way."[115] Sorel insisted paradoxically that "syndicalism is the only organized expression of socialism." Only in syndicalist organizations "can socialists acting individually take an active part in the common struggles of their countries."[116]

Sorel's individualism is not merely a poetic expression of the general-strike myth, but is an active characteristic of that myth which is partly inspired by liberal institutions. It is therefore not surprising that Sorel should attempt to find a philosophical basis for his pluralistic viewpoint, in the years that succeeded the publication of the *Reflections*, in the writings of the American philosopher of pluralism, William James, rather than in Nietzsche or in some "fascist" philosopher of the will to power.

Notes

1. Peter Stearns, *Revolutionary Syndicalism and French Labor* (New Brunswick: Rutgers University Press, 1971), p. 14.
2. Ibid., p. 19. Stearns cautions that conditions were changing.
3. Georges Goriely, *Le Pluralisme dramatique de Georges Sorel.*
4. Sorel, *Insegnamenti*, pp. 52-53.
5. Ibid., p. 392; *FGS*, p. 199.
6. Ibid., p. 392.
7. See Chapter 4, above; Sorel, *Illusions*, chap. 7.
8. Sorel, "Les Syndicats industriels et leur signification," *Revue Socialiste* (July 1902): 44.
9. Ibid. (Aug. 1902): 173.
10. Sorel, *Insegnamenti*, pp. 391-92. Cf. "Le Syndicalisme révolutionnaire," *Mouvement Socialiste* (Nov. 1905): 280.
11. (Paris: Schleicher; reprinted by Gorden and Breach, Paris, 1971). References will be to the 1971 reprint. Cf. Sorel *Insegnamenti*, p. 53.
12. Pelloutier, *Histoire des bourses du travail*, pp. 98-99.
13. The literature on French syndicalism is considerable. In addition to Pelloutier and Peter Stearns, see Paul Louis, *Histoire du mouvement syndical en France* (Paris: Valois, 1947); F. F. Ridley, *Revolutionary Syndicalism in France: The Direct Action of Its Time* (Cambridge: Cambridge University Press, 1970); and Jacques Julliard, *Fernand Pelloutier et les origines du syndicalisme d'action directe* (Paris: Editions du Seuil, 1971).
14. Pelloutier, *Histoire des bourses du travail*, pp. 61-62.
15. Sorel, "Les Dissensions de la social-démocratie allemande à propos des écrits de M. Bernstein," *Revue Politique et Parlementaire* (July 1900): 63 (italics Sorel's).
16. Ibid., p. 63. Sorel uses the English word *self-government.*
17. Pelloutier, *Histoire des bourses du travail*, pp. 116-17.
18. Ibid., p. 117.
19. Ibid., p. 119.
20. Ibid., p. 120.

21. Ibid., p. 109.
22. Ibid., p. 117.
23. Sorel, "Syndicalisme révolutionnaire," pp. 276-77.
24. Sorel, *Insegnamenti*, p. 394.
25. Bernstein, cited in *FGS*, p. 106. No source is given.
26. Sorel, Preface to Serverio Merlino, *Formes et essence du socialisme*, p. xxvii.
27. *FGS*, pp. 107-8. Cf. Sorel, *Insegnamenti*, p. 16.
28. Sorel's Preface to Merlino, pp. xli-xlii.
29. Sorel, "Etude sur Vico," p. 1033.
30. Ibid., p. 1020.
31. Ibid., p. 1037: "The authority of heroic times can perhaps be compared to that of the high Middle Ages. If there is a period in which justice is completely absent, it is here."
32. Ibid., p. 1033.
33. Sorel, *Insegnamenti*, p. 397.
34. *FGS*, p. 89.
35. Sorel, "La Valeur sociale de l'art," *Revue de Métaphysique et de Morale* (1901): 278 (hereafter referred to as "Art").
36. Ibid., p. 273.
37. Ibid., p. 277.
38. Ibid., p. 273.
39. Ibid., p. 275.
40. *FGS*, p. 219.
41. Ibid., p. 220. Compare J. Glenn Gray, who says in regard to World War II: "As one approached the combat area, relations between officers and men became more natural and functional; the spit and polish of army book discipline disappeared. . . . There was a surprising lack of orders from above; each man becomes more or less his own authority. The amount of individual responsibility is both frightening and heartening": *The Warriors: Reflections on Men in Battle* (New York: Harper, 1967), pp. 135-36.
42. Sorel, "Art," p. 277.
43. Ibid., p. 269.
44. Sorel, *Réflexions sur la violence*, p. 378 (*FGS*, p. 222; *Reflections*, p. 243).
45. Sorel, "Art," pp. 272, 274.
46. Sorel, *Introduction à l'économie moderne*, p. 390.
47. Sorel, "Art," p. 251.
48. Ibid., pp. 266-67.
49. Ibid., pp. 270-71.
50. *FGS*, p. 77.
51. Ibid., p. 78.
52. Ibid., p. 214.
53. Ibid., p. 220.
54. Sorel, *Reflections*, p. 144.
55. Ibid., p. 148.
56. Sorel, "Art," p. 276.
57. Ibid., p. 251.
58. Sorel, "Etude sur Vico," p. 1025.
59. Sorel, *Réflexions*, p. 217 (American edition, p. 148).
60. Sorel, "Etude sur Vico," p. 1034.
61. Ibid., pp. 1024-25, citing Vico's *Nouvelle Science* 2.2.1, p. 388.

62. *FGS*, p. 200.
63. Sorel, *Réflexions*, p. 180 (*FGS*, p. 208; *Reflections*, pp. 122-23).
64. Ibid., p. 182 (*FGS*, p. 210).
65. Ibid., p. 217.
66. Sorel, "Quelques objections au matérialisme économique," *Humanité Nouvelle* (June 1899): 659.
67. *FGS*, p. 204.
68. Ibid.
69. Ibid., p. 221.
70. Ibid., p. 205.
71. Ibid., p. 220.
72. Sorel, Preface to Victor Griffuelhes and L. Niel's *Les Objectifs de nos luttes de classe* (Paris: La Publication Sociale, 1909), pp. 7-8.
73. Sorel, "Syndicalisme révolutionnaire," p. 275.
74. Sorel, *Réflexions*, p. 196 (American edition, p. 135).
75. *FGS*, p. 209 (*Réflexions*, p. 177; American edition, p. 125. Sorel's italics).
76. *FGS*, p. 200 (*Reflections*, p. 41).
77. *FGS*, p. 200.
78. Sorel, *Réflexions*, p. 46 (*FGS*, p. 205; American edition, p. 50).
79. Ibid., p. 136.
80. Sorel, *Matériaux*, p. 189. Cf. *Reflections*, p. 240; *FGS*, p. 219.
81. Sorel, *Reflections*, p. 188.
82. Sorel, "Syndicalisme révolutionnaire," p. 277.
83. Sorel, *Reflections*, p. 135. Sorel notes that Marx referred to certain types of socialism as reactionary because they sought to hinder industrial progress (cf. *FGS*, p. 305n36).
84. *FGS*, pp. 78-79. See also the *Lettres à Paul Delesalle*, 19 May 1918 (p. 143), in which Sorel says that according to Marx "capitalism today will be characterized by the predominance of productive organizations as against usury or financial combinations. . . . If the future lies in socialism, according to Marx industrial organization will assume increasing importance in the economy. Bourgeois writers who claim to prove the absurdity of socialism assume, on the contrary, that production can prosper only under the direction of financiers."
85. Sorel, *Reflections*, p. 95.
86. Ibid., p. 136.
87. Ibid., p. 137. Italics are added.
88. See Chapter 4 above.
89. Sorel, *Reflections*, p. 164.
90. Ibid., pp. 164-65.
91. Sorel, *Insegnamenti*, p. 394n. Cf. *FGS*, p. 305n38: "Intellectuals assimilate the attitudes corresponding to the class struggle, what one of them calls 'creative hatred.' The ferocious jealousy of the poor intellectual, who hopes to push the rich speculator to the guillotine, is a bad sentiment containing nothing socialist." J. Glenn Gray, discussing the hateful images of the enemy in modern wars, notes that in World War II many a soldier was appalled to receive letters from home demanding to know how many men he had killed. Gray argues that "the understanding of his opponents' motives, a precondition of sympathy, is usually easier for a trained military man than is the comprehension of the motives of his own political superiors or the civilian mentality of his people. . . . This commonly recognized fact

should surprise nobody, for the military profession, like few others, is a way of life that forms its subjects in relative isolation from modern sentiments and political metamorphoses. When we ask why this image of the enemy grows increasingly unpopular in our day, honest answers are hardly flattering to the anti-militarists": *The Warriors*, pp. 135, 145-46.

92. *FGS*, p. 100.

93. Sorel, *Reflections*, pp. 171-72.

94. Sorel, *Insegnamenti*, p. 54.

95. Sorel, *Reflections*, p. 166.

96. Ibid.

97. Ibid., pp. 167-68.

98. Sorel, "Le déclin du parti socialiste international," *Mouvement Socialiste* (Feb. 1906): 200.

99. Pierre Lasserre, *Georges Sorel, théoricien de l'impérialisme* (Paris: Artisan du Livre, 1928), p. 38. Cf. *FGS*, p. 212.

100. Lasserre, *Georges Sorel*, p. 33.

101. Ibid., p. 92.

102. Ibid., p. 38.

103. Geneviève Bianquis, *Nietzsche en France*, pp. 79, 83.

104. See Chapter 1, n. 74; *FGS*, p. 335n7, citing J. Bourdeau, *Les Maîtres de la pensée contemporaine*.

105. *FGS*, pp. 214-15; Goriely, *Le Pluralisme dramatique de Georges Sorel*, pp. 54-55.

106. Compare Nietzsche's hostility to marriage based on love in *Twilight of the Idols*, section 39 of the chapter entitled "Skirmishes of an Untimely Man": "With the growing indulgence of love matches, the very foundation of marriage has been eliminated, that alone which makes an institution of it. Never, absolutely never, can an institution be founded on an idiosyncrasy": Walter Kaufmann, ed. and trans., *The Portable Nietzsche* (Hammondsworth: Penguin, 1977), p. 544.

107. *FGS*, p. 216. Compare Nietzsche, loc. cit., p. 40, in which, not unlike Sorel, he scoffs at elevating labor into a social question. But Nietzsche also scorns the idea of the dignity of labor.

108. *FGS*, p. 214; *Reflections*, p. 92. Indeed, Lasserre admits in Sorel's theory that we end with "two aristocracies face to face. The class war loses its character of bitterness and hatred. It is reduced to the competition between classes whose rough conflicts of interest would be dominated by a will to peace common to proud men" (*Georges Sorel*, p. 40). But how "imperialistic" is this equilibrium? Sorel notes that when George Pullman attempted a paternalistic regime in his Chicago plant by constructing housing for workers, "the result was the Chicago Pullman strike. . . . Antagonism was born of a philanthropy which was misunderstood." At Pullman's Wilmington plant, where no such attempt was made and whose workers were paid the same salaries as in Chicago, there was no strike (Sorel, review of Paul de Rousiers, "La Vie américaine. Ranches, fermes et usines," *Revue Internationale de Sociologie*, (Oct. 1899), p. 746. The quote is Paul de Rousiers's).

109. *FGS*, p. 213, Sorel's review of Paul de Rousiers, ibid., and of "La Vie américaine: L'Education et la société," in *Revue Internationale de Sociologie* (Feb. 1900): 133.

110. *FGS*, p. 213.

111. Sorel, review of Paul de Rousiers, "La Vie américaine. Ranches,

fermes et usines," pp. 744-45.

112. Sorel, "Le déclin du parti socialiste international," p. 197.

113. *FGS*, pp. 209-210, 335n7.

114. Sorel, "Le Déclin du parti socialiste international," p. 199.

115. Ibid.

116. Ibid., pp. 201-2. It is therefore an oversimplification to argue, as Leszek Kolakowski does, that Sorel sought a rejuvenation of the world "through the breaking of all ties with the dominant culture": "Georges Sorel, Jansenist Marxist," *Dissent* (Winter 1975): p. 71. See above, p. 174, and below, pp. 323-24.

IX
PRAGMATISM, 1909–1921

The paradoxical quality of the social myth set forth in the *Reflections on Violence* is that it reflects history but is not determined by it; it emerges from historical circumstances but rises above the status of mere ideology. Yet the failure of the social myth, which became increasingly obvious in the months following the publication of the *Reflections*, raised questions for Sorel, although he retained his faith in the workers' movement. The relationship between the vision of moral truth that the myth embodied and the social circumstances from which it emerged demanded a more precise theoretical justification than it had received in the *Reflections*. The events in the workers' movement following the *Reflections* seemed to place the social myth in direct confrontation with historical events.

The problem was created by the severe setbacks experienced by the syndicates in a series of strikes undertaken at about the time the *Reflections on Violence* was published. The general strike had lost its poetic character and heroism had been replaced by a series of bloody encounters culminating in the 1908 clashes at Villeneuve-Saint-Georges and Auquonte, during which nine people were killed and sixty-nine wounded. In 1909, Victor Griffuelhes was forced out of his post as the militant head of the Confederation Générale du Travail. When a number of strikes by postmen and railwaymen were broken, it seemed as though ten years of heroic struggle had left the working class disoriented and tired. To Sorel, union activity was now directed more toward raising salaries than toward maintaining an independent existence. The proletariat was becoming bourgeoisified, sapped of its moral strength.[1]

Had "history" treated Sorel cruelly in falsifying the theory of the myth of the general strike as well as the idea of social myths in a general sense? And were such myths, if they did exist, merely subjectivistic illusions? The problem that confronted Sorel was the very practical question of what intersubjective tests exist for determining the validity of myths in particular and of success or failure of social institutions in general.

While he was not fully aware of the content of William James's writings before he began work on the *Reflections* in 1905, Sorel had already made clear in that work that the concept of the social myth could be tested by pragmatic criteria. Sorel's acceptance of these criteria enabled him to continue to accept the idea of the social myth after the particular example of the myth of the general strike had lost its effectiveness among workers. Pragmatism helped add coherence to a theory of social myths that went far beyond syndicalism or a theory of revolt, for it also helped Sorel construct a theory of authority, inspired by Le Play and his followers, based on the experience of the workers' organizations. In 1914, Sorel asserted that "the syndicates appear very much like social authorities that exercise control over the normal means of work."[2] As it turns out, the pragmatism of the *Reflections* is not a prescription for chaos, but anticipates an ordering principle that embodies a continuum between thought and action, between syndicalist pluralism and social participation and between revolution and authority.

I

Sorel's discovery of pragmatism in 1908 did not constitute a radical dissociation from most of his previous modes of thought, but was coincidental with a change of political allegiance toward more conservative views. Although he expressed his intention of abandoning syndicalism, he did not carry through fully on his promise, nor did he break with Marxian viewpoints in certain respects, but instead attempted to reconcile them with William James's pragmatism. Even as late as 1919, Sorel asserted that "pragmatism was in agreement with Marx's historical materialism"[3] (a view shared by Bertrand Russell). However, Sorel's diremptive treatment of social phenomena was in greater agreement with James than with Marx. Sorel, Marx and James all agree that man shapes his own world, but the difference between Sorel's pragmatism and Marxism is that, in Sorel's pragmatic view, we cannot predict scientifically what the future revolution will bring. Marx views the world as being ultimately rational insofar as we consciously shape that world, while James and Sorel are willing to accept the world as a "blooming, buzzing confusion." As Sorel says of the myth of the general strike,

"We are perfectly aware that the historians of the future are bound to discover that we labored under the influence of many illusions, because they will see before them a finished world;"[4] after all, "we know from experience what woe has been caused by false legends which have led people to commit heroic but absurd indiscretions."[5]

How Sorel can take seriously social myths, let alone the general-strike myth, in light of these admissions is explained by Sorel's metaphysical pluralism, for which James provided a systematic statement. For James as well as for Sorel, there will likely be found a "heterogeneity between the ends realized and the ends given."[6] Such a heterogeneity not only renders absurd Renan's positivist debunking of Christianity but confirms the impossibility of Marx's total science. Sorel confesses in the *Reflections* that the content of the myth may be different from the external reality governing it. "In everyday life, are we not accustomed to recognizing that reality differs greatly from the ideas that we had of it before acting? And this does not prevent us from continuing to make resolutions."[7] But since no one can predict just what these absurdities will be in each case, and since no one can anticipate what future historians will say, "nobody can provide us with a means of qualifying our motor images in such a way as to avoid their criticism."[8] The Homeric qualities of the general strike thus retain that mystery of the future which Sorel saw as the tragic dimension of all historical developments.

Even in the *Reflections*, Sorel does not argue that it is entirely fruitless to analyze the social myth, or that any individual can be carried away by any impulse. On the contrary, "of course this picture [of the general strike] must be tested, and that is what I have attempted to do."[9] He proposes to go about this testing process using pragmatic standards. Sorel's separation of the content of myth from its external reality is close to James's distinction between "religious propensities" and the question of a religion's "philosophical significance," or what James calls the existential judgment of religion as opposed to our spiritual judgment of its value.[10]

Richard Vernon takes this to mean that the myth must be understood as the ideas of the participants in social action, who are distinguished sharply from the observers of an action, and that Sorel is looking at the myth of the general strike from the point of view of an observer who is only able to judge the truth of the myth *ex post facto*.[11] How close this comes to making Sorel into a positivist separating fact and value as well as theory and practice is problematic, as I have shown in Chapter 3 and elsewhere.[12] Vernon is certainly correct in asserting that this separation distances Sorel from

Marx, but Sorel does not separate belief from everyday conduct, as is demonstrated by the various ways in which pragmatism is employed in looking at the myth.

The first pragmatic criterion by which James and Sorel judge a belief system is that, in James's words, "beliefs are rules of action. . . . If there were any part of thought that made no difference in the thought's practical consequences, then that part would be no proper element of the thought's significance. To develop a thought's meaning, we need only determine what conduct it is fitted to produce."[13] The "success" of a doctrine is measured by its relation to our day-to-day actions rather than by its inner coherence. Metaphysical discussions of the "essence" or attributes of a doctrine are as meaningless for James as they are for Sorel. What importance do these attributes have for the life of men? If they do not affect conduct, what difference can it make to religious thought whether they are true or false?[14] Sorel can defend the "mediocrity" of American theology on the grounds that such mediocrity is "compensated by the practice of religious experience." Whether beliefs are based on bad theology is much less important than the fact that "they possess the political power of myths . . . giving this term the meaning . . . assigned to it in the *Reflections on Violence*."[15]

Just as James argues, for example, that religious doctrine is valid because it satisfies an inner need, Sorel argues that "it matters little whether the general strike is a partial reality or only a product of the popular imagination. The whole question consists of knowing whether the general strike contains everything that the socialist doctrine expects from the proletariat."[16] As Sorel sums it up, "A system can be celebrated as admissible even while it contains lacunae, grave contradictions, or gross errors, if it suggests to many men a useful tactic to follow in order to conduct what might be called a siege of reality. . . . Many examples show the fruitlessness of philosophies made notable through good and prudent construction, because they halt the mind from undertaking new methods."[17]

Furthermore, Sorel follows James in asserting that a belief cannot be tested on the grounds of the content of the belief itself, but only according to some external standard or function. As an instrumentalist doctrine, pragmatism asserts that something is true or false in relation to some other datum, never "in itself." In this respect pragmatism surmounts the strictly positivist separation of fact and value, because it possesses certain analogies to the actions of the marketplace that link fact, value, and action: one attributes a certain value to a thing; and this is measured partially by our willingness to pay for it, if we can afford it. (1) Like a commodity, a belief has no abstract value but exists only because it is satisfactory to us; (2) it links value to activity in our willingness to perform certain acts (payment of money as well as use) and thus tends to erase differences between our acts and our stated values; and (3) our values and our actions are irrevocably linked to our interests, or, as James puts it, "the true is what is advantageous in our order of thought."[18]

As this linkage is solidified by interest, one final element transcending the positivist separation of fact and value is asserted. Science and belief are linked by what James calls a "preliminary faith." James and Sorel agree that even in the realm of science something more than logic or pure rationality is needed, since preliminary hypotheses are often so weak. In one of his more Bergsonian passages, James says, "Whenever it is a genuine option . . . our passional nature not only lawfully may, but must decide an option that cannot by its nature be decided on intellectual grounds."[19] According to James, not a scintilla of scientific progress can take place unless scientists have great faith in the adequacy of their undertakings and in their contributions to human progress. "Science herself consults her own heart when she lays it down that the infinite ascertainment of fact and correction of false belief are the supreme goods of man."[20] Furthermore, somewhat like Sorel's view of the social myth, this faith, these "values" are irrevocably linked to action. "Unless a preliminary faith exists," some facts cannot appear. Faith in a fact can help create a fact. James envisions a trainload of passengers looted by a few highwaymen because no preliminary faith existed that fellow passengers would aid each other in resistance.[21]

Sorel regards the observer of the general-strike myth as analogous to a physicist who works hard at calculations based on theories that are destined to become outmoded. "The spectacle of modern scientific revolutions is not encouraging for scientists, and has no doubt led many people to proclaim the bankruptcy of science, yet, we would be mad to hand over the management of industry to sorcerers."[22] To proceed scientifically does not mean that we exclude the general strike from serious consideration. "By accepting the idea of the general strike, all the while knowing it is a myth, we operate exactly like a modern physicist who has complete confidence in his science, all the while knowing that the future will regard it as outmoded. It is we who really possess the scientific spirit."[23]

Yet Sorel has judged Marx by Marxian standards, and asserts that pragmatism "ought to be taken pragmatically. . . . The true method to follow for knowing the faults and inadequacies and errors of an important philosophy consists in criticizing it according to its own principles."[24] But Sorel also holds pragmatism up to the mirror of Marxism, just as he has judged Marxism by pragmatic standards, which leads him to insist that the two approaches are very close. James comes under the double scrutiny of pragmatism and of the ideological method of Marx, which are combined quite closely in *De l'utilité du pragmatisme*. The proximity of the two methods is especially apparent in regard to subjectivism, to which in Sorel's view, James comes dangerously close. Since James came under the influence of certain European scholars, he put forth the notion that no theory is an absolute transcript of reality but that any theory may from some point of view be useful. The principal use of an idea is to summarize old facts and to lead to new ones. As James says, "They are only a new-made language, a conceptual shorthand, as someone calls them, in which we write our reports of nature; and languages, as is well-known, tolerate much choice of expression and many dialects. Thus human arbitrariness has driven divine necessity from scientific logic."[25]

Sorel accuses James of imprudence in making such assertions. Sorel himself never argues that science is ultimately ideological; that could lead to moral anarchy and subjectivism. Yet, Sorel regards James as somewhat ideological in his treatment of this subject, saying that James goes to the "extreme left" of pragmatism. In the main, however, Sorel affirms James's good sense, asserting that in other respects he belongs to the "right wing" of pragmatism, "restricting himself to a concern with verification that good sense judges as based on an incontestable reality."[26] According to Sorel, James was forced into his position on the ideological nature of science because he was unable to introduce a genuine pluralism into his theory of knowledge.[27]

Sorel accuses James of a kind of false consciousness wherein his pluralism is really a disguised world-view generated in the American milieu, "from ideological fantasies to historical creations" rather than from artificial nature to science.[28] James's major fault is that he does more than bridge the gap between myth and science; without realizing it, he looks at one in terms of the other. To Sorel, this serves only to cast aspersions on the integrity of science. Thus James depicts science, according to Sorel, as a battlefield of competing dogmas that are, in some sense, parallel to the competing religious sects in America. Due to the conditions of the American experience, James regarded nearly all American sects as "modalities of a single religion."[29] The differences are minor compared to the area of agreement among the faithful:

> Yankees attach little importance to dogmatism; according to them, the essential thing is to be placed in a state wherein one can receive the supernatural cooperation that Christ promised the children of God. In Yankee eyes, religious experience dominates all religion. In Europe (on the other hand) the various churches are far from offering equal recourse to those of their faithful who wish to receive grace of a superior order.[30]

This apparent unanimity in the American spiritual milieu prevented James from seeing the subjectivistic consequences which some interpreters of pragmatism could draw. James's blindness on this point was all the more explicable since James seemed to view the *consensus mundi* among scientists in the same light as "the accord which exists among the faithful" in America.[31] Both realms were therefore distorted by James, who saw excessive unanimity in religious thought and excessive diversity in science.

James's parochialism, according to Sorel, prevents him from seeing the possible subjectivistic and relativistic consequences of his doctrine. As Sorel says:

> The greatest part of our intellectual activity rests on a shifting base and thus favors subjectivism. . . . Condemned to disappear someday, no proposition with its origins in history will be able to impose itself as obligatory on each one of us. William James was scarcely disturbed by this skepticism because, living in a country where traditions are very strong, he saw no reason for waiting for the disappearance of what had appeared in the course of time.[32]

By ignoring the tremendous weight of American liberal ideology in his own theory, James was less sensitive to his parochialism; this rendered pragmatism in his hands "vague, abstract, and subject to innumerable contradictions."[33]

Sorel intends to denature pragmatism in the same way that he denatured the Marxist ideologues. For Sorel, by taking the absolute out of philosophy, James greatly advanced our ability to know truth. He erred in insufficiently recognizing the historicity of his own assumptions. Sorel's is a classic Marxian critique, but almost in reverse: whereas Marx shows us how the relative is masked by the absolute in German philosophy, Sorel shows us how James sees diversity in religion because he is unable to recognize the cultural unanimity of his milieu.

Ironically, this "unmasking" of James ultimately reflects back on Sorel's own theory of syndicalism, if not on the myth of the general strike, when we remember Sorel's statement to the effect that revolutionary syndicalism, in asserting its social pluralism and affirming its diversity and liberty against the bourgeois state, is the "equivalent" of the American Protestant sects.[34] Furthermore, if James is unaware of the historicity of his own view, doesn't Sorel open himself to accusations of subjectivism insofar as he retains the theory of social myths? For although Marxism and pragmatism share the problem of historicism, only pragmatism has the additional problem of subjectivism.

Sorel attempts to fell both problems by constructing a "conservative" social theory of pragmatism that is still faithful to the school of historical law. He does this in effect by emphasizing stability and continuity rather than revolutionary upheavals, as he attempts to account for social change. If no proposition can be tested for its intrinsic truth, Sorel argues, then it must be tested for its "truth value," that is, how it is valued by other men. If the subjective aspects of a proposition are to be tested, one can revert to the kinds of authority which assert a "truth" for a community. To his sociology of virtue, Sorel must add a pragmatic sociology of authority, a socialized pragmatism, to complement the apparent subjectivism of his earlier syndicalism. Given Sorel's own perception of the trade unions as social authorities, this new theory was a natural and simple construction and had always been implicit in his theories. However, since Sorel's theory of syndicalism had already been weakened by both historical and pragmatic measures, he did not rely on the example of the trade unions for his theory of authority. Instead, he turned to the examples found in more traditional authorities and in more venerable myths.

II

Sorel is one of the first to say that in the modern world, authority—even the authority of natural science—is subject to continual crisis by virtue of the very close connection between the organization of knowledge and the historical milieu in which that knowledge arises. He notes, for example, that "Cournot can speak of the science of each people, just as one speaks of political or legal institutions."[35] No master, however illustrious, can ever hope to produce a work possessing as much authority as Euclid's. "The expositions of theories are continually renewed by professors who want to obtain a reputation by giving new demonstrations, by developing doctrines, and by indicating improved applications."[36] Sorel knows that this modern historicist understanding of truth horrifies the metaphysicians and absolutists because they see it as justifying practically anything, as an attitude which "subordinates truth to the arbitrary wills of individuals."[37] This is of course a problem that haunts Sorel in *The Illusions of Progress*, and critics argue that only a universal metaphysics or a rejuvenated Christianity can save the world from moral anarchy if knowledge is to be made completely relative.

Sorel asks the question, originally raised by James, of how knowledge or science can aspire to any degree of authority if it is historically situated. To answer this question, Sorel returns to his previously formulated view of science, reminding us that science is not an individual effort. We no longer employ individual or subjective hypotheses to explain scientific phenomena. The scientific enterprise is a collective or social effort; it is only from this starting point that we can hope to understand its authority. Fundamentally intersubjective, knowledge is relational—like pragmatism itself. Truth is, in James's terms, a "definitely experienceable relation, and therefore describable as well as nameable; it is not unique in kind, and neither invariable nor universal."[38] If it is not universal but socially situated, then truth relates to the social structure; it relates to the authority structures of a society and at times (in Sorel's understanding) seems to coincide with it. Therefore, in Sorel's view, in order to proceed in a truly pragmatic spirit we must "study groups of activities belonging incontestably to the same type, according to the opinion of men versed in these experiences, that can be compared rather approximately to organisms and each one of which relates very clearly to a discernible period."[39]

How closely this method approximates the "organic" one of Durkheim is difficult to say in the light of the outline Sorel gives us. But Sorel's concern with authority, rather than social change, underscores the relatively conservative nature of his interests. The groups of activities he studies produce authoritative opinions; to discern their nature and relationships we must recognize various sets of truths which "correspond" to the opinions of various social groupings. Sorel calls these various groupings *Cités*, which is, as far as we can determine, a general term meaning "community possessing authority," or social authority itself.[40] By this is meant the condition of being an authority as well as the possession of it: an estate. "All the young members of a *Cité* have, in the course of their apprenticeship, acquired a more or less complete confidence in the value of what their elders regard as great works."[41] Every *Cité* can be regarded as a school where one learns to do what the teachers have judged to be worthy of imitation; following that teaching is called wisdom, knowledge, or truth. Thus, truth is the product of our consciousness controlled by "social authorities of incontestable dignity."[42]

Sorel is close to saying that in a *Cité* truth equals authority. That is why Sorel calls pragmatism the "ideological reflection" of what he calls the *Cité savante*, the one *Cité* that has retained its solidarity (hence its authority) in modern Europe: the city of scholars, the scientific estate. The *Cité savante* is, for Sorel, an excellent example of pragmatism in action because it represents the embodiment of the historical genesis of knowledge combined with the stability and continuity needed for any authority in that society.

Sorel notes that important scientific doctrines which are proclaimed revolutionary when they are first developed are often supported with such weak proofs "that if a tribunal of scholars had been called upon to rule on their value, it would have proclaimed them rash."[43] Scientific pragmatic method establishes truth by continuous testing. In defeating continual challenges, the authority of the "victorious" idea is that much stronger; it "pragmatically" offers an extreme stability. After overcoming so many opponents, the prevailing concepts continue to be respected even though grave objections are raised against them. New ideas can triumph only if they prove themselves manifestly more advantageous and present much stronger arguments than those of the old professors. "Thus, there exists in knowledge an historical presumption greatly similar to the presumptions of law."[44]

Sorel argues that new doctrines eventually triumph over the old ones because they make their way in the company of extremely productive methods of investigation leading to results whose utility is demonstrated every day.[45] At a certain point, the competition between new and old ideas reaches a crisis, and the history of scientific crises constitutes the history of scientific change (though not the entire history of science). Knowledge progresses through a succession of these crises, which are analogous to the upheavals produced in a free-market economy. These crises eventually resolve themselves into what Thomas Kuhn called the introduction of new scientific paradigms, and they occur amid jealousies and antagonisms that Sorel sees as being as ferocious as those of the humanists of the Renaissance, with "wars as rich in treachery as those of the barbarians."[46] This new or emergent stage of a doctrine is what Sorel labels its pragmatic stage: a stage rich in good results despite theoretical weaknesses.

Sorel argues that James was misled into regarding this pragmatic stage as the entire history of science, as well as the product of individual researchers, because James mistook periods of change for the entire history of science; there is, however, a hidden stability in the system. Doctrines are created by "proud barons" around whom various scientific and scholarly "clans" are grouped. These barons, whose names are linked with the new discoveries, have only succeeded after undergoing harsh trials, a process of selection so severe that "clan" members "regard themselves as belonging to an elite derived from a selective process whose fairness should be universally admired."[47] Indeed, these coteries organize "solid interest groups" that can impose their precepts on coming generations. Through competition within and among groups, innovations are continuously tested in the most varied ways and "syntheses" appear which appropriately combine the elaborations of current knowledge with the proven acquisitions from the past. When such syntheses have sufficiently matured, the "classical stage" in the development of an idea emerges, a stage in which the ideas that had directed past thinkers are sometimes completely obscured.

What prevents this "classical stage" from degenerating into that Chinese somnolence dreamed of by Auguste Comte[48] is the recurrent competition that prevails between "schools," which often causes scientific systems to disappear with their inventors when disciples alter the teaching of the master. For Sorel, the history of science teaches us that systems so constituted are extremely stable despite their appearance. All this competition among scholars occurs within a framework of common interests that "constrains them from doing anything which would seriously compromise the prestige of science."[49] They must let their most detested adversaries enjoy the title of "scholar" so that they themselves may thoroughly exploit the confidence of the public. That is why scientists ultimately come together to defend one another against the criticisms of laymen. "The passions of a clique do not prevent the existence of a strong sentiment of class solidarity."[50] This is the *Cité savante*. Its authority is further strengthened by the linking of its discoveries to the prosperity of modern production. "Pride, magnified by the flatteries of the clan, compels scientists to imagine that they are called on to lead the world along paths of the highest social as well as technical progress."[51]

Sorel views this "scientific mission" as a "perversion of the souls of scholars,"[52] the ultimate illusion of progress. Scientists are treated obsequiously by courtiers, democratic politicians, and social quacks, who promise a land of milk and honey in the name of science. Sorel condemns 'the frightful triumph of moral materialism, artistic vulgarity, and stupidity in all its forms,"[53] in the *Cité savante*, but admits that this *Cité* attracts to it instincts of discipline and a devotion to productive research rare in contemporary society. With the disappearance of the old social authorities and the triumph of democracy, the *Cité savante* remains one of the last bastions of social authority. This authority doesn't necessarily involve itself in political dealings at all, but it is nonetheless an authority, and one which is "no less solid than it would have been had a law grouped scholars in a privileged corporation which would be given a monopoly over scientific research."[54]

III

In Sorel's discussion of social authority in *De l'utilité du pragmatisme*, one expects Sorel to regard the workers' syndicates as a better example of social authority than the *Cité savante*: syndicates are non-political, concerned with technical and scientific improvement in the workshop, and their members are daily testing new machines to test their practicality. Sorel deals instead with the medieval craft guilds assembled loosely under the heading of the *Cité esthétique* (artistic community), whose Gothic monuments Sorel so much admires.[55]

This *Cité esthétique* created for Sorel an art that, more than any other, merited being called an art of the producers. It was an "aristocracy of professionals," a class in which all members were equal and all acquired a marked predominance in the divided society of the feudal order. "The experience or genius of each member enlightened the corporation, but imposed neither doctrines nor methods."[56] It is superior to the *Cité savante* because of the absence of philosophic dogma; to Sorel, in the medieval craft guilds the poetic spirit dominated the scientific mind, and true symbolism from motives drawn from popular beliefs lay at the foundation of decorative preconceptions "which could not be justified on the grounds of technique, aesthetics, or liturgy."[57]

Like the *Cité savante*, this aesthetic authority was isolated from society. Few if any records exist as to its inner workings, or of the basic symbolism of its decorative ideas; the explanation of its symbolism is hidden from us today. Despite this obscurity, according to Sorel, it is still possible to deduce that this separation from the rest of society possessed advantages and virtues which were demonstrated by the decline of art (in Sorel's view) when the artists sacrificed their splendid isolation and "abandoned the community of artisans to mix with courtiers, humanists, and rich bourgeois" during the Renaissance.[58]

A similar tendency toward the decomposition of art is found in modernity, according to Sorel. When the pragmatic methods of the *Cité esthétique* become pedagogical, when schools of art attempt to impose orthodoxy in methods, they succeed only in uprooting young men who might otherwise have made excellent craftsmen. These schools have thereby helped to ruin superior crafts. Artistic creativity of the kind found in the great guilds cannot be planned or predicted. "Only the unconscious forces of history are in a position to provide an aristocracy of artist-producers."[59]

Sorel thinks more highly of the *Cité esthétique* than he does of the *Cité savante*. The *Cité savante* allies itself with democracy—with the world—in a way that medieval craftsmen would have found shocking. This alliance only helps democracy to further the ruination of all the old social authorities or *Cités*. It is these social authorities whom Sorel sees as preserving the traditions of a culture; only close relations with the life of a glorious *Cité* can maintain these traditions.

At this point Sorel raises the question of the relationship of the strong traditions found in America to the peculiar aura surrounding pragmatic philosophy. Inspired by the accounts of Frederic Le Play's disciple, Paul de Rousiers, concerning social authority in America, Sorel turns to the American aristocracy, whose distinctive characteristics colored William James's moral outlook. This aristocracy, which Sorel calls the American *Cité morale*, is characterized by members who play an "elevated and disinterested role, dedicating to the public good a significant portion of the advantages that they have obtained," and who have "achieved exceptional positions in the economic life of the country as a result of severe selectivity."[60] Here is found *noblesse oblige* where members develop their "sense of social responsibility" on school boards of trustees. These boards are "an effective school of aristocratic government because one learns in them to manage public interests without remuneration."[61] On the other hand, this class raises to its level those social elements (and only those elements) capable and worthy of rising, allowing for a circulation of elites (not Sorel's phrase) which maintains the vigor as well as the authority of "natural aristocracies."[62] Sorel is impressed by Paul de Rousiers's account of a class which emphasizes ability and discourages mediocrity—even in their own children—and which is concerned "much more with helping those with ability . . . than with preventing the incompetent from dying of hunger."[63] Here we find altruism combined with the morality of a race of conquerors extolled in the *Reflections*. This aristocracy exercises its authority without the use of the state or of politicians (whose authority in this land of limited government is, at any rate, small). It is directly through the economy and the society, rather than the state, that the American *Cité morale* supposedly exerts its influence.

According to Sorel, James's vagueness on the problems involved in pragmatic philosophy is due to the fact that James, succumbing to the American tendency to overlook the fact of ruling classes, ignored the influence of the American *Cité morale* in his doctrine. Combined with the extraordinary prosperity in America, this made James ill-disposed to question the process that caused the success of the moral ideas he saw respected around him. James's view on religion, for example, is due to the fact that respect for religion was an unquestioned precept of the American *Cité morale*. "All Yankees agree that fundamental Christian beliefs were very important in creating the prosperity of the States." These convictions appeared to James "as worthy of admiration, as legitimate in the face of criticism, as the most established scientific knowledge can be."[64]

Sorel's admiration for the *Cité morale* leads to his admiration for pragmatism (which appears in Sorel's account to be the ideological reflection of his *Cité morale* as much as it is of the scholarly city). Sorel depicts the American *Cité morale* in full ascendancy, incorporating many if not all of the manly virtues extolled in *Le Procès de Socrate* and the *Reflections*. Like the scholarly and aesthetic cities, it is competitive, resting on historical traditions linked openly to the "trial and error" of competent men and the "free competition of enlightened wills."[65] Experience of this competition gives men wisdom and hence authority. All the *Cités* are products of a long historical development, as is reflected in the opinions of the more experienced individuals composing it. Sorel argues that James has the *Cité morale* in mind when describing what might be called the authority of experience. Sorel quotes James:

> In the long run it is useless to resist experience's pressure; . . . the more of it a man has, the better his position with respect to the truth. . . . [Some] men, having had more experience, are therefore better authorities than others. . . . Some are also wiser by nature and better able to interpret the experience they have had. . . . It is one part of such wisdom to discuss and follow the opinion of our betters. . . . The more systematically and thoroughly such comparison and weighing of opinions are pursued, the truer the opinions that survive are likely to be.[66]

Sorel has used pragmatism as both an explanatory and a normative device in the social sciences. By using his own version of William James's philosophy, Sorel implies that we can comprehend the roles that the various *Cités* play in the moral virtues of the members of a society. Without the "old social authorities" who functioned in the *Cités* and sometimes *as* the *Cités*, neither a conception of truth nor a morality of the producers is possible. "Prosperous peoples" need a *Cité* "in order to maintain their good customs."[67] It is these good customs which constitute the traditions of a social authority. We have noted that all the successful *Cités* Sorel examined are linked by experience to the confidence of the young in the teachings of their elders. These teachings must be linked with actual productive needs and must at the same time protect the *Cité* from decomposition due to external or internal forces.

The pragmatic test for a civilization, for Sorel, boils down to this: is the life of a *Cité*, whether scholarly, aesthetic, or moral, rich in good results? If it is, then we should presume in favor of its traditions. This has the advantage for Sorel, as we shall see shortly, of not accepting every society which exists, which has survived the social struggle, as viable or worthy of emulation. Some societies are better than others, because, among other things, some have traditions which reveal their superiority by their results.

Basic to the life of a viable *Cité* is a superiority due to experience, and since this experience lies at the basis of what we call authority, Sorel is able to employ a pragmatic test for the evaluation of social authority in the modern world. As with any system of social authority, there is presumed here a hierarchical structure depicted in the society as a whole. To Sorel, a *Cité* almost invariably constitutes an "aristocracy"; by all appearances, Sorel means this word in its original sense as the rule of the best—the most heroic and productive. It is not surprising that he should view the *Cité esthétique* as incorporating most, if not all, of his ideals. This "aristocracy of professionals," the American "natural aristocracy," stands apart from society yet is of it—fulfilling its responsibilities according to the canons of the *Cité* rather than of the society at large. When a *Cité* fails to insulate its canons adequately from popular taste or demand, it falls into democratic corruption. Social pluralism must parallel the pluralism in knowledge. This further explains why Sorel scorns the *Cité savante* for its toadying to democratic interests despite its relative coherence and discipline. It therefore cannot match the splendor of the *Cité esthétique*.

Sorel shows himself to be sensitive to the crisis of authority that has plagued the modern world. His essays on pragmatism are an attempt to understand what lies at the bottom of this crisis and to diagnose it. It is his view that the crisis in authority lies, in part, at the basis of the degeneration of modern France. He therefore sets out to depict the decline of the *Cité morale* that formerly ruled France.

Notes

1. Letter to Missiroli, 13 Aug. 1910, in Sorel, *'Da Proudhon a Lenin'*, p. 449.
2. *FGS*, p. 308n75.
3. Sorel, *De l'utilité du pragmatisme*, p. 85n2.
4. Sorel, *Reflections*, p. 149.
5. Sorel, "Art," pp. 254-55.
6. *FGS*, p. 210.
7. Ibid.
8. Sorel, *Reflections*, p. 149.
9. Ibid.
10. William James, *The Varieties of Religious Experience* (New York: Mentor, 1958), pp. 22-23.
11. Richard Vernon, *Commitment and Change: Georges Sorel and the Idea of Revolution* (Toronto: University of Toronto Press, 1978), p. 6.
12. See my "The Social Uncertainty Principle," *Canadian Journal of Political and Social Theory*, 3, no. 3 (Fall 1979): 83-94.
13. James, *The Varieties of Religious Experience*, p. 339.
14. Sorel, "Vues sur les problèmes de la philosophie," p. 586, citing James, *Varieties of Religious Experience*.
15. Sorel, *De l'utilité du pragmatisme*, p. 75n3.
16. *FGS*, p. 211.
17. Sorel, "Vues sur les problèmes de la philosophie," p. 592. Cf. *De l'utilité du pragmatisme*, p. 16.
18. Sorel, *De l'utilité du pragmatisme*, p. 13, citing James, *The Idea of Truth*.
19. William James, *The Will to Believe and Other Essays in Popular Philosophy* (London: Longmans, Green, 1915), p. 11.
20. Ibid., p. 22.
21. Ibid., pp. 24-25.
22. Sorel, *Reflections*, p. 149.
23. Ibid., p. 150.
24. Sorel, *De l'utilité du pragmatisme*, p. 4 and note.
25. William James, *Pragmatism*, cited in *De l'utilité du pragmatisme*, pp. 77-78.
26. Sorel, *De l'utilité du pragmatisme*, p. 78.
27. Ibid., p. 70.
28. Ibid., p. 85.
29. Ibid., pp. 88-89.
30. Ibid., pp. 87-88. Sorel says: "From this point of view, Catholicism in France offers an incontestable advantage over Protestantism due to the care with which its priests uphold Eucharistic piety among the faithful. But it seems that in the United States, most Christian beliefs are about equivalent in producing religious experience having social efficacity. . . . [They are] modalities of a single religion, modalities among which each individual makes a free choice, with the purpose of finding the path which, by reason of the peculiarities of temperament, leads the individual most directly to Christ."
31. Ibid., pp. 89-90.
32. Ibid., p. 92.
33. *FGS*, pp. 277-78; *De l'utilité du pragmatisme*, p. 170.
34. See previous chapter, section V and note 112.

35. Sorel, "A la mémoire de Cournot," *Indépendance* (Oct. 1911).
36. Ibid.
37. Sorel, *De l'utilité du pragmatisme*, p. 179 (*FGS*, p. 281).
38. Ibid., p. 173 (*FGS*, p. 279), citing James, *The Meaning of Truth* (New York: Longmans, Green, 1910), pp. 234-35.
39. Ibid., p. 173 (*FGS*, p. 279).
40. Michel Charzat asserts that these *Cités* are "ideological institutions and devices." But this would seem to make less sense than "authorities" in the light of Sorel's reference to pragmatism as an "ideological reflection" of the *Cité savante*. That is, in Charzat's definition pragmatism becomes an ideological reflection of an ideological institution. See *Georges Sorel et la révolution au XXe siècle* (Paris: Hachette, 1977), p. 197.
41. Sorel, *De l'utilité du pragmatisme*, p. 175 (*FGS*, p. 280).
42. Ibid., pp. 176-77 (*FGS*, p. 280).
43. Ibid., p. 148 (*FGS*, p. 270). Sorel maintains that Galileo was tried more out of a desire to maintain Peripatetic physics than because of theological considerations (*FGS*, p. 360n77).
44. Sorel, "A la mémoire de Cournot," pp. 112-14.
45. Sorel, *De l'utilité du pragmatisme*, pp. 149-50 (*FGS*, p. 270).
46. Ibid., p. 124 (*FGS*, p. 261). Cf. Thomas Kuhn, *The Structure of Scientific Revolutions* (Chicago, University of Chicago Press, 1970).
47. Sorel, *De l'utilité du pragmatisme*, p. 123 (*FGS*, p. 261).
48. See Chapter 2, above.
49. Sorel, *De l'utilité du pragmatisme*, p. 125 (*FGS*, pp. 261-62).
50. Ibid. (*FGS*, p. 262).
51. Ibid., p. 126 (*FGS*, p. 262).
52. Ibid. (*FGS*, p. 262). Cf. "Lyripipii sorbonici moralisationes," *Indépendance* (15 April 1911): 125.
53. Ibid., p. 127 (*FGS*, p. 262).
54. Ibid. (*FGS*, p. 263).
55. The *Cité esthétique* appears to be a transition point between Sorel's reliance on the syndicates and his treatment of historical authorities in *De l'utilité du pragmatisme*. The *Reflections* contains a paragraph on the subject of the *Cité esthétique*, though the latter term is not used: see *FGS*, p. 224.
56. Sorel, *De l'utilité du pragmatisme*, p. 132 (*FGS*, p. 264), citing Viollet-le-Duc, *Dictionnaire raisonné de l'architecture française du XIe au XVIe siècle*.
57. Sorel, *De l'utilité du pragmatisme*, pp. 138-39 (*FGS*, p. 266). Thus "the facade of Notre Dame in Paris owes its beauty to its military symbolism, which connects it closely to the gates of Roman fortresses. The Gallery of the Kings shows us defenders ready to crush any enemies who would advance on the square in front of the church": *De l'utilité du pragmatisme*, p. 141 (*FGS*, p. 267).
58. Sorel, *De l'utilité du pragmatisme*, p. 142 (*FGS*, p. 267).
59. Sorel, *De l'utilité du pragmatisme*, p. 146 (*FGS*, p. 269).
60. Sorel, *De l'utilité du pragmatisme*, pp. 162-63 (*FGS*, p. 275).
61. Sorel, *De l'utilité du pragmatisme*, pp. 162-63 (*FGS*, p. 275).
62. Sorel, *De l'utilité du pragmatisme*, p. 162 (*FGS*, p. 275).
63. Sorel, *De l'utilité du pragmatisme*, p. 163n (*FGS*, pp. 362-63n77).
64. Sorel, *De l'utilité du pragmatisme*, p. 181 (*FGS*, p. 282).
65. Sorel, *De l'utilité du pragmatisme*, p. 185 (*FGS*, p. 284).
66. Sorel, *De l'utilité du pragmatisme*, p. 171 (*FGS*, p. 278), quoting

James's *The Meaning of Truth*.

67. Sorel, *De l'utilité du pragmatisme*, p. 185 (*FGS*, pp. 283-84).

X

THE BOHEMIAN REVOLUTION

During the course of his acquaintance with pragmatic thought, Sorel's attention turned; he abandoned the *Mouvement Socialiste* in the autumn of 1908 and concentrated on the Dreyfus Affair, publishing a book entitled *La Révolution Dreyfusienne* in 1909. Although Sorel was initially a Dreyfusard, in this book he conveyed strong criticism of the Dreyfus movement. Sorel, it seemed, had moved to the right, and this apparent shift was dramatized even before his study of pragmatism; he announced in November 1908 that Maurras's Action Française was "the only serious national movement."[1]

In 1910 Sorel attempted to form *La Cité Française,* an anti-democratic journal which never appeared; in the following year he gravitated to the small but highly influential group of nationalists involved in the publication of the journal *L'Indépendance*, which Sorel was asked to co-edit with Jean Variot. This "pro-royalist" stance, combined with his attack on the Dreyfusards, astonished many commentators; it was difficult to resist dismissing it as just one of Sorel's inconsistencies. Georges Goriely concludes his book on Sorel with an analysis of the *Reflections*, asserting in a postface that Sorel's later political commitments were colored by "so many bizarre and even absurd passionate fixations that only an inexorable spitefulness can explain them."[2] Sorel appeared to support some of these assertions when he said to Croce, "I am a man of the past; I have nothing to say to men who affirm haughtily their Jacobin principles."[3]

Yet, when we examine closely the content of what has been variously called Sorel's "nationalist" or "royalist" sentiments, we come away with the feeling that not very much had changed in Sorel's anti-Cartesian thought over the course of the prewar period. As he said to Dolléans: "One can call me a traditionalist as one can call me a pragmatist, because in the critique of knowledge I attach a major importance to the testimony of historical development. When I sided with Vico against Descartes sixteen years ago I was in a certain sense a traditionalist."[4] It is therefore more likely that Sorel's experiment with monarchism was an extension of his previous disenchantment with Jacobin political democracy in France. When we keep in mind that it is only a certain kind of monarchism which Sorel had in mind, it is reasonable to conclude that Sorel's thought at this time is not only consistent with his sociology of morals but fairly consistent with syndicalism and Proudhonian federalism. This consistency is downplayed or ignored by some writers because they see Sorel's articles and pamphlets as "shockingly inconsistent," as reflecting a change of heart, a "negative streak," lacking in "positive objectives" or his former "enthusiastic inspiration."[5]

With the important exception of a newly formed streak of anti-Semitism coloring Sorel's thought, these accusations are exaggerated. What we see in this period is a recognition of certain inherent virtues in the old French *Cité morale*, the political elite that attained importance in nineteenth-century France; this recognition formed the true essence of Sorel's change of heart. While not as virtuous as the American *Cité morale*, this French moral authority kept certain anti-statist traditions alive; Sorel saw these traditions as being far more compatible with syndicalism, in contrast to the views espoused by the men who had taken over France in the wake of the Dreyfus revolt. Thus, it appears, Sorel is more "positive" in his idea of nineteenth-century French institutions than he was, say, in *The Illusions of Progress*.

In fact, what he is doing is bringing the *Illusions of Progress* up-to-date. In earlier political writings, Sorel criticized the theoretical alternatives to present society; starting with the *Illusions* and continuing with the 1909 book on Dreyfus and his writings in *L'Indépendance*, Sorel centered his attention on a fairly detailed examination of the decomposition of society. This examination provided an historical backdrop to his previous writings. What, Sorel asked, caused the French society's vulnerability (as he saw it) to a decline? The moral framework of *The Illusions of Progress* and *Le Procès de Socrate* was applied to the Dreyfus period. Sorel was to treat the *fin de siècle* in the same manner as his early work on Athenian politics: he analyzed the Dreyfus Affair as the trial of Socrates, the Dreyfusards as the new Sophists; the republican *Cité morale* became loosely parallel to the "old Athenians." The heroic myths surrounding the feudal monarchy, rooted in feudal institutions, became the equivalent of the Aeschylean drama now lost in the headlong rush to establish the omnicompetent statesman.

I

It seems that Sorel's initial attraction to royalism was inspired by ideas later framed in Georges Valois's book, *La Monarchie et la classe ouvrière*, which suggested an alliance between syndicalism and monarchism. This alliance was totally unacceptable to the leader of the Action Française, Charles Maurras, at least at first. Maurras could not accept Sorel's syndicalist views and shared with him only a distrust for democracy.[6] Nevertheless, Sorel, with encouragement from Valois, wrote to Maurras: "Your criticism of contemporary experience well justifies what you have established: 'In modern France, the traditional monarchy would be the sole institution able to carry out the immense tasks that the present theorists of the modern state assign to the government of a great country'."[7] Thanks to the Action Française, Sorel later said, the "*muzzles* which have corrupted everything they have touched" will be removed.[8]

Sorel saw the monarchy chiefly as a means of confronting and strengthening the old republicanism, not of replacing it. His purpose is quite clearly to strengthen the will and the doctrine of the old social authorities whose vitality had been drastically weakened during the Dreyfus period. "I am not a prophet," Sorel said. "I do not know if Maurras will bring back the king of France and that is not what interests me in his thought; what I am concerned with is that he confront the dull and reactionary bourgeoisie in making it ashamed of being defeated and in trying to give a doctrine to it."[9] Sorel's "monarchy" therefore performs some of the same functions as the myth of the general strike—it is a pragmatic means of inculcating the spirit of anticipation and resistance. Thus, he says that the *Cité morale* in France was often at its best during the Empire or during periods when it had to reassert itself: "Liberals are better adapted to opposition than to government; we see this during the first days of the July monarchy."[10]

The important aspect of Sorel's so-called monarchism is that it did not connote an abandonment of either republicanism or syndicalism. In fact, Sorel's thought establishes a continuity among all three concepts, given form by a sort of Marxian medieval nostalgia combined with anti-statism. Sorel asserted that Marx was heavily imbued with "romanticism and consequently the legendary history of the Middle Ages."[11] The idea of class struggle was conceived according to medieval models:

> He conceived social myths by way of viewpoints taken from ideas on the Middle Ages held by the romantics at the beginning of the nineteenth century. Thus, the modern proletariat would be seen as the successor of the weavers of the Italian and Flemish communes. The workers of the Middle Ages were transformed into heroic combatants just as the knights sung by the romantic poets were the personification of the claims of the individual oppressed by the state. The romantics were often quite close to present-day anarchists, whom the socialists have often criticized for having a spirit infused with remnants of aristocratic poetry.[12]

It can be said that Sorel shares in this characterization to the extent that he is anti-statist and romantic himself. "Our republicanism . . . ignores the central organism of the state, which is authoritarian by necessity, and interests itself solely in the less visible but no less essential organisms in which the elite of the people become, through daily practice, disciples of the civic life and protectors of liberties."[13] In Sorel's depiction of the medieval *Cité* we find the link between syndicalism and republicanism, and this pragmatic authority lies at the root of his "royalism."

In *The Illusions of Progress*, Sorel outlined the degeneration of the French monarchy; he underscored the critical standpoint of the centralization of power, with Cartesianism as the court philosophy and the idea of sovereignty as its political theory. In this "monarchist" period, Sorel outlines in more elaborate terms what the consequences of the decline were to be. In a later essay devoted to an Italian translation of Renan's *La Réforme intellectuelle et morale*,[14] he juxtaposes two models of monarchy: a "German model" rooted in medieval pluralism and a "French" example embodying the idea of sovereignty. "The whole secret of our history," wrote Renan, "resides in the struggle between the Gallo-Roman and the Germanic minds, the Gauls having a horror of the divided sovereignty of feudalism, wishing unceasingly to return to the egalitarian administration of the Empire."[15] In tracing the political embodiment of this Germanic tradition, "we find ourself on the terrain of 'barbarian right,' replete with symbols and combining analogies and legal institutions. Unlike the French monarchy, Germanic kingship was entirely legalistic. The Crown belongs to a family who have been 'in some way sequestered from the community,' who have renounced 'all private interest which does not conform to the interest of the nation,' and who are committed to respect scrupulously the rules of heredity in order to avoid the danger of bloody struggles for succession—the ruination of all empires."[16]

Royalty did not execute its tasks directly. "There was no question of sovereignty. Since royalty was a consequence of personal right and an extension of property, the Middle Ages had no idea of the nation envisaged as a source of power. The king is proprietor of his crown,"[17] while the royal court and its budget were strictly constrained by agreements and by the possibility of refusal to pay taxes or to give military service. Around the king was a thriving network of "true republics, the church, universities, religious orders, cities, and corporations of all kinds. Arrayed against the royal power were privileges and customs upon which the king did not dare to infringe."[18] There was therefore little contradiction between these "true republics" and the ideals of the Germanic monarchies—Sorel reminds us of the formula that we would view as contradictory today: "The King, Protector of the French Republics."[19] As Renan said, "There is no electoral system that can give representation like that one."[20] If Gaul, instead of its instincts for equality and uniformity, "had had some slight provincial or municipal spirit; if strong entities, like the Italian cities or the Germanic guilds, could have been formed on our soil; if Lyons, Rouen, or Marseilles had had their *caroccio*, the symbol of civic independence, administrative centralization would have been prevented."[21]

As Sorel implies in the *Illusions of Progress*, the Capetian monarchy had indeed embodied many of these Germanic qualities, and as early as 1904 Sorel extolled it as a new return to heroic culture.[22] Later, the French monarchy lost vitality, while the Germanic monarchy, ruling by symbols more than by force or persuasion, relied heavily on the qualities of the medieval church; these qualities would be conserved in the turbulence of historical change through the respect for old traditions which survived the Lutheran Reformation. Thus, even in Renan's time, while the Catholics at the Saint-Sulpice seminary "admitted the irrational and the miracle only insofar as it was strictly required by Scripture and by church authority," German Catholicism "embraced with a faith analogous to that of the Middle Ages the belief that the miracle is produced abundantly in the present age."[23]

The unity of the complex array of medieval *Cités* and the *Cité catholique* is provided by belief. What the new Royalist-Christian myth needed, according to Sorel, was a component to make it harmonious with feudal-republican virtues. As his friend Charles Péguy put it in 1910, "Our adversaries today want us to hide this mystique of the *ancien régime*, this mystique of old France, that was the republican mystique."[24] Péguy's maxim that "everything begins in mystique and ends in politique"[25] means that in a time when the mystique of the *Cité* remains strong, other mystiques are strengthened symbiotically. "You always speak of the republican degradation. Is there not in the same movement a degradation of monarchism, a royalist degradation parallel and complementary to, symmetrical more than analogous" to the republican degradation?[26] The matter of importance to Péguy is not whether royalism or republicanism carries the day; rather, it is that the mystique of a movement "not [be] devoured by the politics to which it had given birth."[27] The republican politique degrades the republican mystique; the royalist politique undermines the royalist mystique. Furthermore, "when we see what clerical politics has done to the Christian mystique, how can we be astonished at what radical politique has done to the republican mystique?"[28] The mystique of the church of the *Cité catholique* has vanished, just as a mystique of the Republic collapsed under the Dreyfus Affair.

According to Péguy, Christianity in the modern world is no longer what it was. It is no longer a religion "of the depths," of the people. Socially it is nothing more than a religion of the bourgeoisie, a wretched fate for a prominent religion. In a world in which religion is reduced to a political movement, the mystique of Catholicism is shattered. While Sorel attempts to restore bourgeois morals by restoring monarchism, Péguy attempts to restore republican morals by restoring Christianity. The *Cité catholique* has declined, as has the *Cité morale*, since both *Cités* thrive in an atmosphere of opposition. This religious demise goes a long way to explain the demise of socialism. Sorel agrees that syndicalist socialism and Christianity declined together, or at least that the forces that produced a decline in one undermined the other. "The contradiction that historians noted between the secular institutions and monasticism . . . is the image of . . . the contradiction that Daniel Halévy noted between authoritarian scholars and those of the libertarian cooperatives" of the syndicalists.[29]

What the new royalist-republican myth needed was poetic expression, and in Sorel's view this need was fulfilled in 1910 with the publication of Péguy's *The Mystery of the Charity of Joan of Arc.*[30] From this work we can get some idea of what the royalist mythology was for Sorel. In this highly unperformable closet drama, Péguy combines a love for heroism and for national traditions with the mystery that is so much part of the Christian faith. It is thus a defense of the *Cité catholique* as well as a kind of medieval *Cité française*. One could be defended by linking it with the other in the context of the revival of the cult of Joan. *Joan*, revolving around the question of suffering, is a dialogue with three characters: Hauviette, a peasant girl, Madame Gervaise, a nun, and Joan.

Hauviette is a simple soul who takes life as it comes. She is fatalistic about suffering, regarding it as God's will. She accepts the mission of the English soldiers: "They are good Christians," she says. After all, "masses have never ceased; . . . French peasants plough the same fields with just the same care. . . . That is what keeps everything. Work."[31] In Hauviette's hands, labor loses its quality of opposition. It is passive. "If in a little while I were told my day of judgment is going to happen in a half an hour . . . I would go on spinning."

Joan rejects this fatalism. She does not understand why suffering should be allowed, why God has not answered her prayers. Something must be done about it, and she seeks solace from the nun, Madame Gervaise, whose religious quietism, she discovers, is the spiritual counterpart of Hauviette's peasant fatalism. Madame Gervaise argues that war will always tear down churches, but that new ones will be built. "There is still one church which they shall not get at. . . . There is a Church Eternal."[32] Hauviette has severed labor from resistance; Madame Gervaise has separated belief from action.

Joan's agony about suffering, especially Christ's suffering, remains unassuaged. "Those Roman soldiers dared to touch . . . your imperishable body," and such outrages cannot be responded to by the empty charities with which nuns rest content.[33] Joan says that we have been placed in a double bind: we cannot fight because "those who are strongest, those who kill, lose their souls through the murder which they commit. And those who are killed, the men who are weaker, lose their souls through the murder which they suffer."[34] We therefore cannot "kill war" without ingratitude, despair, and perdition. "Since we do not want to kill war, we are accomplices in all this, we who let the soldiers do as they wish. . . . We too, even we, strike crucified Jesus on the cheek."[35]

Madame Gervaise insists that Joan's despair results in an ever-widening circle of guilt and endless damnation, "a dreadful dance of perdition . . . redoublings of damnation, the circles of hell unfolding below circles."[36] Such universalization of guilt replaces the true Christian love with a lie, the false love of the fanatic, while in reality, says Madame Gervaise, "the communication of the Body of Our Lord cures all evils."[37]

At first, Joan appears set on confirming Madame Gervaise's idea. The ever-widening circle of accusation must end by condemning everyone, so Joan starts by condemning herself. If, in order to save the damned, she must abandon her body to the flame, she fervently wishes to do so. Madame Gervaise responds that Joan has blasphemed, that Christ cried out in agony to atone for such suffering. His mission was to establish a Heavenly City—portrayed by Madame Gervaise in her longest speech, a soliloquy which takes up nearly a third of the entire 200-page drama. Christ was a good citizen who founded the Heavenly City and was so respectable as its first citizen that Joseph, a rich man of Arimathea, was willing to donate to Jesus the sepulchre which had been made for him. "You see," says Madame Gervaise, "it is always a good thing to have influential friends. . . . That way, you plainly see, you could not say that [Jesus] was a tramp, a vagrant, a vagabond."[38] Madame Gervaise concludes her portrait of this bourgeoisified Jesus by asserting that it was precisely his sublime innocence and respectability which made the ultimate sacrifice on our behalf possible.

She shows that Joan can no longer condemn herself without making a mockery of Jesus' sacrifice, so Joan turns upon Christianity itself—especially the disciples. They too are guilty. When Jesus told them, "Put up again thy sword into its place: for all they that take the sword shall perish by the sword,"[39] the disciples forsook him and fled. It was they who made a mockery of suffering. Joan concludes that she herself would not have forsaken him despite Madame Gervaise's protestations that anyone would have fled and that Jesus had to die in order to fulfill the Scriptures. Joan repeats several times that neither she nor any good Frenchman would have forsaken Him. "French knights, French peasants, people from our country would never have forsaken him. People from the country of France, people from the province of Lorraine" would have saved him, as would the French saints. To Madame Gervaise's objection that there is but one race of saints, Joan replies sharply that "one always belongs to something and to someone in Christendom." Again, she says that she would not abandon him, that "at heart, I am not a coward."[40]

To act is to save, as a true believer would have done. This is reiterated three or four times, along with many other views. The play is interspersed with responses and comments from other participants, providing it with the rhythm of a litany, giving the impression that Péguy designed it as a kind of national liturgy—a new *Iliad* for the Christian Socialist myth.

Péguy might indeed be seen as more pagan than Christian in this poem, and a few commentators called Péguy's orthodoxy into question: *Joan* was interpreted as an announcement of Péguy's conversion to Christianity. But it was not the believer in Sorel that responded to *Joan*—for Sorel was not one—nor was it the literary critic; Sorel proclaimed himself incompetent at that task. Sorel extolled *Joan* as a national poem. Writing in Maurras's *Action Française*, Sorel says that *Joan* is "destined to occupy an eminent place in the general history of our country. . . . Péguy will be inseparable from the rebirth of French patriotism."[41] To Sorel, it is not the myth of Joan herself that has so pierced the malaise of the French Republic. It is, rather, the myth of patriotism which is accompanied, as it must always be, by some supernatural theme. "To write a great patriotic work, it is suitable to be inspired by ecclesiastical literature."[42] An effort such as Péguy's transcends the clumsy attempts of rationalists and scholars to laicize and materialize the national myths. Péguy has employed fervent praises, lamentations, and supplications. He has united himself with the predramatic genre from whence proceeded the Aeschylean drama "just as does the Catholic liturgy." Everyone knows, Sorel maintains, that ecclesiastical eloquence of any kind has never led to political discourses or pleadings. Lyricism instructs the supernatural; it multiplies the duplications, the progression of images. But to do so the liturgy must not be narrowed by theologians, but, rather, slackened in order to "mix popular representations to orthodox formulas."[43]

II

By late 1910, several months after Péguy's *Joan* had been published, Sorel began to be disillusioned with Maurras. He stated that he was no more concerned with the actual success of royalism than he was with the actualization of the general strike; in both cases, it was the myth that was important. Just as syndicalism had become corrupted by *politique*, Maurras and his followers had confused symbolic anticipation with political utopianism. In Sorel's view, Péguy had used the term *mystique* in a much broader sense than Sorel intended in his concept of myth, which led to ambiguity. "Very often we define *mystique* as a mental illusion which makes us mistake an image or an abstraction for a reality; *mystique* thus understood is almost mystification; and this is exactly what sustains the friends of Maurras."[44] In other words, unlike Sorel's myth, the royalist mystique was not immune from degeneration into ideology. According to Sorel, once Maurras and, especially, Valois adopted the royalist mystique they committed a double error. First, they failed to understand that the Jacobins had a competing "counter-mystique" that was quite separate from the complementary myths of the "true republics" and the Germanic monarchy. This counter-mystique was the illusion or ideology that sustained the republican tradition in the years following the Commune. "The legend of the Commune, and not its reality, has dominated everything that has been produced in French socialism since 1871. For the people, the Commune is the revolt of the Parisians against royalty, and it ended in the massacre of the workers in the name of royalty."[45] Despite the fact that Thiers was the perpetrator of the atrocities, "no reasoning can go against this legend"[46] in an attempt to unite socialism with monarchism.

Maurras had played into the hands of the socialists and democrats. True to the French royalist tradition since Louis XIV, he adopted a mystique that harmonized with the statist idea. To counter democratic *politique*, Maurras had politicized his own mystique and put forth the slogan "Politics first." Thus the legend of the Commune which perceived monarchism only as the statist monarchism of the "Napoleonic legend" that had been "shattered by the experience of the Second Empire,"[47] was reinforced by Maurras's propaganda.

Maurras's cry of "Politics first" meant either a singular lack of devotion to mystique or, at best, a mystique that had been corrupted by the very democratic qualities it opposed. As Sorel stated it, "The modern authors whom Maurras particularly admires (Stendhal, Balzac) possess none of that aristocratic distinction which was the sign of good literature to our ancestors."[48] To Sorel, this meant that Maurras represented not the admirable qualities of monarchism but precisely those aspects which embraced the principle of sovereignty and national will. It was hardly surprising that Maurras should have found this idea of "integral nationalism" compatible with some of the notions of Auguste Comte[49] —a viewpoint utterly alien to Renan's Germanic concept of monarchy and hostile to the very traditions it pretended to defend. True royalty (by which Sorel means Germanic kingship)

> differs above all from tyrannies (such as Bonapartism) by its respect for tradition. The royalist tradition can be engendered only by the activity of its "social authorities." It is curious that the propagandists of the royalist party admire the government of Louis XIV which Le Play regarded as being very harmful. . . . French gentlemen very rarely have the qualities that allow them to fulfill the role of social authorities and consequently of helping the prosperity of a monarchical country."[50]

Without genuine tradition there is no authority; without authority (i.e., power based neither on persuasion nor on force) only force or persuasion can be used. According to the French traditionalists who call themselves monarchists, "Tradition is not nourished by liberty but by recording the decisions of authority." But real tradition, the kind which has taken root, "the tradition which we credit with influencing the formation of our convictions, is the fruit of the free and reasoned efforts of our ancestors."[51]

For Sorel, the present crisis was a crisis of authority; this crisis was not being solved by the Action Française but only exacerbated by a Bonapartism which, by emphasizing popularity based on persuasion and ability based on forcefulness, constituted the antithesis of true authority. As Renan expressed it, "The question of popularity and ability attributed to the personage of the king an importance that it should have only in absolute monarchies."[52] The experience of the nineteenth century, Sorel argues, "shows that none of the three consecutive monarchies had been more favorable than the others to social authorities."[53] No royalist in France, including Maurras, understood or accepted the ideas Renan put forth concerning the monarchical constitution.

This is shown in the misunderstanding surrounding the play *L'Otage* (*The Hostage*), by the Catholic playwright Paul Claudel. In fact, Sorel was one of the few people to have understood what Claudel was attempting to do. Royalist and non-royalist alike interpreted the play as a plea for monarchism, while Sorel understood all too well that it was an explanation of its failure, that is, of the triumph of Bonapartist *politique*. Claudel said that Sorel "understands just what I want to do . . . in this work, which is not an historical but a symbolical or, rather, a synthetic drama."[54] Like Péguy's *Joan*, Claudel's play erases "paltry human individuality" and "executes a kind of liturgy." To Sorel there is a difference between drama which is all flesh-and-blood—all individuals—on the one hand, and mythology (of which *Prometheus Bound* and *Eumenides* are the greatest works, in Sorel's view), on the other. "This mythological drama is the opposite of symbolic literature: in the latter, adventures are invented to illustrate scholastic theories; in the Asechylean drama, ideas are suggested to a mind capable of meditation by means of adventures."[55]

In *L'Otage*, the hero, Georges Confontaine, an ardent royalist of the Napoleonic period, returns from exile. He and his cousin, Sygne, the heroine, vow to remain faithful to each other. In the fight for the Restoration, Confontaine wants the support of the Pope, whom he has rescued from imprisonment and whom he is hiding. Turelure, a ruthless and violent revolutionary who is to become prefect of the Seine, knows Confantaine is protecting the Pope and demands that Sygne marry him or see the Pope arrested. Badilon, a priest and Sygne's confessor, does not understand Georges's feudal ideas and the implication of restored authority outside the ecclesiastical realm. He is terrified by the idea that the emperor, master of the

Pope's person, can create a schism, and he urges Sygne to sacrifice her purity to save the Pope, which she does. *Mystique* is ravaged by *politique*.

Meanwhile, Turelure, realizing that it is to his advantage to fight for the Restoration, betrays Napoleon, and becomes a general. He says that in return for the restoration of Louis XVIII as a constitutional monarch, Georges must also bequeath his lands to the child Sygne has had by Turelure. When Georges attempts to shoot Turelure, Sygne, again following the path of duty, tries to protect Turelure and is mortally wounded. Turelure then kills Georges.

Before Sygne's deathbed, the priest, Badilon, expresses his deepest grief: "All is finished, all is done as He would have it. . . . I have finished my work; I have killed my child for heaven. And I remain alone. The child of my soul has departed and I remain alone, the old useless curé."[56]

Like Péguy's *Joan*, Claudel's play has something heretical about it. Surely the priest's stance in insisting on Sygne's sacrifice of her virtue was unorthodox—a pagan act if ever there was one. Indeed, Georges Confontaine is really not much of a believer; he is a romantic wanting to restore the "old social authorities." He is one of those who "in traversing revolutionary anarchy felt feudal passions reborn in their souls."[57] Like *Joan*, there is little that is historically viable in *L'Otage*. The fictional Pope does not represent a true historical figure but a symbolic *Cité catholique*.

Unlike *Joan*, however, the characters in *L'Otage* are bound by a tragedy which is ironic and fatalistic. The irony is found in the fact that Georges, the fighter for Restoration, "comes to act as the plenipotentiary for the king and is killed by the general who delivers Paris to the Restoration."[58] The fatalism is represented by an overall theme dominating the play, namely, that the social authorities of the feudal age cannot be restored through political action. Turelure, despite his siding with the forces of Restoration for opportunistic reasons, represents not the old order but the new. Thus, interpreting the play, Sorel argues that "what we call the Restoration" was, in fact, the triumph of the Revolution, by which is meant the "new men" who had triumphed when old France was gone. "It was thus convenient [for dramatic purposes] for Sygne to die before the king succeeded; the child that she had presented to Turelure would never know the old France" even though he inherited the property.[59]

In Sygne, according to Sorel, we find a France which has suffered the ruination caused by war and revolution. She is represented in the dialogue as accepting any government which assures civil peace, protects interests, and assures religious toleration. Despite her loyalty to her brother she pleads with him not to become too intransigent, to accept a watered-down constitutional monarchy. As Sorel interprets it, "Having lost hope of seeing a society constituted as conforming to the principles of law, she is content with a regime which surrounds institutions with great prestige."[60]

The interpretation some critics gave to *L'Otage*, that of a monarchist play, was denied by Claudel. He claimed that he was "embarrassed" about publishing it because it would be taken for a reactionary book. "Actually, I've tried to portray many conflicting forces, none of which, not even the Pope who has the principal role, not even God himself, has the field completely to himself."[61]

III

If 1815 saw the failure to revive the royalist *mystique*, the Dreyfus Affair was the death knell for the republican *mystique*: the small caste of republicans who had briefly sustained the love of liberty necessary to true authority was finally driven from power by the events connected with the Affair.

For Sorel, the royal spirit outlined by Renan demands an aristocracy possessing qualities rarely found in French nobility, reduced as they were to being "little more than decoration for the salons." Renan had pointed out to Sorel that since the obligations of aristocracy, "the defense of rights against royalty," had been replaced by the duty to serve the king, the only center of "moral resistance" to sovereignty lies largely in families unconnected with the nobility. To Sorel, the countervailing force of the Germanic aristocracies was exerted by certain bourgeois families who, "proud of having given illustrious sons to industry, letters, and the law, have acquired something of the feudal spirit of the intermediate nobility. In this class the government discovered functionaries who had a moral position that was so strong that the jurists at the head of public agencies could not treat them as mere bookkeepers."[62] This nineteenth-century French *Cité morale* performed its tasks with an independence that no civil-service law could have given it. "Having little taste for the meticulous details of administration, they freely allowed to men of talent the liberty necessary to work productively. . . . Personally interested in maintaining a social order replete with Germanism, they contributed to 'defending the privileges of individuals, to limiting power, to preserving the modern period from the exaggerated idea of the state which was the ruination of ancient societies.'"[63]

This *Cité morale*, the moral authority of the old French republican families, acted as the socially intermediate force during the turbulent years of the nineteenth century. During the days of the Second Empire, this class was more or less isolated from power. The old families who produced such statesmen as Scheurer-Kestner, Cavaignac, and Jules Grévy were almost proud of the fact that they snubbed and were snubbed in turn by the parvenus of the Bonapartist cliques who inherited the political traditions of the Sun King. Full of admiration for Plutarch's heroes, they bitterly condemned monarchy and empire for its luxury. To Sorel, such self-exclusion on the grounds of republican principles as well as interest was admirable.

It is more surprising that Sorel should extol a class which was itself, by Sorel's own account, enamored of the rights of philosophy and knowledge to rule, which protected its children from the hardships of the marketplace, and which was extremely jealous of its heritage. According to Sorel, it thus accorded its sons the birthrights that Sorel missed in the American *Cité morale* and for which American aristocracy was all the better.[64] Nevertheless, it is apparent that Sorel sees the old French ruling elite as better than nothing, that by virtue of the fact that "it took life seriously" it was "worthy of profound respect."[65]

Sorel sees the modern French *Cité morale* as being in a position analogous to that of the old warriors who had lost their authority in post-Periclean Athens. In *Le Procès de Socrate*, Sorel said that the new class of urban oligarchs, devoted to philosophy, had to base their power on persuasion and on force. In both old Athens and twentieth-century France, a decline in authority meant an increase in political propaganda and in the power of the state.

Like the Greek aristocracy depicted in *Le Procès de Socrate*, the younger generation of France by virtue of its inherent rationalism, according to Sorel, made way for its displacement by a class of political parvenus. The new urban oligarchy of Athens had displaced the farmer-warrior class and put forth the notion that "success justifies everything, that there is no moral ideal." Under such a system, social mobility is considerable. "The new urban oligarchs came from all classes, opening their ranks to all capable and intelligent men." Rorel notes how the old-fashioned Aristophanes reproached the modern and urban Euripides for being the son of an herb-peddler and how the well-born Demosthenes criticized Aeschines' humble origins.[66]

Sorel deplores the fact that the old republican aristocracy was being replaced by an intellectual caste whose background made it contemptuous of the old values. In nineteenth-century France, Sorel notes, "The republican world accorded the greatest privileges to birth; it was by reason of his nobility of race that Cavaignac had been able to have a brilliant political fortune."[67] Félix Faure "continued to be a parvenu" despite his long experience with men at the top; and Jules Grévy, a man of the old order, regarded the Franco-Prussian war with alarm because it would mean a dictatorship of the "bohemians."[68]

Sorel notes that Marx, in the *Eighteenth Brumaire*, also considered Louis Napoleon's government to be "an association of bohemians,"[69] and, according to Sorel, the prototype of the politician during the period is found in Emile Olivier—of whom Grévy was no doubt thinking when he made his remark about a government of bohemians. Grévy's disdain for the men who inhabited the court of Louis Napoleon is echoed by Sorel, who notes that Napoleon himself wished to fuse the old France with the new. The Second Empire "worked with great perseverence and efficacity to ruin the prestige still possessed at this time by the *haute bourgeoisie*, on which the parliamentarianism of Louis Philippe rested. This aristocracy, dispossessed of power, did not hide its profound contempt for the new Bonapartist masters of France: it regarded them as political adventurers, stock-market speculators, men without culture and without morals."[70]

Far more than the old republican aristocracy, these new Bonapartist bohemians were analogous to the urban oligarchy of old Athens in another and perhaps more crucial way: they believed themselves entitled to rule by the natural right of intelligence, conveyed to them by philosophy and theory. They thus differed strongly from the American *arrivistes* in their distance from production as well as from practical wisdom. According to Sorel, Olivier, the last premier under the Second Empire, was so transfixed by his own powers of reason that he took his country to war with Prussia on the flimsiest excuses. Ignoring the pragmatic basis of political reality, Olivier "believed that a resolution based on irreproachable arguments produces more or less excellent results in the long run."[71]

Sorel believed that the old Athenian soldiers had given way to a class of young men who inhabited secret clubs, dividing their time between debauchery and philosophy; the old republican aristocrats had given way to young Parisians who frequented salons in which *grandes dames* oversaw discussions of the great questions of the day. The Athenian clubs had undermined the old loyalties that were disastrous for the family and the city; the new bohemians, the men and women of the salons, transmitted the instructions of the *beau monde* to Premier Combes. In France these instructions were obeyed, according to Sorel, with such scrupulousness that "we thus find ourselves in the political world of the eighteenth century carried over into a condition of complete democracy: to a government directed by coteries of courtiers and courtesans."[72]

This transformation of the French elite, according to Sorel, did not take place without a gradual weakening of the spirit of resistance of the old ruling class, just as the younger generation of the old Athenians became increasingly mesmerized by the new rhetors and philosophers, the plays of the subtle Euripides (as against the old legends), as well as the newer religious cults (in Sorel's early account). France was being corrupted by newer teachings, its youth "engaged with a sort of furor on the path of imbecility: the Russian novel, neo-Catholicism, and anarchism greatly contributed to developing in the youth intellectual habits analogous to those one observes in societies arriving at full decrepitude."[73]

As this worship of new teachings reached its full flower, the old French military spirit waned. As in Athens, intelligence had replaced the martial virtues. Sorel maintains that society was convinced that the wars of 1866 and 1870 had demonstrated that nations no longer played a prominent role in the world by virtue of military triumphs. Despite Prussian successes, it was Britain with her small army who appeared to be the great European arbitrator at the Congress of Berlin. As Sorel states it, "The victorious forces of the most colossal empire in Europe had receded before the menaces of the London merchants. . . . The authority that a country can enjoy in Europe can be independent of the glory acquired by its soldiers."[74] After 1870, Gambetta and other leaders came to realize that the idea of glory had little or no effect on the French consciousness. The Franco-Prussian war, in Sorel's eyes, had been too short, "too barren of facts capable of engendering legends,"[75] and it terminated in such a frightful defeat that the whole basis of the French spirit was transformed. Thus Renan called France "the most pacifist country in the world" and noted that "not a single element of the old military life of the country" remained in 1877.[76]

Notwithstanding its internal weaknesses, the French *Cité morale* managed to survive the political turmoils of French life; indeed, according to Sorel, it was through the authority of this *Cité* that the Third Republic survived. It had been intoxicated by the victory that it had won over the *Boulangistes* and it had escaped the worst aspects of the Panama affair, but the weaknesses of French society had been so great that the *Cité morale* relinquished its authority during the most catastrophic event of the *fin de siècle*, the Dreyfus Affair. It was during this controversy that Waldeck-Rousseau organized his 1899 cabinet, which was viewed as the most leftist cabinet since 1848 and hence as Dreyfusard. Though it was rather cautious at first, this "Dreyfus revolution" was, for Sorel, the final triumph of the bohemian class, and, once the full potential of the Affair had become apparent, led to the disintegration of the old social authorities.

The men of letters who formed the vanguard of the radicals and who would profit later from the "Revolution" did not, according to Sorel, generally believe in the value of their own ideas. Like the young Sophists and some of Socrates' followers, their only criterion was success. Thus, "the first Dreyfusards were not highly concerned with Dreyfus himself; the illegality of the sentence did not torment them"[77] and they hardly adored Dreyfus, according to Sorel. Ironically, or perhaps inevitably, Sorel too proclaims that he "did not wish to speak of the innocence or culpability of Dreyfus."[78] He is interested solely in the moral consequences of the Affair. The Affair was nevertheless a bonanza for the Dreyfusards, because they were able to offer "good positions to ambitious men who had really been ardent Dreyfusards by virtue of 'strong passions of racial and religious hatred.' This was a disaster for those who believed they ought to take part in agitation in order to defend great French traditions."[79]

The triumph of the Dreyfus revolution over the old republican aristocracy was, according to Sorel, exemplified by the role that Scheurer-Kestner played. This senator belonged to the old republican aristocracy: he was one of the founders of the République Française and had had the honor of being prosecuted by Napoleon III. Many of the early Dreyfusards were convinced that this distinguished senator was the man who could lead the movement for the re-opening of the case, since he was one of the few men in the establishment who had stood behind Dreyfus. The authority of Scheurer-Kestner was universally respected; he alone might reverse public opinion and create a presumption in favor of Dreyfus's innocence. According to Sorel, events proved contrary to those predictions. Scheurer-Kestner was abandoned by nearly everyone in the *Cité morale* as soon as he discovered his pro-Dreyfus efforts. It was this failure, one that demonstrated the weakness of the entire aristocracy, that paved the way for the forces of democracy. Led by the "new bohemians," the Dreyfusards took cognizance of the state of aristocratic power and ceased to fear the authorities who were constituted above them. A failure of one of their members on one side led to the general breakdown of the old order, largely arrayed on the other side. In short, the failure of Scheurer-Kestner signalled to the bohemians that "the Republican aristocracy was no longer anything but a memory."[80]

The Affair undermined the remaining vestiges of authority in France: the army, the church, and the law itself. The military spirit, which had already been in full retreat, was annihilated by the Affair:

> No serious effort was made to restore in the army the sentiments of honor, camaraderie, and discipline that the system of secret accusation, introduced by General André, had so greatly shaken. High positions were continually given to men who denounced their colleagues and their chiefs; one notes colonels who, in order to be promoted to general, have been obliged to join the Freemasons.[81]

Now, as Sorel had often pointed out, a weakening of the military spirit almost invariably enfeebles the legal spirit,[82] and the Dreyfus revolution weakened the judiciary along with the army. Sorel says that in the course of his research into the Dreyfus case, he was "struck by the contempt the Dreyfusards held for the magistracy, an extraordinary characteristic for those who regard themselves as upholders of the law."[83]

The decree of 12 July 1906, which finally freed Dreyfus, came, according to Sorel, from outside regular channels. The elections of that year were so triumphant for the government that the latter could easily exert pressure on the magistrates. Despite the clarity of the law forbidding the annulment of the Council of War, the government proceeded to do just that. According to Sorel, then, the government of the Third Republic was allowed to interfere with the judiciary as much as was Napoleon III. After the Dreyfus revolution, "magistrates ask only to obey the instructions of the government."[84]

The Dreyfus Affair was as harmful to religious authorities as it was to the secular ones. The revolution which Sorel saw as dragging the judiciary and the army in the dirt also dealt a severe blow to the already waning prestige of the Catholic church. Indeed, an anticlerical posture was part of the general decline of lawfulness.

Official Catholicism was highly unified against a revision of the Dreyfus case. To Sorel, this anti-Dreyfus unity was as grave for the *Cité catholique* as the Dreyfusism of the bohemians was for the *Cité morale*. Pope Leo XIII, despite his bow to liberal Catholicism in the *Rerum Novarum* Encyclical, "hoped again to become sovereign of a little Roman kingdom and he counted on France to realize this chimerical ambition."[85] The Vatican evidently believed that the Dreyfus Affair would allow the Pope to identify himself with the cause of French patriotism. Such opposition only sped the destruction of the church's prestige, once the Dreyfusards had succeeded in mobilizing public opinion to their cause. The success of the Dreyfusards is measured, according to Sorel, by the attack on religious congregations on the part of Waldeck-Rousseau's government.

If the Dreyfus Affair was the Socratic trial of modern France, the Jews increasingly appeared to Sorel as the archetypal bohemian class, the new philosophers or urbanites. "In the Jews who claim to direct our country," he says, "we encounter to a greatly exaggerated degree the faults that were criticized so bitterly until now in the men of Napoleon III." Anti-Semitism is, to Sorel, the "natural consequence" of the traditional anti-Bonapartism of the Republican aristocracy.[86] Sorel regards the Jews as people who should be excluded as zealously as were Orientals in America—and for the same reason: they are a threat to national traditions.

Sorel professes respect for the old Jewish families, and even a grudging admiration for the isolation they endured under the aegis of both necessity and religious dogma.[87] But for Sorel, "the instincts of immoralism are encountered anywhere else, in almost all Jews who have abandoned their national traditions."[88] Sorel seems to argue for separatism, but why does he then say: "Nothing would make anyone dream of regarding Jews as enemies of the country if they consented to live as simple citizens"?[89] How can Sorel extol the particularism of the *Cité d'Israël*, on the one hand, and insist on their living as their fellow citizens do, on the other? It is the classic double bind in which searchers for scapegoats put their victims, claiming that they are snobbish or assimilationist, arrogant or craven, aggressive or lazy, depending upon the mood of the moment. It is certainly one of the most unfortunate aspects of Sorel's thinking, not essential to his body of thought, and inconsistent with his prior view of anti-Semitism[90] as well as his praise of the virtues of family tradition. It is the one area of his thinking in which mean-spiritedness, a "negative streak," really appears.

To be sure, Sorel insists, in contrast to later fascist anti-Semitism, that there is no racial difference in the Jews, that all differences are cultural.[91] Indeed, part of Sorel's answer to Lazare's book *Anti-Semitism* made rather strong claims for the revolutionary tradition of Zionism.[92] Sorel extolled the Jews for their fidelity to tradition in his first book. In 1912, he castigates Lazare's exaggerated claims that modern Zionism inherits the mantle of Lassalle and Marx, and attributes these notions to anonymous sources among the "*grands juifs*." These anonymous sources also, according to Sorel, prepared the Dreyfus revolution. "I am persuaded that the Dreyfus Affair was long ago prepared abroad, that its organization was, at the end of 1897, placed at the disposition of Joseph Reinach, a leading member of the Jewish community who tried unsuccessfully to obtain a revision of the Dreyfus trial thanks to his parliamentary influence."[93] But scholarship[94] is convincing on the point that most French Jews were both highly assimilationist, secular, staunch defenders of the Republic, and even, at first, anti-Dreyfus. Sorel, it is true, is inveighing more against men like Lazare, but the reaction of the French Jews to Lazare's Zionism was lukewarm at best.

Sorel's misguided writings on Jews in this period can perhaps be dismissed as caused by the passions of that moment. They certainly smack of that demagogic creative hatred against which he expends so much of his writing energy. At any rate, the only thing that can be said in defense of Sorel is that he was anything but alone among Frenchmen, that his anti-Semitism was shared by many members of various political views, and that such rhetoric was common currency at this time. That his anti-Semitism was circumstantial is also supported by the fact that most anti-Semitic references in Sorel's published works are found within an extremely short time-span—about two years. *La Révolution dreyfusienne* (1909) contained hardly any anti-Semitic references; almost all his anti-Jewish writing of any extent is found in the pages of *L'Indépendance*. Except in private correspondence after 1913, very few references to the Jewish Question are found.[95] Indeed, Sorel later questioned the utility of anti-Semitism as a political or mythical device.[96]

Occasionally the old anti-Semitism reasserted itself. Sorel would later contrast the "profound gravity of Péguy with the chatter of the Jewish writers who exerted a 'friendly control' over him. . . . Péguy feared them because . . . it would not have been difficult to induce three hundred Jewish subscribers to stop their subscriptions [to Péguy's *Cahiers*]." Péguy was constrained to publish attacks on Bergson because "the rich *ghetto* had a long-held grudge against Bergson for not having been a militant Dreyfusard."[96] This is a clear reference to the anti-Bergsonian Julien Benda, a fellow habitué of Péguy's shop whom Péguy suspected Sorel of plotting against when Benda's novel, *L'Ordination*, failed to win the 1912 Prix Goncourt. Péguy implied that Sorel's anti-Semitism was the motivation behind the "plot."[97] In any case, the Benda fracas was the pretext if not the cause of Péguy's excommunication of Sorel from the weekly bookshop symposia after November of 1912.[98]

Sorel denied a plot, asserting that Benda's failure was due to the offenses to Catholicism in his work.[99] Indeed, the roots of the split were the deep personal and philosophical differences between the two men. Sorel's own critique of the concept of *mystique* was reciprocated by later Péguyites, one of whom later says: "Péguy is a *mystique* and Sorel, despite the role he assigns to myths, is only a *politique.* There came a time when dialogue between them was no longer possible."[100] Yet Sorel was profoundly distrustful of the "conservative" ideologies with which he is commonly associated in the immediate pre-war period. In 1914 Sorel resigned from *L'Indépendance*, expressing his disgust with its "piplets nationalistes" and its "reactionary" character.[101] By then he was to turn to other things.

Notes

1. Jean Variot, ed., *Propos de Georges Sorel* (Paris: Gallimard, 1935), p. 27. The conversation was dated 14 November 1908.
2. Georges Goriely, *Le Pluralisme dramatique de Georges Sorel*, p. 223.
3. Letter to Croce, 22 September 1914, in *Critica* 27, no. 1 (20 Jan. 1929): 51.
4. Eduard Dolléans, "Le Visage de Georges Sorel," *Revue d'Histoire Economique et Sociale* 26, no. 2 (1947): 106-7, citing letter of 13 October 1912.
5. James H. Meisel, *The Genesis of Georges Sorel*, p. 204; Vernon, *Commitment and Change*, p. 15.
6. Eugen Weber, *Action Française* (Stanford: Stanford University Press, 1962), p. 74.
7. Pierre Andreu, *Notre maître Georges Sorel*, p. 61.
8. Sorel, "La Disfatta dei 'muffles.'" *Divenire Sociale* (16 July 1909); reprinted in *Aspects de la France* (1 Dec. 1949).
9. Jean Variot, *Propos de Sorel*, p. 27 (14 Nov. 1908).
10. Sorel, "Trois problèmes," p. 229, citing Daniel Halévy, *Luttes et problèmes: Apologie pour notre passé.*
11. Sorel, *Lettres à Paul Delessalle*, 9 May 1918, p. 139.
12. Ibid., 26 July 1918, p. 159.
13. Sorel, "Trois problèmes," p. 262, citing Halévy, *Luttes et problèmes.*
14. Sorel, "Germanismo e storicismo di Ernesto Renan," *Critica* 29 (Mar., May, Sept., Nov. 1931).
15. Ernest Renan, *Essais de morale et de critique* (6th ed., Paris: Calmann-Lévy, n.d.), p. 43. A précis appears in "Germanismo e storicismo" (Sept.): 359.
16. Sorel, "Germanismo e storicismo" (Nov.): 438, citing Renan's *Questions contemporaines* (Paris: Lévy, 1868), pp. 16-17.
17. See Renan, *Questions contemporaines*, p. 14.
18. Ibid., p. 15.
19. "Germanismo e storicismo" (Nov.): 440-41.
20. Renan, *La Réforme intellectuelle et morale*, pp. 48-49.
21. Renan, *Essais de morale*, p. 37.
22. Review: Flach, *Les Origines de l'ancienne France*, *Revue Générale de Bibliographie* (Feb. 1904): 82.
23. Sorel "Germanismo e storicismo" (May): 204, citing Renan's *Souvenirs d'enfance et de jeunesse*, pp. 273-74.
24. Péguy, *Notre jeunesse* (Paris: Gallimard, 1957), p. 34.
25. Ibid., p. 31.
26. Ibid., p. 32.

27. Ibid., p. 31.
28. Ibid., p. 33.
29. Sorel, "Trois problèmes," p. 278.
30. Péguy, *The Mystery of the Charity of Joan of Arc*, trans. by Julien Green (New York: Pantheon, 1950) (hereafter cited as *Joan*).
31. Péguy, *Joan*, p. 42.
32. Ibid., p. 72.
33. Ibid., p. 73.
34. Ibid., p. 28.
35. Ibid., pp. 74-75.
36. Ibid., pp. 78-79.
37. Ibid., p. 80.
38. Ibid., pp. 136, 140.
39. Ibid., p. 170.
40. Ibid., p. 208.
41. Sorel, "Le Réveil de l'âme française: Le Mystère de la 'Charité de Jeanne d'Arc' de Péguy," *Action Française* (Apr. 1910). In Eric Cahm, *Péguy et le nationalisme français* (Paris: Cahiers de l'Amitié Charles Péguy, 1972), p. 164.
42. Ibid., p. 165.
43. Ibid., p. 166.
44. Sorel, "Le Patriotisme actuel en France," *Resto del Carlino*, 28 September 1910. Reprinted in *Feuillets d'amitié Charles Péguy,* no. 6 (1949): 13.
45. Sorel's letter to Valois in Valois, *La Monarchie et la classe ouvrière* (Paris: Nouvelle Librarie Nationale, 1914), p. 70.
46. Ibid., p. 71.
47. Ibid.
48. *FGS*, p. 344.
49. See Charles Maurras, *Oeuvres capitales* (Paris: Flammarion, 1954), vol. 3, pp. 484-86.
50. *FGS*, p. 366n107.
51. Ibid., p. 284.
52. Renan, *Questions contemporaines*, p. 35.
53. Sorel, "Germanismo e storicismo" (Sept.): 363.
54. Paul Claudel, letter to Gide, 21 June 1911, in *The Correspondence between Paul Claudel and André Gide, 1899-1926*, trans. by John Russell (London: Secker and Warburg, 1952), p. 165.
55. Sorel, "'L'Otage' de Paul Claudel," *Indépendance* (July 1911): 394.
56. Paul Claudel, *L'Otage* (Paris: Gallimard Folio, 1939), p. 138.
57. Sorel, "'L'Otage' de Paul Claudel," p. 396.
58. Ibid.
59. Ibid., p. 398.
60. Ibid.
61. Claudel, letter to Gide, 20 April 1910, in *Correspondence*, p. 125.
62. Sorel, "Germanismo e storicismo" (Nov.): 441.
63. Ibid.
64. *FGS*, pp. 275-78.
65. Sorel, "Le Monument Jules Ferry," *Indépendance* (Mar. 1911): 3.
66. *FGS*, pp. 68-69.
67. Sorel, *La Révolution Dreyfusienne*, p. 58.
68. Ibid.
69. Ibid., p. 64.

70. Ibid.
71. Sorel, "Les Responsabilités de 1870," *Indépendance* (July 1911): 184.
72. Sorel, *La Révolution Dreyfusienne*, p. 56.
73. Sorel, "Aux temps Dreyfusiens," *Indépendance* (Oct. 1912): 51.
74. Sorel, "Le Monument Jules Ferry," pp. 9-10.
75. Sorel, "L'Abandon de la revanche," *Indépendance* (April 1911), p. 91.
76. Ibid., citing Renan's *La Réforme intellectuelle et morale*, pp. 23, 25-26.
77. Sorel, "Trois problèmes," p. 226.
78. Sorel, letter to Croce, 10 May 1909, in *Critica* 26, (20 May 1928): 195. Cf. "Lettre à *Action Française*," 6 June 1910, reprinted in Cahm, *Péguy*, pp. 180-81.
79. Sorel, "Trois problèmes," p. 229, citing Halévy, *Apologie pour notre passé*.
80. Sorel, *La Révolution Dreyfusienne*, pp. 63-64.
81. Sorel, "Le Patriotisme actuel en France," p. 10.
82. Sorel, "Trois problèmes," p. 276.
83. Sorel, *La Révolution Dreyfusienne*, p. 44.
84. Ibid., pp. 44-45.
85. Ibid., p. 52.
86. Sorel, "Urbain Gohier," *Indépendance* (1 Jan. 1912): 315.
87. Sorel, "Quelques prétentions juives," *Indépendance* (May 1912): 218.
88. Ibid. (June 1912): 325.
89. Ibid., p. 332.
90. See, for example, Sorel's review of Lombroso's *L'Antisémitisme*, *Revue Internationale de Sociologie* (April 1899): 301, and of Bonomelli's *Contre l'antisémitisme*, *Revue Générale de Bibliographie* (April 1904): 182.
91. Sorel, "Quelques pretentions juives" (June 1912): 324-25.
92. Bernard Lazare, *Anti-Semitism: Its History and Causes* (London: Britons, 1967), chap. 12.
93. Sorel, "Aux temps Dreyfusiens," p. 42.
94. See Hannah Arendt, *The Origins of Totalitarianism*. Part I: *Anti-Semitism* (New York and Cleveland: World, 1958). Arendt notes the highly assimilationist and even conservative behavior of most Western European Jews. A book which expresses its indebtedness to Arendt and confirms most of her findings is Michael R. Marrus, *The Politics of Assimilation: A Study of the French Jewish Community at the Time of the Dreyfus Affair* (Oxford: Clarendon Press, 1971).
95. Sorel, *Lettres à Paul Delesalle*, 25 May 1921, p. 229.
96. Sorel, "Charles Péguy," in *Da Proudhon a Lenin*, pp. 62-63.
97. Daniel Halévy, *Péguy et Les Cahiers de la Quinzaine*, trans. Ruth Bethell (London: Dobson, 1946), p. 171.
98. Marcel Péguy, "La Rupture de Charles Péguy et de Georges Sorel d'après des documents inédits," *Cahiers de la Quinzaine* (Paris: 1930), pp. 19-21.
99. Sorel, letter to Lotte, 21 December 1912, in *Feuillets de l'amitié Charles Péguy*, no. 33, May 1953, p. 10.
100. Jean Ominus, "Péguy et Sorel," in ibid., no. 77, May 1960, p. 7.
101. Sorel letter to Lotte, 25 February 1914, in ibid., no. 34, July 1953, p. 12; Variot, *Propos de Georges Sorel*, p. 41.

XI

THE EUROPEAN IDEOLOGIES, 1914–1922

Sorel's greatest period of despair was during World War I and its aftermath. By then, as we have noted, Sorel had been largely disabused of his syndicalist hopes, and his desire for a revived republican aristocracy seemed doomed to frustration. Socialism was "dead and buried," syndicalism "impotent,"[1] and Sorel declared to Croce that "I no longer believe, with Bergson, in a regeneration of the French spirit."[2] Indeed, Bergson himself, in Sorel's view, had "exhausted the essential aspects of his philosophy"[3] and had degenerated into platitudes. As Sorel complained to Croce, "Among us there is not a single man with something serious to say."[4] Claudel and Péguy were denounced as "empty spirits,"[5] while the syndicalist chiefs had betrayed their followers "in order to avoid military employment and to obtain good positions."[6] Since Sorel had already written off the royalists,[7] there remained in France no thinker or group on which Sorel could pin his hopes for the future. The emptiness of spirit in France meant to Sorel that if France were victorious in the war, the result would only be the "definitive triumph" of the "godless school" of Jacobinism.[8]

The temper of Sorel's approach during this period, which is normally presented as one which shows his credulity, moved one commentator to ask if Sorel was a "monstrous bungler."[9] This greatly exaggerates the case. Sorel's condemnation of the war as fought for the basest possible motives reveals a skepticism that is as profound as any found in his previous writings. Sorel had always regarded the problem of evil as "the stumbling block of modern thought,"[10] and this awareness of evil not only pervaded Sorel's view of the war but produced his skepticism about the great ideological movements of the postwar era.

Sorel's experimentation with foreign ideologies emerged from his sense of despair for his own civilization; it led him to look elsewhere—first to Germany, then to Russia, and finally to Italy—for a new center of regeneration. That is why this period represents Sorel's greatest output in writings on current affairs and his smallest in the realm of theory. What we find is not so much credulity as a renewed searching, a mental experimentation, if you will, with the new twentieth-century ideological movements. His treatment and testing of these movements often resulted in contradictory testimony; despite a lingering sympathy for the goals of the Soviet Republic, the result was skepticism.

I

In *Reflections on Violence*, Sorel condemns the fact that "the ideology of a timorous humanitarian middle class, professing to have freed its thought from the conditions of its existence, is grafted onto the degeneration of the capitalist system." Aside from a great extension of proletarian violence, Sorel sees only one occurrence that would halt this degeneration: "a great foreign war, which might renew lost energies, and which in any case would doubtless bring into power men with a will to govern."[11] Though Sorel said that such an "hypothesis" seemed far-fetched in 1906, he took quite a different view of the First World War from his earlier theoretical position. It is safe to say of the Great War that during and after the event and until his dying day, Sorel did not have a single good thing to say about it. Throughout his writings of this period, Sorel implies that the First World War violated Proudhon's rules of war. He states explicitly that it was imperialist; whatever the theoretical position in favor of struggle, Sorel's repugnance for the war was far stronger than that of most of his humanitarian contemporaries.

Sorel's opposition to the war was not on strictly humanitarian grounds and was certainly not pacifist. Ultimately, his opposition took the form of a Proudhonian hostility to wars of brigandage, but this framework caused him some difficulty at the outset of the conflict because the motives for the war were not readily apparent to him. Thus in August 1914 he thought that the German Emperor would keep the peace in order to keep the prosperity of his country. He was as unable to understand the motives that drove the Emperor to war at a time when all Europe was grouped against him as he was to determine the basis of the Entente Cordiale, especially England's interests on behalf of the alliance.[12]

Soon, however, Sorel turned to the opinion that Germany, the land of productivity and progress, was being in a sense exploited by

France, the land of plutocracy and of "the Jacobin spirit which favors it."[13] Indeed, to Sorel:

> The powers of the Entente pursue a war of rapine, intended to give to bourgeois idlers the means of appropriating the product of labor of the most industrious country in Europe. . . . I am increasingly convinced that this war is a struggle of the bourgeoisie against labor; and this leads me to ask if the German socialists have not given proof of a unique perspicacity in recognizing the true character of this war from the very beginning.[14]

He extolled certain German socialists such as Legien and certain trade-union chiefs for their resistance to the war. Sorel excoriated Kautsky and the other "intellectual prattlers" in the German Social Democratic Party for giving in to the warmongers and hence for setting themselves against the working classes of Germany.[15] "The latter," he said in 1917, "still resist. Here [in France] they do not."[16]

Sometimes Sorel confuses an admiration for Germany *en bloc* with an admiration for the industrial spirit of Germany. When even the working classes of France are condemned for cooperating in the war, Sorel's unit of analysis appears to be the nation instead of the social class. Thus he extols Germany as the new Rome, while France has degenerated from its old, serious *Romanité* to a frivolous *Latinité*.[17]

Basically, however, Sorel reverts to the Proudhonian view of unjust wars based on pillage, as he censures the underlying motive for ruling-class enthusiasm for the war. Sorel depicts the modern ruling classes as analogous to the ruling classes at the time of Napoleon. "In spite of his parsimony, the emperor was constantly short of money. In order to create a class of 'social authorities' he found it necessary to furnish very heavy subsidies to his high functionaries . . . so that their silly prodigality never ceased to create problems for the Empire."[18] In Sorel's view, many military problems would have been averted if Napoleon and his soldiers had not been weighted down with the loot of battle. Sorel takes it as axiomatic that the modern Jacobin class is imitating the actions of Napoleon, thereby leading the country to ruin. The ruling classes think that "the only way, indeed, to contain a conquered nation is to destroy it by plundering the rich classes and to make of the country a vast *mezzadria* with a population divided into two parts, making the most numerous and poor class participate in the spoils of the rich class."[19] Sorel affirmed that such an attitude held by the ruling class would lead only to the degeneration of the victorious side; the revenge and booty incorporated in the Versailles Treaty strengthened his opinion. "How," he asked, "can a peace be concluded which imposes on

Germany more humiliating and more onerous terms than those which Napoleon imposed at Tilset after conquering Prussia?"[20]

But does the First World War provide adequate confirmation of Sorel's distinction between good and bad wars, that is, wars fought either for glory or for autonomy, and those fought for brigandage and/or revenge? Against Sorel, it could be argued that wars fought for gain are less onerous and more limited than those fought for national greatness. Was Wilson's entry into the war on the basis of a crusade for democracy really less honorable than Sorel's Proudhonian standards? Sorel argues that the Calvinist myth, praised in the *Reflections on Violence*, that so galvanized the virtuous authorities of the Swiss cantons, had in Wilson's hands been transformed into the ideology of modern, demagogic democracy. "The treaty of Versailles has cast discredit on the era of Presbyterian democracy. A great part of public opinion, having come to abandon easily the principles that it had proclaimed necessary for the pacification of Europe, believes that its great probity rendered it an easy victim of shrewd politicians."[21]

Perhaps inadvertently, Sorel appears here to be confessing the inevitable failure of myth. In a struggle between the violence of myth and the brutality of power, power seems destined to win. Sorel has admitted that the glorious Calvinist myth has been transformed into a justificatory ideology of modern democracy, a democracy Sorel had always juxtaposed to myth. Thus, Sorel's analysis of American entry into the war concludes by rejecting the myth as a unit of analysis. He approaches the war as motivated by brutal, materialist aims, merely masked by Calvinism: America's entry into the war was to insure the success of the two great powers of the Entente; to obtain most-favored-nation status in the new Europe; to gain access to Russian mineral resources; to prevent Japan from entering China; and to prepare a military force for a war against Japan.[22] Some political realists might argue that had American goals indeed been that clear-cut, the world might have been spared considerable grief.

In any case, is this mixture of Calvinist mythology (or ideology) and pragmatism (imperialism) any different from Sorel's own assertion that "social myths in no way prevent a man from profiting by the observations which he makes in the course of his life, and form no obstacle to the pursuit of his normal occupations" or that Protestant sectarians whose exaltation was fed by myths were "nonetheless quite practical men"?[23] Sorel's treatment of the war was not without insight, but it was almost totally devoid of any discussion of myths. Sorel can affirm the susceptibility of myth to testing, but the limits to myth are so vague, the contours so mysterious, that it is difficult to distinguish myth from ideology, especially since Sorel himself noted that "there are rarely myths that are perfectly free from any hint of utopianism."[24] This admission gives Sorel free rein to decide for or against certain beliefs on grounds of his own choosing, that is, on either Bergsonian or historical grounds, on the terrain of myth or that of practical politics.

The one cutting edge that seems best to distinguish good myth from bad ideology, that differentiates action based on the sublime from that based on interest, appears to be the way politicians—especially democratic politicians—put an idea to use. The extraordinary hostility Sorel showed toward democratic regimes stems from his repeated belief that politics, and especially democratic politics, pollutes everything it touches. At times, an undercurrent in Sorel's writings seems to imply that democracy is the political form which is most easily set against myth and against which myth is most powerless. This is one of the pillars of his rather pessimistic vision of Europe's future. At the time of the First World War, all European countries appeared to Sorel to be in the process of democratization: "In a word, we are entering a radical-socialist era which could last for half a century," he said in 1914.[25] Four years later, he asserted that "the victory of the Entente was a triumph for demagogic plutocracy."[26]

II

One of the more troublesome areas of Sorel's thought is found in its relation to fascism. Looking at Sorel's writings as a whole, we see an ambiguous stance in the face of this new European phenomenon. In a letter to Croce, and in the course of several conversations, Sorel made complimentary references to Mussolini's leadership. On the other hand, numerous letters express Sorel's criticism of the fascists, sometimes referring to their repressive tactics, sometimes to their weak leadership, sometimes to their demagogy.

This ambiguity is par for the course in Sorelian thought, and it reflects both the complexities of Sorel's theory and the fact that, prior to 1922, fascism was an almost completely unknown quantity in European politics. Indeed, Sorel notes the "large number of discordant and contradictory elements" in fascism.[27] J. L. Talmon, Jack Roth, A. James Gregor, and others have tended to stress Sorel's affinities with fascism. Gregor notes that Sorel's view of myth, which is based on the will of the moral agent and is stridently opposed to the limits of both positivism and rationalism, was embraced by Mussolini, who saw the myth as a means of converting the population into a compact, anti-democratic revolutionary mass. Mussolini derived from Sorel the theory that "the history of society is the history of group conflict," that the state was the executive agency of a dominant minority. Furthermore, Mussolini, like Sorel and Pareto, was an anti-rationalist. "Men, particularly the mass, were motivated by sentiment rather than reason." Thus, Mussolini was inspired by Sorel's view that "a revolutionary social element (in this case the proletariat) can accede to dominance only if organized and directed by an elite which effectively mobilizes sentiment through a compelling social myth . . . cast in images appropriate to warfare."[28] Finally, Mussolini acknowledged his debt; everything he was, he asserted, he owed to Sorel. "He is an accomplished master who, with his sharp theories on revolutionary formations, contributed to the molding of the discipline, the collective energy, the massed power of the fascist cohorts."[29]

Prior to the war, Sorel returned the compliment and praised Mussolini. "Believe me," he is reported to have said to Variot, "you will perhaps see him one day at the head of a sacred battalion, sword-bearer of the Italian banner. He is an Italian of the fifteenth century, a condottiere. No one realizes it yet, but he is the only man capable and energetic enough to redress the weaknesses of the government."[30] During the war, Sorel is reported to have said that Mussolini had "an astonishing comprehension of the Italian masses and he had invented something which is not in my books, the union of the national and the social, which I have studied but never understood. This discovery of that which is both national and social and which is at the base of his method is purely Mussolinian, and I do not think I have inspired him either directly or indirectly."[31] It is interesting that Sorel, who had flirted with French nationalism before the war, should dissociate himself from fascism's unification of nationalism and socialism and that, as he interpreted it, Mussolini's nationalism was different from his own. His praise for the fascists as "the most original social phenomenon in Italy"[32] was simultaneously a partial dissociation from fascism.

The supposed originality of fascism may have been the basis of Sorel's appreciation of it. He said that Mussolini was far more disinterested than Bonaparte, for Napoleon "created an aristocracy on the old model . . . created only a sham."[33] Mussolini, on the other hand, had an originality comparable to Lenin's. The two men, "so different from one another in their social ideas, come together in the form of almost perfect leaders of their people, whom they serve and are not served by."[34] Both men, he said, possessed political genius that far surpassed that of any of their contemporaries.

In order to understand Sorel's views on Mussolini, we must try to keep in mind the function of symbolic leadership that he had developed in the prewar period. Sorel's contempt for Napoleon's "old-fashioned" aristocracy was a contempt for an elite that had long lost the independence it had enjoyed under the Capetians. Sorel's appreciation of Mussolinian leadership appears to echo his admiration for the Capet monarchy, i.e., he sees it as a limited, symbolic leadership that kept the plurality of society intact and whose true meaning was not understood by the modern monarchists, who attempt to derive political power from symbolic power. Gregor and other writers, who argue that Sorel "comes close to fascism,"[35] fail to distinguish symbolic leadership, as an oppositionist construction, from statism. Such opposition is suggested in Sorel's assertion that "the fascists have as their occult but real chief, the king," but Sorel implies that this symbol is mistaken, because it confuses force with violence. The king, Sorel notes, had "forced Italy to go to war in the hope of causing the ruination of socialism."[36]

When we recall the Sorelian distinction between force and violence, it appears that Sorel perceived fascism as destructive insofar as it gave itself over to the repressive characteristics of state power. "Italy," he wrote, "seems increasingly oriented toward a regime which resembles Ireland; the fascists operate on the model of the Black-and-Tans."[37] There is little doubt that this statement signified a condemnation of the fascists, since Sorel regarded the Black-and-Tans as instruments of the "Anglo-American financial alliance" victimizing Ireland.[38] As agents of force rather than violence, the fascists were not directed toward establishing a new form of social authority, as Sorel had once hoped the syndicates would do. Instead, the fascists, in attacking the Italian Workers' Councils, only forced all the socialists to join with the old socialist parliamentarians of Bombacci,[39] with consequences which Sorel saw as "disturbing for the future of Italy."[40]

With some perspicacity, Sorel saw fascism as a European rather than an Italian phenomenon and he was, to say the least, not entirely pleased about it. To Delesalle he wrote that the fascists treated their socialist opponents "as the Jacobins were treated by the Thermidorians." Indeed, "all Europe is undoubtedly destined to experience a new *Thermidorism*, and perhaps we are happy to be let off with a few trials that are more ridiculous, than deadly."[41] The situation in Italy, he implied, degenerated in proportion as the fascists assumed greater importance.[42] "The disorder of the fascists who suppress the state can easily lead Italy back to the Middle Ages; for it appears that the fascists are no better balanced than the futurists, who certainly contributed to making the Italians lose their heads during this past year."[43]

It appears, furthermore, that Sorel admired neither the fascist myth nor the manner in which it was propagated. In the early days of the war he complained that the "oracles of Mussolinian socialism" imagine "that it is enough to have eloquent declamations in order to create a popular ideology."[44] In regard to demagogic appeals, it would appear that Mussolini was making the same mistake as Maurras had been in the days before the war. Like the Action Française, the fascists missed the opportunity to engage in the kind of violence Sorel admired. "The results of this war are so deplorable that I ask myself how the people cannot demonstrate their indignation against the victors. This would have been a fine opportunity for the fascists to become the representatives of the young Italy; but they do not seem to have been aware of the role that circumstances offered them. It leads to the question of whether their leaders have not betrayed them."[45]

Considerable confusion is visible in Sorel's attitude toward leadership. Gregor quite rightly notes that Sorel does not meet all the criteria of proper fascism. For one thing, Mussolini went far beyond Sorel in arguing that the social myth "could not provide the strategic program of the party leadership. The leadership requires a specific knowledge that governs and is adequate for action. For those who conceive socialism in terms of Sorel's myth, nothing obtains other than acts of faith. . . . Mussolini opposed the realistic Guicciardini to the visionary Sorel."[46] In one respect this is quite wrong, of course, because Sorel's early writings do discuss the development of alternative socialist institutions, but it is quite right to assert that the development of fascist political parties was guided by presuppositions quite different from those lying behind Sorel's federalism. In this regard Mussolini and his communist opponent Antonio Gramsci, who was also indebted to Sorel, had similar criticisms. As Gramsci put it, theoretical syndicalism "relates to a subordinate group which is prevented by this theory from ever becoming dominant, of developing beyond the economico-corporative phase in order to raise itself to the phase of ethico-political hegemony in civil society and of the domination of the state."[47]

It is likely, then, that Sorel's admiration for Mussolini's leadership and/or fascism is due to an apparent change of heart regarding its character, that is, it is couched in terms of Sorel's opposition to the alliance between fascism's socialist opposition and the state. Sorel notes the alliance of peasant socialists with the state against the fascists;[48] it is in their role as opponents of state power that Sorel wrote to Missiroli that "the fascists are not completely wrong to invoke my opinions because their power demonstrates the value of violence triumphant."[49] If we assume that for Sorel violence is equivalent to rebellion and juxtaposed to force, his letter to Missiroli, though seemingly pro-fascist, interprets the fascists as a potential alternative to state repression: "their violence can be substituted advantageously for state force which permits the socialists to terrorize the bourgeoisie. The fascists have had the idea of substituting themselves for this same state and of upholding the national independence conquered by Garibaldi. . . . We find ourselves at the beginning of a movement which should reverse the parliamentary edifice which has become increasingly useless with each passing day. I predict that one day the fascists will change this state of affairs radically."[50]

Indeed, there is some indication that Sorel regarded the fascists as surrogate syndicalists in a more literal sense than the one implied above. That is, not only did he view them as counter-force rather than force, but he saw them as the embodiment of working-class sentiments that were found in Italy and which led Sorel to anticipate Italy as the source of a great European renewal. Insofar as Mussolini's leadership corresponded to those sentiments, Sorel looked upon it with some sympathy. But it was the workers' councils arising throughout Italy that he viewed as corresponding "perfectly to the emerging sentiments of the proletariat of that country."[51] The movement to establish workers' councils in the Fiat plant was "more important than all the writings published in *Neue Zeit*."[52]

In any event, aside from a couple of letters, little evidence exists to mark Sorel's sentiments as pro-fascist. These letters and the oral accounts of Variot and Michels are outweighed by the far more numerous anti-fascist statements found in his correspondence. Jack Roth argues rather generally that, as reflected in his correspondence, Sorel became pro-Mussolini only after 1920.[53] Now this change, if it did occur, had to take place between June of 1921, when he was still making anti-Mussolini remarks, and the letter written to Croce in late August, 14 months before Mussolini's triumph, when his political "genius" appeared to be bearing fruit. Discounting the prewar statements in favor of Mussolini, there is some evidence that Sorel was disturbed by fascist street tactics even as late as 8 November.[54]

In any event, the spottiness of the evidence for such a transformation, at a time when Sorel's correspondence diminished, leaves many lacunae. It is unfortunate that nearly all of Sorel's discussion of fascism takes place in letters which in any case speak very little of fascist doctrine at all. Much of Sorel's writing in this period is journalistic rather than theoretical, addressed to current events rather than transcendent questions. Sorel did not really know what Mussolini stood for. In speaking sympathetically to Roberto Michels of Mussolini, Sorel asked, "Does anyone know where he is going? In any case he will go far."[55]

There remains the question of how great the debt of fascist ideology and practice to Sorel really was, and to what extent Sorel was responsible for spreading ideas that made acceptance of fascism easier. Here we enter the troublesome area of whether an individual can be condemned by the actions of his followers.

Jack Roth maintains that what in Italy was called "*Sorelismo* both directly and indirectly figured significantly in the origins of Fascism"; but Roth is careful to distinguish between *Sorelismo*, "an organized and vulgarized Italian transformation of the pre-war Sorelian movement," and Sorel's original ideas. He further notes that other groups may have arrived at fascism by routes other than Sorelismo and concludes that Sorel played a somewhat "biblical" role in the formation of fascism, a role not wholly dissimilar to that played by Marx in communist debates. Thus, there was a Sorelian opposition to fascism as well as a group of men calling themselves Sorelians who favored it; and both sides quoted Sorel to support their position. As Roth says, "Sorel could be for Libya or against it, for intervention or against it."[56]

It should be noted that most discussions of Sorel's influence on fascism center on the fascist movement before it had come to power in Italy. This early movement was more diverse and decentralized (hence more amenable to Sorelianism) than it was after its capture of the state machinery.[57] Since Sorel died before he could see the consequences of fascism in power, the only testimony we have as to how he would have viewed fascism is from his most loyal followers, whose trustworthiness may not have been any greater than that of Marx's followers. The best testimony, the one which is certainly the closest to Sorel, is that of Edouard Berth, for whose *Méfaits des intellectuels* Sorel had written a preface in 1914. In a foreword to the second edition of this book, written four years after Sorel's death, Berth said:

> The war irretrievably shattered Maurrasisme; and this is undoubtedly why a man like Valois cannot remain in the ranks of the Action Française. Valois at present wants to instigate a movement similar to Italian fascism in France, but the conditions of France are not those of Italy; fascism is an entirely Italian phenomenon, and I do not think that a "French fascism" has a future. . . . We must not forget the radical difference that separates *fascist violence* from *Sorelian violence*.

> The latter is the true violence, that which tends to destroy the traditional state and institute a *free order.* The former is, in a word, only a bourgeois force tending, on the contrary, to restore the traditional state and consequently to consolidate the bourgeois order. . . . Neither fascism nor communism has succeeded in restoring national or revolutionary values except in a rather regressive regime.[58]

In 1931, Berth wrote: "It is thus absolutely vain and ridiculous to want to transform Sorel into 'the spiritual father of fascism.' . . . One thing ought to be most clear: proletarian violence has nothing to do with either Blanquist or fascist violence; its acts are only comparable to the acts of war of an army on the march."[59] It might be added that to confuse Sorelianism with fascism is to make the same mistake as to single out war, rather than the internal state terror which Sorel abhorred, as the single most characteristic trait of fascism.[60]

III

It is probable that Sorel's interest in fascism stemmed from his concern with militant syndicalist and working-class sentiments that were strong in Italy, although in his view such sentiments were suppressed in Germany and had vanished in France; and his corresponding admiration for workers' councils led Sorel to admire not only Italy but the Soviet experiment in Russia as well.

The Russian Revolution renewed Sorel's hopes for a return, of sorts, to the syndicalist ideals he had more or less abandoned after 1909. Sorel is far less equivocal about Lenin's new republic of soviets than he was about Mussolini (although even there he had some doubts). In March of 1917, he dismissed the early stages of the Russian Revolution as "analogous to the position France had been in from 1792 to 1794. The Cadets are the new Girondins, very partial to the war. . . . It is unlikely that the Cadets are more adept than the Girondins at directing the Revolution; they work for an extreme left of demagogues. . . . The poor Czar seems condemned to imitate Louis XVI."[61] The working classes in Russia were duped by the democrats, as were the Parisian workers in 1848.

When the Bolshevik Revolution triumphed against all odds, Sorel returned to myth. The Revolution appeared to him to demonstrate again that an exceptional act motivated by a powerful myth enables a movement to "force" history. Such attempts may fail, according to Sorel, but he insisted that in the case of Soviet Russia, "the ideology of the new proletarian state will never perish; it will survive by merging with the myths which will take their substance from the popular accounts of the struggles sustained by the Republic of Soviets against the coalition of capitalist powers."[62] The Soviet myth subsists, in Sorel's view, on popular legends sustained by great writers like Gorki, in whose eyes "there exists no great difference between the preachers of the Christian faith who have justified their testimony by their martyrdom, and the revolutionaries who have proved their disinterested and intrepid devotion to the interests of the people and to liberty and truth."[63]

Sorel argues that Lenin's great insight was to recognize the power of the "protest against an oligarchy whose greatest concern had been not to appear Russian."[64] This power of rebellion gave Lenin "the moral authority enjoyed by men who have won, through their services, the confidence of the people; at every instant, the responsible persons of the revolution are obliged to defend it against the instincts which always impel humanity toward the lowest spheres of life,"[65] that is, toward natural nature. The construction of an artificial nature in Russia required Lenin to demonstrate to the producers, through his moral authority, "the value of certain rules derived from the experiences of a highly developed capitalism"[66] without relying on the superstition of the automatic mechanism of *laissez-faire*. For Sorel, then, the construction of Russian industry is the great Bolshevik task; in this he seems to be in agreement with the Bolsheviks themselves. Thus, he insists that the sole means of testing the validity of the Russian experiment, that is, "the only really important question that the philosopher may consider, is whether [Lenin] is directing the orientation of Russia toward the construction of a republic of producers, capable of embodying an economy as progressive as that of our capitalist democracies."[67]

In the last months of Sorel's life, the productive criteria he had set up to test the validity of the Russian experiment seemed to deny many previous hopes. Sorel admitted the possibility that Bolshevism had attained results opposite to those that had been intended: that the Republic of Soviets had not, for example, reversed the traditional absenteeism of Russian workers; and that there had been in fact a terrible diminution in the productivity of labor.[68]

> It seems that the Soviet legislators first had the idea of giving to workshop councils a task that did not have to be determined by business directors. But experience has shown that the Russian workman is very far from having in the workshop a principle of intelligent cooperation, and it is therefore necessary to rule with central direction. . . . It can therefore be said with good cause that industrial parliamentarianism has been a failure in Russia,

just as the parliamentarianism of the Duma had failed.

The failure to recognize the Russian peasant's "instinctive repugnance" for collective work was, to Sorel, the greatest mistake of Bolshevism, and he noted the failures of agricultural cooperation due to "total popular indifference."[69]

Nor did Sorel view these failures as an excuse for central direction. He criticizes the "democratic illusions" of the new Russian elite and condemns it for promoting industrial concentration and state direction. "The militarization of work," which was the bureaucratic response to the failures of workers' control, "belongs more to the category of measures of public safety proper to a tottering democracy than it does to the regular organization of scientific production. From an economic point of view, the rural population of Italy is at an infinitely higher level than that of the Russian proletariat."[70]

Sorel almost certainly separated the myth of Russia and the myth of Lenin from the political realities of Russia and the doctrine of Lenin, of which he knew very little. "Berth has given me a copy of *Left Wing Communism: An Infantile Disorder*," he complained to Delesalle. "This work appears rather obscure to me because I don't know enough of the situation in Russia to understand Lenin's polemic well enough."[71] If Sorel had such difficulty in comprehending Lenin's political masterpiece, it is unlikely that he understood much else by him. Sorel shows no more comprehension of the doctrines of Lenin than he did of Mussolini's ideas. He judged both these figures as statesmen and historical figures rather than as political theorists. As with fascism, Bolshevism—insofar as it was viewed favorably—was viewed in the light of Proudhonian criteria. "Syndicalism was the slippery slope to Bolshevism,"[72] Sorel thought, and despite his admiration for Lenin and the Soviet experiment, to the very last Sorel never failed to reaffirm his essential Proudhonism. In his last major article, *Ultime meditazioni* (1920),[73] one finds further suggestions as to the reason for his apparent inconsistencies in viewing the new ideologies. Sorel says that even the Soviet system, if it is a success, will not be copied in Western Europe. The importance of national traditions, that is to say, historical considerations, is crucial in determining the success of any movement. Once again, he argues, only a supreme act of will can force a break in these historical traditions. Revolutionary socialism itself has become weakened: "Only revolutionary socialism is able to favor the development of proletarian justice. It is not to be deplored enough that Marxism has produced the almost complete ruination of the attempt made by Proudhon to lead this field. I, for my part, find this result dreadful, since the sentiment of justice is also dying in the bourgeois world."[74]

Here we see that Sorel has not only cut himself off from modern ideologies, but has, through the success of these ideologies, seen the failure of Proudhonism as well; there is little doubt that the modern totalitarian movements in power would have revealed to Sorel, had he lived, their incompatibility with Proudhon's federalist principles. What sympathy he did reveal for these movements is more than mitigated by the theoretical objections made against them by his more loyal successors, in the name of Sorelian principles. Sorel's hostility to statism, Jacobinism, demagogy, terrorism, and intellectual elitism could only have led him to the hostility to totalitarianism found in his follower, Berth. There is even less doubt that had he sympathized with these movements in power, his sympathy would have been no longer-lasting than it was for his other "allegiances." Sorel's greatest virtue, as well as his greatest weakness, is that his Proudhonian position effectively cut him off from the possibility of any long-lasting commitment to a political movement. He was far too much of a liberal to favor centralized state direction (or party direction); too much of a conservative to sympathize with any wholesale reconstruction of society in the name of some theory; far too much of a nationalist to sympathize with a communist international; and too much of a syndicalist to excuse the fascist cooptation of trade unions. In short, Sorel's pluralism precludes any long-term acceptance of the unitary ideologies necessary to modern authoritarian movements.

Part of the confusion that identifies Sorel with fascism is his inclination to "sympathize" with a movement in order to understand it, but this sympathy is part of the tool kit of the social analyst rather than the politician. Sorel criticizes his subjects from within rather than from without; this is a methodological, not an ideological, stance, and the methodology ultimately precludes a political commitment. Thus Sorel comes from within Marxism to present us with a Marxian criticism of Marx—only to reject Marx. His "progressive" criticism of the idea of progress assumes a cyclical view of history. His republican criticism of radicalism terminates in implacable hostility to the Jacobin tradition and despair for the fate of the Republic. The irony is that ultimately his temporary sympathy for his subjects led to a detachment from all of them, a critical detachment closely approximating that of the philosophers whom he scorned.

Sorel's perspective is most valuable, then, as a tool for the criticism of ideologies and social phenomena, rather than as an alternative social system. In this respect it is negative and, in being negative, possesses a certain instability. The Sorelian viewpoint is rather like a highly unstable chemical substance: it can be benign or highly explosive, depending on the method by and the context within which it is used. Used properly, it is invaluable for handling the modern assumptions of political movements, as well as the nineteenth-century assumptions of twentieth-century social science.

Notes

1. Sorel, letter to Missiroli, 10 August 1914, in *'Da Proudhon a Lenin'*, p. 502. Cf. his letter to Missiroli, 13 August 1910: "Syndicalism has [now] slid down the same incline that socialism has already traveled—toward a pure outbidding by demagogues" (*'Da Proudhon a Lenin'*, p. 449).

2. Sorel, letter to Croce, 8 April 1915, in *Critica* 27, no. 2 (20 March 1929): 120.

3. Sorel, letter to Missiroli, 17 January 1915, in *'Da Proudhon a Lenin'*, p. 537.

4. Sorel, letter to Croce, 18 July 1915, in *Critica* 27, no. 2 (20 March 1929): 123.

5. Sorel, letter to Croce, 25 April 1915, in ibid., p. 120.

6. See Sorel's letter to Missiroli, 15 May 1917, in *'Da Proudhon a Lenin'*, p. 621.

7. See Chapter 10.

8. Sorel, letter to Croce, 5 May 1915, in *Critica* 27, no. 2, (20 Mar. 1929): 121.

9. Claude Polin, Preface to Georges Sorel's *Réflexions sur la violence* (9th ed., Paris: Rivière, 1972), p. vii. Polin is actually fairly sympathetic to Sorel.

10. Sorel, letter to Croce, 27 November 1909, in *Critica* 26, no. 5 (20 Sept. 1928): 336.

11. Sorel, *Reflections*, p. 86.

12. Sorel, letter to Missiroli, 10 August 1914, in *'Da Proudhon a Lenin'*, pp. 500-501.

13. Sorel, letter to Missiroli, 30 August 1914, in ibid., p. 507.

14. Sorel, letter to Missiroli, 8 September 1916, in ibid., p. 606.

15. Sorel, letter to Missiroli, 15 May 1917, in ibid., p. 620.

16. Sorel, letter to Missiroli, 15 May 1917, in ibid., p. 621.

17. Sorel, letter to Missiroli, 24 October 1914, in ibid., p. 516 (italics are Sorel's).

18. Sorel, "Le Guerre di brigantaggio," in *'Da Proudhon a Lenin'*, p. 98 (reprint of an article of 7 June 1919).

19. Ibid., p. 101, and letter to Missiroli, 8 September 1916, in *'Da Proudhon a Lenin'*, p. 606. See also the letter to Missiroli, 5 July 1915, in *'Da Proudhon a Lenin'*, p. 572, in which he refers to the German policy toward Belgium as "brutal."

20. Sorel, letter to Missiroli, 8 September 1916, in *'Da Proudhon a Lenin'*, p. 607.

21. Sorel, "Calvinismo politico," 12 June 1921, in ibid., p. 36. Cf. *Lettres à Delesalle*, 29 May 1918, p. 147, in which Sorel calls Wilson a "sinister *farceur* in the clutches of a demagogic plutocracy."

22. Sorel, letter to Missiroli, 15 May 1917, in *'Da Proudhon a Lenin'*, p. 619.

23. Sorel, *Reflections*, p. 125 and note.
24. *FGS*, p. 205.
25. Sorel, letter to Missiroli, 10 August 1914, in *'Da Proudhon a Lenin'*, p. 502.
26. *FGS*, p. 246.
27. Sorel, *Lettres à Delesalle*, 18 April 1921, p. 223.
28. A. James Gregor, *The Ideology of Fascism* (New York: Free Press, 1969), p. 69; cf. pp. 115, 119.
29. Ibid., p. 116, citing de Begnac's *Palazzo Venezia: Storia di un regime* (Rome: La Rocca, 1950), p. 118.
30. Pierre Andreu, *Notre maître Georges Sorel*, p. 109n. This speech was quoted to Andreu by Variot, who had inadvertently omitted it from his book, *Propos de Georges Sorel.*
31. Ibid.
32. Sorel, letter to Croce, 26 August 1921, in *Critica* 28, no. 3 (20 May 1930): 195.
33. Andreu, *Notre maître Georges Sorel*, p. 109n.
34. Variot, *Propos de Georges Sorel*, p. 86.
35. See J. L. Talmon, "Sorel's Legacy," *Encounter* (Feb. 1970).
36. Sorel, *Lettres à Delesalle*, 19 March 1921, p. 215.
37. Sorel, *Lettres à Delesalle*, 26 Feb. 1921, p. 210. Cf. Sorel's letter to Missiroli, 11 March 1921, in *'Da Proudhon a Lenin'*, p. 727; letter to Croce, 25 March 1921, in *Critica* 28, no. 3 (20 May 1930): 194.
38. Sorel, letter to Missiroli, 7 May 1916, in *'Da Proudhon a Lenin'*, p. 599.
39. Sorel, letter to Missiroli, 30 January 1921, in ibid., p. 726.
40. Sorel, letter to Missiroli, 22 January 1921, in ibid., p. 724.
41. Sorel, *Lettres à Delesalle*, 9 April 1921, pp. 218-19 (Sorel's italics).
42. Ibid., 24 March 1921, p. 217.
43. Sorel, letter to Missiroli, 21 June 1921, in *'Da Proudhon a Lenin'*, p. 733.
44. Sorel, letter to Missiroli, 9 December 1914, in ibid., p. 529.
45. Sorel, letter to Missiroli, 21 June 1921, in ibid., p. 733.
46. Gregor, *The Ideology of Fascism*, p. 118.
47. Antonio Gramsci, *The Modern Prince and Other Writings* (New York: International, 1957), p. 154.
48. Sorel, *Lettres à Delesalle*, 13 July 1921, p. 236.
49. Sorel, letter to Missiroli, 16 April 1921, in *'Da Proudhon a Lenin'*, p. 731.
50. Sorel, letter to Missiroli, September 1921, in Missiroli's "Prefazione" to *L'Europa sotto la tormenta* (Milan: Corbaccio, 1932), p. *xxxiii.*
51. Sorel, "I Consigli operai" (22 Mar. 1921), in *'Da Proudhon a Lenin'*, p. 343.
52. Sorel, "Il Massimalismo Italiano ai miei compagni d'Italia," in ibid., pp. 172-73. The oppositionist character of Sorel's view of fascism is highlighted in Sorel's approving reference to a letter from Enrico Leone: "The communists," Leone said, "are much further from us [than the fascists] because of the communist, statist and dictatorial concepts" (*Lettres à Delesalle*, p. 222). Sorel regarded Leone as a most consistent and steadfast socialist libertarian.
53. Jack Roth, "Sorel on Lenin and Mussolini," *Contemporary French Civilization* 2, no. 2 (Winter 1978): 244.

54. See Sorel's *Lettres à Delesalle*, 8 November 1921, p. 237.

55. Sorel, "Lettere a Roberto Michels," *Nuovi Studi di Divitto Economia e Politica* (Feb. 1929): 293n4.

56. Jack Roth, "The Roots of Italian Fascism: Sorel and Sorelismo," *Journal of Modern History* 39, no. 1 (Mar. 1967): 30.

57. For a discussion of this point, see Edward Tannenbaum, "The Goals of Italian Fascism," *American Historical Review* 74, no. 4 (Apr. 1969): 1183. Tannenbaum says that fascist syndicalism was a "perversion" of Sorelian revolutionary syndicalism "from any point of view" (p. 1192).

58. Edouard Berth, *Les Méfaits des intellectuels* (2nd ed., Paris: Rivière, 1926), pp. 21n, 29, 38.

59. Berth, *Du 'Capital' aux 'Réflexions sur la violence'*, p. 194.

60. See Hannah Arendt, *The Origins of Totalitarianism*, part 3. The author notes that the chief characteristics of totalitarian regimes are ideology and terror. Sorel opposes terror, and his hostility to the ideologies of totalitarian regimes is shown in his opposition to the rule of intellectual elites.

61. Sorel, letter to Missiroli, 5 March 1917, in *'Da Proudhon a Lenin'*, p. 613.

62. Sorel, *Reflections*, p. 280.

63. Sorel, "Lénine d'après Gorki," *Revue Communiste* (11 Jan. 1921): 410.

64. Sorel, *Reflections*, p. 282.

65. Ibid., p. 281.

66. Ibid.

67. Ibid., p. 284.

68. Sorel, "Economia Sovietica" (14 April 1921), in *'Da Proudhon a Lenin'*, p. 344.

69. Ibid., pp. 346-47.

70. Ibid., p. 347.

71. Sorel, *Lettres à Delesalle*, 12 February 1921, p. 207.

72. Ibid., 7 July 1921, p. 234.

73. In *'Da Proudhon a Lenin'*, pp. 413-34. For various reasons, this article did not appear until 1928.

74. Ibid., p. 433.

XII

CONCLUSION: SOREL AND THE CRITIQUE OF TOTALITY

In this work I have attempted to argue that Sorel has been misconstrued by many contemporary analysts, that he has been relegated to the position of an historical curiosity or a precursor of fascism. This kind of classification obscures Sorel's utility as a critic of modern Marxism. There are several reasons for this misunderstanding, many of which are related. His association with fascism is of course one. Another is Sorel's reputation as a theorist of violence: in this turbulent century, Sorel's name appears with irregular frequency when terrorism, bloodshed, revolution, and mayhem appear on the scene; almost invariably, it is his *livre standard* which is invoked. Another cause of confusion is the awkward relationship that Sorel has with Marxism. The decomposition of Marxism proclaimed by Sorel now seems to have taken place in the Western world. Yet in the academies of the English-speaking world, Marxist analytical approaches have gained a toehold in departments which had heretofore ignored it or been implacably hostile to it. Insofar as Sorel's writings appear to be within the Marxian tradition, he is regarded as either irrelevant to contemporary reality or hostile both to the "abstract empiricism" of mainstream social science and to the Marxian alternatives.

In Western countries which still have strong Marxist parties, a different viewpoint has recently emerged. In 1977, a publishing event of some importance occurred in Paris: the House of Hachette presented to the world Michel Charzat's *Georges Sorel et la révolution au XXe siècle.*[1] The importance of this is not so much that it represents the publication of the first book on Sorel in France in fifteen years, but that this generally positive treatment should have come from a member of the executive committee of the French Socialist Party. When we remember that in a general way the PSF is the heir of Jules Guesde and Jean Jaurès, the event borders on the hilarious.

Until now, the French intellectual and publishing establishment has largely ignored Sorel. Today, only the *Reflections on Violence* remain in print in Sorel's native country. Reprints and translations of Sorel are much more readily available outside France—especially in Italy. Why this should be the case is unclear. Explanations range from the assumption that the luminaries of French Marxism disdain Sorel's "fascist" company and have sent him to literary Coventry, to the view that Sorel, in his ideological itinerary reminding French intellectuals of their own fashion-consciousness, operates as the gadfly of European ideological movements, a sort of counter-cyclical trendy.

Yet, on the continent Sorel's reputation has now been enhanced by the recognition that his critique of Marxism and his peculiar brand of socialism are increasingly relevant to the problems of the socialist and communist parties of Latin Europe. Not only Charzat but Jean Elleinstein of the French Communist Party, as well as numerous Italian Euro-Communists, have expressed interest in Sorel. Here I will sketch briefly some of the reasons why Sorel's reputation has become enhanced recently in his own land, as well as elsewhere. I am going to try to show that Sorel is now generally agreed to have criticized violence more than he advocated it, and that his approach is generally linked to an attack on the concept of totality as a viable framework for the study of institutions. This will not hide the fact that some of the efforts to revive Sorel—including Charzat's—have been somewhat misguided and that the institutions most likely to benefit from a Sorelian analysis could well to be found altogether outside the socialist movement.

I

Two statements by Sorel may represent two poles of his position in regard to the most important question posed by modern social-science methodology: the question of totality. In the *Saggi di critica del marxismo*, Sorel claims that Hegelian dialectic possesses a fundamental fault:

> It considers only perfect states almost as would a physiologist who focuses on the egg and then the adult without trying to follow development from one to the other little by little. We are in the presence of a series of catastrophic metamorphoses. Under the influence of dialectical concerns, the study of real relations and practical solutions is naturally set aside. The greatest

> mistake of the theorists of the dialectic is in placing social transformation in a mysterious realm and consequently culminating "in a veritable supernatural belief in the creative power of force." . . . Marx and Engels were veritable Blanquists for a great part of their lives.[2]

The other statement, written six years later, asserts that the philosophy of pessimism is necessary in approaching the problems of society. The pessimist, Sorel says, "regards social conditions as forming a system chained together by an iron law to whose necessity we must submit *in toto* and which will disappear only if a catastrophe sweeps everything away."[3] Now these two statements—one pluralistic and one holistic, one gradualist, the other catastrophic—might be taken to represent Sorel's internal contradictions. However, in the context of his thought, and even accepting that the statements were made at different times, they may be viewed in a much more refined light. The second statement reflects the realization that the Marxian concept of totality is at the same time the guiding myth of the Marxian movement; that, shorn of philosophical refinements, the idea of totality stems directly from "psychological laws" which impel us to "classify, group, and connect phenomena, but which do not give us facts."[4] That is why the social myth emerges from the recesses of our deepest psychology and why Sorel concedes the *mythical* utility of the concept of totality. To the orthodox Marxist, presentation of the concept of totality in such a pessimistic way represents the ultimate debunking of the Marxist framework. Sorel's work retains an ambiguous position in the world of Marxology because it treats the concept of totality as myth, a treatment that is ultimately alien to the Marxian outlook.

Seen in this light, the sensitivity of Marxists is not difficult to fathom. In recent years, the methods of analysis of leading Marxist theoreticians have, in diverse ways, come increasingly to rely on the concept of concrete totality in order to preserve Marxism from irrelevance.[5] Especially in the postwar years, most Western Marxists have paid comparatively little attention to the idea of raw exploitation and the inevitable catastrophic revolution that is deemed so important by dialectical materialism, focusing instead on Marxism as an ethical rebellion, as a humanist critique of the prevailing system of domination.[6] Modern Marxists' view of socialism as an ethical phenomenon is a little closer to Sorel than was the mechanistic thinking of the turn-of-the-century Marxists.

It is one of the peculiar ironies in the fate of Sorel's writings that his political theory has survived in part because his notion of ethics played an important role in the theories of Georg Lukács. Lukács' early writings were greatly influential in the development of Marxist humanism as well as of the so-called Frankurt School of Critical Theory, yet Sorel did not accept the possibility of a transcended alienation as a realistic socialist goal. The concept of transcended alienation (as we saw in Chapter 3) relies implicitly on the Hegelian idea of totality, which Sorel's pragmatism went so far to condemn. For Lukács, the ethical reform of socialism is only "the subjective side of the missing category of totality which alone can provide an overall view."[7] Lukács attributes the non-totalistic reformulation of socialism, as Labriola did before him, to a Kantian dualism between "objective economic laws" and the ethics of the subject. In Lukács' view, the unfortunate result of this dualism is the acceptance of fatalistic economic laws, on the one hand, and an attempt, on the other, to change the world at its only remaining free point, namely, man himself. Such an ethic remains abstract, in Lukács' view, because "it fails to be truly active in its creation of objects. It is only prescriptive and imperative in character."[8] The separation of subject and object, theory and practice, noumena and phenomena, can only be transcended by focusing the known totality upon the reality of the historical process and by confining it to this. For Lukács and for his humanistic successors, this boils down to a criticism advanced from the standpoint of the universally exploited class.[9]

To Lukács and his humanist successors, Sorel's solution to this subject-object problem is a pseudo-solution—a mythical one, if you will. Indeed, as we have said above, since there is no transcended alienation *in toto* for Sorel, we are left with recurrent attempts to bridge the gap between subject and object which arises not out of the capitalist system, but out of the nature of things, that is, out of a dualism which results from the struggle between artificial and natural nature. All we can hope for, in Sorel's view, is a series of pragmatic hypotheses or "rules of prudence," which make no attempt to be comprehensive, on how work ought to be conducted. Any attempt at total transformation based on total understanding is utopian. Unity of thought and action is limited to this junction of practical thought with everyday work and experimentation, and to poetic images linked with revolutionary activity. The complete unification of philosophical theory and practice is impossible for Sorel; on this ground alone he tends to be unsatisfactory to most Marxists. Richard Vernon has described this bifurcation as based on a retrospective vision and a prospective vision; it is the division between history as an accomplished fact and the future as poetry, which Sorel established in his insistence (in his work on Renan) upon the radical separation of theological and historical investigations.[10] This ultimate dividing line between past and future, the interdiction of projections of the past into the future which constitutes the stumbling block of both progressive and utopian thought, makes Sorel far too pessimistic for Marxists.

Yet, as we have pointed out, Sorel vaguely anticipated the humanist defense of Marxism. He was aware that Marx looked forward to the day when, as Sorel expressed it, "work will be the primary need of life. . . . When we have learned to resort to tasks which are at once useful and aesthetic in order to overcome suffering instead of demanding a fleeting escape in distractions." Present civilization, in Marx's view, would "give way to an idealized Greece. . . . The newspapers of social democracy would give the proletarians an education capable of assuming the triumph of rationalism in a hyper-Hellenic world."[11] In his later writings, Sorel came to criticize Marx for a virtually Platonic idealism in which the proletariat in large industry are seen as equivalent to the warriors of the *Republic*.[12] This accusation seems less far-fetched when we note that some Marxist critics have recently undertaken to criticize Lukács's idea of alienation (or "reification," in Lukács's term)[13] as demanding a totality that is utterly Hegelian, if not Platonic, in its idealism. Theodor Adorno expresses one such view: "The thinker may easily comfort himself by imagining that in the dissolution of reification, of the merchandise character of things, he possesses the philosopher's stone. But reification itself is the reflexive form of false objectivity; centering theory around reification, a form of consciousness, makes the critical theory idealistically acceptable to the reigning consciousness. This is what raised Marx's early writings—in contradistinction to *Das Kapital*—to their present popularity, notably with theologians."[14]

Gareth Steadman Jones goes further in his attack on Lukács. The theory of totality cancels out any distinction whatever between objectification and alienation. There remains here a sort of ascribed universal consciousness, wherein class consciousness is sufficient to alter class situation, and power ultimately becomes ideological.[15] As Sorel expressed it earlier in regard to Marx, "The idea which carries man toward reason, according to Hegel, will, according to Marx, achieve its beneficent work in imposing the unity required by rationalism where only plurality, the detestable fruit of chance, reigned before. Marx understood that this passage from heterogeneity to homogeneity . . . will result henceforth from ideological causes."[16]

But most Marxists are unhappy with such a view of totality. Rather than be satisfied with Sorel's mythic diremptive view, they attempt to rescue the concept of the whole determining the parts.

Sorel thus makes a distinction between this idealism and a fragmented totality which, in Karel Kosik's terms, "hypostasizes the whole before the parts and makes the whole into a myth."[17] Kosik attempts to turn this problem around by defending the idea of totality as the context or milieu in which social phenomena occur, phenomena which influence each other reciprocally. Without this common-sense view of totality, the whole is certainly likely to be rendered into the myth that "neo-romantic thought" makes of it. "Totality does not mean all the facts but reality as a structured dialectical whole in which or from which any fact can be rationally understood." Such a view, Kosik argues, "has nothing in common with the holistic, organicist" viewpoint.[18]

As we have tried to show, theoretical understanding may be achieved, according to Sorel, only if we dirempt or abstract a phenomenon from its totality. The totality itself is of dubious theoretical value, and what we have termed Sorel's uncertainty principle makes it difficult or impossible to define. As he showed in the *Illusions of Progress*, totality as an oceanic historicism leads to grave sophisms; in his revolutionary writings, Sorel demonstrated that it was impossible to view the future in the same way as the past and, consequently, that separate methods for studies of the past and of the future are necessary. Finally, as Sorel's own understanding of social science makes clear, once our understanding is based on symbolic diremption, it is not really feasible to reconstruct the broken unity of a phenomenon, for the interior and exterior of a phenomenon cannot be grasped simultaneously without distortion.

The idea of plurality has undergone a revival in Marxist literature thanks to the writings of Louis Althusser, who has attempted to adapt Lévi-Strauss's idea of structuralism to Marxism. Althusser is noteworthy because in his critique of totality, he also attacks the humanist Marxism preeminent in Western Marxist circles. Althusser maintains that there is an "epistemological break" between the early "humanist" Marx and the later "scientific" Marx, which in turn distinguishes the "ideological" from the "scientific" components of Marxism.[19] Althusser argues that ideologies are part of a totality that is "decentered," i.e., beyond the intelligibility of the subject, while true knowledge or science requires an intending subject.[20] This led one writer to assert that Althusser changes Marx's view of ideology: "Marx did not criticize theories because they fostered certain human interests, but because they solidified class society. To Marx, the theory of the proletariat de-legitimizes existing class rule and was hence different from ideology." This de-legitimization was not enough to establish Marxism as a science, the argument continues.

It has simply answered certain subjective necessities of the mobilization of the masses. What makes Marxism a science for Althusser is not that it led to revolution but that it does not conceptualize society from the situated presence of any of its members. The theoretical advance of Marx came from the purely theoretical production of concepts that revealed the hidden structure of capitalism.[21] This knowledge can only be gained from science, whose goal it is to probe systematically the hidden structure. For Althusser, the separation of subject and object means that no true (i.e., total) knowledge can be gained from alienated labor. On the other hand, Althusser may not really have strayed very far from Marx, for in the 1844 Manuscripts Marx maintained that in the early stages of socialist society members of the oppressed class could realize themselves only as members of a certain class, not as fully developed and wholly conscious individuals. There is in Marxism an extremely cloudy understanding of just when ideology as the self-interest of the proletariat gives way to a science of the totality; that is, when crude communism as universal jealousy gives way to true communism.[22] Only in the communistic stages of society is such a total understanding possible, and without such a total understanding, that is, with science still linked to partial interests, science retains ideological blinders.

In adopting this stance, Althusser inclined toward Sorel's uncertainty principle. For Althusser, total knowledge can only be gained from science, whose goal it is to probe "the hidden structure" of reality, i.e., of the reality of commodities. It is this "structure in dominance" that is the object of study; one cannot single out any single element of it for examination. Moreover, substructure and superstructure are highly interrelated and reciprocally interdependent, with the substructure dominant only in "the last instance." For Althusser, contradictions exist on many levels, not just on the economic base. Dialectic is transformed into "structure," which becomes totally objective—that is, without human intentionality. History now becomes the transformation of one structure into another, and one cannot single out one element of the totality, for the structure itself is supreme.[23]

Michel Charzat maintains that Althusser's substitution of a pluralist for a monist conception of history approximates Sorel's. In both, the Hegelian dialectic is replaced by a "combinatory" of diverse possibilities taking root in the organic co-penetration of legal and economic factors:

> Indeed, for Sorel, social reality advances in the framework of a "milieu" or "bloc," that is, a field of solidified forces which unites inseparably in civil society the infrastructure and the

> superstructure. This "milieu," which realizes the permanent symbiosis between the economic "base" of society and its politico-legal "summit," limits or paralyzes the social movement independently of the individual consciousness of men. The Sorelian rejection of all determinism in nature and society leads, paradoxically, to the absolute conditioning of the individual by the historical bloc. A position which, *mutatis mutandis*, anticipates the analysis of the French structuro-Marxist school.[24]

For Sorel and for Althusser, in Charzat's view, relations (the field of forces) are not directly observable realities; they are levels of reality which exist separately from the visible relations which men establish among themselves.[25]

Sorel urged Marxists to investigate this field of forces, but he did not infuse his ideas with a new concept of totality, as Althusser does. Althusser, in trying to understand the total structure, calls for a new science of totality. For Sorel, totality can only be understood and acted upon mythically; it is useless from a scientific point of view, for it is as scientifically unfathomable as the myth itself and demands diremption. For Althusser, "specific structures of historicity . . . since they are merely the existence of determinate social formations (arising from specific modes of production) articulated as social wholes, have no meaning except as a function of the essence of those totalities, i.e., of the essence of their particular complexity."[26] For Sorel, as we have seen, to deduce a knowledge of specifics from the so-called knowledge of the whole is to fall into the ultimate rationalist fallacy. Furthermore, Sorel draws no sharp line between ideology and science. As Sorel's depiction of scientific authority reveals, science is always mixed with concrete interests, often of the most vulgar kind. In linking competing methodologies with scientific schools, Sorel separates myth and science less thoroughly than Althusser does. Ironically, in fragmenting totality more thoroughly than Althusser does, Sorel fragments thought and practice less. The myth is not relegated to a decentered totality; it is the main focus of the unity of revolutionary practice and thought in a society with highly individualistic wish-images. Sorel knew that diremptions often could provide only a symbolic knowledge of what history creates. With this knowledge, "reason should clarify practice so as to help guide us as wisely as possible in our day-to-day difficulties."[27] On the other hand, science, like art and philosophy, flourishes only when infused with overwhelming vitality. If it is not to become static, science should be filled with confidence in its invincibility. In this respect, as we have noted, science itself resembles Sorel's social poetry more than a little.

II

Not only does Sorel raise methodological criticisms to the idea of totality, but by his emphasis on concrete institutions he stresses the importance of mediating forces in social development more than Marx did. Hegel's emphasis on the state was criticized by Marx as ideology. Unfortunately, Marx never replaced Hegel's state—which had the incomparable advantage of being an accomplished fact—with anything more concrete than the working class and the political party as agencies of the revolution. Even in the immediate revolutionary situation, criticisms abound that too much stress was placed both by Marx and by his humanist followers on the proletariat *en bloc*, that is, on a still-to-become universal class and on a political party whose historical significance was only *posited*.[28] We are left, in this case, with mediating forces that are still abstractions, or at best still in the process of a development about whose future we can only guess.

Sorel is aware of the ambiguities of Marx, whose monist prejudices were balanced by such "pluralistic writings" as the *Eighteenth Brumaire*. But in Sorel's eyes such pluralities were self-negating in the Marxian framework; Marx saw history primarily as the conflict of classes rather than of other groupings, and anticipated that these class antagonisms would someday be transcended. At that time, according to Sorel, social groups serving as a framework for social analysis would be abolished and nothing would replace them. Marx became "intoxicated with the hope that a day would come when diremption would be without an object."[29]

After the war, Sartre criticized Marxists for their unitary view of the proletariat and their failure to view history through concrete mediating institutions. In his view, the concept of totality was exploited by capitalism and bureaucracy as a device for conformity and domination.[30] Sartre was aware that Marxists had failed adequately to appreciate the historical forcefulness of nationalism. It was, after all, nationalism and diverse local sympathies that had divided the proletariat in the first place, and the failure to develop a universal class was closely related to the fact that the sympathies of the proletariat often lay outside the "class-in-itself."

For this reason, several generations of Marxists simply could not come to grips with nationalism and patriotism or see them as anything but a vulgar false consciousness. Thus they could not adequately explain the rise of fascism. Indeed, much of the criticism against Sorel's "fascism" is that he, more than any other theorist, attached socialism to religious, national, or local institutions—the real mediating forces of social life.[31] The question in regard to such an identification is whether or not it really views these institutions as properly "mediating" in the Hegel-Marx sense at all. Certainly no attempt is made by Sorel to construct a universal class out of diverse national classes—any more than he would reconstruct the broken unity of diremption. In all instances he despaired of the possibility of gaining "perceptions of future totalities." In Sorel's writings the mediating force has replaced the totality and become the end in itself.

This view is suggested by Theodor Adorno, who in attempting to rescue the idea of totality ends by transforming the idea into a concrete institution, a mediating totality. Totality as a "mediation of all social facts is not infinite. By virtue of its very systematic character, it is closed and finite. In the democratically governed countries of industrial societies, totality is a category of mediation, not one of domination and subjection." For Adorno, this means that other kinds of societies, "non-capitalist enclaves," can exist in capitalist societies.[32]

Such mediating totalities, it could be argued, are not really totalities in any meaningful sense: they are partial institutions which in Adorno's view connect to the larger society by performing a system-maintenance role. Non-capitalist enclaves are functional prerequisites for the maintenance of the capitalist system.

Do such mediating forces play any role in Sorel's own system? Sorel was never so brash as to deny the existence of totality. His own writings are replete with such terms as "civilization," "decadence," "bourgeois society." He did, however, consistently deny both the possibility of understanding that totality in anything but the most general outline and the possibility of deducing from the whole an understanding of particulars. Conversely, the essence of diremption is to start with a particular segment of society, a segment that is incapable of informing us of the whole from which it is derived.

Mediating institutions do appear to Sorel to constitute a functional prerequisite to the transformation of the larger society, rather than its system-maintenance. Syndicalism plays a role which extends beyond the reform of syndicates, that is, as an aristocratic agent of civilizational restoration. The "violence" of the syndicates sometimes approximates Lewis Coser's later formulation: "Conflict with another group leads to the mobilization of the energies of group members, and hence to increased cohesion of the group."[33] Not only could Sorel proclaim that the promotion of social peace was disastrous for the middle classes, but he argued that proletarian violence tends to restore to the bourgeoisie the warlike qualities it formerly possessed. Conflict benefits both the oppressed and the oppressor.

"If a united and revolutionary proletariat confronts a rich middle class, eager for conquest, capitalist society will have reached its historical perfection."[34]

To speak of capitalist society, even in Sorel's terminology, is to speak of a larger social whole; here Sorel is going against his own grain by predicting the moral outcome of a battle not yet waged, an almost inevitable consequence of attempting to depict an historical genealogy of morals. Looked at another way, however, Sorel is content with a moral improvement of the microcosm into institutions themselves dirempted from the totality, or of mediating institutions that are ends in themselves. As I have elsewhere suggested, the nature of Sorel's departure from Marx makes him particularly useful as a critic of those forces in society that Marxists would dismiss as irrelevant and meaningless.[35] This dismissal stems partly from the exclusionary quality that these institutions impose upon themselves—in a manner not unlike the "corporate exclusiveness resembling the local or racial spirit" which Sorel attributes to the syndicalists.

Sorel's theory is particularly applicable to the Black Muslims in America. This curious sect possesses a forcefulness whose power lies in its severance from the larger social totality. Here too one finds an apocalyptic myth harnessed to the application of practical tasks and an ethic of labor. Here too one finds a form of "violence" that invites charges of fascism. The fate of the Black Muslims presents an excellent pragmatic test of whether one can meaningfully dirempt a movement from the larger totality.

The Black Muslims have made an attempt to separate themselves as an autonomous socio-moral authority—to the point of demanding a land of their own. They wish to separate themselves from white society, rather than to integrate with it as the "main line" black pressure groups desire to do. They argue that "the international conception of honor, pride and dignity is not concerned with individuals within a country but is rather concerned with your work and value as part of an established nation."[36] The idea of separation is bolstered by a vision of conflict with the white world. Underscoring the vision is the idea that the white world, much like Sorel's bourgeois world, is in a state of decay, and that to attach oneself to it is to board a sinking ship. Its rule will last no longer than a period necessary "for the chosen of Allah to be resurrected from the *mental* death imposed upon them by the white man." Blacks must be freed from the white ideology, the Christian religion, which has poisoned them, taught them self-hatred, and legitimized their subordinate position by teaching forgiveness to the oppressor.[37] For this reason the Muslims are at least ambivalent toward black intellectuals who, they argue, have been brainwashed by the white man, and have, furthermore, given their education back to their white teachers instead of teaching in black schools and colleges, where they are most sorely needed. Muslims have established their own parochial schools, including in the curriculum their own cultural subjects.

The reaction among most whites (as well as many blacks) toward the separation of Muslims from the white world has often been couched in terms of democracy. C. Eric Lincoln quotes a black insurance executive as saying that the Muslims have done a "definite disservice to the effort being made in the realm of human relations to make democracy in its fullest sense a reality."[38] Muslim hostility to such views, as well as the strident tone of the Black Muslim press, has produced a counter-hostility in the white community. Despite some bloodletting between Muslims and whites (mostly police), however, Lincoln argues that "few open battles have been joined so far. The Black Muslims do not pretend to love the white man but they avoid outright antagonism. They shun the white community entirely, regarding it as irredeemable and unreformable,"[39] just as Sorelian syndicalists shunned the bourgeois state. Yet this prudence is matched by a highly volatile secessionist myth of a black state, a vaguely held vision of a black exodus only specific enough to suggest that several American states might be transferred to black control (and even this specific program has been fudged in recent years). Such doctrines are, according to Lincoln, "myths . . . outside the realm of the true or untrue. They are subject neither to the rules of logic nor to the techniques of scientific investigation."[40]

Accompanying this apocalyptic vision, the Muslims promote the idea of trade and buying among themselves. In addition to numerous small shops, they operate department stores, bakeries, restaurants, and several large farms; they are planning a low-rent housing project and hospital in Chicago.[41] As with Sorel's Yankee Protestants and English sectarians, the Muslims combine a sort of millenarianism with what is popularly called "the Protestant ethic." Since American blacks find it relatively difficult to create and sustain their own businesses, the Muslim doctrine that "Heaven demands hard work," that "we must get away from the idea of depending on others," that "fear, cowardice and laziness are our greatest enemies," are very practical.[42] In the words of one commentator, the target of Black Islam's most bitter denunciations is not the white man, but the "slave mentality of the lower-class so-called Negro."[43] The result is a morality that condemns conspicuous consumption and identifies and glorifies the productive virtues and the working class.

An ascetic life-style is bolstered by a doctrine which asserts: "Each working day is to be considered a learning experience against the time when the Black Nation will operate its own factories, farms and other enterprises."[44]

In the Black Muslim credo, the productive virtues are linked to strong family values. Sexual morality is defined in puritanical terms, and philanderers are answerable to the quasi-judicial militia, the Fruit of Islam.[45] No Muslim woman may be alone in a room with any man not her husband; provocative dress and most cosmetics are forbidden. The role of each sex is designated, the man being assigned traditional masculine tasks—not the least of which is the role of warrior.

The Fruit of Islam is a military organization, a sort of reserve fighting corps, "a phalanx of black men ready to wage open war against the entire white community in case of white provocation."[46] Lincoln refers to the "pent-up militancy of the true believer" as forming the basis of the military sentiment of members of the FOI, and the words "pent-up" are appropriate.[47] While the threat of violence is constant, the Muslims are extremely hesitant to precipitate violence (in the common meaning of the term); they discourage spontaneous brutality, and often disavow earlier Muslim street conflicts.[48] On the contrary, again in Lincoln's words, violence "belongs to the future, in which the present believers are not likely to participate. Unanticipated violence on the other hand may occur at any moment. The Muslims display a kind of contained aggressiveness, which may occasionally provoke violence without actually initiating it."[49]

Thus what is manifestly a battle plan is in fact violence sublimated toward labor, practical activity, and ego reinforcement. "The black man is thereby rescued from the condition of suffering from a missing heritage and lost identity. In thus being infused with a zeal, a confidence and a sense of means and goals, the Muslims fabricate the wherewithal to overcome racial defeat, despair and self-destroying self-hate."[50] If we are to believe Malcolm X, the moral results of this sustained critical tension are impressive: when a man becomes a Muslim, "no matter how bad his morals or habits were before, he immediately takes upon himself a profound change which everyone admits."[51] Malcolm X rid himself of his drug addiction, and Muslim success among alcoholics and former habitual criminals is greater than that resulting from the activities of civilian social and police agencies.

The similarities between Muslim and Sorelian themes extend to the criticisms made against both: it is said that the Muslims constitute a sort of Black Fascism, or at least reveal totalitarian tendencies. Lincoln speculates that the Fruit of Islam approaches totalitarianism more closely as it diverts more and more attention to internal policing of morals rather than to resisting threats from outside. Furthermore, Eric Hoffer emphasizes the importance of hatred and "devils" for the true believer.[52] Both Arendt and Hoffer discuss the heavy criminal element in totalitarian movements. Finally, the power structure of the Fruit of Islam suggests that onion-like arrangement together with a fluid concept of general authority which is characteristic of mass movements.[53]

Two things must be emphasized here. First, the role and elite nature of the FOI (as opposed to its military ethos) find no corresponding element in Sorel; any totalitarianism in Black Islam may turn out to be the greatest point of separation between the Muslims and Sorelismo. Second, Black Islam has had to resort to internal policing methods precisely because the cleavage between it and the white world has markedly softened; that is, it has recently seen its role as a social authority weakened and must replace this authority with internal coercion. The Muslims' problem is that, as with Sorel's syndicates, the critical tension necessary for sustaining the movement is in a state of highly delicate balance. If upset one way, the movement risks being absorbed into the larger totality by being killed with kindness. To verge too far in the other direction, to resort to brutality, risks degeneration into the "politico-criminal association" Sorel warned against. Both the Muslims, in their way, and Sorel, in his, wish to avoid these temptations. The Muslims, as well as French syndicalism, have been accused of inclining in both directions at various times.

In regard to the first danger, that of being brought into the present system, Michael Parenti has argued that, like most chiliastic forces, the Muslims will become detached from the notions that prompted them, and that "despite their loftiest visions, prophets become bishops, reformers become bureaucrats, and conspirators become commissars."[54] In short, in reaching for some kind of respectability, the sect has, in Troeltsch's terms, become a church in which exclusiveness has been replaced by catholic inclusiveness.[55] But if it is tempted by the outside world, the movement must either bolster internal discipline or risk degeneration. As social authority is threatened, internal policing is stepped up or threats from outside reintroduced or concocted. Lewis Coser notes that "despotism is related to lack of cohesion; it is required for carrying out hostilities when there is insufficient group solidarity to mobilize energies of group members."[56] He notes that violence becomes more intense as proximity between antagonists increases.[57] It would seem as a corollary that violence would decrease in proportion as groups succeed in establishing autonomy for themselves vis-à-vis the greater society. Thus Coser posits that "loosely structured groups, and open societies, by allowing conflicts, institute safeguards against the type of conflict which would endanger basic concerns and . . . core values."[58] But it is these "values" which Muslims and syndicalists have wished to transvalue. This notion of conflict goes to the heart of the paradox of both syndicalists and Muslims. By separating themselves from society through the rhetoric of violence, these groups avoided the brutality and conflict of armed revolutionaries and/or politico-criminal associations. The separation may at the same time preserve the autonomous values of the insurgent group but also risk that autonomy by removing external threats. Precisely the correct distance from external threat is necessary. In other words, the autonomous group is seriously threatened with degeneration if its autonomy is too complete. Coser's answer to this problem is similar to Sorel's: the ideology preaching separation lessens conflict, but an ideology "in which participants feel that they are merely representatives of a group fighting not for themselves but for ideals . . . [is] likely to become more radical and merciless."[59] Hence the more autonomous the group, the less threat; the less threat, the more important becomes the social myth in order to dispel a relaxation or a breaking down of internal authority.

The movement must sustain a certain limited contact with the greater society but only on one level, that of lending veracity to the myth itself. Although it is apparent that the larger society has little or no functional need for the Black Muslims, it is less apparent that the Muslims do not rely on the larger totality to sustain their own inner cohesion. Despite the fact that Sorel's theory of the myth is presented as virtually autonomous, it relies on the daily experiences of the proletariat in their places of work. This allows a recognition of antagonists where none existed before. In Coser's terms, conflict establishes relations.[60] In doing so it establishes both an equilibrium and a test for power. Consequently, on a psychological level, another of Coser's propositions seems realized: "Struggle may be an important way to avoid conditions of disequilibrium by modifying the basis of power relations."[61]

It could be argued that Sorel's syndicates and the Black Muslims reject both the group basis of liberal politics and fascist street-fighting in favor of a social "cold war." Sorel posits a sort of moral continuity between the extremes of participation and brutality. By enticing the autonomous group into the greater society, brutality increases within the group to uphold its stance vis-à-vis the outside world. As Sorel expressed it:

> All the efforts of the "worthy progressives" only brought about results in flat contradiction to their aims; it is enough to make one despair of sociology! If they had any common sense, and if they really desired to protect society against an increase in brutality, they would not drive the Socialists into the necessity of adopting the tactics which are forced on them today; they would remain quiet instead of devoting themselves to "social duty"; they would bless the propagandists of the general strike, who as a matter of fact endeavor to *render the maintenance of socialism compatible with the minimum of brutality*. But these "well-intentioned" people are not blessed with common sense; and they have yet to suffer many blows . . . before they decide to allow socialism to follow its own course.[62]

The same words could be used to apply to a social policy with regard to the Black Muslims. The continuity between brutality and accommodation (echoed in the Coserian principle that certain types of conflict cement the prevailing order) is visible in the fate of the Black Panther party. The Panthers, in contrast to the Muslims, engaged in *open* violence while simultaneously engaging in *political* action. To Lincoln their fate suggests the continuity between open violence and the prevailing order: "For the Panthers and other radical groups, the source of corruption which breeds the confrontation is 'the system' or 'the establishment.' Hence, the problem is a political one which can be resolved by displacing the existing system with a more perfect one. For the Muslims, the root problem is theological rather than political. The imperfections of the white man's system are but the imperfections of the individual, the race, the religion—writ large on the pages of human intercourse."[63] Lincoln suggests that, whatever their shortcomings, the Muslims have survived the now moribund Panthers because they were not seeking favors from the system, in the form of demands and demonstrations of force, as the Panthers were. There is an implied distinction here between a Muslim-style defense force and the urban guerrillas whom the Panthers emulated.[64]

Sorel himself suggests that the seductive lure of political respectability is often all-powerful. He was to be disappointed in the performance of the syndicates after 1909; today, Parenti suggests that the Black Muslims too will perhaps fall victim to a desire for respectability.[65] But whatever the ease with which the autonomous social authority is corrupted, the Sorelian ethic still represents a stage of development of certain groups. Indeed, it should perhaps be said that, despite his own pessimism, Sorel's failure was to underestimate the transitory nature of these moral agencies in modern life: his idea of social entropy has been proved all too clearly. Sorel's creative tension may require such a delicate balance that attainment, even for the briefest time, is nearly impossible. But this is true of most political principles: liberty, autonomy, self-government, as well as Sorel's favorite whipping-posts, democracy and progress. All of these require a delicate balance, and all of them can claim a history of abuses, bloodletting, and carnage that makes Sorelismo seem pacific by comparison. There remains a distinct possibility that balance is an important but necessary stage in the moral and political development of a people. Is Sorel correct in saying that the apocalyptic qualities of a movement can coexist with its organizational stability, of is Parenti right in suggesting with Max Weber that "stability and longevity . . . can only be secured at the expense of the impulsive and charismatic"; that is, when the apocalyptic movement is "too weak to achieve its dream yet too functional to disappear" does it go the way of the early Church of the Bolshevik party?[66]

III

Now the question remains as to whether Sorel's focus on specific mediating forces in place of the abstractions of socialism or our Sorelian focus on the concrete institutions of the Black Muslims, in place of the relatively abstract democratic principles of "integration," "equality," and the like, obscures rather than illuminates our understanding of the larger society. The problems with Sorel's procedure are seen once the totality of bourgeois society, for instance, is "dirempted" into discrete moments of capitalist development in Marx's account of modern European capitalism: usury, exchange, and manufacture. Sorel's analyses of and condemnation of capitalist society as an economic process focus on usury and exchange capital as if the development of capitalism had stopped at those instances. One wonders here whether the basis of Sorel's understanding was obscured by the very fact that he was caught up in one or another of the "theoretical axes" that had eliminated everything outside their own purview; that is, his failure to reintegrate the diremption into the concrete totality had created as many illusions as it eliminated.

If Sorel believed in the necessity of mediating institutions in socialism to a far greater extent than was true of orthodox socialists, he also underscored the importance of the totality in its mythical form, of the will toward totality. Ultimately these two tendencies would clash. On the one hand, the Bolshevik revolution, whose mythic power Sorel not only analyzed but to which he succumbed, attained an historical power that, at one level of analysis, annihilated the mediating institutions that Sorel had spent a lifetime in defending. Lenin's success in galvanizing the vanguard of western Marxism through anticipation of a future totality had beaten Sorel at his own game. On the other hand, this Leninistic transformation from sect to church was self-negating, for it substituted for the myth the worst kinds of pseudo-science. Once international socialism became identified with the new Rome of the Soviet Union, that is, with a concrete mediating institution, the man whom Lenin had condemned as a "notorious muddlehead" was partially vindicated. Once the Bolshevik revolution, unbeknownst to Sorel, was shown to have relied all too heavily on both the ideology and the updated institutions of Jacobinism—on progress, on the state, and on terror—the ghastly consequences of the annihilation of the soviets were readily revealed. For what was the Bolshevik state but an attempt to replace the soviets with a "concrete totality"?

Many of the questions originally raised by the Bolsheviks have recurred in regard to the revolutions of the Third World. Yet in the underdeveloped countries, emancipation from the colonial experience has inevitably lent a more concrete tone to the expressions of socialism; they are tied to nation, to religion, and even to ethnicity. How these new, mediating institutions moderate or affect the concept of totality as reflected in the theoreticians of these revolutions is an interesting question.

One facet of this relationship is the notion of purification. The literature of revolution in emerging countries is replete with the awareness that it is not merely justice, socialism, or independence that is being sought, but emancipation from the moral corruption and decadence that are the legacy of the past. This moral stance, however, does not necessarily immunize the subject from taking on a totalistic or even totalitarian character. To give one noteworthy example: the great cultural revolution engineered by Mao Tse-tung was inspired in part by the belief held by "the great helmsman" that a period of moral decline had set in, resulting from the bureaucratic mentality of the communist cadres. One purpose of the revolution was to upset these cadres and to infuse them with a new sense of moral purpose. The totalitarian methods employed, as well as the disruption of production that ensued, made this revolution far from purely Sorelian, but it does raise further questions about the compatibility of the idea of moral regeneration and a revolution relatively free of brutality.

Perhaps no writer in the third world, or, for that matter, anywhere in our time, has been portrayed as being inspired by Sorelian ideas so much as Frantz Fanon. Yet some commentators find little evidence that Fanon was influenced by Sorel in the way Camus had been. (Indeed, nowhere does this African theorist of violence explicitly hark back to Sorel. Rather, he acknowledges being inspired by Hegel's master-slave relationship and by Sartre.) Yet if Fanon was not inspired by Sorel, he was spurred on by the revolutionary myth of Negritude—the complex of values of black peoples worked out by Leopold Sedar Senghor. "These values," Senghor says, "are essentially informed by intuitive reason, because this sentient reason, the reason which comes to grips with things, expresses itself emotionally, through that self-surrender, that coalescence of subject and object; through myths, by which I mean the archetypal images of the collective soul." All men live by these archetypal images. "Negritude itself is a myth (I am not using the world in any pejorative sense), but a living dynamic one."[67]

To this myth, too, Fanon adds respect for the local authorities of the revolution—authorities inextricably linked to the laboring process and disdainful of Europeanized party intellectuals who claim to know better than the true natives. "The traditional chiefs are ignored, sometimes even persecuted. . . . The old men, surrounded by respect in all traditional societies and usually invested with unquestioned moral authority, are publicly held to ridicule." Fanon asserts that these chiefs ought to make of village history a harmonious whole, "at one with the decisive action to which they call on the people to contribute."[68] The social authorities and the peasantry are "a coherent people who go on living as it were statically, but who keep their moral values and their devotion to the nation intact."[69] If the men coming from the cities do not "learn their lessons in the hard school of the people," if "the men at the head of things distrust the people of the countryside," they are destined to relate only to the colonizers and are likely to become political heirs of the imperial power.[70] The result is a species of revolutionary continuity in which the political parties "share the optimism of the settlers," and whose new order consists in a mere transfer of power from a white oligarchy to a black one.

Fanon's "revolutionary conservatism" is demonstrated again in his explanation of the function of the veil in North African culture. The progressive colonial forces who mingle socially with Westernized native couples (the woman no longer veiled) in Fanon's view perform a cultural rape which should be defended against, at least in the early stages of revolt, by reasserting traditional values.[71] At one level of analysis, this assertion appears to be a restatement of Sorel's "psycho-erotic law," transmogrified into directly Freudian terms. Rather than linking political emancipation to sexual emancipation, Fanon seems to be echoing the classic view that a repressed libido is the price we pay for civilizational integrity.

But this is not to last for Fanon. The women are indeed emancipated through their own revolutionary activity, and that activity means not a continued restraint but a form of catharsis through violence. To be given the revolution is to continue the form of colonial dependency; one must take the revolution through violence—it is only through violence that true emancipation, true self-responsibility is realized. Thus Fanon says:

> At the level of individuals, violence is a cleansing force. It frees the native from his inferiority complex and from his despair and inaction; it makes him fearless and restores his self-respect. *Even if the armed struggle has been symbolic and the nation is demobilized through a rapid movement of decolonization*, the people have the time to see that the liberation has been the business of each and all and that the leader has no special merit. . . . The people . . . show themselves to be jealous of the results of their action and . . . rebel against any pacification. From now on the demagogues, the opportunists and the magicians have a difficult task.[72]

Here appears Fanon's concurrence with Sorel. Not only did both regard the symbolic power of violence as being more important than the real thing, but both look for redemption outside politics rather than mere redistribution of power within it.[73]

Yet some commentators argue that Fanon's resemblance to Sorel is superficial; that his cathartic violence is different from the "mythical" view of Sorel;[74] that Fanon desired a total *release*, a material victory for the oppressed, while Sorel foresaw social movements in which the old society is not *necessarily* overthrown and which in any case anticipate continued tension, a continued form of psychological repression. Finally, the struggle, according to Fanon, would benefit only the oppressed, not the oppressor, as in Sorel's view.[75] These criticisms are correct as far as they go, but they tell us more about their critics than they do about Fanon or Sorel.

Fanon has been somewhat hampered from proclaiming himself indebted to Sorelian influences by his French leftist mentors, who have damned Sorel for his "fascist utterances," to use Sartre's words. This is curiously unfair, given the paucity of evidence for sustaining a case for Sorel's continuing support of Mussolini—especially considering Sartre's own admission that, along with Engels and Fanon, Sorel was responsible for bringing "the process of history into the clear light of day."[76]

David Caute continues this almost fearful view that Sorel "had become a bad name on the left" and implies that Sartre's condemnation "supports the view that Fanon would not have acknowledged any debt to Sorel."[77] Caute fears that to associate Fanon with Sorel would be to make Fanon into a "black neo-Fascist." Caute then muddles the evidence for Sorel's "fascism" by asserting that Sorel in a very few years went "from admiration of Lenin to admiration of Mussolini,"[78] when we know he admired Lenin at the end. After showing some interesting differences between Fanon and Sorel, Caute proudly concludes, "So much for Fanon the black neo-Fascist."[79] It is a highly dubious logic that assumes that dissociation from Sorel is dissociation from fascism per se.

Sorel's "fascism" is also due to his association with the social myth. It is amusing to read Renate Zahar's assertion that "while Fanon, whose stance is determined by humanist considerations and the desire to enlighten, is averse to myth and analyzes conditions scientifically, myth occupies a central position in Sorel's thought."[80] Yet Zahar also says that "the contrast elaborated by Negritude between the technological civilization of the whites organized along lines of rationalism and expediency, and the black soul abandoning itself to feeling and giving rise to true humanity, is reminiscent of the Bergsonian distinction between intelligence and intuition."[81] On these grounds, however, Sorel the technocrat-engineer, the conqueror of natural nature, is closer to both science and rationality than Fanon. Zahar admits that Fanon "passionately postulated authenticity and analyzed the function of Negritude . . . as both an historical and psychological necessity." Yet she attempts to sever him from this "Bergsonian" view by asserting that Fanon had "certain misgivings about its irrational elements." Zahar continues that "according to Fanon the writer's falling back on the past only has a meaning if it is linked in a concrete manner with present-day realities; otherwise culture remains mere folklore."[82] But surely Sorel would have agreed. David Caute's own criticism of Sorel establishes that the social myth is "only a means of acting on the present," while for Fanon "it is also a means of overthrowing the present."[83] Yet Sorel would not have objected to the overthrow of the present order through the proletarian general strike.

The difference between Sorel and Fanon consists in the fact that Fanon appears less concerned with subjective moral regeneration and more concerned with the cathartic effects of genuine brutality than does Sorel. It is this difference which enables the genuine rather than false contrasts between Sorel and Fanon to survive. For example, Fanon looks upon the struggle between colonists and natives as a struggle between absolute good and absolute evil. "The Manicheism of the settler produces a Manicheism of the native. . . . For the native, life can only spring up again out of the rotting corpse of the settler."[84] This "scientific" and "humanitarian" viewpoint (to use Zahar's jargon) is replete with the spirit of hatred and revenge that Sorel wished to purge from revolutionary movements. "Make no mistake about it," says Sartre in his introduction to Fanon, "by this mad fury, by this bitterness and spleen, by their ever-present desire to kill us, by the permanent tensing of powerful muscles which are afraid to relax, they have become men. . . . Hatred, blind hatred which is as yet an abstraction, is their only wealth."[85] Whether it is Sorel or Sartre's Fanon (or is it Fanon's Sartre?) who has more fully embraced the "fascist" spirit, I leave the reader to decide.

Another argument, made by David Caute, is that Fanon wished to resolve the conflict between settler and native while Sorel's creative tension did not necessitate real material overthrow—merely its anticipation.[86] The desire for genuine resolution in the form of violence as a catharsis is Fanon's more than Sorel's. It is closer to Sartre's Jacobin heritage than to Sorel's puritanical syndicalism. Sartre insists that Fanon's violence, like Achilles' lance, heals the wounds it inflicts.[87] As Irene Gendzier points out, revolutions and coups in Africa hardly demonstrate this purification. Few Algerians have justified the Battle of Algiers, she says, on the ground that it would "cleanse" its participants of colonialism. On the contrary, Gendzier maintains that Fanon, a man who wished to bear witness to his rebirth as a free man, projected his own wish-images onto the larger canvas of the Algerian revolution.[88]

The differences between Sorel and Fanon are differences of perspective. Sorel was haunted by the problem of *praxis*; he could not make up his mind whether he wanted to be on the inside looking out or to remain on the outside as a disinterested servant and observer. Fanon wanted passionately to be a participant observer—the kind of professional revolutionary Sorel distrusted; Sorel looks on the general-strike myth from the outside as a "disinterested servant of the proletariat," while Fanon, distrustful of the Jacobinism of the urban nationalist revolutionaries, ends by embracing it. Sorel and Fanon hold mirrors up to each other by their very differences. Fanon represents the moral futility of Jacobinism, while Sorel demonstrates the ease with which his philosophy of violence becomes unbalanced in a Jacobin direction; Fanon did not realize his view was a myth, while Sorel discovered the shortcomings of the social myth in short order.

IV

The bloodthirstiness of Fanon's and especially of Sartre's theories of Third World revolution leads back to the question of the kind of revolution called for by revolutionary theory. What is the relationship between the idea of totality and that of violence? Is a diremption not only a viable means of social analysis but a viable ethical stance as well?

We have stated in Chapter 7 that Sorel's *Reflections on Violence* is less violent that superficial observers would have it; that his thought constitutes (among other things) an ethical evaluation of violence. Perhaps the first writer to recognize this fact clearly was Walter Benjamin who, writing in Sorel's later years, commented on the "highly ingenious arguments" whereby Sorel's "rigorous conception of the general strike as such is capable of diminishing the incidence of actual violence in revolutions."[89] With this consideration in mind, it is instructive to remember that Sorel was concerned about a dilemma that has plagued political theory for the last three millennia: the problem of violent foundation of a new juridical order. This problem was posed by Niccolò Machiavelli, another theorist who has often been compared to Sorel: both were concerned with the restoration of military virtues and both devoted a considerable amount of their writing to the use of "violence" to reform a corrupt society.[90] But there is one area in which Sorel is responding to a problem posed by Machiavelli in a way which invites comparison with Camus's theories. In the *Discoursi*, Machiavelli distinguishes two kinds of political qualities involved in the founding of a republic. The founder-legislator of a republic, he argues, "should concentrate all authority in himself, and a wise mind will never censure anyone for having employed any extraordinary means for the purpose of establishing a kingdom or constituting a republic. It is well that, when the act accuses him, the result should excuse him." But in seeming contradiction to the "Machiavellian" ruthlessness necessary for the founding of a republic, the great Florentine—ever the prudent republican—insists that the lawgiver-founder should not leave this founding authority to heirs or to anyone else. "For mankind being more prone to evil than to good, his successor might employ for evil purposes the power which he had used only for good ends. Besides, it will not endure long if the administration remains on the shoulders of a single individual; it is well, then, to confide this to the charge of the many."[91] Ultimately, Sorel must cope with this moral problem, the dilemma of combining the violence of a founder, who is usually acting in a corrupt situation, with the "good" qualities needed for the continuance of a republican form of government. Romulus, Moses, Lycurgus, Solon—to use Machiavelli's examples—may have possessed these double qualities; few others have.[92]

Rousseau stated the problem in a somewhat different way. For him the problem appeared almost insurmountable: "For a young people to be able to relish sound principles of political theory and to follow the fundamental principles of statecraft, the effect would become the cause; the social spirit which would be created by these institutions would have to preside over their very foundation; and men would have to be, prior to law, what they should become by means of law."[93] Foundation is a circular problem: that which starts in force cannot change to law, and that which is pre-social cannot start with law, which is social. Since law is based on reason, reason cannot be used to found a republic any more than force can. "Therefore the legislator, being unable to appeal to either force or reason, must have recourse to an authority of a different kind, able to restrain without violence and persuade without convincing."[94]

Part of the confusion surrounding the modern understanding of Sorel centers on the function of violence in regard to this problem of foundation. The common understanding of Sorel, such as that held by Fernand Rossignol, is that, like Machiavelli, Sorel wishes to "force history." Rossignol quotes Sorel, who asks "what the great tsars would have done had they been threatened by revolts similar to those which the Republic of *soviets* is obliged to overcome quickly if it does not wish to commit suicide; they certainly would not have recoiled from the most terrifying severities. . . . Lenin is not, after all, a candidate for the prize for virtue awarded by the French academy; he is accountable only to Russian history."[95] Here, by giving this quote out of the context of Sorel's thought, Rossignol makes it appear that Sorel justifies any means to the establishment of a stable and long-lasting regime.

Yet, as we have seen in most of his writings, Sorel is aware of the need to place strictures on this kind of apology for violence if tyranny is not to succeed tyranny. Thus, in the same essay on Lenin, Sorel condemns Lenin's opponents for violating "the true laws of war defined by Proudhon." These laws, as we have seen, are not Machiavellian but are rooted in a kind of sublimation of violent instincts in the form of production. Although Machiavelli, too, was concerned with the problem of deriving virtue from violence, Proudhon's and Sorel's solutions to that problem are closer to those of Camus than of Lenin.

Sorel's response to this challenge, despite his misguided admiration for Lenin, is based on the denial of a total revolution in anything but myth. To make concrete the totality in institutional form is to bring together all the agencies of force which he sought so avidly to distinguish from violence. I have suggested that Sorel's distinction between force and violence is updated in Albert Camus's distinction between rebellion and revolution. Rebellion for Camus commences with a concrete subject which exists in a state of tension with the social milieu. With Sorel, the concrete interests of this rebellion are what keep it from being submerged in the totality and thus preserve an arena of freedom. Camus, too, harks back to the *élan vital* of syndicalism. He asserts that if syndicalism wants a revolution, "it wants it on behalf of life, not in defiance of it. That is why it relies primarily on the most concrete realities—on occupation, on the village where the living heart of things and of men is to be found."[96] The political revolution, on the other hand, "starts from doctrine and forcibly introduces reality into it," while syndicalism "is the negation, to the benefit of reality, of bureaucratic and abstract centralism."[97] The political revolution is both utopian and historicist, which is to say, total. It has an end vision, the pursuit of which justifies any means, and this justification is embodied in a theory of historical progress. Camus states that "Sorel was perfectly correct in saying that the philosophy of progress was exactly the philosophy to suit a society eager to enjoy material prosperity," and adds that the idea can be used to justify conservatism as well as Marx's scientific messianism.[98] The logic of history exemplified by progressive revolutionary theories gradually leads itself "to mutilate man more and more and to transform itself into objective crime."[99]

Camus emphasizes the nihilistic consequences of progress more than Sorel does, but like Sorel he believes that there is a revolutionary continuity between the political revolution and the *ancien régime*. "The contemporary revolution believes that it is inaugurating a new world when it is really only the contradictory climax of the old one. . . . Capitalist society and revolutionary society are really one and the same thing."[100]

As distinct from political revolution, true rebellion denies a future of reconciliation in which all problems are resolved. "Rebellion's demand is unity; historical revolution's demand is totality."[101] True rebellion embodies both freedom and limits by insisting on the primacy of human liberation over justice. The progressive illusion that the end justifies the means because the ends are certified is replaced by a rebellion in which the means become the end. Since rebellion is itself an act of realized freedom, the very act of rebellion must be based on respect for freedom; it therefore limits its excesses by restricting the rebel's freedom in the face of the freedom of others. True rebellion "says yes and no simultaneously."[102] Mere affirmation or mere negation terminates in a continuum of quietism or murder. But when both are combined in rebellion, they moderate each other, as well as rebellion itself. Moderation consists in a continued tension between affirmation and negation; moderation is in fact "nothing but pure tension. . . . But its smile shines brightly at the climax of interminable effort. . . . Moderation born of rebellion can only live by rebellion. It is a perpetual conflict, continually created and mastered by the intelligence. It does not triumph either in the impossible or the abyss."[103] As for Sorel, the rebellious movement is everything, the end is nothing. Revolution must not anticipate realizing itself in some future utopia "but in terms of the obscure existence that is already made manifest in the act of insurrection. This rule is neither formal nor subject to history; it is what can best be described by examining it in its pure state—in artistic creation." Thus Camus says, "I rebel, therefore we exist."[104] Camus's paradoxical view that violence is never justified but is sometimes necessary is resolved by insisting that the rebel himself must be guided by a moral rule to balance the amorality of "history" and that this morality must consist partly in the realization that violence must be viewed as a moral and individual responsibility.

The paradox of the Camus viewpoint—and that of Sorel, from which it is partly derived—is that it represents inversely the paradox of the Marxian theory, that an emphasis on action reestablishes the contemplative stance. If the movement is everything and the end is nothing, the philosophical stance must be outside the movement. That is why Sorel could proclaim himself a "disinterested servant of the proletariat"[105] without inconsistency. This disinterestedness has the paradoxical effect of moving all rational theory away from revolutionary activity. No external guide to revolutionary activity is needed because none is called for. The independent dignity of the revolutionary theorist is reestablished, while at the same time uniting thought and action in the myth.

In the Marxian view, the professed unity of theory and practice ultimately leads to the question of what role the theorist actually does play in revolutionary movements. It was Sorel's contention that such a viewpoint leads Marxists to assume that historical development possesses the qualities ascribed to it by contemplation. While Marxism proclaims the unity of theory and practice, it really starts in theory and by proclaiming certain ends terminates in thought via action. The unity of theory and practice is self-negating.

Indeed, the ultimate defense of Marx raised by his partisans is that Marx rejected the world of contemplation for the political world of *praxis*. As one of these partisans has stated:

> Marxist theory was not produced *outside* the working-class movement. It was produced *inside* the working-class movement. True, it was produced by intellectuals. . . . But . . . they were precisely those who linked their fate with the working class, formed organizations to institutionalize that union, and participated in the class struggle. . . . What they gained from the working class were a number of experiences not readily available to most bourgeois intellectuals and which do not emerge spontaneously from the activity of theoretical work: the experience of exploitation and repression, the experience of the struggle against these realities, the experiences of the successes and failures of that struggle. . . . Marx learned from the initiatives of the communards, of the need for the proletariat to smash the bourgeois state . . . in the failure of 1848 . . . the necessity of permanent revolution.[106]

In increasingly dissociating himself from this viewpoint, Sorel left himself open to the charge of "idealism." Yet it was Marx who is said by Sorel to have been the idealist. How does Marx as an observer of the events of the Commune and of 1848 differ from Sorel as an observer of the Commune, of the Dreyfus Affair, of World War I, from which it may be said that he had "learned something"? Sorel cannot be said to have been an ardent activist because he shared in the agonies of his civilization. Nor is Marx the publicist a practitioner in the Marxist sense. Marx cannot be called a practitioner just because he actively polemicized in the pages of the *Neue Reinische Zeitung*, any more than Sorel can be called an ardent activist by virtue of his editorship of *L'Indépendance*. If the humanist Marx—the Marx of the 1844 Manuscripts—can be said to have been the mature Marx, then the groundwork of Marxian theory was largely produced from a contemplative stance, as a philosophical commitment brought about by conversations with French socialists, whose economic theory was perfected at the desks of the British Museum. In Sorel's view it is absurd romanticism to envision Marx as a practitioner of the barricades and the factory floor, when his primary activity was in the political struggles of workers' parties. In his later writings, Sorel rejects not only philosophy but the view that to be political is to be a practitioner in the Vicoian sense. Politicians *make* nothing, in Sorel's view, and despite differences, they have far more in common with contemplative intellectuals than they do with engineers, inventors, and proletarians; that is why utopias slide easily into practical and corrupt reforms. He who makes nothing cannot possibly unify theory and practice. The dualism of thought and action which Marxists accuse their opponents or heretics of reviving is impossible to escape once any philosophical enterprise is admitted to the movement. In Sorel's view, accusing one's opponents of being Hegelians or nasty neo-Kantians is insufficient to resolve this dilemma. This does not exclude Sorel from that criticism, for he became caught himself in this rhetorical Tar Baby.

The bitterness and sense of betrayal felt by Sorel in the World War I period are characteristic of men who proclaim the glories of engagement but who are detached enough to realize the futility of Marx's unity of philosophy and practice. That is why Sorel oscillates from engagement to disinterest. This double stance results in the irony of a tale told by Lucien Jean, approvingly reviewed by Sorel himself. A voyager, arriving among peasants, preaches the cult of heroism. "Men generally lack happiness and beauty," because they spend their lives in "superfluous efforts without definite end and for derisory causes," the traveler says. To which the peasants respond by going about their business, proclaiming his cult useless because "the exultation which you offer us we find in everything around us," in the life and needs of the working world itself.[107] Sorel lauds the insights of this fable, but it is a critique of all intellectuals—including himself.

In this criticism of intellectuals and the exposure of the moral bankruptcy of the Jacobin tradition lies the true value of the Sorelian analysis. The ambiguity of Sorel's position with regard to the place of the intellectual derives from the necessity of his criticizing the very group of which he was so eminent a representative. To criticize the intellectual caste is to criticize the entire concept of the theory aspect of the union of theory and practice. Sorel's is a criticism which has seen Marxism in many of the most advanced Western countries confined to tiny groups of academic adepts, which has seen planners of various stripes exposed to the scorn of the people whom they have striven to protect. The failure of syndicalism, the potential weakening of would-be Sorelian movements, can only enlarge the wounds that Sorel's own knife has opened.

Notes

1. The cover extols Sorel as the "pioneer of non-dogmatic Marxism, apostle of the direct-action labor movement currently called self-government in industry."
2. *FGS*, pp. 161-62.
3. Ibid., p. 195.

4. Ibid., p. 139.

5. For an exposition of this theme see, for example, Karel Kosik, "The Concrete Totality," *Telos*, no. 4 (Fall 1969): 35.

6. The literature on this subject is vast. See, for example, Bertel Ollman, *Alienation*. Robert Tucker, *Philosophy and Myth in Karl Marx* (Cambridge: Cambridge University Press, 1963), takes a more critical view of this theme, projecting it onto Marx himself. See also Herbert Marcuse, *Reason and Revolution* (Boston: Beacon, 1960), and Adam Schaff, *Marxism and the Human Individual* (New York: McGraw-Hill, 1970).

7. Georg Lukács, *History and Class Consciousness*, trans. by Rodney Livingstone (Cambridge: MIT Press, 1971), p. 38.

8. Ibid.

9. For an exposition of this theme, see Gareth Jones, "The Marxism of the Early Lukács," *Western Marxism: A Critical Reader* (London: Verso Editions, 1978), p. 11, and cf. pp. 17, 41.

10. Richard Vernon, ed., *Commitment and Change*, pp. 7-8.

11. *FGS*, pp. 242-43.

12. Ibid.

13. See Lukács, *History and Class Consciousness*, p. 89: "Fragmentation of the object of production necessarily entails the fragmentation of its subject."

14. Theodor Adorno, *Negative Dialectics* trans. E. B. Ashton (New York: Seabury, 1973), p. 190, cited in Martin Jay, "The Concept of Totality in Lukács and Adorno," in Shlomo Avineri, ed., *Varieties of Marxism* (The Hague: Nijhoff, 1975), p. 163.

15. Jones, "The Early Lukács," p. 17. Jones, like Sorel, is quick to point out the catastrophic consequences of this Hegelianized thinking. "There is no room" in Lukács's model "for conceiving the possibility of a dominated class which is . . . uneven and impure. . . . The proletariat is necessarily always at one or another . . . extreme. . . . Lukács's model itself remains securely trapped within the problematic of the Second International belief in the final cataclysmic economic collapse of capitalism" (ibid., pp. 41-42).

16. *FGS*, p. 241.

17. Kosik, "The Concrete Totality," p. 49.

18. Ibid., pp. 37, 49.

19. See Louis Althusser, *For Marx*, trans. Ben Brewster (New York: Vintage, 1970), esp. pts. 5 and 6.

20. Ibid., p. 102.

21. Mark Poster, *Existential Marxism in Postwar France* (Princeton: Princeton University Press, 1975), pp. 344-45.

22. See Karl Marx, *Early Writings*, p. 153.

23. See Louis Althusser and Etienne Balibar, *Reading Capital*, trans. Ben Brewster (2nd ed., London: New Left Books, 1977): "Just as there is no production in general, there is no history in general, but only specific structures of historicity, based in the last resort on the specific structures of the different modes of production" (p. 108). See also Althusser, *For Marx*, p. 111.

24. Michel Charzat, *Georges Sorel*, pp. 175-76.

25. Ibid., p. 179.

26. Althusser and Balibar, *Reading Capital*, pp. 108-10.

27. *FGS*, p. 228.

28. See Jones, "The Early Lukács," p. 17.

29. *FGS*, p. 241.

30. Poster, *Existential Marxism*, p. 296, citing Sartre, *Critique de la raison dialectique.*

31. Meisel in *The Genesis of Georges Sorel* prudently distances Sorel from fascism (pp. 217-33). However, I think he misjudges Sorel in his claim that Sorel "was too firmly anchored at his internationalist and laborist moorings to ride the tide of the new nationalism" (p. 23). As we have seen, Sorel argued that decentralization and localism were to be the hallmarks of the post-bourgeois era.

32. Adorno, *Negative Dialectics*, p. 107.

33. Lewis Coser, *The Functions of Social Conflict* (New York: Free Press, 1956), p. 95.

34. Sorel, *Reflections*, p. 92.

35. *FGS*, pp. 59-60.

36. Elijah Mohammed, *Message to the Blackman* (Chicago: Muhammad Mosque of Islam No. 2, 1965), p. 223.

37. C. Eric Lincoln, *The Black Muslims in America* (Boston: Beacon, 1973), pp. 79-80. See also the excellent account of black eschatology in E. U. Essien-Udom, *Black Nationalism: A Search for Identity in America* (New York: Dell, 1965), chap. 5.

38. Lincoln, *Black Muslims*, p. 149; cf. Essien-Udom, *Black Nationalism*, pp. 328-32.

39. Lincoln, *Black Muslims*, p. 186.

40. Ibid., p. 70.

41. Ibid., p. 96.

42. Michael Parenti, "The Black Muslims: From Revolution to Institution," *Social Research* 31, no. 2 (Summer 1964): 185.

43. Ibid.

44. Lincoln, *Black Muslims*, p. 95.

45. Ibid., p. 84.

46. Ibid., p. 222.

47. Ibid., p. 225.

48. Ibid., pp. 221-22.

49. Ibid., p. 228. Compare Essien-Udom, *Black Nationalism*: "The possibility of spontaneous eruptions of violence between whites and blacks . . . cannot be denied. It exists in spite of Muhammad's movement. The movement, however, tends to stop the believer's aggression from finding expression in acts of violence against both whites and Negroes" (p. 312).

50. Parenti, "The Black Muslims," p. 192.

51. Quoted by Lincoln, *Black Muslims*, p. 85.

52. Eric Hoffer, *The True Believer* (New York: New American Library, 1951), pp. 85-86.

53. For a description of this authority structure see Hannah Arendt, *The Origins of Totalitarianism*, pp. 364ff.

54. Parenti, "The Black Muslims," p. 194.

55. Ernst Troeltsch, *The Social Teaching of the Christian Churches.* (New York: Harper, 1960).

56. Coser, *The Functions of Social Conflict*, p. 95.

57. Ibid., pp. 71-72.

58. Ibid., p. 80.

59. Ibid., p. 118.

60. Ibid., p. 128.

61. Ibid., p. 137.

62. Sorel, *Reflections*, p. 188 (italics are Sorel's).

63. Lincoln, *Black Muslims*, p. 275.

64. James Petras criticizes Régis Debray for his scorn of the defense tactics of Bolivian miners as "shallow." Debray argues that the miners' defeat "proves" that the self-defense policy was wrong. Debray criticizes movements "having some contact with the masses while holding high . . . abstract Revolutionary Strategy—so high that it is neither related to popular problems nor relevant to the living social forces which create a base of support for evolutionary struggles": "Debray: Revolutionary or Elitist?" in *Régis Debray and the Latin American Revolution*, ed. Leo Huberman and Paul Sweezy (New York: Monthly Review Press, 1968), p. 108.

65. Parenti, "The Black Muslims," p. 194.

66. Ibid., p. 193.

67. Leopold Sedar Senghor, "What Is Negritude?" in James A. Gould and Willis H. Truitt, eds., *Political Ideologies* (New York: Macmillan, 1972), pp. 417-18.

68. Frantz Fanon, *The Wretched of the Earth*, trans. Constance Farrington (New York: Grove, 1966), p. 91.

69. Ibid., p. 101.

70. Ibid., p. 102.

71. Frantz Fanon, *A Dying Colonialism*, trans. Haakon Chevalier (New York: Grove, 1967), p. 62.

72. Fanon, *Wretched of the Earth*, pp. 73-74 (italics added).

73. I. Gendzier, *Frantz Fanon: A Critical Study* (New York: Pantheon, 1973), p. 202.

74. Ibid., p. 204.

75. David Caute, *Frantz Fanon* (London: Fontana, 1970), p. 86.

76. Jean-Paul Sartre, Preface to *The Wretched of the Earth*, pp. 12-13.

77. Caute, *Frantz Fanon*, p. 86.

78. Ibid.

79. Ibid., p. 87.

80. Renate Zahar, *Frantz Fanon: Colonialism and Alienation* (New York: Monthly Review Press, 1974), p. 86.

81. Ibid., p. 62n2.

82. Ibid., pp. 70-71.

83. Caute, *Frantz Fanon*, pp. 86-87.

84. Fanon, *The Wretched of the Earth*, p. 72.

85. Sartre, Preface to Fanon, p. 15.

86. Caute, *Frantz Fanon*, p. 86.

87. Sartre, Preface to Fanon, p. 25.

88. Gendzier, *Frantz Fanon*, pp. 201-2.

89. Walter Benjamin, *Reflections* (New York: Harcourt, Brace, 1978), p. 292.

90. See Neal Wood, "Some Reflections on Sorel and Machiavelli"; James Meisel, *The Genesis of Georges Sorel*, p. 98.

91. Machiavelli, *The Prince* and the *Discourses*, ed. Max Lerner (New York: Modern Library, 1950), I.ix, pp. 138-39.

92. Ibid., p. 140.

93. Rousseau, *The Social Contract* and *The Discourses*, trans. G. D. H. Cole (New York: Dutton, 1950), p. 40.

94. Ibid., p. 40.

95. Fernand Rossignol, *Pour connaître la pensée de G. Sorel*, p. 261, citing Sorel's *Reflections*, p. 284.

96. Albert Camus, *The Rebel*, p. 298.

97. Ibid.

98. Ibid., pp. 193-94.

99. Ibid., p. 246.

100. Ibid., p. 272.

101. Ibid., p. 251.

102. Ibid., p. 250.

103. Ibid., p. 301.

104. Ibid., p. 250.

105. Sorel, *Matériaux*, dedicatory page. See in general Vernon, *Commitment and Change.*

106. Norman Geras, "Althusser's Marxism: An Assessment," *Western Marxism: A Critical Reader*, pp. 268-69.

107. Sorel, *Matériaux*, pp. 301-2.

BIBLIOGRAPHY

PRIMARY SOURCES

This list includes most books and articles written by Sorel that are known to me. When a book includes articles formerly published, the book title has been listed. The place of publication of books, unless otherwise stated, is Paris. Order is chronological, by date of first publication.

Books

Contribution à l'étude profane de la Bible. Ghio, 1889.

Le Procès de Socrate. Alcan, 1889.

D'Aristote à Marx, ed. Eduard Berth. Rivière, 1935. (Originally published in *Ere Nouvelle* in 1894, as "L'Ancienne et la nouvelle métaphysique.")

La Ruine du monde antique. Rivière, 1901, 1925, 1933. (Originally published in large part in *Ere Nouvelle*, 1894.)

Essai sur l'église et l'état. Jacques, 1902.

Introduction à l'économie moderne. Jacques, 1902. Second ed., Rivière, 1922.

Saggi di critica del marxismo. Palermo: Sandron, 1902. Reprinted Rome: Samonà e Savelli, 1970.

Le Système historique de Renan. Jacques, 1905. Reprinted Geneva: Slatkin, 1971.

Insegnamenti sociale della economia contemporanea. Palermo: Sandron, 1906.

La Décomposition du Marxisme. Rivière, 1908. (Translated into English as *Decomposition of Marxism* and published as an appendix to Irving Louis Horowitz, *Radicalism and the Revolt against Reason*; New York: Humanities Press, 1963.)

Les Illusions du progrès. Rivière, 1908. Four subsequent editions. (Translated into English by John and Charlotte Stanley as *The Illusions of Progress*; Berkeley and Los Angeles: University of California Press, 1969.)

Réflexions sur la violence. Rivière, 1908. Six subsequent editions.

(Translated into English by T. E. Hulme and J. Roth as *Reflections on Violence*; New York and London: Macmillan, 1950.)

La Révolution Dreyfusienne. Rivière, 1909, 1911.

Matériaux d'une théorie du prolétariat. Rivière, 1919, 1921.

De l'utilité du pragmatisme. Rivière, 1921, 1928.

Propos de Georges Sorel, ed. Jean Variot. Gallimard, 1935.

Lettres à Paul Delesalle, ed. André Prudhommeaux. Grasset, 1947.

'Da Proudhon a Lenin' e 'L'Europa sotto la tormenta', ed. Gabriele de Rosa. Rome: Edizioni di Storia e Letteratura, 1974.

Articles, Prefaces to Books, Book Reviews

1886

"Sur les applications de la psychophysique." *Revue Philosophique* 22.

1887

"Le Calcul des probabilités et l'expérience." *Revue Philosophique* 23.

1888

"De la Cause en physique." *Revue Philosophique* 24.

"Les Représentants du peuple à l'armée des Pyrénées-Orientales en 1793." *Revue de la Révolution* 13 (Sept., Oct., Jan. 1889).

Review

Vidal, "Histoire de la Révolution dans les Pyrénées-Orientales." *Revue de la Révolution* 11 (April).

1890

"Contributions psycho-physiques à l'étude esthétique. Notes et discussions." *Revue Philosophique* 29-30.

1891

"Les Girondins du Roussillon." *Bulletin de la Société Agricole, Scientifique et Littéraire des Pyrénées Orientales* (Perpignan).

"Sur la géométrie non-euclidienne. Notes et discussions." *Revue Philosophique* 30.

1892

"Essai sur la philosophie de Proudhon." *Revue Philosophique* 33-34.

"Fondement scientifique de l'atomisme." Annales de Philosophie Chrétienne.

"François Ducruix—Contribution à la psychologie des Maratistes." *Bulletin de la Société Agricole, Scientifique et Littéraire des Pyrénées Orientales* (Perpignan).

"La Physique de Descartes." *Annales de Philosophie Chrétienne.*

1893

"La Bonne Marche des locomotives à grande allure." *Revue Scientifique* 51.

"Le Crime politique d'après M. Lombroso." *Revue Scientifique* 51.

"Deux nouveaux sophismes sur le temps." *Annales de Philosophie Chrétienne.*

"Une Faute de crime politique." *Archivio di Psichiatria e Scienze Penali* 14, p. 452.

"La Femme criminelle d'après M. Lombroso." *Revue Scientifique* 52.

"La Position du problème de M. Lombroso." *Revue Scientifique* 51.

"Science et socialisme." *Revue Philosophique* 35.

1894

"Le Mouvement de la voie des chemins de fer." *Revue Scientifique* 53.
"La Psychologie du Juge." *Archivio di Psichiatria e scienze penali* 15.

Reviews

Coucelle-Seneuil, "La Société moderne," in *Ere Nouvelle* (January).
Fiaux, "Les Maisons de tolérance; leur fermature" (March).
"Le Journal d'un philosophe," in *Ere Nouvelle* (March).
Masseron, "Danger et necessité du socialisme," in *Ere Nouvelle* (March).
Strada, "Philosophie de l'impersonalisme méthodique," (March).
"Compte rendu du Congrès international des travailleurs des voies ferrées européennes tenu à Zurich, 1893," in *Ere Nouvelle* (April).
Guyot, "Les Principes de '89 et le socialisme," in *Ere Nouvelle* (April).
Demolins, "Quel est le devoir présent?" in *Ere Nouvelle* (May).
Laveleye, "Essais et études," in *Ere Nouvelle* (May).
Roguenant, "Le Grand Soir," in *Ere Nouvelle* (May).
Mazimann, "Le Socialisme de l'avenir ou la mutualité par l'état," in *Ere Nouvelle* (June).
George, "La Condition des ouvriers; lettre ouverte au Pape Léon XIII," in *Ere Nouvelle* (July).
Laurent, "Les Bissexués," in *Ere Nouvelle* (July).
Espinas, "Leçon d'ouverture d'un cours d'histoire de l'économie sociale," in *Ere Nouvelle* (August).
Leverdays, "La Centralisation," in *Ere Nouvelle* (August).
Leverdays, "Politique et barbarie," in *Ere Nouvelle* (August).
Daudet, "Les Morticoles," in *Ere Nouvelle* (September).
"Discours de distribution des prix," in *Ere Nouvelle* (September).
Jay, "Etude sur la question ouvrière en Suisse," in *Ere Nouvelle* (October).
Tolstoy, "L'Esprit chrétien et le patriotisme," in *Ere Nouvelle* (October).
Manaceine, "L'Anarchie passive et le comte Léon Tolstoi," in *Ere Nouvelle* (November).
Tarroux, "Luttes sur le socialisme," in *Ere Nouvelle* (November).

1895

"Les Théories de M. Durkheim." *Devenir Social* (April-May).
"L'Eglise et le travail manuel." *Devenir Social* (September) (signed "B").
"La Métaphysique évolutioniste de M. Brunetière." *Devenir Social* (September) (signed "B").
"La Superstition socialiste." *Devenir Social* (November).
"L'Evolution moderne de l'architecture." *Revue Scientifique* 3 (4th series).
"Les Théories pénales de MM. Durkheim et Tarde." *Archivio di Psichiatria e Scienze Penali* 16.

Reviews

Rignault, "Les Premières Formes de la religion," in *Devenir Social* (May) (signed "X").
Ferrero, "Les Lois psychologiques du symbolisme," in *Devenir Social* (June) (signed "X"). Depasse, "Du travail et de ses conditions," in *Devenir Social* (August).

Geblesco, "La Propriété rurale à Rome, en France, en Roumanie," in *Devenir Social* (August).

Laveleye, "Essais et études," in *Devenir Social* (August).

Legrain, "Dégénérescence et alcoolisme," in *Devenir Social* (October) (signed "G").

Molinari, "Science et religion," in *Devenir Social* (October).

Zolla, "Questions agricoles d'hier et d'aujourd'hui," in *Devenir Social* (October) (signed "B").

Brutailes, "Etude sur la Chambre de Commerce de Guyenne," in *Devenir Social* (November) (signed "X").

Le Bon, "Psychologie des foules," *Devenir Social* (November).

Torreilles and Desplanque, "L'Enseignement élémentaire en Roussillon," in *Devenir Sociale* (signed "X").

1896

"Etudes d'économie rurale." *Devenir Social* (January-February) (signed "F").

"La Science dans l'éducation." *Devenir Social* (February-May).

"Progrès et développement." *Devenir Social* (March) (signed "B").

"L'Idéalisme de M. Brunetière." *Devenir Social* (June) (signed "David").

"Les Sentiments sociaux." *Devenir Social* (August-September) (signed "X").

"Economie sociale catholique." *Devenir Social* (October) (signed "B").

"Etude sur Vico." *Devenir Social* (October-December).

"La Dépression économique." *Devenir Social* (November) (signed "F").

Reviews

"Annales de l'Institut International de Sociologie," in *Devenir Social* (January).

Office du Travail, "Statistique des grèves et des recours à la conciliation et à l'arbitrage survenus pendant l'année 1894," in *Devenir Social* (January) (signed "G").

Schuler, "Economistes classiques et leurs adversaires," in *Devenir Social* (January) (signed "X").

Lourbet, "La Femme devant la science contemporaine," in *Devenir Social* (February) (signed "X").

Rumelin, "Problèmes d'économie politique et de statistique," in *Devenir Social* (February) (signed "J. David").

Pioger, "La Question sanitaire dans ses rapports avec les intérêts et les droits de l'individu et de la société," in *Devenir Social* (March) (signed "G").

Renard, "Critique de Combat," in *Devenir Social* (March).

Nordeau, "Paradoxes psychologiques," in *Devenir Social* (April) (signed "B").

Virgili, "Il Problema agricolo e l'avvenire sociale," in *Devenir Social* (April) (signed "F").

Pareto, "Cours d'économie politique," in *Devenir Social* (May).

Say, "Contre le socialisme," in *Devenir Social* (May) (signed "X").

Lapouge, "Sélection sociale," *Devenir Social* (June) (signed "X").

Levy, "Réglementation de la production du charbon," in *Devenir Social* (June) (signed "G").
Fouillée, "Le Mouvement idéaliste et la réaction contre la science positive," in *Devenir Social* (July).
"Annales de l'Institut de Sociologie," in *Devenir Social* (August).
Labriola, Antonio, "Del materialismo storico," in *Devenir Social* (August).
Ferri, "Socialisme et science positive," in *Devenir Social* (December) (signed "David").

1897

"La Science de la population." *Devenir Social* (February).
"Contre une critique anarchiste." *Devenir Social* (May) (signed "H").
"Sur la théorie Marxiste de la valeur." *Journal des Economistes* (May).
"La Loi des revenus." *Devenir Social* (July).
"Sociologie de la suggestion." *Devenir Social* (August-September) (signed "X").
"Die Entwicklung des Kapitalismus." *Sozialistische Monatshefte* (October).
"Pro e contro il socialismo." *Devenir Social* (October).
"Der Ursprung des Staatssozialismus in Deutschland." *Sozialistische Monatshefte* (November).
Preface to Antonio Labriola, *Essais sur la conception matérialiste de l'histoire.* (French trans., Giard et Brière; partial translation in Labriola, *Socialism and Philosophy*, Chicago: Kerr, 1911.)

Reviews

Avenel, "Le Mécanisme de la vie moderne," in *Devenir Social* (January) (signed "E. G.").
Balicki, "L'Etat comme organisation coercitive de la société politique," in *Devenir Social* (February) (signed "E. G.").
Fouillée, "Le Mouvement positiviste et la conception sociologique du monde," in *Devenir Social* (February).
Guyot, "L'Economie de l'effort," in *Devenir Social* (February).
Payot, "De la croyance," in *Devenir Social* (February) (signed "X").
Molinari, "La Viriculture," in *Devenir Social* (March) (signed "David").
Niceforo, "Il Gèrgo nei normali, nei degenerati e nei criminali," in *Devenir Social* (March).
Office du Travail, "Statistique des grèves et des recours à la conciliation et à l'arbitrage survenus pendant l'année 1896," in *Devenir Social* (April) (signed "G").
Ferrero, "L'Europa giovane," in *Devenir Social* (May) (signed "J. David").
Lerda, "Il Socialismo e la sua tattica," in *Devenir Social* (May) (signed "B").
Pareto, "Le Cours d'économie politique II," in *Devenir Social* (May).
Lubbock, "L'Emploi de la vie," in *Devenir Social* (June) (signed "E").
Caruso-Casa, "La Questione siciliana degli zolfi," in *Devenir Social* (July) (signed "F").
Virgili, "La Sciopero nella vita moderna," in *Devenir Social* (August) (signed "G").

1898

"Ein sozialistischer Staat." *Sozialistische Monatshefte* (January).

"L'Avenir socialiste des syndicats." *Humanité Nouvelle* (March-May) (reproduced as Chapter 1 of *Matériaux d'une théorie du prolétariat*).

"Was man von Vico lernt." *Sozialistische Monatshefte* 2 (June).

"Betrachtungen über die materialistische Geschichtsauffassung." *Sozialistische Monatshefte* (July-September) (Chapter 1 of *Saggi di critica del marxism*).

"La Necessità e il fatalismo del marxismo." *Riforma Sociale* (Milan, August) (Chapter 2 of *Saggi di critica del marxismo*).

"Der amerikanische Kapitalismus." *Sozialistische Monatshefte* (December).

"La Crise du socialisme." *Revue Politique et Parlementaire* (December).

"Il Giuri e la crisi del diritto penale." *Scuola Positiva nella Giurisprudenza Penale* (December).

Preface to Serverio Merlino, *Formes et essence du socialisme* (Giard et Brière).

Reviews

Renard, "Le Régime socialiste," in *Ouvrier des Deux Mondes* (May).

Destrée and Vandervelde, "Le Socialisme en Belgique," in *Ouvrier des Deux Mondes* (1 June).

"Annali di statistica" (Rome), in *Revue Internationale de Sociologie* (November).

Bosco, "La Statistica civile e penale," in *Revue Internationale de Sociologie* (November).

Guesde, "Le Socialisme au jour le jour," in *Revue Internationale de Sociologie* (November).

Von Kol, "Socialisme et liberté," in *Revue Internationale de Sociologie* (November).

Loria, "La Costituzione economica odierna," in *Revue Internationale de Sociologie* (December).

1899

"Dove va il marxismo?" *Rivista Critica del Socialismo* (January).

"Marxismo e scienza sociale." *Rivista Italiana di Sociologia* (January) (Chapter 6 of *Saggi di critica del marxismo*).

"Dommatismo e pratica." *Rivista Critica del Socialismo* (March).

"Morale et socialisme." *Mouvement Socialiste* (March).

"Y a-t-il de l'utopie dans le Marxisme?" *Revue de Métaphysique et de Morale* (March) (Chapter 5 of *Saggi di critica del marxismo*).

"Il Vangelo, la Chiesa e il socialismo." *Rivista Critica del Socialismo* (April, May) (final chapter of *La Ruine du monde antique*).

"L'Ethique du socialisme." *Revue de Métaphysique et de Morale* (May).

"L'Evoluzione del socialismo in Francia." *Riforma Sociale* (June).

"Quelques objections au matérialisme économique." *Humanité Nouvelle* (June-July) (reprinted in *Saggi di critica del marxismo*, Chapter 4).

"Il Socialismo e la teoria delle razze." *Rivista Critica del Socialismo* (July) (Chapter 3 of *Saggi di critica del marxismo*).

"Socialismo e rivoluzione." *Rivista Popolare di Politica* (15 July).

"Le Idee giuridiche del marxismo." *Rivista di Storia Filosofia del Diritto* (8

August) (reprinted in *Saggi di critica del marxismo*, Chapter 7).
"Les Divers Types des sociétés cooperatives." *Science Sociale* (September).
"La Scissione socialista in Francia." *Rivista Critica del Socialismo* (Rome, October).
"Socialismo e democrazia." *Rivista Critica del Socialismo.*
"Le Spirito pubblico Francia." *Rivista Popolare di Politica*, Vol. 5.
Reviews
Cavalieri, "Funzioni publiche e atti amministrativi," in *Revue Internationale de Sociologie* (January).
Ferrari, "La Liberta politica e il diretto internazionale," in *Revue Internationale de Sociologie* (January).
Mansuetus, "Le Sens commun et son application aux sciences," in *Revue Internationale de Sociologie* (January).
Rousiers, "Les Industries monopolisées aux Etats-Unis," in *Mouvement Socialiste* (15 January).
Carbone, "Lo Statuto e le teoriche su la revizione," in *Revue Internationale de Sociologie* (February).
Le Bon, "La Psychologie du socialisme," in *Revue Internationale de Sociologie* (February).
Pintor, "Sovranita populari o sovranita degli ottimi," in *Revue Internationale de Sociologie* (February).
Villa, "Sui metodi delle scienze morali," in *Revue Internationale de Sociologie* (February).
Lichtenberger, "Le Socialisme et la révolution française," in *Mouvement Socialiste* (1 February).
Bulletin Bibliographique, "Les Revues," in *Mouvement Socialiste* (15 February; 1 March; 15 March; 1 April; 15 April; 1 May; 15 May; 1 June).
Fournière, "L'Idéalisme social," in *Revue Internationale de Sociologie* (March).
Colajanni, "L'Italia nel 1898," in *Mouvement Socialiste* (1 March).
Fédération des Jeunesses Socialistes du Midi, "Aux jeunes," in *Mouvement Socialiste* (1 March).
Hariou, "Leçons sur le mouvement social," in *Mouvement Socialiste* (1 March).
Vandervelde, "L'Influence des villes sur les campagnes," in *Mouvement Socialiste* (1 March).
Le Bon, "La Psychologie du socialisme," in *Mouvement Socialiste* (15 March).
Baratono, "Sociologia estetica," in *Revue Internationale de Sociologie* (April).
Berryer, "Le Monopole de l'alcool," in *Revue Internationale de Sociologie* (April).
Demolins, "L'Education nouvelle," in *Revue Internationale de Sociologie* (April).
Groppali, "La Genesi sociale del fenòmeno scientifico," in *Revue Internationale de Sociologie* (April).
Lamperière, "Le Rôle social de la femme," in *Revue Internationale de Sociologie* (April).

Lombroso, "L'Antisémitisme," in *Revue Internationale de Sociologie* (April).

Panizza, "Le Tre Leggi. Saggio di psicofisiologia sociali," in *Revue Internationale de Sociologie* (April).

Delesalle, "Les Conditions du travail chez les ouvriers en instruments de précision de Paris," in *Mouvement Socialiste* (1 April).

Ferri, "Contro l'utopia reazionaria," in *Mouvement Socialiste* (15 April).

Gide, "Si les institutions sociales sont un mal social," in *Mouvement Socialiste* (15 April).

Platon, "La Démocratie et le régime fiscal à Athènes, à Rome et de nos jours," in *Revue Internationale de Sociologie* (May).

Demolins, "L'Education nouvelle," in *Mouvement Socialiste* (1 May).

Rambaud, "Histoire des doctrines économiques," in *Mouvement Socialiste* (1 May).

Maxweiler, "La Participation aux bénéfices," in *Mouvement Socialiste* (15 May).

Chironi, "L'Individualismo e la funzione sociale del diritto," in *Revue Internationale de Sociologie* (June).

Deslinières, "L'Application du système collectiviste," in *Revue Internationale de Sociologie* (June).

Direzione Generale della Statistica (Rome), "Statistica giudiziaria penale par l'anno," in *Revue Internationale de Sociologie* (June).

Racioppi, "Forme di stato e forme di governo," in *Revue Internationale de Sociologie* (June).

Ragnisco, "I dolori della civilità e il lori significato," in *Revue Internationale de Sociologie* (June).

Claudel, "Essai de synthétique," in *Revue Internationale de Sociologie* (July).

Combothecra, "La Conception juridique de l'état," in *Revue Internationale de Sociologie* (July).

Dina, "L'Ultimo Periodo del principato longobardo e l'origine del dominio pontificio in Benevento," in *Revue Internationale de Sociologie* (July).

Simons, "Synthèse sociologique," in *Revue Internationale de Sociologie* (July).

Marx, "Critique de l'économie politique," in *Revue Internationale de Sociologie* (August-September).

Office du Travail, "Résultats statistiques du recensement des industries et professions," in *Revue Internationale de Sociologie* (August-September).

Tangorra, "Il Controllo fiscale nell' amministrazione finanziaria," in *Revue Internationale de Sociologie* (August-September).

Posada, "Gli studi sociologici in Ispagna," in *Revue Internationale de Sociologie* (October).

Rossi, "L'Animo della folla," in *Revue Internationale de Sociologie* (October).

Rossi, "Genio e degenerazione in Mazzini," in *Revue Internationale de Sociologie* (October).

Rousiers, "La Vie américaine. Ranches, fermes et usines," in *Revue Internationale de Sociologie* (October).

Boilley, "De la production industrielle," in *Revue Internationale de Sociologie*

(November).
Wechniakoff, "Savants, penseurs et artistes: biologie et pathologie comparées," in *Revue Internationale de Sociologie* (November).

1900

"Uber die kapitalistische Konzentration." *Sozialistische Monatshefte* 4 (February-March).
"I Postulati del Manifesto Comunista." *Rivista Popolari di Politica* 6, nos. 5 and 6 (15 March, 15 April).
"Les Polémiques pour l'interprétation du marxisme." *Revue Internationale de Sociologie* (April-May) (reprinted in *Saggi di critica del marxismo*, Chapter 9).
"Alcune previsioni stoiche di Marx." *Rivista Popolari di Politica* 6, no. 8 (30 May).
"Le Elezioni municipali a Parigi." *Rivista Popolari di Politica* 6, nos. 10 and 11 (31 May, 15 June).
"Costruzione del sistema della storia seconda Marx." *Riforma Sociale* (June) (Chapter 8 of *Saggi di critica del marxismo*).
"Les Dissensions de la social-démocratie allemande à propos des écrits de M. Bernstein." *Revue Politique et Parlementaire* (July).
"Le Système des mathématiques." *Revue de Métaphysique et de Morale* (July).
"Les Aspects juridiques du socialisme." *Revue Socialiste* (October-November).
"L'Economie sociale à l'exposition." *Mouvement Socialiste* (November).
"Les Facteurs moraux de l'évolution." *Questions de morale* (Alcan).
"La Science et la morale." *Questions de morale* (Alcan).

Reviews

Croce, "Materialismo storico ed economica marxistica," in *Revue Internationale de Sociologie* (January).
Rousiers, "La Vie américaine. L'Education et la société," in *Revue Internationale de Sociologie* (February).
Direzione Generale della Statistica (Rome), "Annali de statistica," in *Revue Internationale de Sociologie* (June).
Dugard, "De l'éducation des jeunes filles," in *Revue Internationale de Sociologie* (June).
Office du Travail, "Résultats statistiques du recensement des industries et professions," vol. 2, in *Revue Internationale de Sociologie* (June).
Todd, "Le Gouvernement parlementaire en Angleterre," 2 vols., in *Revue Internationale de Sociologie* (June and December).
Saito, "La Protection ouvrière au Japon," in *Revue Internationale de Sociologie* (July).
Direzione Generale della Statistica, "Statistica della elezioni generali politiche del 10 guigno 1900," in *Revue Internationale de Sociologie* (October).
Direzione Generale della Statistica, "Statistica degli scioperi durante l'anno 1898," in *Revue Internationale de Sociologie* (October).
Sitta, "La Populazione della republica argentina," in *Revue Internationale de Sociologie* (October).

Ferraris, "Socialismo e riforma sociale nel morente e nel nascente secolo," in *Revue Internationale de Sociologie* (November).

Giroud, "Cempius. Education intégrale. Coéducation des sexes," in *Revue Internationale de Sociologie* (November).

Boulard, "Le Collectivisme intégral," in *Revue Internationale de Sociologie* (December).

Garnier, "La Terre éternelle," in *Revue Internationale de Sociologie* (December).

Pagano, "Le Forme di governo e loro evoluzione popolare," in *Revue Internationale de Sociologie* (December).

1901

"Conseils du travail et paix sociale." *Mouvement Socialiste* (January).

"Les Grèves de Montceau." *Pages Libres* (March).

"Economie et agriculture." *Revue Socialiste* (March-April).

"Proudhon." *Pages Libres* (4 May).

"Quelques mots sur Proudhon." *Cahiers de la Quinzaine*, no. 130 of the second series (June).

"Pour Proudhon." *Pages Libres* (8 June).

"La Propriété foncière en Belgique." *Mouvement Socialiste* (October).

"La Valeur sociale de l'art." *Revue de Métaphysique et de Morale.*

Reviews

Cutrera, "La Mafia e i mafiosi," in *Revue Internationale de Sociologie* (February).

Direzione Generale della Statistica, "Annuario statistico italiano," in *Revue Internationale de Sociologie* (February).

King, "Textbook de l'Institut des Actuaires de Londres," in *Revue Internationale de Sociologie* (February).

Lorini, "Il Profitto," in *Revue Internationale de Sociologie* (February).

Office du Travail, "Répartition des forces motrices à vapeur et hydroliques en 1899," in *Revue Internationale de Sociologie* (February).

Office du Travail, "Statistique des grèves, 1899," in *Revue Internationale de Sociologie* (February).

Saint-Clair, "Lettres d'un militant," in *Revue Internationale de Sociologie* (February).

Ministère du Commerce, "Les Associations professionelles ouvrières," vol. 2, in *Revue Internationale de Sociologie* (May).

Ministère du Commerce, "Neuvième session du Conseil Supérieur du Travail," in *Revue Internationale de Sociologie* (August-September).

Direzione Generale della Statistica, "Annali di statistica," in *Revue Internationale de Sociologie* (October).

Korn, "L'Alcoolisme en France et le rôle des pouvoirs publics dans la lutte contre le cabaret," in *Revue Internationale de Sociologie* (October).

Office du Travail, "Répartition des forces motrices en 1899," vol. 2, in *Revue Internationale de Sociologie* (October).

1902

"Jean Coste." *Cahiers de la Quinzaine* (February).

"Idées socialistes et faits économiques au XIXe siècle." *Revue Socialiste* (March-May).

"Storia e sciencia sociale." *Rivista Italiana di Sociologia* (March-June).

"Le Matérialisme historique." *Bulletin de la Société Française de Philosophie* (20 March).

"Soziale Ideen und Organisation der Arbeit." *Sozialistische Monatshefte* (June).

"Les Syndicats industriels et leur signification." *Revue Socialiste* (July-August).

"La Crise de la pensée catholique." *Revue de Métaphysique et de Morale* (September).

Preface to Fernand Pelloutier, *L'Histoire des bourses du travail* (Schleicher).

Reviews

L'Institut International de Statistique, *Bulletin* 12, in *Revue Internationale de Sociologie* (February).

Office du Travail, "Poisons industriels," in *Revue Internationale de Sociologie* (February).

Ministère Belge de l'Industrie et du Travail, "Recensement général des industries et des métiers," in *Revue Internationale de Sociologie* (March).

Ministère Belge de l'Industrie et du Travail, "Statistique des salaires dans les mines de houille," in *Revue Internationale de Sociologie* (March).

Ministère du Commerce Française, "Résultats statistiques du recensement des industries et professions," vol. 4, in *Revue Internationale de Sociologie* (March).

Office du Travail, "Statistique des grèves, 1900," in *Revue Internationale de Sociologie* (March).

1903

"Qu'est-ce qu'un syndicat?" *Pages Libres* (March).

"Sur divers aspects de la mécanique." *Revue de Métaphysique et de Morale* (November).

"A propos de l'anticléricalisme." *Etudes Socialistes.*

"Le Compagnonnage." *Etudes Socialistes.*

"Léon XIII." *Etudes Socialistes.*

"Nouveaux réquisitoires de M. Brunetière." *Etudes Socialistes.*

"Observations sur le régime des chemins de fer." *Etudes Socialistes.*

Reviews

Le Bon, "Psychologie de l'éducation," in *Revue Générale de Bibliographie* (January).

Schmoller, "Politique sociale et économie politique," in *Revue Générale de Bibliographie* (January).

Vigouroux, "L'Evolution sociale en Australasie," in *Revue Générale de Bibliographie* (January).

Bourgeois, "La Liberté de l'enseignement," in *Revue Générale de Bibliographie* (March).

Faguet, "Le Libéralisme," in *Revue Générale de Bibliographie* (March).

Grappe, "J-H. Newman," in *Revue Générale de Bibliographie* (March).
Huguet, "Le Rachat des chemins de fers suisses," in *Revue Générale de Bibliographie* (March).
Pareto, "Les Systèmes socialistes," in *Revue Générale de Bibliographie* (March).
Chaine, "Les Catholiques français," in *Revue Générale de Bibliographie* (July).
Charléty, "Histoire de Lyon," in *Revue Générale de Bibliographie* (July).
Delp, "Le Suffrage classifique," in *Revue Générale de Bibliographie* (July).
Denis, "Les Vrais Perils," in *Revue Générale de Bibliographie* (July).
Dunand, "Etudes critiques sur l'histoire de Jeanne d'Arc," in *Revue Générale de Bibliographie* (July).
Gay, "Histoire de Vallais," in *Revue Générale de Bibliographie* (July).
Guyot, "Le Trust de pétrole aux Etats-Unis," in *Revue Générale de Bibliographie* (July).
Krigg, "Vieux papiers," in *Revue Générale de Bibliographie* (July).
Delarue, "Le Clergé et le culte catholique en Bretagne pendant la Révolution," in *Revue Générale de Bibliographie* (September).
Dufourcq, "La Christianisation des foules," in *Revue Générale de Bibliographie* (September).
Dussaud, "Les Nouvelles Clauses et conditions générales imposées aux entrepreneurs des ponts et chaussées," in *Revue Générale de Bibliographie* (September).
Funck-Brentano, "La Famille fait l'Etat," in *Revue Générale de Bibliographie* (September).
Leon, "Fleuves, canaux, chemins de fer," in *Revue Générale de Bibliographie* (September).
Besse, "Le Cardinal Pie," in *Revue Générale de Bibliographie* (November).
Carnegie, "L'Empire des affaires," in *Revue Générale de Bibliographie* (November).
Faulquier, "Frédéric Ozanam," in *Revue Générale de Bibliographie* (November).
Ghio, "Notes sur l'Italie contemporaine," in *Revue Générale de Bibliographie* (November).
Seilhac, "Le Monde socialiste," in *Revue Générale de Bibliographie* (November).

1904

"Due anni di anticlericalismo in Francia." *Rivista Popolari di Politica* 10.
"La Morte di Waldeck-Rousseau." *Rivista Popolare di Politica* 10.

Reviews

Bourdeau, "Les Maîtres de la pensée contemporaine," in *Revue Générale de Bibliographie* 2 (January).
Brunetière, "Cinq lettres sur Ernest Renan," in *Revue Générale de Bibliographie* 2 (January).
Dunand, "Etude historique sur les voix et visions de Jeanne d'Arc," in *Revue Générale de Bibliographie* 2 (January).
Guyot, "Gaspillages regressifs et dépenses nécessaires," in *Revue Générale*

de Bibliographie 2 (January).

Isaiff, "Les Grands Hommes et le milieu social," in *Revue Générale de Bibliographie* 2 (January).

Péguy, "Cahier de l'inauguration du moment de Renan à Treguier," in *Revue Générale de Bibliographie* 2 (January).

Rappoport, "La Philosophie de l'histoire," in *Revue Générale de Bibliographie* 2 (January).

Allard, "Les Chrétiens ont-ils incendié Rome sous Néron?" in *Revue Générale de Bibliographie* 2 (February).

Bréhier, "Les Origines du crucifix dans l'art religieux," in *Revue Générale de Bibliographie* 2 (February).

D'Adhémar, "La Philosophie des sciences et le problème religieux," in *Revue Générale de Bibliographie* 2 (February).

Ermoni, "La Bible et l'archéologie syrienne," in *Revue Générale de Bibliographie* 2 (February).

Flach, "Les Origines de l'ancienne France," in *Revue Générale de Bibliographie* 2 (February).

Houtin, "L'Américanisme," in *Revue Générale de Bibliographie* 2 (February).

Loisy, "Le Quatrième Evangile," in *Revue Générale de Bibliographie* 2 (February).

Payot, "Cours de morale," in *Revue Générale de Bibliographie* 2 (February).

Flornoy, "La Moricière," in *Revue Générale de Bibliographie* (March).

Gondal, "Au temps des Apôtres," in *Revue Générale de Bibliographie* 2 (March).

Lionnet, "Un Evêque social. Kettler," in *Revue Générale de Bibliographie* (March).

Bonomelli, "Nomen, crimen. Contre l'antisémitisme," in *Revue Générale de Bibliographie* (April).

Cetty, "Oeuvres sociales et ouvriers en Allemagne," in *Revue Générale de Bibliographie* (April).

Delaisi, "L'Eglise et l'empire romain," in *Revue Générale de Bibliographie* (April).

Leroy, "Le Droit civil et le droit nouveau," in *Revue Générale de Bibliographie* (April).

Paulus, "Les Juifs et le Messie," in *Revue Générale de Bibliographie* (April).

Rébillon, "L'Eglise au Moyen-Age," in *Revue Générale de Bibliographie* (April).

Salomon, "Mgr. Dupanloup," in *Revue Générale de Bibliographie* (April).

Smets, "Catéchétique ou méthodologie religieuse," in *Revue Générale de Bibliographie* (April).

Weulersse, "Le Japon d'aujourd'hui," in *Revue Générale de Bibliographie* (April).

Luchaire, "L'Eglise et le seizième siècle," in *Revue Générale de Bibliographie* (May).

Brizon, "L'Eglise et la Révolution française," in *Revue Générale de Bibliographie* (June).

Fachan, "Historique de la rente française et des valeurs du trésor," in *Revue Générale de Bibliographie* (June).
Fremont, "Lettres à l'abbé Loisy sur quelques points de l'Ecriture-sainte," in *Revue Générale de Bibliographie* (June).
Garriguet, "L'Association ouvrière," in *Revue Générale de Bibliographie* (June).
Houtin, "Un Dernier Gallican," in *Revue Générale de Bibliographie* (June).
Jellineck, "L'Etat moderne et son droit," in *Revue Générale de Bibliographie* (June).
Laberthonnière, "Le Réalisme chrétien et l'idéalisme grec," in *Revue Générale de Bibliographie* (June).
Musset, "L'Eglise de France au XVIIe siècle," in *Revue Générale de Bibliographie* (June).
Lassalle, "Théorie systématique des droits acquis," in *Revue Générale de Bibliographie* (July).
Delattre, "Autour de la question biblique," in *Revue Générale de Bibliographie* (August).
Doellinger, "La Papauté," in *Revue Générale de Bibliographie* (August).
Duchesne, "Autonomies ecclésiastiques," in *Revue Générale de Bibliographie* (August).
Duchesne, "Les Premiers Temps de l'état pontifical," in *Revue Générale de Bibliographie* (August).
Leclercq, "L'Afrique chrétienne," in *Revue Générale de Bibliographie* (August).
Rocquigny, "Le Prolétariat rural en Italie," in *Revue Générale de Bibliographie* (August).
Bréhier, "La Querelle des images," in *Revue Générale de Bibliographie* (September).
Ermoni, "L'Agape dans l'église primitive.—L'Eucharistie dans l'église primitive," in *Revue Générale de Bibliographie* (September).
Ermoni, "Le Baptême dans l'église primitive," in *Revue Générale de Bibliographie* (September).
Menger, "L'Etat socialiste," in *Revue Générale de Bibliographie* (September).
Bertrand, "L'Egalité devant l'instruction," in *Revue Générale de Bibliographie* (October).
Labench, "Le Christianisme dans l'empire perse," in *Revue Générale de Bibliographie* (October).
Péguy and Zangwill, "Chadgadya," in *Revue Générale de Bibliographie* (October).
Turinaz, "Encore quelques mots sur les périls de la foi," in *Revue Générale de Bibliographie* (October).
Dufourcq, "Saint Irénée," in *Revue Générale de Bibliographie* (October and December).
Bourget and Salomon, "Bonald," in *Revue Générale de Bibliographie* (December).
Bremond, "Newman," in *Revue Générale de Bibliographie* (December).
Calmes, "L'Apocalypse devant la tradition et devant la critique," in *Revue*

Générale de Bibliographie (December).
Ferrero, "Grandeur et décadence de Rome," in *Revue Générale de Bibliographie* (December).
Lodiel, "Nos raisons d'être catholiques," in *Revue Générale de Bibliographie* (December).
Turmel, "Tertullien," in *Revue Générale de Bibliographie* (December).
Viollet, "L'Infaillibilité du Pape et le Syllabus," in *Revue Générale de Bibliographie* (December).
Waldeck-Rousseau, "Le Testament politique de Waldeck-Rousseau," in *Revue Générale de Bibliographie* (December).

1905

"Conclusions aux *Enseignements sociaux de l'économie moderne*." *Mouvement Socialiste* (July).
"Le Syndicalisme révolutionnaire." *Mouvement Socialiste* (November).
"Lo Sciopero generale." *Divenire Sociale* (December).
Preface to Georges Castex, *La Douleur physique* (Jacques).
"La Restaurazione giacobina in Francia." *Rivista Popolare di Politica* 11.

Reviews

Ansiaux, "Que faut-il faire de nos industries à domicile," in *Revue Générale de Bibliographie* (January).
De Broglie, "Monothéisme, hénothéisme, polythéisme," in *Revue Générale de Bibliographie* (January).
De Leener et al., "Le Charbon dans le Nord de la Belgique," in *Revue Générale de Bibliographie* (January).
Lemonnyer, "Epîtres de saint Paul," in *Revue Générale de Bibliographie* (January).
Chaussin, "Le Bénitier d'argent," in *Revue Générale de Bibliographie* (February).
Crick, "Le Procès du libre échange en Angleterre," in *Revue Générale de Bibliographie* (February).
Joran, "Université et enseignement," *Revue Générale de Bibliographie* (February).
Naquet, "L'Anarchie et le collectivisme," in *Revue Générale de Bibliographie* (February).
Dessignolle, "La Question sociale dans Emile Zola," in *Revue Générale de Bibliographie* (March).
Guiraud, "Etudes économiques sur l'antiquité," in *Revue Générale de Bibliographie* (March).
Un Jurisconsul, "La Séparation de l'église et de l'état," in *Revue Générale de Bibliographie* (March).
Métin, "La Révolution et l'autonomie locale," in *Revue Générale de Bibliographie* (March).
Blondel, "Histoire et dogme," in *Revue Générale de Bibliographie* (April).
Demolins, "Classification sociale," in *Revue Générale de Bibliographie* (April).
Frémont, "Les Principes, ou essai sur le problème des destinées de l'homme," in *Revue Générale de Bibliographie* (April).

Pautigny, "Justin. Apologies," in *Revue Générale de Bibliographie* (April).
Tavernier, "La Religion nouvelle," in *Revue Générale de Bibliographie* (April).
Tixeront, "Histoire des dogmes," in *Revue Générale de Bibliographie* (April).
Bourdeau, "Socialistes et sociologues," in *Revue Générale de Bibliographie* (August).
D'Adhémar, "Le Triple Conflit. Science, philosophie, religion," in *Revue Générale de Bibliographie* (August).
Desjardins, "Catholicisme et critique," in *Revue Générale de Bibliographie* (August). Ermoni, "Les Premiers Ouvriers de l'Evangile," in *Revue Générale de Bibliographie* (August).
Ferrero, "Grandeur et décadence de Rome. Jules César," in *Revue Générale de Bibliographie* (August).
Guieyesse, "La France et la paix armée. La conférence de La Haye," in *Revue Générale de Bibliographie* (August).
Le Roy, "Qu'est-ce qu'un dogme?" in *Revue Générale de Bibliographie* (August).
Nouvelle, "L'Authenticité du quatrième Evangile," in *Revue Générale de Bibliographie* (August).
Saint-Paul, "Architecture et catholicisme," in *Revue Générale de Bibliographie* (August).
Huret, "En Amérique. De San-Francisco au Canada," in *Revue Générale de Bibliographie* (September).
Lavergne, "Monsieur le maire," in *Revue Générale de Bibliographie* (September).
Viollet, "Infaillibilité et Syllabus," in *Revue Générale de Bibliographie* (September).
De Lapparent, "Science et apologétique," in *Revue Générale de Bibliographie* (October).
Goyau, "Moehler," in *Revue Générale de Bibliographie* (October).
Leclercq, "L'Espagne chrétienne," in *Revue Générale de Bibliographie* (October).
Poincaré, "La Valeur de la science," in *Revue Générale de Bibliographie* (October).
Allard, "Dix leçons sur le martyre," in *Revue Générale de Bibliographie* (November).
Baudrillart, "L'Eglise catholique. La Renaissance. Le Protestantisme," in *Revue Générale de Bibliographie* (November).
Binet, "L'Ame et le corps," in *Revue Générale de Bibliographie* (November).
Brémond, "Newman. Psychologie de la foi," in *Revue Générale de Bibliographie* (November).
De Broglie, "Les Fondements intellectuels de la foi chrétienne," in *Revue Générale de Bibliographie* (November).
De Montessus de Ballore, "Le Radium," in *Revue Générale de Bibliographie* (November).
Duhem, "La Théorie physique," in *Revue Générale de Bibliographie* (November).

Picard, "La Science Moderne et son état actuel," in *Revue Générale de Bibliographie* (November).

Sortais, "Le Procès de Galilée," in *Revue Générale de Bibliographie* (November).

Fouillée, "Eléments sociologiques de la morale," in *Revue Générale de Bibliographie* (December).

Sertillanges, "Socialisme et christianisme," in *Revue Générale de Bibliographie* (December).

1906

"Il Tramonto del partito socialista internationale." *Divenire Sociale* (January).

"Le Déclin du parti socialiste international." *Mouvement Socialiste* (February).

"Le Elezioni in Francia." *Divenire Sociale* (April).

"Le Idee di uguaglianza." *Divenire Sociale* (April).

"La Storia ebraica e il materialismo storico." *Divenire Sociale* (May).

"Grandeur et décadence de Rome." *Mouvement Socialiste* (July, and February 1907).

"L'Unita dei riformisti e dei 'rivoluzionari' tradizionali." *Divenire Sociale* (August).

"A proposito del Congresso di Roma." *Divenire Sociale* (October).

"Roberto Owen." *Divenire Sociale* (November).

"Cattolizi contra la Chiesa." *Divenire Sociale* (December).

"L'Industria urbana." *Rivista Popolare di Politica* 12.

Reviews

Duhem, "Les Origines de la statique," in *Revue Générale de Bibliographie* (January).

Bremond, "Newman. Essai de biographie psychologique," in *Revue Générale de Critique et de Bibliographie* (February).

Fourier, "Contribution à l'étude du socialisme français," in *Mouvement Socialiste* (February).

Pacheu, "Du positivisme au mysticisme," in *Revue Générale de Critique et de Bibliographie* (February).

Bureau, "Le Paysan des fjords de Norvège," in *Mouvement Socialiste* (March).

Dujardin, "La Source du fleuve chrétien," in *Revue Générale de Critique et de Bibliographie* (March).

Leclère, "Le Mysticisme catholique et l'âme de Dante," in *Revue Générale de Critique et de Bibliographie* (March).

Rouse-Ball, "Histoire des mathématiques," in *Revue Générale de Critique et de Bibliographie* (March).

Grasset, "Le Psychisme inférieur," in *Revue Générale de Critique et de Bibliographie* (April).

Labriola, Antonio "Scritti varii di filosofia e politica," in *Mouvement Socialiste* (April).

Deslandres, "Le Concile de Trente et la réforme du clergé catholique au XVIe siècle," in *Revue Générale de Critique et de Bibliographie* (May).

Ferrero, "Grandeur et décadence de Rome. La Fin d'une aristocratie," in *Revue Générale de Critique et de Bibliographie* (May).

Grasset, "Les Limites de la biologie," in *Revue Générale de Critique et de Bibliographie* (May).

Babeuf, "La Doctrine des égaux," in *Mouvement Socialiste* (June).

Frémont, "Les Principes ou Essai sur le problème des destinées de l'homme," in *Revue Générale de Critique et de Bibliographie* (June).

Giraud, "Questions d'histoire et d'archéologie chrétienne," in *Revue Générale de Critique et de Bibliographie* (June).

Rouquette, "L'Inquisition protestante," in *Revue Générale de Critique et de Bibliographie* (June).

Turmel, "Saint Jerôme," in *Revue Générale de Critique et de Bibliographie* (June).

Vandervelde, "Le Socialisme et l'agriculture," in *Revue Générale de Critique et de Bibliographie* (July).

Prins, "De l'esprit du gouvernement démocratique," in *Revue Générale de Critique et de Bibliographie* (August).

Stapfer, "Sermon laïque ou propos de morale et de philosophie," in *Mouvement Socialiste* (September).

Batiffol, "Etudes d'histoire et de théologie positive," in *Revue Générale de Critique et de Bibliographie* (October).

Dolléans, "Le Caractère religieux du socialisme," *Revue Générale de Critique et de Bibliographie* (October).

Giraud, "Anticléricalisme et catholicisme," in *Revue Générale de Critique et de Bibliographie* (October).

Modeste, "Vers l'éducation nouvelle," in *Revue Générale de Critique et de Bibliographie* (October).

Vacandard, "Etudes de critique et d'histoire religieuse," in *Revue Générale de Critique et de Bibliographie* (October).

Brunetière and Labriolle, "Saint Vincent de Lérins," in *Revue Générale de Critique et de Bibliographie* (November).

Giraud, "Pascal, *Pensées*," in *Revue Générale de Critique et de Bibliographie* (November).

Houtin, "La Question biblique au XXe siècle," in *Revue Générale de Critique et de Bibliographie* (November).

Baille, "Qu'est-ce que la science?" in *Revue Générale de Critique et de Bibliographie* (December).

Brémond, "Newman. Le Développement du dogme chrétien," in *Revue Générale de Critique et de Bibliographie* (December).

Chollet, "La Morale est-elle une science?" in *Revue Générale de Critique et de Bibliographie* (December).

De Lapparent, "La Providence créatrice," in *Revue Générale de Critique et de Bibliographie* (December).

Ferrero, "Grandeur et décadence de Rome. Antoine et Cléopâtre," in *Revue Générale de Critique et de Bibliographie* (December).

Giraud, "Livres et questions d'aujourd'hui," in *Revue Générale de Critique et de Bibliographie* (December).

Sueur, "Intellectualisme et catholicisme," in *Revue Générale de Critique et de Bibliographie* (December)

Valois, "L'Homme qui vient. Philosophie de l'autorité," in *Revue Générale de Critique et de Bibliographie* (December).

1907

"La Démocratie." *Bulletin de la Société Française de Philosophie* (March).

"Le Pragmatisme." *Bulletin de la Société Française de Philosophie* (April).

"Le Prétendu Socialisme juridique." *Mouvement Socialiste* (April).

"Les Cahiers de jeunesse de Renan." *Mouvement Socialiste* (May).

"L'Idéa di libertà." *Divenire Sociale* 3 (June).

"Jean-Jacques Rousseau." *Mouvement Socialiste* (June).

"La Crise morale et religieuse." *Mouvement Socialiste* (July).

"Critique de 'L'Evolution créatrice.'" *Mouvement Socialiste* (October, November, December, and January, February 1908).

Reviews

Batiffol, "L'Avenir prochain du catholicisme en France," in *Revue Générale de Critique et de Bibliographie* (January).

D'Azambuja, "La Grèce ancienne," in *Revue Générale de Critique et de Bibliographie* (January).

De Montesquiou, "Le Système politique d'Auguste Comte," in *Revue Générale de Critique et de Bibliographie* (January).

Dimier, "Les Maîtres de la contre-révolution au XIXe siècle," in *Mouvement Socialiste* (January).

Maurras, "Le Dilemme de Marc Sangnier. Essai sur la démocratie religieuse," in *Revue Générale de Critique et de Bibliographie* (January). Also in *Mouvement Socialiste* (August).

Vacandard, "L'Inquisition," in *Revue Générale de Critique et de Bibliographie* (January).

Dolléans, "Robert Owen," in *Revue Générale de Critique et de Bibliographie* (February).

Faguet, "Le Socialisme en 1907," in *Revue Générale de Critique et de Bibliographie* (February). Also in *Mouvement Socialiste* (May).

Glotz, "Etudes juridiques et sociales sur l'antiquité grecque," in *Revue Générale de Critique et de Bibliographie* (February). Also in *Mouvement Socialiste* (June).

Janssens, "La Philosophie et l'apologétique de Pascal," in *Revue Générale de Critique et de Bibliographie* (February).

Prat, "Origène," in *Revue Générale de Critique et de Bibliographie* (February).

Lorieux, "L'Autorité des Evangiles," in *Revue Générale de Critique et de Bibliographie* (April).

Moulard and Vincent, "Apologétique chrétienne," in *Revue Générale de Critique et de Bibliographie* (April).

Roguenant, "Patrons et ouvriers," in *Revue Générale de Critique et de Bibliographie* (April).

Saintyves, "Le Miracle et la critique historique," in *Revue Générale de Critique et de Bibliographie* (April).

D'Adhémar, "Les Variations des théories de la science," in *Revue Générale de Critique et de Bibliographie* (May).

Houtin, "La Crise du clergé," in *Revue Générale de Critique et de Bibliographie* (May).

Le Roy, "Dogme et critique," in *Revue Générale de Critique et de Bibliographie* (May).

Donop, "Commandement et obéissance," in *Mouvement Socialiste* (July).

Giraud, "Ferdinand Brunetière. Notes et Souvenirs," in *Mouvement Socialiste* (July).

Montesquiou, "Le Système politique d'A. Comte," in *Mouvement Socialiste* (July).

Brément, "Cerbet," in *Mouvement Socialiste* (August).

Brunetière, "Questions actuelles," in *Mouvement Socialiste* (August).

Guyot, "La Démocratie individualiste," in *Mouvement Socialiste* (August).

Auguy, "Les Systèmes socialistes d'échange," in *Mouvement Socialiste* (October).

Bainville, "Bismarck et la France," in *Mouvement Socialiste* (October).

Combasieu, "La Musique, ses lois, son évolution," in *Mouvement Socialiste* (October).

Brunetière, "Discours de combat," in *Mouvement Socialiste* (November).

Bruyssel, "La Vie sociale et ses évolutions," in *Mouvement Socialiste* (November).

Thomas, "Le Second Empire," in *Mouvement Socialiste* (November).

"L'Année sociologique," in *Mouvement Socialiste* (December).

1908

"La Decadenzia parlementare." *Divenire Sociale* (May).

"Morale e socialismo." *Divenire Sociale* (May).

"La Politique américaine." *Mouvement Socialiste* (June).

"Les Intellectuels à Athènes." *Mouvement Socialiste* (September).

"Le Modernisme dans la religion et dans le socialisme." *Revue Critique des Livres et des Idées.*

Reviews

Garriguet, "Régime de la propriété," in *Mouvement Socialiste* (February).

Gayau, "Kettler," in *Mouvement Socialiste* (February).

Fonsegrive, "Ferdinand Brunetière," in *Mouvement Socialiste* (February).

Newman, "Grammaire de l'assentiment," in *Mouvement Socialiste* (February).

Orano, "Cristo e Quirino," in *Mouvement Socialiste* (April).

Boutroux, "Science et religion dans la philosophie contemporaine," in *Mouvement Socialiste* (May).

Eichthal, "La Liberté individuelle du travail et les menaces du législateur," in *Mouvement Socialiste* (May).

Ghio, "Cours d'économie politique," in *Mouvement Socialiste* (June).

Journal Reviews

"La Crise américaine," in *Mouvement Socialiste* (February).

"L'Allemagne économique et financière au début de 1908," in *Mouvement Socialiste* (April).

"La Crise de l'apprentissage," in *Mouvement Socialiste* (April).
"La Discussion générale du projet d'impôt sur le revenue," in *Mouvement Socialiste* (April).
"L'Impuissance parlementaire," in *Mouvement Socialiste* (July).

1909

"La Religion d'aujourd'hui." *Revue de Métaphysique et de Morale* (May).
"La Disfatta dei 'muffles.'" *Divenire Sociale* (6 July); reprinted in *Aspects de la France*, 1 December 1949.
"La Russia e Clemenceau." *Divenire Sociale* (August).
"Il Dolori dell'eria presente." *Divenire Sociale* (October).
"Gli intellectuali contro gli operari." *Divenire Sociale* (December).
"La Maturita del movimento sindicale." *Divenire Sociale* (December).
"La Leçon du malheur." *Almanach de la Révolution.*
Preface to Victor Griffuelhes and L. Niel, *Les Objectifs de nos luttes de classe.*

1910

"Le Mystère de la 'Charité de Jeanne d'Arc' de Péguy." *Action Française* (April); reprinted in Eric Cahm, *Péguy et le nationalisme français* (Paris: Cahiers de l'amitié Charles Péguy, 1972).
"Le Patriotisme actuel en France," *Resto del Carlino*, (28 September); reprinted in *Feuillets d'amitié Charles Péguy*, no. 6 (1949): 13.
"Vues sur les problèmes de la philosophie." *Revue de Métaphysique et de Morale* 18 (December).
Preface to Arturo Labriola, *Karl Marx: L'Economiste, le socialiste* (Rivière).

1911

"Le Monument Jules Ferry." *Indépendance* (March).
"L'Abandon de la revanche." *Indépendance* (April).
"Lyripipii sorbonici moralisátiones." *Indépendance* (15 April).
"L'Otage de Paul Claudel." *Indépendance* (July).
"Les Responsabilités de 1870." *Indépendance* (July).
"Si les dogmes évoluent." *Indépendance* (September).
"Sur la magie moderne." *Indépendance* (September).
"A la mémoire de Cournot." *Indépendance* (October).
"Une Critique des sociologues." *Indépendance* (October).
"Le Democrazia antiche." *Rassegna Contemporanea* (November).
"Trois problèmes." *Indépendance* (December).
Preface to E. R. A. Seligman, *L'Interprétation économique de l'histoire* (Rivière; originally published in English as *The Economic Interpretation of History*).
"Psychologie politique." *Bulletin de la Semaine.*

Reviews

Bourdeau, "Entre deux servitudes," in *Indépendance* (1 March).
Croce, "Ce qui est vivant et ce qui est mort dans la philosophie de Hegel," in *Indépendance* (1 March).
Cromer, "Impérialisme ancien et moderne," in *Indépendance* (1 March).
Lagrange, "Quelques remarques sur l'*Orpheus* de M. Salomon Reinach," in *Indépendance* (1 March).
Pareto, "Le Mythe vertuiste et la littérature immorale," in *Indépendance* (1

March).
Schinz, "Antipragmatisme," in *Indépendance* (1 March).
Seligman, "L'Interprétation économique de l'histoire," in *Indépendance* (1 March).
Tyrrel, "Le Christianisme à la croisée des chemins," in *Indépendance* (1 March).
Alfassa, "Coopération et socialisme en Angleterre," in *Indépendance* (1 April).
Bricout, "La Science des religions et la foi chrétienne," in *Indépendance* (1 April).
Le Bon, "Psychologie de l'éducation," in *Indépendance* (1 April).
Leclère, "Pragmatisme, modernisme, protestantisme," in *Indépendance* (1 April).
Van Laak, "Harnack et le miracle," in *Indépendance* (1 April).
Gebhart, "Les Jardins de l'histoire," in *Indépendance* (15 April).
Gebhart, "La Vieille Eglise," in *Indépendance* (15 April).
Cazamian, "L'Angleterre moderne, son évolution," in *Indépendance* (1 May).
Lasserre, "La Philosophie de M. Bergson," in *Indépendance* (1 May).
Lombroso, "Hypnotisme et suggestion," in *Indépendance* (1 May).
Pirenne, "Les Anciennes Démocraties des Pays-Bas," in *Indépendance* (1 May).
Bainville, "Louis II de Bavière," in *Indépendance* (15 May).
Euchen, "Les Grands Courants de la pensée contemporaine," in *Indépendance* (15 May).
Gebhart, "Souvenirs d'un vieil Athénien," in *Indépendance* (15 May).
Newman, "Saints d'autrefois," in *Indépendance* (15 May).
Ruskin, "Praeterita. Souvenirs de jeunesse," in *Indépendance* (15 May).
Mathiez, "Rome et le clergé français sous la Constituante," in *Indépendance* (1 June).
Maze-Sencier, "L'Erreur primaire," in *Indépendance* (1 June).
Chevrillon, "Nouvelles Etudes anglaises," in *Indépendance* (15 June).
Meyer, "Ce que mes yeux ont vu," in *Indépendance* (15 June).
Gaultier, "La Pensée contemporaine," in *Indépendance* (1 July).
Seillière, "Barbey d'Aurevilly," in *Indépendance* (1 July).
Filon, "L'Angleterre d'Edouard VII," in *Indépendance* (1 August).
Guiraud, "Histoire partiale et histoire vraie," in *Indépendance* (1 August).
Dom Besse, "Le Catholicisme libéral," in *Indépendance* (15 August).
Flach, "La Poésie et le symbolisme dans l'histoire des institutions humaines," in *Indépendance* (15 August).
Houtin, "Un Prètre marié," in *Indépendance* (15 August).
Fiaux, "Armand Carrel et Emile de Girardin," in *Indépendance* (1 September).
Harmignie, "L'Etat et ses agents," in *Indépendance* (1 September).
Platon, "Pour le droit naturel," in *Indépendance* (1 September).
Ollivier, "L'Empire libéral," in *Indépendance* (1 September).
Seilière, "Les Mystiques du néo-romantisme," in *Indépendance* (15

September).
Boutroux, "William James," in *Indépendance* (1 October).
Brunetière, "Etude sur le XVIIIe siècle," in *Indépendance* (1 October).
Crispi, "Archives et papiers personnels de Crispi," in *Indépendance* (1 October).
Meynier, "L'Afrique noire," in *Indépendance* (1 October).
Montesquiou, "Le Réalisme de Bonald," in *Indépendance* (1 October).
Harman, "Domination et colonisation," in *Indépendance* (15 October).
Laberthonnière, "Positivisme et catholicisme," in *Indépendance* (15 October).
Charles-Brun, "Le Régionalisme," in *Indépendance* (1 November).
Gebhart, "De Panurge à Sancho Pança," in *Indépendance* (1 November).
Giraud, "Les Maîtres de l'heure," in *Indépendance* (1 November).
Giraud, "Pages choisies des Mémoires d'Outre-Tombe," in *Indépendance* (1 December).
Loisy, "A propos de l'histoire des religions," in *Indépendance* (1 December).
Brunetière, "Lettres de combat," in *Indépendance* (15 December).
Philippe, "Lettres de jeunesse," in *Indépendance* (15 December).
Reinach, "Histoire de l'Affaire Dreyfus," Tome VII, in *Indépendance* (15 December).

1912

"Urbain Gohier." *Indépendance* (1 January).
"La Rivolta ideale." *Indépendance* (1 April).
"Quelques prétentions juives." *Indépendance* (1, 15 May, 1 June).
"Aux temps Dreyfusiens." *Indépendance* (1 October).

Reviews

"A l'enseigne de l'idéal," in *Indépendance* (1 January).
Bernard, "Les Idées révolutionnaires dans les campagnes du Boubonnais," in *Indépendance* (1 January). Poncare, "Les Sciences et les humanités," in *Indépendance* (1 January).
Radziwell, "Quarante-cinq ans de ma vie," in *Indépendance* (1 January).
Meyer, "Aux ordres d'Arthur Meyer," in *Indépendance* (1 February).
Lebourt et Batiffol, "Les Odes de Salomon," in *Indépendance* (15 February).
Proudhon, "Lettres de Proudhon à Gustave Chaudey," in *Indépendance* (15 February).
Archimbault, "Renouvier," in *Indépendance* (1 March).
Bridge, "L'Impérialisme britannique," in *Indépendance* (1 March).
Gautherat, "Gobel: Evêque Metropolitain constitutionnel de Paris," in *Indépendance* (1 March).
Jacquier, "Le Nouveau Testament dans l'église chrétienne," in *Indépendance* (1 March).
Lantivy-Tredion, "La Question bretonne," in *Indépendance* (1 March).
Lemaître, "Pages choisies," in *Indépendance* (1 March).
Piepenbring, "Jésus et les apôtres," in *Indépendance* (1 March).
Collas, "Jean Chapelain," in *Indépendance* (15 March).

Frère Léon, "Le Miroir de la perfection du bienheureux François d'Assise," in *Indépendance* (15 March).

Mornet, "Les Sciences de la nature au XVIIIe siècle," in *Indépendance* (15 March).

Vacondard, "Etudes de critique et d'histoire religieuse," in *Indépendance* (15 March).

Vincent d'Indy, "Béethoven," in *Indépendance* (15 March).

Gebhart, "Contes et fantaîsies," in *Indépendance* (1 April).

Hallays, "En Flanant. A travers la France," in *Indépendance* (1 April).

Lothin, "Quételet," in *Indépendance* (1 April).

Mondolfo, "Il Materialismo storico in Frederico Engels," in *Indépendance* (1 May).

Palhories, "Nouvelles orientations de la morale," in *Indépendance* (1 May).

Tixeront, "Histoire des dogmes dans l'antiquité chrétienne," in *Indépendance* (1 May).

Hémon, "Bersot et ses amis," in *Indépendance* (1 June).

Aventino, "Le Gouvernement de Pie X," in *Indépendance* (August).

Demange, "Notes d'un voyage en Grèce," in *Indépendance* (August).

Gillouin, "La Philosophie de M. Henri Bergson," in *Indépendance* (August).

Giraud, "Nouvelles études sur Chateaubriand," in *Indépendance* (August).

Poulpiquet, "L'Objet intégral de l'apologétique," in *Indépendance* (August).

Preaudau, "Michel Bakounine," in *Indépendance* (August).

Schopenhauer, "Mémoires sur les sciences occultes," in *Indépendance* (August).

Thureau-Dongin, "Newman catholique," in *Indépendance* (August).

Gaultier, "Comment naissent les dogmes," in *Indépendance* (October).

Mollat, "Les Papes d'Avignon," in *Indépendance* (October).

Cor, "Essais sur la sensibilité contemporaine," in *Indépendance* (1 November).

Deploige, "Annales de l'Institut Supérieur de Philosophie de Louvain," in *Indépendance* (November).

Gardeil, "La Credibilité et l'apologétique," in *Indépendance* (November).

Gillet, "Histoire artistique des ordres mendiants," in *Indépendance*. (December).

Houtin, "Histoire du modernisme catholique," in *Indépendance* (November).

Hill, "L'Etat moderne et l'organisation internationale," in *Indépendance* (December).

Ollivier, "L'Empire libéral," in *Indépendance* (December)

Pujo, "Pourquoi on a étouffé l'affaire Valensi," in *Indépendance* (December).

1913

Preface to Italian translation of Ernest Renan, *La Réforme intellectuelle et morale*, later published under the title "Germanismo e storicismo di Ernesto Renan," *Critica* 29 (March, May, September, November 1931).

Reviews

Gebhart, "Les Siècles de bronze," in *Indépendance* (January).

Giraud, "Maîtres d'autrefois et d'aujourd'hui," in *Indépendance* (January).

Marcault, "L'Art de tromper, d'intimider et de corrompre l'électeur," in *Indépendance* (January).

Dunayer, "Fouquier-Tinville," in *Indépendance* (February).

Garcia-Calderon, "Les Démocraties latines d'amérique," in *Indépendance* (February).

Lenôtre, "Blancs, bleus et rouges," in *Indépendance* (February).

Palhories, "Saint-Bonaventure," in *Indépendance* (February).

Tonquedec, "L'Immanence, Essai critique sur la doctrine de Maurice Blondel," in *Indépendance* (March).

Vincent, "Les Institutions et la démocratie," in *Indépendance* (March).

1914

Preface to Edouard Berth, *Les Méfaits des intellectuels* (Rivière).

1915

Preface to Mario Missiroli, *Il Papa in guerra* (Bologna).

"Uno guidizio di Giorgio Sorel su l'intervento dell' Italia," *Avanti*, (15 May).

"Il destino dell' Austria," *Avanti*, (16 May).

1919

"Charles Péguy." *Ronda* (April).

"Proudhon." *Ronda* (September).

"Respublica litteratorum." *Lettres* (October).

1920

"Gambetta et Madame Adam." *Ronda* (5 May).

"La Chine." *Revue Communiste* (15 July).

"Cristianesimo greco e Europa moderna." *Ronda* (8-9 August).

"Le Bolchévisme en Egypte." *Revue Communiste* (7 September).

"Le Travail dans la Grèce antique." *Revue Communiste* (7 November).

"Irlande et Egypte." *Tempo* (7 December).

"La Correspondenza di Thiers." *Ronda* (12 December).

1921

"Lénine d'après Gorki." *Revue Communiste* (11 January).

"Le Génie du Rhin." *Revue Communiste* (14 April).

"La Neutralita Belga in teora e in practica." *Ronda* (6 July).

"Proudhon e la rinascita del socialismo." *Ronda* (11-20 November).

1922

Interview, *Humanité* (9 March 1922).

"Jeremy Bentham et l'indépendance de l'Egypte." *Revue Le Mercure de France* (April) (with L. Auriant).

1923

"Pagine inédite." *Opere e il giori* (1 February 1923).

Letters

To Eduard Berth, extracts from thirty-seven of which are in *Feuillets d'amitié Charles Péguy* no. 77 (May 1960) and *Cahiers du cercle Proudhon* no. 5 (1913) (166).

To Benedetto Croce, 1895-1921, *Critica* 25-28 (1927-1930) (343).

Lettres à Paul Delesalle, edited by André Prudhommeaux (Paris: Grasset, 1947) (64).

To Edouard Dolléans, *Revue d'histoire économique et sociale* 26, no. 2 (1947) (1).

To Guglielmo Ferrero, *Pensiero Politico*, no. 1 (1972) (27).

To Daniel Halévy, *Fédération* (November 1947) (2).

To Hubert Lagardelle, *Homme Réel* (February 1934) (2).

To Lanzillo, in Johannet, *Itinéraires d'intellectuels* (Paris, 1921) (11).

To Joseph Lotte (edited by Pierre Andreu) *Feuillets d'amitié Charles Péguy*, nos. 33, 34 (May-July, 1953) (14).

To Roberto Michels, *Nuovi Studi di Diritto, Economia e Politica* (Rome, September-October 1929) (5).

To Mario Missiroli (edited by Gabriele de Rosa), in Georges Sorel, *'Da Proudhon a Lenin' e 'L'Europa sotto la tormenta'* (Rome: Edizioni di Storia e Letteratura, 1974) (243) and "Preface" to *L'Europa sotto la tormenta* (Milan: Corbaccio, 1932) (1).

To Vilfredo Pareto (edited by Gabriele de Rosa), *Carteggi Paretiani* (Rome: Edizioni di Storia e Letteratura, 1964) (17).

To Georges Valois, in Valois, *La Monarchie et la classe ouvrière* (Nouvelle Librarie Nationale, 1914) (1).

BOOKS AND ARTICLES ON SOREL

Andreu, Pierre. *Notre maître Georges Sorel.* Paris: Grasset, 1953.

Angel, Pierre. *Essais sur Georges Sorel.* Paris: Rivière, 1937.

Ascoli, Max. *Georges Sorel.* Paris: Rivière, 1921.

Bentham, David. "Sorel and the Left." *Government and Opposition* 4, no. 3 (Summer 1969).

Berlin, Sir Isaiah. "Georges Sorel." *Times Literary Supplement* (31 December 1971).

Berth, Edouard. *Les Derniers Aspects du socialisme.* Paris: Rivière, 1923.

_____ *Du "Capital" aux "Réflections sur la violence".* Paris: Rivière, 1932.

_____ *La Fin d'une culture.* Paris: Rivière, 1927.

_____ *Guerre des états ou guerre des classes.* Paris: Rivière, 1924.

_____ "Préoccupations métaphysiques des physiciens modernes." *Mouvement Socialiste* (February 1906).

_____ "Le Système historique de Renan." *Mouvement Socialiste* (August 1907).

Charzat, Michel. *Georges Sorel et la révolution au XXe siècle.* Paris: Hachette, 1977.

Ciria, Alberto. "Georges Sorel." In *Separata de la revista del instituto de ciencias sociales.* Barcelona: Diputacion Provincial, 1968.

Curtis, Michael. *Three against the Third Republic: Sorel, Barrès, and Maurras*. Princeton: Princeton University Press, 1959.

Dolléans, Eduard. "Le Visage de Georges Sorel." *Revue d'Histoire Economique et Sociale* 26, no. 2 (1947).

Freund, Julien. "Une Interprétation de Georges Sorel." *Cahiers Vilfredo Pareto* 14, no. 36 (1976).

Freund, Michael. *Georges Sorel: Der revolutionäre Konservatismus*. Frankfurt am Main: Klostermann, 1932.

Giacalone-Monaco, Tommaso. *Pareto e Sorel*. 2 vols. Padua: Cedam, 1960.

Goriely, Georges. *Le Pluralisme dramatique de Georges Sorel*. Paris: Rivière, 1962.

Hamilton, James Jay. "Georges Sorel and the Inconsistencies of a Bergsonian Marxism." *Political Theory* 1, no. 3 (August 1973).

Horowitz, Irving Louis. *Radicalism and the Revolt against Reason*. New York: Humanities Press, 1963.

Humphrey, Richard. *Georges Sorel: Prophet without Honor*. Cambridge: Harvard University Press, 1951.

Johannet, René. "L'Evolution de Georges Sorel." In *Itinéraires d'intellectuels*. Paris: Nouvelle Librairie Internationale, 1921.

Kolakowski, Leszek. "Georges Sorel, Jansenist Marxist." *Dissent* (Winter 1975).

Lasserre, Pierre. *Georges Sorel, théorician de l'impérialisme*. Paris: Artisan du Livre, 1928.

Lytle, Scott H. "Georges Sorel: Apostle of Fanaticism." In E. M. Earle, ed., *Modern France*. Princeton: Princeton University Press, 1951.

Meisel, James H. *The Genesis of Georges Sorel*. Ann Arbor: George Wahr, 1951.

Nye, Robert A. "Two Paths to a Psychology of Social Action: Gustave Le Bon and Georges Sorel." *Journal of Modern History* 45, no. 3 (1973).

Ominus, "Péguy et Sorel," *Feuillets d'amitié Charles Péguy*, no. 77 (May 1960).

Péguy, Marcel. "La Rupture de Charles Péguy et de Georges Sorel d'après des documents inédits." *Cahiers de la Quinzaine* (Paris, 1930).

Pirou, Gaetan. *Georges Sorel*. Paris: Rivière, 1927.

Rossignol, Fernand. *Pour connaître la pensée de Georges Sorel*. Paris: Bordas, 1948.

Roth, Jack. "Revolution and Morale in Modern French Thought: Sorel and the Sorelians." *French Historical Studies* 3, no. 2 (June 1963).

_____ "The Roots of Italian Fascism: Sorel and Sorelismo." *Journal of Modern History* 39, no. 1 (March 1967).

_____ "Sorel on Lenin and Mussolini." *Contemporary French Civilization* 2, no. 2 (Winter 1978).

Rouanet, S. P. "Irrationalism and Myth in Georges Sorel." *Revue of Politics* 26 (January 1964).

Sartre, Victor. *Georges Sorel, élites syndicalistes et révolution prolétarienne*. Paris: Editions Spes, 1937.

Stanley, John L. "Sorel and the Social Uncertainty Principle," *Canadian Journal of Political and Social Theory* 3, no.3 (Fall 1979).

_____, ed. *From Georges Sorel*, New York: Oxford University Press, 1976.

Talmon, J. L. "Sorel's Legacy." *Encounter* (February 1970).

Variot, Jean. *Propos de Georges Sorel.* Paris: Gallimard, 1935.

Vernon, Richard. *Commitment and Change: Georges Sorel and the Idea of Revolution.* Toronto: University of Toronto Press, 1978.

Wanner, Jean. *Georges Sorel et la décadence.* Lausanne: F. Roth, 1943.

Williams, George Huntston. "Four Modalities of Violence, with Special Reference to the Writings of Georges Sorel." *Journal of Church and State* 16, nos. 1 and 2 (Winter and Spring 1974).

Wood, Neal. "Some Reflections on Sorel and Machiavelli." *Political Science Quarterly* 83 (March 1968).

OTHER WORKS

Adorno, Theodor. *Negative Dialectics*, trans. E. B. Ashton. New York: Seabury, 1973.

Alexander, Peter. "Ernst Mach." In *Encyclopedia of Philosophy*, vol. 5. New York: Collier-Macmillan, 1967.

Althusser, Louis. *For Marx*, trans. Ben Brewster. New York: Vintage, 1970.

Althusser, Louis, and Etienne, Balibar. *Reading Capital*, trans. Ben Brewster. London: New Left Books, 2nd ed., 1977.

Anderson, J. K. *Military Theory and Practice in the Age of Xenophon.* Berkeley, Los Angeles, and London: University of California Press, 1970.

_____ *Xenophon.* New York: Scribners, 1974.

Arendt, Hannah. *The Origins of Totalitarianism.* New York and Cleveland: World, 1958.

Aristotle. *The Politics*, ed. and trans. Sir Ernest Barker. New York: Oxford University Press, 1958.

Avineri, Shlomo. *The Social and Political Thought of Karl Marx.* Cambridge: Cambridge University Press, 1970.

Benda, Julien. *The Treason of the Intellectuals*, trans. Richard Aldington. New York: Norton, 1969.

Benjamin, Walter. *Reflections.* New York: Harcourt, Brace, 1978.

Bergson, Henri. *Creative Evolution*, trans. Arthur Mitchell. New York: Modern Library, 1944.

_____ *Introduction to Metaphysics*, trans. T. E. Hulme. Indianapolis: Bobbs-Merrill, 1949.

_____ *Matter and Memory*, trans. Nancy Paul and Scott Palmer. London: Unwin, 1911.

_____ *Time and Free Will*, trans. Pogson. London: Unwin, 1910.

Bernstein, Eduard. *Evolutionary Socialism*, trans. Edith C. Harvey. New York: Schocken, 1961.

Berth, Edouard. *Les Méfaits des intellectuels.* 2nd ed., Paris: Rivière, 1926.

Bianquis, Geneviève. *Nietzsche en France.* Paris: Alcan, 1929.

Bohm-Bewark. *Karl Marx and the Close of His System.* New York: Augustus Kelly, 1949.
Brown, Raymond E. *The Gospel according to John.* Garden City: Doubleday, 1966.
Burnham, James. *The Machiavellians: Defenders of Freedom.* Chicago: Regnery, 1943.
Byrnes, Robert Francis. *Anti-Semitism in Modern France.* New Brunswick: Rutgers University Press, 1950.
Cahm, Eric. *Péguy et le nationalisme français.* Paris: Cahiers du l'Amitié Charles Péguy, 1972.
Camus, Albert. *The Rebel*, trans. Arthur Bower. New York: Vintage, 1968.
Caute, David. *Frantz Fanon.* London: Fontana, 1970.
Charlton, D. G. *French Positivist Thought in the Nineteenth Century.* Oxford: Clarendon, 1959.
Chevalier, Jacques. *Henri Bergson.* New York: Macmillan, 1923.
Chroust, Anton-Herman. *Socrates, Man and Myth: The Two Socratic Dialogues of Xenophon.* London: Routledge and Kegan Paul, 1957.
Clark, Terry, ed. *Gabriel Tarde: On Communication and Social Influence.* Chicago: University of Chicago Press, 1969.
Claudel, Paul. *L'Otage.* Paris: Gallimard Folio, 1939.
Claudel, Paul, and André Gide. *The Correspondence between Paul Claudel and André Gide, 1899-1926*, trans. John Russell. London: Secker and Warburg, 1952.
Cole, G. D. H. *A History of Socialist Thought.* Vol. 3. London: Macmillan, 1956.
Colletti, Lucio. *From Rousseau to Lenin.* London: New Left Books, 1972.
Comte, Auguste. *Introduction to the Positive Philosophy*, ed. and trans. Frederick Ferré. Indianapolis: Bobbs-Merrill, 1970.
Coser, Lewis. *The Functions of Social Conflict.* New York: Free Press, 1956.
Davis, J. K. *Athenian Propertied Families.* Oxford: Oxford University Press, 1971.
Delebecque, Eduard. *Essai sur la vie de Xénophon.* Paris: Klincksieck, 1957.
Durkheim, Emile. *The Rules of the Sociological Method*, trans. Sarah Solovay and John H. Mueller. New York: Free Press, 1966.
______. *Le Suicide.* Paris: Alcan, 1897.
Engels, Frederick. *Anti-Dühring*, English edn. Moscow: Foreign Languages Publishing House, 1959.
Essien-Udom, E. U. *Black Nationalism: A Search for Identity in America.* New York: Dell, 1965.
Fanon, Frantz. *A Dying Colonialism*, trans. Haakon Chevalier. New York: Grove, 1967.
______ *The Wretched of the Earth*, trans. Constance Farrington. New York: Grove, 1966.
Foulon, Maurice. *Fernand Pelloutier.* Paris: La Ruche Ouvrière, n.d.
Gay, Peter. *The Dilemma of Democratic Socialism.* New York: Collier, 1962.
Gendzier, I. *Frantz Fanon: A Critical Study.* New York: Pantheon, 1973.
Geras, Norman, "Althusser's Marxism: An Assessment." *Western Marxism:*

A Critical Reader. London: Verso Editions, 1978.
Gomperz, Theodor. *Greek Thinkers*, trans. G. Berry. London: John Murray, 1949.
Gramsci, Antonio. *The Modern Prince and Other Writings*, trans. Louis Marks. New York: International, 1957.
Gray, J. Glenn. *The Warriors: Reflections on Men in Battle*. New York: Harper, 1967.
Gregor, A. James. *The Ideology of Fascism*. New York: Free Press, 1969.
Griffuelhes, Victor, and L. Niel. *Les Objectifs de nos luttes de classe*. Paris, 1909.
Guthrie, W. K. C. *Socrates*. Cambridge: Cambridge University Press, 1971.
Habermas, Jurgen. *Knowledge and Human Interests*, trans. J. J. Shapiro. Boston: Beacon, 1971.
Halévy, Daniel. *Apologie pour notre passé*. Paris: Rivière, 1911.
——— *Péguy and Les Cahiers de la Quinzaine*, trans. Ruth Bethell. London: Dobson, 1946.
Harbold, William H. "Justice in the Thought of Pierre-Joseph Proudhon." *Western Political Quarterly* 22, no. 4 (December 1969).
Hayak, Edward von. *The Counter-Revolution in Science*. New York: Free Press, 1969.
Hegel, G. W. F. *The History of Philosophy*, trans. E. S. Haldane. New York: Humanities Press, 1955.
Hoffer, Eric. *The True Believer*. New York: New American Library, 1951.
Huberman, Leo, and Paul Sweezy, eds. *Régis Debray and the Latin American Revolution*. New York: Monthly Review Press, 1968.
Jacobitti, Edmund E. "Labriola, Croce, and Italian Marxism." *Journal of the History of Ideas* 36, no. 2 (1975).
James, William. *The Meaning of Truth*. New York: Longmans, Green, 1910.
——— *Pragmatism*. New York: Longmans, Green, 1914.
——— *The Varieties of Religious Experience*. New York: Mentor, 1958.
——— *The Will to Believe and Other Essays in Popular Philosophy*. New York: Longmans, Green, 1915.
Jay, Martin. "The Concept of Totality in Lukács and Adorno." In Shlomo Avineri, ed., *Varieties of Marxism*. The Hague: Nijhoff, 1975.
Joll, James. *The Second International, 1889-1914*. New York: Harper and Row, 1966.
Jones, Gareth. "The Marxism of the Early Lukács." In *Western Marxism: A Critical Reader*. London: Verso Editions, 1978.
Julliard, Jacques. *Fernand Pelloutier et les origines du syndicalisme d'action directe*. Paris: Editions du Seuil, 1971.
Kosik, Karel. "The Concrete Totality." *Telos* no. 4 (Fall 1969).
Kuhn, Thomas. *The Structure of Scientific Revolutions*. Chicago: University of Chicago Press, 1970.
Labriola, Antonio. *Essais sur la conception matérialiste de l'histoire*. Paris: Gordon and Breach, 1970.
——— *Socialism and Philosophy*. Chicago: Kerr, 1911.

Labriola, Arturo. *Karl Marx. L'Economiste, le socialiste.* Paris: Rivière, 1910.

Lazare, Bernard. *Anti-Semitism: Its History and Causes.* London: Britons, 1967.

Le Bon, Gustave. *The Crowd.* New York: Viking, 1960.

_____ *Les Opinions et les croyances.* Paris: Flammarion, 1911.

_____ *La Psychologie politique et la défense sociale.* Paris: Flammarion, 1910.

_____ *The Psychology of Revolution.* New Brunswick: Transaction Books, 1979.

_____ *The Psychology of Socialism.* New Brunswick: Transaction Books, 1981.

Lichtheim, George. *Marxism: An Historical and Critical Study.* New York: Praeger, 1962.

_____ *Marxism in Modern France.* New York: Columbia University Press, 1966.

Lincoln, C. Eric. *The Black Muslims in America.* Boston: Beacon, 1973.

Louis, Paul. *Histoire du mouvement syndical en France.* Vol. 1. Paris: Valois, 1947.

_____ *Histoire du socialisme en France.* Paris: Rivière, 1946.

Lukács, Georg. *History and Class Consciousness*, trans. Rodney Livingstone. Cambridge: MIT Press, 1971.

Machiavelli, Niccolò. *The Prince* and the *Discourses*, ed. Max Lerner. New York: Modern Library, 1950.

Marrus, Michael R. *The Politics of Assimilation: A Study of the French Jewish Community at the Time of the Dreyfus Affair.* Oxford: Oxford University Press, 1971.

Marx, Karl. *Capital.* Vol. 1. New York: Modern Library, n.d.

_____ *Early Writings*, ed. T. B. Bottomore. New York: McGraw-Hill, 1964.

Marx, Karl, and Frederick Engels. *The German Ideology*, trans. R. Pascal. New York: International Publishers, 1947.

_____ *Selected Works*, 2 vols. Moscow: Foreign Languages Publishers, 1958.

Maurras, Charles. *Oeuvres capitales.* Paris: Flammarion, 1954.

Merlino, Serverio. *Formes et essence du socialisme.* Paris: Giard et Brière, 1898.

Meyer, J. P. *Political Thought in France from the Revolution to the Fourth Republic.* London: Routledge and Kegan Paul, 1943.

Michels, Roberto. *Political Parties.* Glencoe: Free Press, 1960.

New Left Books, ed. *Western Marxism: A Critical Reader.* London: New Left Books, 1978.

Nietzsche, Friedrich. *The Birth of Tragedy* and *The Genealogy of Morals*, trans. Francis Golffing. New York: Doubleday-Anchor, 1956.

_____. *The Portable Nietzsche*, ed. and trans. Walter Kaufmann. Hammondsworth: Penguin, 1977.

Nye, Robert A. *The Origins of Crowd Psychology: Gustave Le Bon and the Crisis of Mass Democracy in the Third Republic.* London: Sage, 1975.

Ollman, Bertell. *Alienation: Marx's Conception of Man in Capitalist Society.* Cambridge: Cambridge University Press, 1971.

Parenti, Michael. "The Black Muslims: From Revolution to Institution." *Social Research* 31, no. 2 (Summer 1964).

Péguy, Charles. *Marcel: Premier dialogue de la cité harmonieuse.* Paris: Gallimard, 1973.

——— *The Mystery of the Charity of Joan of Arc*, trans. Julien Green. New York: Pantheon, 1950.

——— *Notre jeunesse.* Paris: Gallimard, 1957.

——— *Notre patrie.* 37th ed., Paris: Gallimard, 1950.

——— *Péguy tel qu'on l'ignore*, ed. Jean Bastaire. Paris: Gallimard, 1973.

Pelloutier, Fernand. *L'Histoire des bourses du travail.* Paris: Gordon and Breach, 1971.

Phillips, D. C. *Holistic Thought in Social Science.* Stanford: Stanford University Press, 1976.

Plato. *Euthyphro*, *Apology*, *Crito*, trans. F. J. Church. Indianapolis: Bobbs-Merrill, 1956.

——— *Phaedrus*, trans. R. Hackforth. Indianapolis: Bobbs-Merrill, 1952.

Poster, Mark. *Existential Marxism in Postwar France.* Princeton: Princeton University Press, 1975.

Pritchett, W. Kendrick. *The Greek State at War*, Vol. 1. Berkeley, Los Angeles, London: University of California Press, 1974.

Proudhon, Pierre-Joseph. *De la capacité politique des classes ouvrières.* Paris: Lacroix, 1873.

———. *De la justice dans la révolution et dans l'église.* Paris: Lacroix, 1868-1870.

——— *La Guerre et la paix.* Paris: Lacroix, 1869; new edition, Paris: Rivière, 1927.

——— *L'Idée générale de la révolution au XIXe siècle.* Paris: Lacroix, 1867.

——— *Philosophie de la misère.* Paris: Lacroix, 1875.

——— *La Pornocratie ou les femmes dans les temps modernes.* Paris: Lacroix, 1875.

——— *Selected Writings of Pierre-Joseph Proudhon*, ed. Stewart Edwards, trans. Elizabeth Frazer. New York: Doubleday, 1969.

——— *Système des contradictions économiques.* Third edition, Paris: Lacroix, 1867.

———. *Théorie de la propriété.* Second edition, Paris: Lacroix, 1866.

Renan, Ernest. *L'Antéchrist.* Paris: Calmann-Lévy, 1899.

——— *Les Apôtes.* 27th ed., Paris: Calmann-Lévy, 1925.

——— *L'Eglise chrétienne.* 5th ed., Paris: Calmann-Lévy, 1899.

——— *Essais de morale et de critique.* 6th ed., Paris: Calmann-Lévy, n.d.

——— *Les Evangiles et la seconde génération chrétienne.* 11th ed., Paris: Calmann-Lévy, 1922.

——— *Feuilles détachées.* Paris: Calmann-Lévy, 1892.

——— *Histoire du peuple d'Israël*, vols. 4, 5. Paris: Calmann-Lévy, 1893.

——— *Marc-Aurèle et la fin du monde antique.* 8th ed., Paris: Calmann-Lévy, 1899.

_____ *Questions contemporaines*. Paris: Lévy, 1868.

_____ *La Réforme intellectuelle et morale*. 14th ed., Paris: Calmann-Lévy, n.d.

_____ *Saint Paul*. 15th ed., Paris: Calmann-Lévy, n.d.

_____ *Souvenirs d'enfance et de jeunesse*. Paris: Calmann-Lévy, n.d.

_____ *La Vie de Jésus*. 59th ed., Paris: Calmann-Lévy, n.d.

Ribot, Théodule. *La Psychologie des sentiments*. 13th ed., Paris: Alcan, 1930.

Ridley, F. F. *Revolutionary Syndicalism in France: The Direct Action of Its Time*. Cambridge: Cambridge University Press, 1970.

Ritter, Alan. *The Political Thought of Pierre-Joseph Proudhon*. Princeton: Princeton University Press, 1969.

Rousseau, Jean-Jacques. *The Social Contract* and *The Discourses*, trans. G. D. H. Cole. New York: Dutton, 1950.

Sartre, Jean-Paul. *Critique de la raison dialectique*. Paris: Gallimard, 1960.

Schaff, Adam. *Marxism and the Human Individual*, trans. Olgierd Wojtasiewicz. New York: McGraw-Hill, 1970.

Schweitzer, Albert. *The Quest for the Historical Jesus*, trans. W. Montgomery. New York: Macmillan, 1968.

Seligman, E. R. A. *L'Interprétation économique de l'histoire*, trans. H.-E. Barrault. Paris: Rivière, 1911.

Senghor, Leopold Sedar. "What Is Negritude?" In James Gould and Willis H. Truitt, eds. *Political Ideologies*. New York: Macmillan, 1972.

Stearns, Peter. *Revolutionary Syndicalism and French Labor*. New Brunswick: Rutgers University Press, 1971.

Sternhell, Zev. *La Droite révolutionnaire 1885-1914*. Paris: Editions du Seuil, 1978.

Strauss, Leo. *Xenophon's Socrates*. Ithaca: Cornell University Press, 1972.

_____. *Xenophon's Socratic Discourse: An Interpretation of the 'Oeconomicus'*. Ithaca: Cornell University Press, 1970.

Tannenbaum, Edward. "The Goals of Italian Fascism." *American Historical Review* 74, no. 4 (April 1969).

Tarn, W. W. *Hellenistic Military and Naval Developments*. Cambridge: Cambridge University Press, 1930.

Thomas, Paul. "Marx and Science." *Political Studies* 24, no. 1 (1976).

Troeltsch, Ernst. *The Social Teaching of the Christian Churches*, trans. Olive Wyon. New York: Harper, 1960.

Tucker, Robert. *The Marxian Revolutionary Idea*. New York: Norton, 1969.

_____ *Philosophy and Myth in Karl Marx*. Cambridge: Cambridge University Press, 1963.

Weber, Eugen. *Action Française*. Stanford: Stanford University Press, 1962.

_____ *The Nationalist Revival in France, 1905-1914*. Berkeley: University of California Press, 1959.

Wilson, Nelly. *Bernard Lazare: Anti-Semitism and the Problem of Jewish Identity in Nineteenth Century France*. Cambridge: Cambridge University Press, 1978.

Wood, Neal. "Xenophon's Theory of Leadership." *Classica et Mediaevalia*

25, no. 1 (1964).
Woodcock, George. *Pierre-Joseph Proudhon*. London: Routledge and Kegan Paul, 1956.
Xenophon. *Cyropaedia*, trans. Walter Miller. Cambridge: Loeb Classical Library, 1947.
——— *Minor Works*, trans. J. S. Watson. London: Bell, 1878.
——— *Oeconomicus*. In Leo Strauss, *Xenophon's Socratic Discourse*. Ithaca: Cornell University Press, 1970.
——— *Recollections of Socrates and Socrates' Defense before the Jury*, trans. Anna S. Benjamin. Indianapolis: Bobbs-Merrill, 1965.
Zahar, Renate. *Frantz Fanon: Colonialism and Alienation*. New York: Monthly Review Press, 1974.

INDEX

CPSIA information can be obtained
at www.ICGtesting.com
Printed in the USA
BVHW031141111120
593079BV00006B/60

9 780520 303874